ISBN 978-1-332-32986-1
PIBN 10314911

1 MONTH OF
FREE
READING

at

www.ForgottenBooks.com

By purchasing this book you are eligible for one month membership to ForgottenBooks.com, giving you unlimited access to our entire collection of over 1,000,000 titles via our web site and mobile apps.

To claim your free month visit:
www.forgottenbooks.com/free314911

English
Français
Deutsche
Italiano
Español
Português

www.forgottenbooks.com

Mythology Photography **Fiction**
Fishing Christianity **Art** Cooking
Essays Buddhism Freemasonry
Medicine **Biology** Music **Ancient**
Egypt Evolution Carpentry Physics
Dance Geology **Mathematics** Fitness
Shakespeare **Folklore** Yoga Marketing
Confidence Immortality Biographies
Poetry **Psychology** Witchcraft
Electronics Chemistry History **Law**
Accounting **Philosophy** Anthropology
Alchemy Drama Quantum Mechanics
Atheism Sexual Health **Ancient History**
Entrepreneurship Languages Sport
Paleontology Needlework Islam
Metaphysics Investment Archaeology
Parenting Statistics Criminology
Motivational

To Hugh Wiley
With the compliments
of A. ...

QUESTIONED DOCUMENTS

A STUDY OF QUESTIONED
DOCUMENTS WITH AN
OUTLINE OF METHODS BY
WHICH THE FACTS MAY BE
DISCOVERED AND SHOWN

BY

ALBERT S. OSBORN

EXAMINER OF QUESTIONED DOCUMENTS

WITH AN INTRODUCTION

BY

PROFESSOR JOHN H. WIGMORE

AUTHOR OF

"WIGMORE ON EVIDENCE"

———

TWO HUNDRED ILLUSTRATIONS

———

THE GENESEE PRESS

THE POST EXPRESS
PRINTING COMPANY
ROCHESTER NEW YORK

INTRODUCTION

A CENTURY ago the science of handwriting-study did not exist. A crude empiricism still prevailed. This hundred years past has seen a vast progress. All relevant branches of modern science have been brought to bear. Skilled students have focussed upon this field manifold appurtenant devices and apparatus. A Science and an Art have developed. A firm place has now been made for the expert witness who is emphatically scientific, and not merely empiric.

Each age has its crimes, with the corresponding protective measures,—all alike the product of the age's conditions. In each age, crime takes advantage of conditions, and then society awakes and gradually overtakes crime by discovering new expedients. In modern history—since Charlemagne and the beginning of the re-civilization of Europe, some twelve hundred years ago—there have been two great epochs in the history of documents. In the first, skin-parchment is the vehicle, and writing is an esoteric art for the monkish few. Forgery flourished in the middle ages, chiefly as a successful method of acquiring land-titles. The forged Decretals of Isidorus come down to us as a typical imposition of that age. In the next epoch, paper is made, then printing is invented, and education in writing becomes gradually almost universal. Amidst these new conditions, the falsifier again outstrips society for a while. A Chatterton and a Junius can baffle the community. Well down into the 1800s, the most daring impositions remain possible. But society at last seems to have overtaken the falsifier once more. Science and art, in the mass, are more than a match for the isolated individual. We have now apparently entered further upon a somewhat variant documentary epoch,—that of the typewriting machine. But even this, with its novel possibilities, will remain within the protective control of science. —as the present book shows.

The feature of Mr. Osborn's book which will perhaps mark its most progressive aspect is its insistence upon the reasons for an opinion,—not the bare opinion alone. If there is in truth a science (and not merely an individual empiricism), that science must be based on reasons, and these reasons must be capable of being stated and appreciated. Throughout this book may be seen the spirit of candid reasoning and firm insistence on the use of it. I believe that this is the spirit of the future for the judicial attitude towards experts in documents. If judges and lawyers can thoroughly grasp the author's faith in the value of explicit, rational data for expert opinions, the whole atmosphere of such inquiries will become more healthy. The status of the expert will be properly strengthened, and the processes of a trial will be needfully improved.

The book abounds in the fascination of solved mysteries and celebrated cases. And it introduces us to the world-wide abundance of learning in this field. French and German investigations are amply drawn upon. Psychology, mathematics, and literature, as well as chemistry, photography, and microscopy, are made to serve. The reader arises with a profound respect for the dignity of the science and the multifarious dexterity of the art.

JOHN H. WIGMORE.

Northwestern University
Law School, June 1, 1910.

IN the words of Epicharmus, which are the motto
of this work, "Mind sees, and Mind hears; all
things else are deaf and blind." It is not
merely by looking at a plant, or a mineral, or an
animal, that any one really sees it. This is true of
all the productions of nature, and it is equally true
of whatever is elevating, or beautiful, or graceful,
or minute, in the works of man. It is true of a
cathedral, a statue, or a picture, of Grecian vases or
of ancient coins. It is likewise true of handwriting.
—*Hon. Edward Twistleton, in Handwriting of
Junius, p. lxxv (1871).*

CONTENTS

PAGE

Introduction   vii

Contents   xi

Preface   .   .   xv

Author's Introduction   xix

CHAPTER I.

Care of Questioned Documents

CHAPTER II.

Classes of Questioned Documents   6

CHAPTER III.

Standards of Comparison   .   16

CHAPTER IV.

Photography and Questioned Documents   .   36

CHAPTER V.

The Microscope and Questioned Documents   70

CHAPTER VI.

Instruments and Appliances   89

CHAPTER VII.

Movements, Line Quality, and Alignment in Writing   105

CHAPTER VIII.

Pen Position, Pen Pressure, and Shading   .   126

CHAPTER IX.

Arrangement, Size, Proportions, Spacing, and Slant in
    Writing   .   .   .   141

CHAPTER X.

Writing Instruments   .   154

CHAPTER XI.

Systems of Writing and Questioned Documents   .   168

CHAPTER XII.

Variation in Genuine Writing   .   .   196

CHAPTER XIII.

Individual and General Characteristics in Writing   206

CHAPTER XIV.

Variety of Forms in Handwriting and Mathematical Cal-
    culations Applied to Questioned Handwriting .   217

CHAPTER XV.

Simulated and Copied Forgeries   .   .   236

CHAPTER XVI.

Traced Forgeries   .   266

CHAPTER XVII.

Anonymous and Disputed Letters   .   302

CHAPTER XVIII.
Ink and Questioned Documents   .   330

CHAPTER XIX.
Paper and Questioned Documents   .   363

CHAPTER XX.
Sequence of Writing as Shown by Crossed Strokes   .   375

CHAPTER XXI.
Writing over Folds in Paper   .   394

CHAPTER XXII.
Erasures and Alterations in Documents   .   404

CHAPTER XXIII.
Questioned Additions and Interlineations   422

CHAPTER XXIV.
Age of Documents   .   .   431

CHAPTER XXV.
Questioned Typewriting   .   .   437

CHAPTER XXVI.
A Questioned Document Case in Court   .   .   466

Appendix   479

Bibliography   483

Index   489

THE late Mr. Justice Miller of the United States Supreme Court declared that the difficulties in determining questions of fact are greater and more common than those that occur in determining questions of law, and other judges have testified to the same experience. It is therefore eminently desirable that aid should be sought by the triers of fact in all accessible sources where authentic advice is likely to be found.—*Moore on Facts, Vol. I, p. v, 1908.*

PREFACE

THE purpose of this book is to assist in the discovery and proof of the facts in any investigation or legal inquiry involving the genuineness of a document.

Definite methods of procedure are given for investigation of the many important questions relating to the various kinds of questioned documents and the attempt has been made to reduce to order the known facts and underlying principles of the various branches of the subject. It has been the aim to make as brief as possible if not wholly to avoid those abstruse discussions, particularly of unsettled questions, which so often render technical treatises of little practical value.

The work contains the proved results of the latest investigations and it is confidently thought will furnish some suggestions and render some immediate assistance to one having an actual case in hand. Nothing of importance connected with the various questions has been purposely omitted, but that which is not likely to be of actual use has been given no place.

The book has been in course of preparation for a number of years and a large part of it has grown out of actual cases involving the questions discussed and has been tested and amended by application to many such cases.

Illustrations have been introduced where it is thought they are really helpful and make clearer the points under consideration, but merely curious illustrations of general interest as well as long discussions of noted cases have been purposely omitted. Although there is much general interest in many of the subjects treated the work is not primarily intended for the popular reader, but is designed as a working treatise.

Definite instructions regarding the investigation of the several classes of questioned documents are given; the chapters on photography and the use of the microscope outline specific methods and give practical directions that in any case can at once be put in operation; the chapter on typewriting as evidence is the result of study, experience and investigation in this important new field; the method outlined for the measuring and recording of ink tints makes it possible in many cases to present conclusive testimony on the subject of the age of writing, and the special application of stereoscopic photography to the subject of questioned documents makes it possible to present delicate and almost hidden facts in a most conclusive manner.

Some of the various topics treated are necessarily very closely related and some slight repetitions have been permitted to remain in order that the separate chapters may furnish more available assistance by being more complete in themselves. The exhaustive index with cross-references will be helpful to one who is investigating some special phase of the various subjects treated.

A number of dated legal references, with brief excerpts from opinions, will be found in connection with various discussions throughout the work. While these references to the law are from the most authoritative sources, they are not printed primarily for the purpose of giving the law, but because of their bearing on the discussion of the merits of the particular subjects to which they refer.

The many excellent digests and text-books now available give the law of questioned documents according to the latest decisions in the various states, and this book is designed not to give the law on the subject but to assist in that most important part of the trial of a case, the proving of the facts.

It is of course essential to know the law, but it is certainly true that many lawyers are inclined to spend much time looking up old legal opinions that may have only the remotest connection with the proof of a case in court and neglect to qualify themselves on the most fundamental and elementary questions connected with the actual facts they must prove.

It is astonishing how often and in how many ways questions regarding handwriting and allied subjects enter into trials of issues in courts of law and it is hoped that what is here presented may in such inquiries assist in furthering the ends of justice.

The book is especially designed for the use of the lawyer, but, it is thought, will also be useful to the banker, the business man, or to any one who may be called upon to investigate the genuineness of a document.

ALBERT S. OSBORN.

New York,
    April 5, 1910.

UPON principle, therefore, as well as from the necessity of the case, proof of handwriting, under proper restrictions, is, as has been seen, everywhere admitted. Moreover, as has been well said, it seems that this kind of evidence, like all other probable evidence, admits of every degree of certainty, from the lowest presumption to the highest moral certainty.— *American and English Encyclopædia of Law, Vol. XV, 2d Ed., p. 283.*

AUTHOR'S INTRODUCTION

GENUINE documents are sometimes suspected and attacked and no doubt are occasionally set aside as fraudulent, while on the other hand great numbers of fraudulent documents undoubtedly wholly escape suspicion and pass as genuine. A suspected document in the natural course of events sooner or later gets into the hands of a lawyer or, as frequently occurs, he may be the one who first suspects it as he is usually the first to pass judgment upon it. He must consider the question and end the inquiry or decide upon a more extended investigation.

If the interests of justice are to be fully served the lawyer at this point should know, at least in a general way, what initial steps to take in order to test the genuineness of the instrument. He should know what to look for and how to look at it and should know what can be shown and how to show it; and a portion of this preliminary work he should be able to do himself and do promptly.

Questions of this character and of the greatest importance may arise in the midst of a trial when a prompt decision is imperative and immediate knowledge is doubly valuable. Some one has said that every man should know enough law to know when he ought to consult a lawyer, and it is equally true that a lawyer should know at least enough of the study of questioned documents to be able to determine with promptness and certainty how far such a subject of inquiry should be carried.

The lawyer should have this special knowledge in order also that he may be able to utilize effectively testimony on the subject that he may wish to present; that he may be qualified to test in advance the force and truth of such testimony, and, finally and most important of all, that he may be prepared to cross-examine adverse witnesses with intelligence and skill.

A case is always in grave danger if an attorney is trying by the aid of witnesses to get before a jury that which he himself does not clearly understand. Such a lawyer will often prejudice his cause in the mind of the court, annoy and disconcert his own witnesses, confuse the jury and lose his case because he proves too little, or, what may be far worse, attempts to prove too much.

The successful lawyer is he who not only knows the law but knows the facts, and when he is able to quote the first and prove the second he is ready for trial. A jury instinctively distrusts a lawyer who does not seem to understand clearly the facts of his own case.

The vast increase in the use of documents is one of the characteristics of modern civilization, and as all such documents are subject to forgery, spurious papers are constantly being produced ranging in importance from one dollar orders to one hundred thousand dollar notes; from five dollar checks to five million dollar wills.

It would be well if there could be devised a better method of safeguarding and transferring important property interests than by the almost exclusive use of written documents, but no immediate change seems probable. In many instances the disposition of millions of dollars depends upon the correct identification of a single signature. This great opportunity is a temptation that it seems impossible for some to resist who would not commit an ordinary crime.

In these days the estates of deceased persons are the especial prey of bold adventurers, and nearly every term of court has forgery cases of high or low degree. The proportion of this class of crime has undoubtedly greatly increased in recent years.

Forgeries vary in perfection all the way from the clumsy effort which any one can see is spurious, up to the finished work of the adept which no one can detect. The perfect forgery would naturally be successful, and might not even be suspected, but experience shows that the work of the forger is not usually well done and in many cases is very clumsy indeed.

A number of causes lead to this result, the chief of which is that fortunately the one who produces a criminal forgery is rarely the skillful one qualified to do it well, and also because a crime of any kind is an unnatural and unusual act. Forgers frequently do not exercise what would seem to be ordinary precaution, but no doubt overlook one part of the process because such intense attention is given to other parts, and it is probably true that they are sometimes more bold because in so many cases ineffective procedure and inadequate means have been provided for the detection and proof of forgery.

In numerous states, even at this late day, the common-sense practice of admitting genuine writings expressly for the purpose of comparison with a questioned writing is not allowed. In such jurisdictions only writings "in the case for other purposes" can ordinarily be used, a limitation which makes the proof of forgery difficult, ties the hands of those who seek to show the facts, encourages crime and assists the criminal. The United States Federal Courts still follow this antiquated rule in criminal cases.

This procedure is a curious inheritance projected into the present day practice and its continuance is one of the curiosities and misfortunes of legal procedure. In these jurisdictions where no standards are admitted writing in many cases must be proved by those alone who are said "to know a handwriting," and the spectacle is too often presented of one line of tottering old men and women, who saw some one write many years before, all testifying that they think a certain writing is genuine and another similar line testifying that from their recollection it is not genuine. Such witnesses many times may not be able to see well enough to get the papers right side up and such "proof" is often a veritable farce.

It would certainly be better to put in evidence a sufficient number of good standards of writing and, with even a fairly intelligent jury, have no testimony whatever but let the jury examine for themselves, rather than depend upon such "recollection" testimony alone. It is possible "to know a handwriting," but such a knowledge is not gained by inexperienced observers by a mere casual glance at a writing seen, it may be, many years before. To say that such a person knows a handwriting is a ridiculous legal fiction.

Expert testimony, on any subject, that is merely the statement of an opinion may be of but little value and often is not worth the time that it consumes in a court of law. But in proportion as such testimony is clear and logical and of a nature that permits it to be illustrated in a tangible manner it becomes valuable. A mere opinion any one can give, but an opinion based on accurate and intimate knowledge, if logically presented and adequately illustrated, will not only bear the fierce light that beats upon the witness-box but will be clarified and strengthened the more it is attacked.

In an inquiry relating to a document attention is directed to a material, visible thing, and, with proper and adequate standards, methods of procedure are possible that cannot be employed in many investigations in which expert testimony is necessary.

It is obvious that the duty of the competent and honest expert in such cases is first, by applying to the question his special knowledge and his experience in similar cases, to determine what is the fact in the matter at issue. Then methods must be devised and means employed whereby the fact can best be shown and proven so that an impartial and competent observer will reach a correct conclusion.

The real expert, who is in fact what the word implies, when guided and assisted by the competent lawyer, will make the facts themselves testify and stand as silent but convincing witnesses pointing the way to truth and justice. In order that this end may be obtained with certainty the lawyer as well as the witness should master the subject.

In connection with the discussion of the methods of investigation of the various questions attention has specifically been called to the limitations of technical ability. It is disagreeable but necessary to keep in mind the ignorant pretender and the conscienceless perjurer who, in partnership with the attorney who engages and pays them, bring so much discredit upon the administra-

. tion of the law as applied to scientific inquiries. No
other remedy is so effective against this evil as thorough
technical knowledge of the subjects discussed. While it
may never be possible to label and bar out the unworthy,
it is hoped that a way may be found for the courts
officially to recognize those who are qualified and worthy
and thus render more effective their assistance in discovering and proving the facts.

In a legal controversy regarding a questioned document the contention of one party must be right and the
other wrong; there can be no middle ground. The one
purpose of this book is to assist, as in a scientific inquiry,
in discovering and proving the fact. Not a line has purposely been included in these pages to give aid and com-
fort to those on the wrong side whose interests impel
them to attempt to prevent the truth from being discovered and shown in a court of law.

It is hoped that the book will, at least in some slight
degree, assist in bringing about an improvement in the
methods of using expert testimony regarding documents that will make it easier in every possible way to
find and prove the fact in all courts of all states.

CHAPTER I.

From the moment that the genuineness of a document is questioned it should be handled and cared for in such manner as not to impair in the slightest degree its value as evidence. This precaution may seem unnecessary, but it frequently happens that through carelessness or ignorance the evidential value of a document of great importance is seriously impaired and important interests are thus imperiled. As early as practicable the exact physical condition of every part of a suspected document should be carefully observed in detail and made a matter of definite, written record and thereafter the document should be preserved as far as possible in exactly the condition it is in when first suspected. It is usually of especial interest to one of the parties to insist that the document be properly protected and cared for.

Numerous negative directions are necessary. Such a document should not be cut, torn nor mutilated in any manner in the slightest degree; it should not be touched with an eraser of any kind nor with pen, pencil or sharp instrument of any character. It should not be folded in any new place; should not be folded and unfolded unnecessarily; should not be wet nor dampened and, except by special permission, no chemicals should be placed upon papers of the opposing party in such a way as to injure or deface them and such tests should be made only by those properly qualified. To avoid even the

[1]

possibility of pencil marks being made upon such a document those examining it should not be allowed to point closely at letters or any parts of it with a pencil. Sharp pointed dividers or measuring instruments should not be put upon a questioned writing except with the greatest care and only by those skilled in the use of such instruments and a tracing should not be made of it except under proper supervision and with a very soft pencil and the very lightest pressure.

A folded document of any kind that is being investigated, such as a note, check, draft, legal paper or letter, should be unfolded and kept flat in a suitable envelope or receptacle made of heavy paper. This should be done in order to avoid the necessity of folding and unfolding the document every time it is examined, which procedure will inevitably break the paper at the folds and also change the condition of the folds as shown when the genuineness of the paper is first questioned.

Small disputed documents, such as checks, notes and similar papers, should be kept unfolded in suitable envelopes as stated, and it is an excellent plan to place them between the two leaves of a folded sheet of stiff blank paper, cut a trifle larger when folded than the documents, so that they can be held in this folded sheet and not directly in the hand or between the thumb and finger as such papers are usually held. Such papers if held and handled in the ordinary way will inevitably become soiled, defaced and covered with finger marks.

If the document is of a fragile character, and especially if it is to be handled by attorneys, witnesses, court and jury in a protracted trial, it is highly important that in every case it be placed between two pieces of clear glass, cut slightly larger than the document and fastened together with binding tape at one end and a rubber band placed around the opposite end. This method permits examination of both sides of the paper and if thus protected a document will not be injured by any amount of handling. The paper can easily be removed when necessary by simply removing the band at one end of the glass covers. In order to reduce the weight and bulk of the

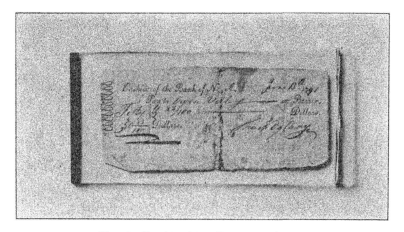

Fig. 1—Double Glass Document Covers

exhibits where there are numerous disputed documents it may be better to use transparent celluloid with card backing instead of the glass, and if there is no writing on the back of the sheet one glass cover attached to a stiff card of the same size as the glass will be sufficient.

A questioned document should not be exposed to moisture of any kind; should not be exposed long to strong sunlight or left out in the air uncovered, and should not be carried in the pocket where it may be affected by bodily moisture or become worn, wrinkled or soiled.

In examining a questioned document with a microscope having no stage, but a special foot that allows the instrument to be placed anywhere on the paper, special care should be taken not to soil, wrinkle or fold the document. To avoid the necessity of placing the microscope directly upon the document itself it is an excellent plan to place over the document during the examination a good strong sheet of paper from the middle of which a suitable aperture has been cut. The type of microscope just mentioned not only makes it possible to examine the middle or any portion of a large sheet of paper or page of a book, which is not possible with the ordinary instrument, but also thus avoids the danger of injuring a document by folding it in such a way as to get it on the ordinary microscope stage.

If, as is often the case, the exact condition, character, tint and shade of the ink have any bearing on the question of genuineness, it is particularly important to guard the document carefully from excessive light, heat and moisture, as such exposure may seriously affect ink conditions. Many fireproof safes, especially when new, are somewhat damp and a questioned document involving the question of the age of ink should not be kept in such a receptacle.

It has been proposed in connection with certain inquiries regarding the sequence of crossed ink lines that an ordinary letter-press copy be made of the part in dispute. This should never be allowed. Such a test will not ordinarily furnish any information of value and, what is more serious, will probably make it impossible thereafter to ascertain the fact by any method whatever. Certain foreign technical books describe numerous impracticable methods of examination in disputed document cases that would inevitably deface if not actually destroy a document. These experiments should, of course, not be allowed[1].

If a disputed document becomes torn or mutilated in any way, or if it is in this condition to begin with, it should not be pasted on an opaque card. It is well in such a case to fasten the pieces together at the margins with a few small strips of transparent adhesive tissue and then put the repaired document between sheets of glass as already described.

In important inquiries it is usually advisable as early as possible to put a disputed document in the custody of the court or some public officer where, under proper restrictions, all parties may have access to it.[2]

Finally, the court stenographer should especially be cautioned when marking a questioned document as an exhibit, not to write, paste a label, or put a rubber stamp impression on it at any place where there is writing on either side of the paper.

---

[1] If this has also been in vain there is still a last but heroic method which under all circumstances injures the document if it does not destroy it, and may therefore be made use of only with special consent of the court. This is the reproduction of the removed writing by heat up to the time when the paper begins to coal or turns black.—Der Nachwies von Schriftfälschungen, etc., von Dennstedt und Voightländer (1906).

[2] We think the better practice is to direct that the deed should be placed in the custody of the county clerk with permission to the plaintiff to inspect it and, if he desires, to have it photographed.—Beck vs. Bohm, 95 N. Y. App. Div. 273 (1904).

CHAPTER II.

Documents are attacked on many grounds and for various reasons, but the great majority of questioned papers are included in the following classes:

(1) Documents with questioned signatures.

(2) Documents containing alleged fraudulent alterations.

(3) Holograph documents questioned or disputed.

(4) Documents attacked on the question of their age or date.

(5) Documents attacked on the question of materials used in their production.

(6) Documents investigated on the question of typewriting:

    (a) With a view to ascertaining their source.

    (b) With a view to determining their date.

(7) Documents or writings investigated because they identify some person through handwriting:

    (a) Anonymous and disputed letters.

    (b) Superscriptions, registrations and miscellaneous writings.

A brief description of these more common classes of suspected documents is here given in connection with a few general suggestions regarding a preliminary examination of such papers, and this brief outline will also serve as a general survey of the whole subject.

[6]

The most common disputed document is that of the first class and may be any one of the ordinary commercial or legal papers such as a check, note, receipt, draft, order, contract, assignment, will, deed, or similar paper the signature of which is under suspicion. In this class are found the traced forgery and the forgery produced by the simulating or copying process. In such a document the signature only may at first be attacked, but many different things may show the fraudulent character of the instrument, and everything about it that in any way may throw light on the subject should as early as possible be carefully investigated.

At first view the signature should be critically examined and compared with genuine signatures and, at this time or later, no writings should be used for comparison by those who are to testify that cannot be legally proved as standards of comparison. In such an examination it is necessary to determine whether the writing in question shows the absence of divergent writing characteristics and the presence of the genuine writing habits and characteristics of the alleged writer to a sufficient extent to warrant the conclusion that the writing is genuine, or the absence of a sufficient number of such characteristics of genuineness and the presence of divergent characteristics to such an extent as to lead to the conclusion that the writing is not genuine. This preliminary examination should not be hastily made and judgment should be reserved until every phase of the examination is completed. It is desirable in many instances to make the examination at two sittings with some time intervening that the steps may be carefully reviewed when the mind and vision are unwearied.

The color and character of the ink of a questioned signature should on first view always be carefully observed under suitable magnification and compared with the ink on all other parts of the document and, if conditions warrant it, with standard inks of the alleged age of the document. If the ink is apparently fresher than the age of the document would seem to warrant, a careful color reading of it should be made and recorded.

The document if handwritten should also be examined to see if it was continuously written by the same writer. The size, shape, color and characteristics of the paper on which the document is written should be carefully observed and the watermark examined, if any appears, if these questions may by any possibility have the slightest bearing on the question of genuineness. Attention should also be given to typewriting, seals, erasures or changes, interlineations, discolorations, thumb-tack or pin holes, and to printing when conditions seem to require it, even although it may at first appear that the signature alone is questioned.

Not infrequently the attempt is made to hide the evidences of forgery in a fraudulent document by some alleged accident or condition by which the paper is partially defaced or torn, or it may be badly soiled or discolored so as to make it more difficult to show its real character. Such a condition is an additional reason why the document should be subjected to an even more rigid examination than would otherwise be given it.

In the second class of questioned documents are included all those in which it is alleged some alteration has been made by erasure, addition, interlineation or substitution by reason of which the effect or value of the document is materially changed. In connection with this class of documents questions may arise regarding the order or sequence of writing as shown by crossed lines, age of writing, continuity of writing, erasures and changes, identity of ink, identity of pen and pen condition, self-consciousness or unusual care in writing, and, under certain conditions, the question may arise whether writing preceded or followed the folding of the paper. This important class of questioned documents also includes all varieties of "raised" checks, drafts and notes as well as fraudulent interlineations in contracts, deeds, wills and other legal papers.

The third class of suspected papers comprises those in which the writing of an entire written document is all questioned. Such complete documents, if fraudulent, are usually vulnerable in many possible particulars and should be subjected to the most searching scrutiny including consideration of paper, watermarks, ink, pens, style or system of writing, natural variation or variety in writing, wording, subject-matter, seals, folding and ruling. Holograph documents are more fully discussed in the chapter on simulated forgeries.

Tickets of many kinds are frequently forged or counterfeited, as are also rare stamps, valuable manuscripts, certificates, letters of introduction and recommendation, letters of credit, diplomas, marriage certificates, marriage contracts, court papers, book plates, and especially autographs and letters of famous people, and also commissions, discharges and many other kinds of documents, some of which would be included in the third class named above, but which cannot all be discussed in this place.

The fourth class of questioned documents includes those in which the age of an instrument or the age of some part of it is investigated, or a paper in which the comparative age of different parts may have some bearing on the question of its genuineness. Interesting papers of this class are often brought forward which purport to be ancient documents of great importance, and which, it is usually claimed, were found in some strange place or under peculiar conditions, and these circumstances are, as a rule, minutely detailed.

Documents have frequently been shown to be false because they were dated many years before the paper was made on which they were written, and this is only one illustration of the fifth class of questioned documents or those shown to be fraudulent by the examination of materials. Other matters for investigation under this head are, type printed forms, lithographed forms, typewriting, seals, envelopes, stamps, or any tangible thing that may have a date value.

A comparatively new class of questioned papers is included under the sixth division and this interesting subject is discussed in the chapter on questioned typewriting.

The seventh class of questioned documents are of great variety, and of all disputed papers they are perhaps most frequently brought under investigation. This class includes all documents, papers, writings or instruments which by their handwriting and contents tend to identify some person. The most common documents of this class are all kinds of anonymous and disputed letters. These may be ordinary letters offered as evidence, but usually are abusive, warning, obscene, or scurrilous communications, or any of the great variety of blackmailing, black-hand, and threatening letters which so frequently become the subject of legal inquiry.

Another important class of letters which it frequently becomes important to identify are those written by persons under suspicion or arrest, for the purpose of diverting suspicion from the writers. A suspected letter should be subjected to the most comprehensive and thorough examination, which, in many cases, will conclusively identify its author or show the fraudulent character of the document if it is fraudulent.

It will be seen in considering these various classes of disputed papers that there are two related but quite distinct questions regarding handwriting. The first question is whether a certain writing is genuine or forged. In such a case the writing is usually denied by the writer, or those who represent him, and the question to be determined is whether it is genuine writing, an imitation of genuine writing, or a wholly different writing. The second handwriting question in such inquiries, as outlined in the heading, is whether a certain writing will serve to identify the writer. Such writing may be and usually is disguised. If disguised then the question is, did the writer attempt to hide his personality and fail to do so, or is the writing not disguised and actually the writing of another person? In this class are included disguised anonymous letters and also ordinary letters and papers offered as evidence that by their writing serve as a means of identification.

In disguised writing the effort of the writer is directed to the exclusion of personal writing characteristics by the adoption of characteristics foreign to his own writing. The problem in the examination of such writing is to discover and weigh against each other involuntary and unconscious genuine characteristics and voluntary adopted or foreign characteristics.

A simulated writing[1] is one in which the attempt is made to copy or imitate the writing of another as is done in an ordinary signature forgery. To be entirely successful it is obvious that such writing by one who knows how to write, involves a double process and must not only contain the features of the writing imitated, but must also exclude the writer's own personal writing characteristics. A writing that is simply disguised, as is usually the case in anonymous letters, is one in which the writer only seeks to hide his own personality without assuming that of any other particular person. It is reasonable to expect that a simulated writing will resemble in some degree the writing it seeks to imitate, and it is equally apparent that a disguised writing will differ in some measure from the usual writing of one who thus attempts to hide his own personality.

The simple question sometimes arises whether a complete letter or other document containing considerable matter, and which is written rapidly and freely, is in the actual handwriting of a certain writer admitted specimens of whose writing of a similar character are shown. In such an inquiry it is simply necessary to determine to what an extent all the variable characteristics and habits of two natural and undisguised handwritings will accidentally coincide. With sufficient disputed and

---

[1] Simulate. To assume or have the mere appearance or form of, without the reality; assume falsely or fraudulently the condition or character of; act or take on a form in imitation of; counterfeit; imitate.—Standard Dictionary.

standard writing of this class by the same writer, proof of identity reaches such a degree of certainty that it often leads to confession or disappearance of the writer.

In any considerable quantity of writing it is usually possible to discover and show clearly whether a writing is natural and free or whether it is unnatural and feigned. A feigned hand is almost certain to be inconsistent with itself in important features and will not be free and rapid. If such a writing is free and rapid it is certain to show, when carefully analyzed, many of the characteristics of the natural writing of the writer no matter what disguise is employed.

When a signature is shown to be fraudulent the question naturally arises as to who committed the forgery. This question is usually asked in every such case, but cannot often be answered with much certainty, judging from the writing alone. It is much easier to show that a fraudulent signature is not genuine than it is to show that such a writing is actually the work of a particular writer. A forgery is a more or less successful imitation of the writing of another and it is seldom that the forger will incorporate in the few letters of a single signature a sufficient number of the characteristics of his own writing to serve to identify him positively as the writer.

When the attempt is made simply to disguise a quantity of writing, as in anonymous letters, the problem is a very different one and it is usually possible to show with much certainty who was the writer, but where only a signature is forged by imitation or tracing it is usually very difficult to discover from the writing itself who actually did write it, unless, as occasionally happens, the forgery is practically an undisguised specimen of the writing of the forger. The defects or shortcomings in a fraudulent signature are frequently of a character that point toward the writing of the forger, but alone are not often sufficient to identify him positively. It thus follows that it is much easier to prove forgery in a civil case or to establish the crime of uttering a forged paper than, from the writing alone, to fix the crime of forgery on some individual.

The degree of certainty of proof of forgery, or proof of identity through handwriting, necessarily differs enormously in different cases and under differing circumstances and ranges all the way from a mere conjecture to conclusive proof.[1] In some cases the basis for any conclusion whatever may be very meager on account of the nature of the question and an opinion is but little more than a mere conjecture and is of little value as evidence. Then again, such evidence may be so confirmatory of itself in its various phases, so cumulative in force when the many conditions are considered, that it is irresistibly convincing to a logical and unprejudiced mind.[2] In many cases handwriting in sufficient quantity and kind may afford the most positive and conclusive evidence of human identification.

[1] Upon principle, therefore, as well as from the necessity of the case, proof of handwriting, under proper restrictions, is as has been seen, everywhere admitted. Moreover, as has been well said, it seems that this kind of evidence, like all probable evidence, admits of every degree of certainty from the lowest presumption to the highest moral certainty.—American and English Encyclopedia of Law, Second Edition, Vol. XV. 283 (1903).

[2] From every standpoint from which the examination of the evidence has been considered, and the disputed points therein investigated, the mind of the court has been irresistibly led to the conclusion that the signatures of Philinda Terwilliger to the deed X and to the will were never signed by her, and that both of said signatures are false and forged.—Green vs. Terwilliger, 56 Fed. 384, 407 (1892).

A document suspected of being fraudulent should be subjected to an immediate and thorough examination. The value of promptness is especially urged. Important interests are sometimes endangered by a delay of only a few days and many questions regarding documents may arise that require the earliest possible attention if the true conditions are to be known with certainty and shown with clearness. It may seem unnecessary to make this suggestion, but in many instances such preliminary examinations are not only of the most hasty and superficial character, but are so long postponed that much of their value is lost. The preliminary examination should not only be prompt, but also should be thorough.

The procedure often followed would seem to indicate a belief that after incessant but utterly unsystematic and purposeless staring at a document it would in some mysterious way proclaim itself as false or true, as good or bad, and frequently the hope seems to be entertained that the answer will appear even to the unskilled and the inexperienced. One might as well expect to obtain by the same procedure an interpretation of the ancient inscriptions on an Egyptian obelisk.

CHAPTER III.

One of the first steps in the investigation of a suspected or disputed writing should be the seeking out of genuine writings with which it may be compared. Strange to say, in many instances this common sense proceeding is long delayed even in those jurisdictions where standard writings are admitted.

Unfortunately this rational method cannot be followed at all in those states and courts where only "writings in the case for other purposes" can be used for comparison. Under this peculiar and unfortunate condition it is usual that only very inadequate if not wholly improper standards are available and under such conditions it is not surprising that so-called proof of handwriting is often a mere farce. The frequent outcome of this old practice has been briefly discussed in the introduction of this book.

England changed the old practice by statute in 1854, and Massachusetts and Connecticut, to their honor be it said, have from the first permitted comparison of handwriting with properly proved standard writing, but the courts of numerous states, strange to say, have refused to change the practice. The average man is perfectly astounded to learn that a writing cannot be proved by going out and getting undoubtedly genuine writing to compare it with. New York did not change the practice until 1880, Pennsylvania did not make the change until

[16]

1895, and all the courts of several states and the United States federal courts in all the states in criminal cases, are still under the old procedure[1].

One of the principal objections to the ancient procedure was not necessarily that no writing whatever was available for comparison, but because that which might be available, that happened to be "in the case for other purposes," sometimes was worse than none as an exclusive basis of comparison. Many important cases have been tried with only one standard signature for comparison, and that not only of a different class, but sometimes

---

[1] The whole subject of handwriting comparison is most ably discussed in that valuable collection of legal information entitled Lawyers' Reports Annotated and known to every lawyer as "L. R. A." In an extended note (62 L. R. A. 818) much valuable information on the subject will be found.

In connection with another exhaustive and scholarly discussion of the subject, Prof. John H. Wigmore gives in his great work, Wigmore on Evidence (1904-1907), a list of the states that permit the introduction of standards of comparison in handwriting cases. From these two sources, in connection with recent inquiry on the subject, a list of the states is given with date of change from the old common law practice. The dates mostly refer to the years when statutes were passed, but in a few states the change was made by judicial decisions. In a few instances the date is somewhat uncertain, but the date given is approximately correct. West Virginia passed the statute admitting standards in 1907, and the Illinois legislature passed such a statute at its last session (1909), but because of some technical irregularity it will be necessary to submit the matter to the legislature again. It is surprising to many to know how new a thing real handwriting comparison is in most courts of law.

The list, including the recent changes, is as follows:

California, 1872; Colorado, 1893; Connecticut, 1791; Delaware, 1881; Florida, 1892; Georgia, 1895; Iowa, 1851; Kansas, 1872; Kentucky, 1886; Louisiana, 1866; Maine, 1822; Maryland, 1888; Massachusetts, 1813 and earlier; Minnesota, 1886; Mississippi, 1874; Missouri, 1895; Montana, 1895; Nebraska, 1867; New Hampshire, 1852; New Jersey, 1877; New York, 1880; Oklahoma, 1900; Ohio, 1863; Oregon, 1892; Pennsylvania, 1895; Rhode Island, 1872; South Dakota, 1905; Tennessee, 1889; Vermont, 1832; Virginia, 1884; Washington, 1896; West Virginia, 1907; Wisconsin, 1898.

The states still continuing the old practice unchanged or in which the procedure is mixed or doubtful are: Alabama, Arkansas, District of Columbia, Idaho, Illinois, Indiana, Michigan, New Mexico, North Carolina, South Carolina, Texas, Utah, and the Federal Courts.

written *thirty years* or more before or after the date of the disputed writing.

Under this old practice where the standard writing came into the case "by accident," it is not to be wondered at that such testimony often deserved the criticism it received and the whole history of the subject has been clouded by this unfortunate procedure.

Under the modern practice, permitting the introduction of writings for the purposes of comparison, abuses may creep in and justice be defeated, but this possibility is greatly reduced as compared with results under the old rules. With a competent judge and counsel of intelligence no unfairness to either side will result from the modern practice and the truth will be much more likely to prevail. Certain simple precautions may be necessary for the guidance of those who have not had experience with handwriting cases.

A questioned signature may be so unnatural as writing and so drawn and patched that its fraudulent character is quite evident when these things alone are clearly shown, and in some cases the exact identity of two or more signatures to a disputed document may in itself be sufficient to show their intrinsic fraudulent character, but the real nature of a disputed writing, in most cases, must finally be legally determined by actually comparing it with other writings which are proved or admitted to be genuine.

It is obvious that the best standards of comparison are those of the same general class as the questioned writing and as nearly as possible of the same date. Such standards should, as a rule, include all between certain dates covering a period of time both before and after the date of the writing in dispute. The amount of writing necessary for comparison differs in different cases, but enough should always be obtained to show clearly the writing habits of the one whose writing is under investigation. A positive conclusion that a signature is fraudulent can sometimes be reached by comparison with a small amount of genuine writing, especially, as stated above, if the disputed signature is a bungling forgery that is suspicious in itself. More standard writing may, therefore, be necessary as a basis for positive opinion that a writing is genuine than is necessary to show that it is fraudulent.

Several signatures should always be obtained, if possible, before any final decision is rendered, five signatures always constituting a more satisfactory basis for an opinion than one, and ten being better than five. It is not often helpful to use more than fifty to seventy-five, except in unusual cases, and it is not usually desirable to use those of widely different dates if sufficient contemporary writings of the right class can be obtained.

Notwithstanding the common practice of bankers in this regard, it is always dangerous to base a positive conclusion that a suspected signature is genuine on a comparison of it with only one genuine signature. For comparison with a disputed letter one good complete standard letter may be sufficient, but in such an inquiry more should always be obtained if possible. Many errors in the examination of questioned writing are due to the fact that an adequate amount of standard writing is not obtained before a final decision is given. The competent examiner will decline to give any opinion until a satisfactory basis for such an opinion is available.

As stated at the beginning, the writings most to be depended upon as standards are always those bearing dates nearest to the date of the disputed writing and of the same general class. This is true for the reason that writing of different individuals varies in differing degrees as written at different times and for different purposes, and the only way to learn of these habits of writing of any writer is through standard writing.

Some writers have formal business signatures for checks, legal documents and important papers, and careless or unconventional signatures for familiar letters or similar writings, although, as a rule, these two classes of signatures are used interchangeably to some extent by most writers. It is obvious that the conditions last named would affect the value of either class of such writings as exclusive standards of comparison with a writing of the other class. Certainly with the average writer there is no appreciable difference in signatures due alone to the fact that they are attached to ordinary business documents of varying degrees of importance.

The signatures of the great majority of writers do not differ in general style from their other writing and in such cases it is entirely proper to compare signatures and general writing, such as the body writing of letters and other written documents. The signatures of some writers, however, differ in certain radical and pronounced particulars from their general writing, in which case signatures should be compared only with signatures and general writing with general writing. In many instances, however, the writing of signatures influences general writing in certain very significant particulars. Peculiar formations, combinations or individual habits which become fixed by being often repeated in frequently written signatures may unmistakably affect general writing where such letters, forms or combinations appear. In such a case writing other than signatures may be particularly valuable for comparison with a peculiar questioned signature, or genuine signatures as standards may become very useful in identifying the author of such a disputed letter or a general writing by such a writer.

The most significant writing characteristics persist to a greater or less extent under whatever circumstances writing is produced, but here again the habits of different individuals vary greatly. A conclusion that two sets of writings are not by the same hand, as in signature inquiries, should mainly be based upon comparisons with writings of the same class, but a conclusion that two sets of writings are by the same writer, as in anonymous letter cases, may be greatly enforced and confirmed if writings produced under very different conditions all show many identical characteristics.

Unusual conditions under which signatures are written may affect their value as standards of comparison. Hastily written, careless signatures, like those in express or telegraph messenger's books, for instance, should, of course, not be used exclusively for comparison with a questioned signature unless it is supposed to have been written under similar conditions of haste and lack of care.

The acceptability of standards may also be affected by the age of the person whose writing is in question or the age of the writer when the disputed writing is alleged to have been produced. Handwriting is individualized from the very beginning of learning to write, but such development becomes much more pronounced as soon as writing is used to any considerable extent for practical purposes and its distinct individuality develops much earlier with some writers than with others. Even after a writing becomes distinctively individualized it will gradually change in numerous particulars, the extent of the change depending upon the amount of writing done, the occupation, habits and environment of the writer.

With one who writes but little and whose surroundings continue the same, changes will be but slowly developed, while the writing of one who writes much will often show a gradual but constant evolution in certain particulars so that a careful examination by dates will show the development, even in a small signature, of certain definite, permanent characteristics which begin at a certain time and continue through certain definite periods of time. This chronological fact often becomes very important in examining a questioned document which purports to have been produced at some remote time. The writing of a fraudulent document of this character is often modeled after writing of a later period and sometimes its spurious character may thus be conclusively shown.

The most significant form characteristics of pencil writings are in general character the same as those in pen writings by the same individual and a questioned document in pencil may properly be compared in this particular with pen writing, but the standards of comparison in such a case should, if possible, include pencil writing. Shading, pen pressure, pen position and line quality characteristics are not exactly the same in pen and pencil writing, but such differences will not render one kind of writing entirely useless as a proper standard for comparison with the other, but would tend to weaken its value. Some writers make considerable distinction between their pen and pencil writing, while others do not, and this fact also should always be determined and considered.

Pencil writing is usually produced with more finger action than pen writing, especially by one who usually writes with the arm motion, and a pencil is usually grasped more firmly than a pen and, as a rule, such writing also requires more pressure on the paper, which may interfere somewhat with free action. With some writers, however, pencil writing is nearly always careless and rapid and much inferior to their pen writing. It will thus be seen that similarities between pen and pencil writings may be very significant as indicating identity, as in anonymous letter inquiries, but certain differences in speed, pen pressure or shading would not necessarily be conclusive as indicating lack of identity.

Physical conditions may affect the acceptability of standards. Many forgeries are committed in attempts to obtain the property of those who were advanced in years at the time it is alleged the writing in dispute was done, and sometimes sickness or weakness through age during a certain definite period of time may affect such aged writers so as to render writings made before or after a certain definite date improper and undesirable as exclusive standards of comparison. Signatures produced during a period of great weakness would, of course, not be proper for exclusive comparison with writing at a subsequent period under normal conditions.

If questioned writing purports to be by an aged writer it is especially desirable that the standards should not only be near the date of the writing in question, but it should also, if possible, be shown that they were written under similar health conditions. A severe illness may so affect an aged writer as to render all previous signatures improper as standards of comparison with a later writing unless this fact is understood and given due consideration.

It is sometimes found that a signature to a fraudulent document, bearing a date of a number of years previous, may not accord with the physical condition of the writer on the date it bears. It can sometimes be definitely shown that on the exact date of a disputed document the alleged writer not only did not write, but was physically unable to do so. This subject is further discussed in the chapter on variation in genuine writing.

Request writings and forced writings are not usually the best standards of comparison, but may be of very great value where writings serve to identify a person, this being especially true with illiterate persons and those unaccustomed to writing. If circumstances are favorable suspected anonymous letter writers, or those who deny any writing of considerable length, should sometimes be asked to write the disputed matter from dictation or typewritten copy under as nearly as possible the same conditions as those under which it is alleged or suspected that it was produced. The same kind of pencil or pen should be used and also paper of the same size, ruling and quality. Such writing should, if possible, be obtained in such maner that it is not strained, unnatural and self-conscious. If considerable writing is done and included in it is all or part of the disputed writing, some of such writing is quite certain to be in a natural style. Innocent parties do not often object to furnishing specimens of their writing and suspected parties may not dare to refuse or, as is very frequently the case, may be entirely unconscious of the fact that their writing is full of peculiar individual characteristics.

It is sometimes a good plan to incorporate into such request writing matter apparently on some outside subject, but including words, expressions, letters, names and combinations that are found in the questioned writing. Under these conditions a writer is more apt to write in a natural way the matter in question than if he is asked to write that alone. A small amount of writing produced by anyone when the question of writing is in the mind, is apt to be somewhat self-conscious and unnatural so that a larger quantity should be written to overcome this difficulty.

If it appears that the writer is endeavoring to write a disguised hand, the same matter should be dictated twice and written on different papers, and matter should be dictated that is not understood by the writer, which matter may be joined with simple words or letters and figures which can be written rapidly and will be more likely to be written freely.

Depositors' bank signatures are in many instances the most undesirable standards with which to compare a questioned writing because of the conditions under which the signatures are usually written. Such writing is often done while the writer is standing and with a strange pen and in an unaccustomed place, and formerly such signatures were written in a big book and now are usually put on a small card. But what is frequently more disturbing than these conditions is the consciousness of the fact that the signature is being written to be used for comparison, which, with many writers, as stated above, tends to produce a self-conscious, unnatural signature. With only one such signature for comparison it is not strange that forged papers may be paid at a bank when handwriting comparison alone must be depended upon.

A change should be made in the method of securing such signatures for comparison and with inactive accounts they should undoubtedly be renewed from time to time, particularly with old people, and with such accounts more than one signature should always be procured and kept for comparison. Two paid checks or vouchers, drawn in the ordinary course of business, would serve very much better as standards than those usually employed. Decisions on handwriting, with most unfortunate results, are made by bankers on standards of comparison that would be considered inadequate by the most competent and experienced handwriting examiners.

Standards of comparison offered in court should be carefully scrutinized throughout by one capable of making such an examination in order to discover possible forgeries offered as standards and also to see if such proposed standards show evidences of retouching, tampering or changes of any kind which the signatures may not have contained as originally written. The attempt may be made to introduce as standards, not only addi-
nal forgeries by which to prove forgeries, but genuine

signatures which have been fraudulently changed to make them conform to the signature of a disputed document.

These changes in genuine signatures may be made by actually erasing by chemicals or by abrasion portions of a genuine signature and then restoring the parts in the manner desired, or may be the retouching and patching of undoubtedly genuine signatures in order to explain and excuse such retouching in a disputed writing. Fortunately such evidences of erasures and retouching done at a different time and by a different hand are, as a rule, perfectly evident when carefully examined. The line or pen strokes composing such signatures should be carefully examined throughout with the microscope in good light, and suspicious signatures should be objected to by counsel and excluded by the court. With an attorney fairly alert and reasonably well qualified on the subject no abuse on this score need be feared.

The question as to what are proper and adequate standards of comparison may arise in the consideration of certain so-called tests which are sometimes proposed in connection with handwriting testimony. Unfortunately such tests are in some instances manifestly unfair and their sole purpose is thus to divert attention from the main facts and destroy the effect of damaging testimony. No competent and honest witness will refuse to submit to a fair test and no witness should be compelled to submit to a test that is not fair.

The inquiry is sometimes made whether several test signatures or words on a sheet were written by one, two or more writers. This at first may seem like a proper question and an answer may be insisted upon, but there may be and usually is no suitable basis for an opinion in such an inquiry on account of the lack of proper and sufficient standards. A competent and experienced examiner will not give a positive opinion in any such matter until comparison can be made with a sufficient quantity of standard writing, unless, as may be the case, the existing fact is perfectly evident by a mere inspection.

If, however, a witness has given a positive opinion on the main question in dispute based on an equally slender foundation, as unfortunately may be the case with the presumptuous or the inexperienced, then a test which is really parallel in character to the original inquiry, may be entirely proper and allowable. Much of the discredit that has been brought upon handwriting testimony has resulted from rash attempts to give opinions in the absence of proper standards. This unfortunate practice is undoubtedly due, in a measure, to the bank custom, already referred to, of keeping only one signature for handwriting comparison.

Writing characteristics of any handwriting as determined and classified in a thorough examination are, (1) permanent, or fixed, (2) usual or common, (3) occasioual, and (4) exceptional or accidental. It therefore follows that a handwriting has a certain field of possible and expected variation and without a sufficient quantity of standard writing significant habits cannot be determined, and the value and force of characteristics cannot be definitely known. It is usually through ignorance, but sometimes through pretension, that the attempt is voluntarily made to differentiate the various signatures of a specially prepared test group, as described above, with no other standards for comparison than the various signatures themselves. All of such signatures may be disguised and they are quite likely to be unnatural and may be simulated from one model, and with no fixed habits and characteristics for comparison it can easily be seen what presumption it may be to give any opinion whatever. The case is not at all parallel with the comparison of a disputed writing with a sufficient quantity of proved, genuine writings or an adequate number of naturally written, genuine signatures.

In such inquiries the fact should always be brought out and emphasized that tests to be fair and of value must be parallel in nature with the main question at issue. Because one signature is pronounced a forgery it is not to be assumed that any forgery, no matter how skillfully executed, should necessarily be discovered at sight or even by study. Like counterfeits of any kind they may be good enough to deceive the most skillful, but this does not prove that a bungling forgery is genuine nor does it follow that if a definite opinion can be given in one case it must be in the other.

To insist on a positive opinion under any test is saying, in effect, that one who is not able and willing to answer correctly every question or solve every problem is therefore not qualified to answer any question or solve any problem. Such a method of proving either competency or incompetency would not be permitted in any properly conducted scientific inquiry. The competent man in any field of inquiry does not hesitate to acknowledge his limitations and he should not be forced to do that which he does not assume to be able to do.

If the pretender or the unskilled witness presumes to

give opinions offhand and without a proper and adequate foundation, as unfortunately is sometimes the case, it is right and proper that such ignorance and pretension should be exposed by proper tests similar in character to the main inquiry. Often such witnesses are utterly unable to separate the actual signature in dispute from the genuine signatures in the case when all are presented in the form of photographs, especially if the size of the signatures has been somewhat changed.

Some of those who testify from recollection and pretend to "know a handwriting" will often make the most absurd errors on the simplest tests. They not only cannot pick out the disputed signature when all are photographed, but in many instances actually cannot distinguish the very writing in question in the case from the standard signatures, if the signatures are mixed up and shown out of their connection with other matter or in irregular order. Such practical tests are perfectly proper and may show most conclusively the unreliable character of such testimony.

Just a further word is added to this chapter regarding the long discussion, in fact covering several centuries, of what in legal phrase was known as "comparison of hands." The point at issue first was whether any comparison of any kind in a legal contention would be permitted, and later, as we have seen, the question arose as to the admission of genuine writings for purposes of comparison. The fact that in early days only an occasional juryman could read and write no doubt had an important bearing on the subject. Many of the old practices are now as obsolete as "Benefit of Clergy" or indictments for witchcraft.

Some knowledge of the ancient discussion is necessary to a full understanding of some of the later rulings
on the subject. For instance, one of the reasons at first
for objecting to the admission of writings for comparison was that under the still older law any comparison
whatever was deemed improper, and the influence of
this old rule can be traced through the decisions long
after the rule itself was changed.

Incident to the long struggle to get genuine writings
admitted for comparison in handwriting cases numerous
queer arguments were developed. For nearly seventy-
five years now one of these has trickled down through
the decisions, which, in brief, is the contention that in
making a comparison "recollection" of a handwriting
is more to be depended upon than the most thorough
and extended study and direct comparison of the disputed writing with any number of genuine examples.

It is not probable that the same argument would be
seriously applied to anything else under heaven, but in
solemn legal form it has been made to apply to handwriting. The peculiar doctrine is now nearly obsolete,
but still appears now and then in some opinion or some
text-book that harks back to the old precedents.

Mr. Justice Coleridge, of the King's Bench, is in
great measure responsible for the emphasis on this reasoning which was definitely formulated in 1836, not
directly on this particular subject but in an argument
to show that standard writings should not under any
conditions be admitted for comparison. The case was
Doe d. Mudd vs. Suckermore (5 Ad. & El. 705) and, as
the title of the case would seem to suggest, the opinion
has not tended to clarify the stream of justice.

As part of this argument against the admission of standard writings, and mainly for the purpose of showing that they were not necessary or desirable, the opinion vaguely says: "The test of genuineness ought to be the general resemblance, not to the formation of the letters in some other specimen or specimens, but to the general character of the writing."

The contention in simpler words seems to be that such judgments must depend upon an impression of a handwriting as a whole and a certain indescribable intuition that excludes all analysis and necessarily jumps to a conclusion. Few things are more misleading or deceptive than general resemblance or "general character" in writing and nearly all errors in such examinations are, as a matter of fact, made by those who literally follow this improper method. This vague and fallacious argument, however, has been quoted with approval in scores of legal opinions.

Even before the date of this decision the weakness of the argument, then under discussion in the courts of this country and England, was pointed out in Lyon vs. Lyman, 9 Conn. 55 (1831), by an able Connecticut judge who, on an appeal to set aside a verdict because writings had actually been compared by a witness, disposes of what he calls the "feeble objection" in these sensible words:

"The first class of witnesses had seen the defendant write. They believed it to be his handwriting; but on cross-examination, they said they did not know that they were sufficiently acquainted with it to *determine* it to be his, except by comparing it with the writings proved to be genuine. Surely, the objection here was entirely to the weight of their testimony and not to its admissibility. A fair paraphrase of their testimony is, that they *believed* it to be his handwriting from having seen him write. This, according to the second position, would render the testimony admissible. But they *knew* it to be his, by comparing it with his other writings . . .

"But I forbear. It has always appeared to be a very feeble objection; and I rejoice to see it overruled. The motion ought to be denied."

It is to be regretted that the author of this opinion was not then a judge of England's highest court.

Many text writers and many judges have from the first refused to follow Mr. Justice Coleridge and have spoken in plain terms on the question[1], but the rule laid

---

[1]Prof. Wigmore, already quoted at the beginning of this chapter, closes his able discussion of the questions of "comparison of hands" and admission of standard writings, as follows:

The argument of Mr. Justice Coleridge that "the English law has no provisions for regulating the manner of conducting the inquiry" illustrates that perverse disposition of the Angle-Saxon judge—the despair of the jurist—to tie his own hands in the administration of justice, to deny himself, by a submission to self-created bonds, that power of helping the good and preventing the bad which an untechnical common sense would never hesitate to exercise. The enlightened procedure on this subject is that which had subsequently been introduced in England by the statute of 1854, that which the Court of Massachusetts had already adopted from the beginning and that which now prevails by statute in many of our jurisdictions, namely, the method of addressing all evidence of genuineness [of standards] to the judge and of leaving the control of its length, its quality, and its effect to the trial judge's discretion.—Wigmore on Evidence, Vol. III. Sec. 2000 (1904).

An admirable example of the absurdity to which the admission of knowledge evidence at the same time with the exclusion of comparison evidence, has led is shown in the case of Smith v. Sainsbury (1832) 5 Car. & P. 196; the court implying (something that it could not believe) that greater certainty could be obtained by evidence from the shadowy standard in the witness's mind, than from actual juxtaposition.—L. R. A. Note, 62 L. R. A. 818 by L. B. B. (1904).

It would seem as if the following discussion of the matter from a leading Minnesota case would be conclusive:

In general, and from necessity, the authenticity of handwriting must be subject to proof by comparison of some sort, or by testimony which is based upon comparison, between the writing in question

down in Mudd vs. Suckermore continued in force in England till 1854, and in this country generally till late in the last century and, as we have already seen, is still the law in numerous states and the question as to whether it is preferable, all things considered, to prove writings

---

and that which is in some manner recognized or shown to be genuine. This is everywhere allowed, through the opinions of witnesses who have acquired a knowledge, more or less complete, of the handwriting of a person, as by having seen him write or from acquaintance with papers authenticated as genuine. In such cases the conception of the handwriting retained in the mind of the witness becomes a standard for comparison, by reference to which his opinion is formed, and given in evidence. It would seem that a standard generally not less satisfactory, and very often much more satisfactory, is afforded by the opportunity for examining, side by side, the writing in dispute and other writings of unquestioned authenticity; and, this, we think is in accordance with the common judgment and experience of men.— Morrison vs. Porter, 35 Minn. 435. Dickinson, J. (1886).

In many cases it is more satisfactory to allow a witness to compare the writing in issue with other writings of unquestioned authority as to genuineness, than to compare it with the standard which he may have formed or retained in his mind from a knowledge of the party's handwriting.—Green vs. Terwilleger, 56 Fed. 384 (1892).

Abstractly reasoning upon this kind of proof it seems plain that a more correct judgment as to the identity of handwriting would be formed by a witness by a critical and minute comparison with a fair and genuine specimen of the party's handwriting, than by a comparison of seen signatures with the faint impression produced by having seen the party write, and even then, perhaps, under circumstances which did not awaken his attention; hence the greater necessity for such a standard, as without it no possible legal conclusion could be reached.—Reid vs. Warner, 17 L. C. Rep. 485 (1867).

I think in all the cases where little weight is recommended to be given to the opinion of experts of handwriting, a clear distinction is to be drawn between the mere opinion of the witness and the assistance he may afford by pointing to the marks, indications and characters in the writings themselves, upon which the opinion is based, and that the caution applies to cases where opinions conflict and the alleged forgery is admittedly executed with great skill, and the detection is unquestionably difficult.—19 Nova Scotia 279 (1886).

No clearer and more effective discussion of the subject has appeared than that of Hon. Edward Twistleton in the great work on the Junius Letters. He says:

"Comparison of handwritings, as an instrument for ascertaining who is the handwriter of a disputed document, seems very superior to the declaration of a witness as to his belief, however familiar he may be with the hand of the supposed writer. If there are sufficient materials for comparison, this superiority is great, even when there is

by recollection or by using standards, is actually still under discussion.

This question of general appearance or "general character" in handwriting is treated more at length in a subsequent chapter on individual and general characteristics of writing and also in the chapter on simulated forgeries.

----

no disguise; and in the case of a really good disguise, the superiority is overwhelming.

"A witness who declares such belief can only form his opinion from comparison; but one of the terms of the comparison is withdrawn from the knowledge of others. That term of comparison exists simply in the memory of the witness, who has the type of a particular handwriting present to his mind. But the value of this type depends wholly upon the correctness of his original observations, and on the accuracy of his memory. Unless he has previously studied a handwriting for the express purpose of comparison, his conclusions can scarcely ever be more than a strong mental impression of resemblance. For others, his opinion derives all its value from authority. He cannot go through the proofs of what he asserts; others cannot see what he thinks he sees in his mind's eye; and, if he has made a mistake in his type, his error cannot be proved to exist. Moreover, if he has to deal with a thoroughly well disguised hand, the general type in his mind ceases to have much value.

"The case is very different in the comparison of documents presented to the eyes of those who are to judge respecting them. Here they know both the terms of the comparison. Ultimately, their conclusions need not rest upon authority at all. A general expert in handwriting may point out coincidences in documents which a volunteer would not have observed, if the documents had been in his possession during a long series of years; but those coincidences are outward objective facts, the common property of experts and volunteers.

"If the expert has skill in analyzing his own impressions, he can go through the proofs of everything which he asserts and can make others see what he sees. If he makes a mistake, his error admits of proof. Hence the case with which he deals, however complicated, becomes merely one of reasoning, in which internal circumstantial evidence is applied to demonstrate a disputed fact."—Hon. Edward Twistleton in Handwriting of Junius, pp lxi, lxii (1871).

CHAPTER IV.

Photographs are useful in nearly every questioned document investigation, and in many cases it is impossible without them to present the facts to a court and jury in an effective, convincing manner. In such an inquiry a tangible thing is under examination for the purpose of determining which of two conflicting interpretations is the correct one, and if the investigation is to be thorough and complete, certain instruments and illustrations are necessary to bring into view and make plain and clear the physical facts which constitute the evidence upon which the final conclusion is based. The photographic camera is one of these instruments.

Photographs often make clear what may otherwise be hidden or indistinct and this alone is sufficient reason for their use. In many different ways they are helpful; and some of the various uses are here described and some technical directions are given for the most effective illustration of a few of the numerous questions that may arise regarding disputed documents.

In the first place every questioned document should be promptly photographed in order that a correct and permanent record may be made of it and its condition.

---

[1]This chapter, in part, first appeared in The Albany Law Journal, Vol. 63, No. 7, and is reprinted here by permission. Up to the date of its recent discontinuance The Albany Law Journal was the oldest law publication in America. Complete files covering its long history are to be found in the leading law libraries.

The photographic record may be of great value in case of loss or mutilation of the original document or in the event of any fraudulent or accidental changes being made in it or of any changes due to natural causes.

Photographs should also be made of disputed documents for the more important reason that they may be of great assistance in showing the fraudulent character of the papers, or on the contrary may be of distinct value in establishing the genuineness of documents wrongfully attacked.

Those especially who question the genuineness of a paper should insist on their right to photograph it and if the request is refused a petition to the proper tribunal for an order should be promptly made. Nor should the parties who do not have possession of a document be compelled to accept unsuitable photographs made by the opposing parties, but they should insist on having the photographing done satisfactorily.

It is sometimes contended by those who object to photographs that in some way they supplant the original document in dispute and serve as a sole basis for a final conclusion. This is, of course, not the fact, for their purpose is to illustrate, test and interpret the original, and with their aid this is done without danger of injuring or entirely destroying it.

Even with the utmost care a disputed paper seldom goes through a protracted trial without being soiled, torn and broken and if the original document itself and it alone is to be handled, tested, measured and examined by court, jury and witnesses day after day, it is almost certain to be so defaced and injured that finally it may be difficult to determine from the paper itself whether it is genuine or not.

The ways in which photographs may be helpful and illuminating in questioned document investigations are so numerous that only the more important are here described.

The most important reason for making photographs of a disputed document is because by this means the writing in question can be accurately enlarged so that every characteristic can be clearly and properly interpreted whether the facts so shown point to genuineness or to fraud. Writing in natural size is, in most instances, too small for critical study and even a slight enlargment is often of great assistance in showing the facts. In some inquiries the facts can be successfully denied if they are not shown by properly made enlarged photographs.[1]

Another purpose in photographing a document is by this means to provide any number of perfectly accurate

---

[1]We have ourselves been able to compare these signatures by means of photographic copies and fully concur (from evidence "oculis subjecta fidelibus") that the seal and the signature of Pico on this instrument are forgeries.—Luco vs. U. S., 23 Howard (1859).

The magnified photographic copies of the genuine signatures of the defendant, and of the disputed signature, which was submitted to the inspection of the jury, were, we think, in connection with the testimony of Mr. Southworth, admissible in evidence. It is not dissimilar to the examination with a magnifying glass. Proportions are so enlarged thereby to the vision, that faint lines and marks, as well as the genuine characteristics of handwriting which perhaps could not otherwise be clearly discerned and appreciated, are thus disclosed to observation and afford additional and useful means of making comparisons between admitted signatures and one which is alleged to be only an imitation.—Marcy vs. Barnes, 16 Gray, Mass. 161 (1860).

The administration of justice profits by the progress of science, and its history shows it to have been almost the earliest in antagonism to popular delusions and superstitions. The revelations of the microscope are constantly resorted to, in protection of individual and public interests. It is difficult to conceive of any reason why, in a court of justice, a different rule of evidence should exist, in respect to the magnified image, presented in the lens in the photographer's camera, and permanently delineated upon the sensitive paper. Either may be reproductions of it, thus affording unlimited opportunity for study, comparison and investigation by any number of examiners, which would not be possible by using the original paper alone.   Photographic duplicates also enable court and jury to see, understand and weigh testi-

distorted or erroneous through imperfect instruments or manipulation, but that would be apparent or easily proved.   If they are relied upon as agencies, for accurate mathematical results in mensuration and astronomy, there is no reason why they should be deemed unreliable in matters of evidenc.   Wherever what they disclose can aid or elucidate the just determination of legal controversies, there can be no well formed objection to resorting to them.—Frank vs. Chemical Nat. Bank, 5 Jones & S., 26 N. Y. Sup. Ct. (1874), aff. 84 N. Y. 209.

Enlarged copies of a disputed signature or writing, and of those used as comparisons, may be of great aid to a jury in comparing and examining different specimens of one's handwriting.   Characteristics of it may be brought out and made clear by the aid of a photograph or magnifying glass which would not be discernible by the naked eye.   As well object to the use of an eye-glass by one whose vision is defective.—Rowell vs. Fuller, 59 Vt. 688 (1887).

Enlarged photograph copies proven to have been correctly made, of the will and of the signatures of Philinda Terwilliger. . . . . were admitted in evidence.   These copies were of great assistance and value to counsel in their arguments and have materially aided the court in its investigation in comparing and examining the different specimens of handwriting exhibited in the original document.—Green vs. Terwilliger, 56 Fed. Rep. 384 (1892).

The mere momentary enlargement of the signatures one by one by each juror for himself with the aid of a magnifying glass, giving different effects according to the place where he holds the glass, must be regarded as a poor substitute for the permanent enlargement of all the signatures alike by magnified copies which are the same to all the jurors and do not vary on different examinations.—Editorial Comment by "B. A. R.," in L. R. A., 35:813 (1897).

The defense caused the signature of Governor Armijo to the alleged grant and one existing on one of the documents offered as a standard of comparison, to be photographically enlarged.   After proving by the photographer by whom the photographs were made the accuracy of the method pursued and the results obtained by him, the enlarged photographs were tendered and were admitted in evidence over objection.   The ruling was correct.—U. S. vs. Ortis, 176 U. S. Supreme Court (1899).

Appellees had the signature in contest and two other signatures of the testator, one at the foot of a check, and the one on the back of a note, both clearly genuine, enlarged and reproduced by photography.   These photographs were exhibited to the jury after proof by the photographers of their accuracy.   Appellant complains of the admission of the photographs.   But they were only a more enduring form of exhibiting the signatures to the jury as under a magnifying glass.—First National Bank vs. Wisdom's Ex'rs. 111 Ky., 63 S. W. Rep. 461 (1901).

mony regarding a document as it is being given, which cannot be done without such assistance, as all could not see the original paper at the same time.

Another reason for photographing a document is that photographs can be cut apart in any way necessary or desirable and the various parts classified for comparison as cannot be done without some means of making accurate duplicates of the original paper. The real significance of many writing characteristics cannot be clearly understood until parts to be compared are classified and all brought within the angle of vision.

Except in the case of those specially skilled, the eye is almost totally unable to carry unfamiliar form or color impressions, and but very few are able properly to note even the most conspicuous resemblances or differences in objects that cannot be examined close together[1]. Objects that are really different apparently differ more and more the closer together they are placed; or, if similar, appear to be more and more alike as they are brought together. In showing dissimilarity or identity in two sets of writings the cumulative force of such grouped writing characteristics is, in many instances, irresistible. The logical way to determine whether things are alike or different is to examine them side by side, and photographs make this possible in comparing writings. As

[1]When the original is produced, but it is desired also conveniently to collate specimens by photographic groupings (as by placing many specimens in juxtaposition on a single sheet), the original is not literally unavailable, in the sense of being tangibly beyond procurement. Nevertheless there are still lacking and unproduced to instantaneous perception the minute resemblances and differences which appear upon close juxtaposition and fade from memory in the operation of passing from one document to the others. Hence the photographic juxtaposition does, in strict sense, "produce" these otherwise unavailable minutiae, and such a grouping is therefore allowable without even any deviation from technical principle.—Wigmore on Evidence, Vol. I. Sec. 797 (1904).

FIG. 2—Document Camera on Special Stand in vertical position. Object board removed and instrument arranged for photographing books or any bulky objects.

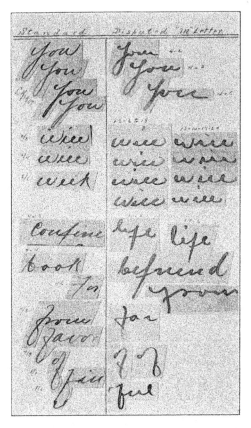

Fig. 3—Grouped comparison of portions of anonymous letter and standard letter by suspected writer, showing method of comparison by juxtaposition.

Professor Wigmore so well points out, the original itself is not available for examination, or rather for the best examination, until by means of photographs comparison is made possible.

There are certain microscopic conditions in connection with certain inquiries that even cannot be clearly seen except under proper magnification. Such facts may be vital, and are none the less facts notwithstanding their smallness and need only to be seen to be appreciated.

In jury cases particularly it is sometimes very difficult if not entirely impossible to prove such conditions because of the difficulty of showing them. Here again photography renders great assistance. Properly made photo-micrographs of such parts give court and jury in permanent form the transitory view that can only be seen by one at a time by the use of the microscope. Such enlarged photographs are sometimes absolutely conclusive; they are silent but convincing witnesses of fact and not of opinion and cannot be successfully disputed.

Many other conditions may arise under which photography is useful. One of these is the necessity of deciding whether a writing was continuously written under

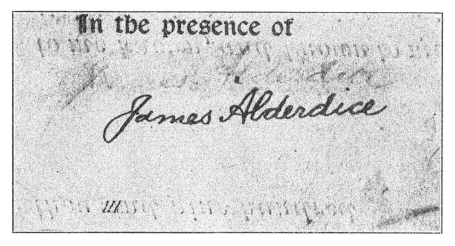

Fig. 4—A chemically erased signature reproduced by photography after subjection to fumes of ammonia sulphide. Case of People vs. Alderdice. Photo. by Drummond, New York City.

the same conditions or whether it contains an added fraudulent portion. The photographic lens and sensitized photographic plate will distinguish and make permanent record of differences in tint that the human eye does not see clearly until pointed out in this way. A photograph, in such an inquiry as that just described, may thus be indispensable as a means of pointing the way to the truth. This phase of photographic work is discussed more at length in the chapter on ink.

Photographs may also be useful in showing delicate discolorations, due to chemical erasures or other fraudulent changes, which otherwise might be overlooked, denied or misinterpreted. Ordinary photographic plates render yellow tints as shades of black, and as many discolorations have a yellow tinge, a photograph will show such conditions with great clearness.

This tendency to make black of yellow is also of great value in photographing old and faded yellow writing or writing made to simulate it. A photograph in such case reproduces the original with accuracy of form and also makes it more legible, thus giving an opportunity for study and comparison that the original does not afford. In some cases the indistinctness of the writing in question is its strongest defense and as soon as it is clearly photographed, and especially if it is suitably enlarged, it immediately becomes vulnerable from many points. In such cases photographs are not merely desirable; they are necessary.

Photography is also helpful in determining whether erasures by abrasion have been made in a document. If

Fig. 5—Transmitted light photograph of portions of note for three hundred thousand dollars, in W. M. Rice case (New York), dated back twenty years, showing careful erasure of printed figures of a later dated note form.

they have been made and the paper was afterwards rubbed down and refinished, it may, in certain rare cases, be difficult to show the fact, but by this process of erasure

FIG. 6—Transmitted light photograph, showing erasure by abrasion. "Mar. 4" on opposite side of sheet.

a portion of the paper has been removed, rendering the field of the erasure more transparent, and a photograph of the document by transmitted light may show conclusively that an erasure has been made.

Erasures by abrasion or by an ordinary rubber eraser may sometimes be shown very clearly and recorded in permanent form by a photograph taken with the paper placed obliquely to the plane of the lens and plate and inclined at just the right angle of reflection to show differences in the reflected light from different portions of the paper surface. Such erasures should be promptly photographed, particularly in cases when the handling of the paper may obliterate or render indistinct conditions that originally may be very clearly seen.

Transmitted light photography is very useful in the examination of water-marks. It also furnishes one method of determining the identity or difference in

papers by showing arrangement of the fibres and the
markings of the wire gauze and dandy-roll with such

Fig. 7—Enlarged transmitted light photographs of dated watermarks
in writing paper.

distinctness as to render comparison of these characteristics easy that otherwise would be very difficult if not
impossible.

Where the question is one of continuity of strokes or
of retouching of the writing, a photograph by trans-

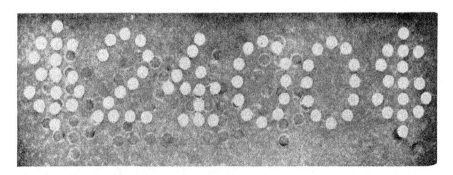

Fig. 8—Transmitted light photograph showing original check punch characters 24 filled up and 2400 punched over the same field.

mitted light will show plainly the uneven distribution of ink in interrupted strokes and the presence of the added ink film in retouched strokes. In retouched writing the added ink, which may make a line twice as thick in certain places, may not change the color of the writing in the least when viewed by direct light, but will simply change its thickness, and this difference will be plainly discernible in a transmitted light photograph for the reason that the added ink film will make the line just so much more opaque at that point.

The principle of stereoscopic photography, as applied to the microscopic investigation of questioned documents, apparently has not been employed hitherto, and illustrations such as those described below have not actually been presented in a court of law, but there cannot be a valid objection to a method that certainly would tend to promote the ends of justice.

The principle of the stereograph is that of the two-eyed view or binocular vision, by which means things are seen exactly as they are. Depth, or the third dimension in a stereo-photograph, is shown by taking two views of the same object or scene from slightly different points of view, just as the two eyes see, and then by looking at these two views at once, as united in the stereoscope, there is carried to the brain the same sense of depth and distance as is conveyed when the two eyes see the actual scene.

The stereographic photo-micrograph shows conditions in connection with certain questioned document cases with remarkable distinctness. In any inquiry where it is desirable to show depth or solidity, such a photograph is of very great value. Questions of this kind arise regarding the sequence of crossed lines, and also as to whether a writing across a fold preceded or followed the folding of the paper, this sometimes being a question of vital importance.

Certain conclusions regarding paper fiber and the relation of ink to it and changed conditions in paper surface due to erasures and changes, may be effectively illustrated in this manner. Stereoscopic illustrations may also be very helpful when the question arises as to whether typewriting was done on a certain individual machine, the letters of which show certain bruises and imperfections. Seals and impressed designs of any kind can by this same method of illustration be shown very clearly. These are all microscopic questions, and in the absence of the necessary instruments or of appropriate illustrations, it may be impossible to show the existing facts.

To be of any value for these purposes, stereoscopic photographs must be made in greatly enlarged form and the ordinary stereoscopic camera cannot be used. The special apparatus necessary carries only a single lens, with which two slightly different views are made of the same object, and by this means the same result is obtained as in simultaneous views with the two lenses of the regular stereoscopic camera. Two lenses cannot be used for this work, as it would be impossible to bring the lenses close enough together under the required magnification.

The degree of enlargement desirable in such photographs naturally depends upon the conditions, but ranges from twenty-five to seventy-five diameters for practical work.   It cannot be understood without actual trial with what realism certain delicate microscopic conditions can thus be illustrated[1].

Several highest courts of appeal have answered affirmatively the question whether stereoscopic photographs, and the stereoscope to view them, may be used in court. These decisions relate to ordinary stereoscopic photographs, but the principle is the same as in the new application of the stereoscopic idea just described[2].

---

[1]Stereoscopic photographs of the character described herewith can be made with any good document camera.   The cut-outs (see Fig. 23) in the back of the document camera, should be used to cover either the right or left half of the plate, and the important part of the image should be focused about one and one-half inches from the center of the whole plate and the first exposure made.   The cut-out is then reversed and the object is moved sufficiently in an exact horizontal direction so that the image on the ground glass has moved over about three inches on the plate from the point where the first exposure was centered and the second exposure is made.   The distance between the two views, which is governed by the distance the object is moved, determines the depth or perspective of the resulting illustration and this can be regulated as may be desired.   For observation with the ordinary stereoscope the negative or the print must be reversed as with any stereoscopic view.

If desirable the two views can be made on different plates by marking on the ground glass the exact center of the first image and then, before exposing the second plate, moving the object as far as is necessary to produce the desired depth or perspective.

This simple method of making micro-stereoscopic photographs, requiring no complicated apparatus, has been worked out after many experiments and produces results that seem to be the same as though two simultaneous views were made from two view points.   The method is, of course, applicable only to inanimate objects.

[2]"The next contention of the appellant is that the court erred in admitting in evidence a stereoscopic view of the south side of the bridge and the embankment; also one of State St. west of the bridge showing the surface of the roadway or street and west end of the bridge.   The court also allowed in evidence a stereoscope to aid the jury in the examination of the views.   .   .   .

There was no error in this action of the court.   It is a common practice to admit a plan or picture shown to be a correct representation by preliminary proof, to aid the jury in a proper understanding of the case, and we do not see any difference in the application of the rule whether the picture is made by hand or by the art of photography, the real question being whether the view be a correct representation."—Rockford vs. Russell, 9 Ill. App. 229 (1881).

Fig. 9.—Stereoscopic Photo-Micrograph of impressed seal on white paper lighted by side light. This illustration when viewed in the ordinary stereoscope shows with what startling clearness delicate detail can thus be shown. This method may be employed to advantage in any inquiry into which depth or the third dimension enters. This illustration will be found on detached sheet on inside of back cover of this book convenient for examination with ordinary stereoscope.

Objections to the use of photographs in court are based upon the theory that they may be distorted and not true representations of the original, and it is also asserted that the original affords the best means for study and comparison and that no reproducton of it is necessary.

Photographs may be distorted and may be dishonest, and if they cannot be properly proved, or verified by comparison with the original, they should be excluded. If there is any doubt about the accuracy of photographs they can be made by both parties, and in questioned document cases they can easily be verified by comparison with the original paper which is at hand. On account of the latter fact there is not the legitimate objection to photographs of a questioned document that may arise over photographs of a different nature which cannot be compared and verified by judge, jury and opposing counsel.

The best modern lenses will make photographic reproductions with the utmost accuracy. They render straight lines as such, or possess the quality described as rectilinear; they are without astigmatism and reproduce without distortion. By these qualities involuntary distortions and inaccuracies are entirely eliminated and an objection to photography is removed that might have been valid in the early days of the art. Lenses are now made so accurately that they are certified by the government Bureau of Standards as "making reproductions without distortion." There are as good reasons for objecting to the use of an ordinary magnifying glass or the microscope as to an enlarged photograph, since such photographic reproduction is simply the enlarged view in permanent form.

The real reason for most objections to photographs is that they do well just what it is intended they should do, that is, assist in showing the facts. Some ancient opinions recite a long array of conditions that may make photographs dangerous in courts of law, but not one of

Fig. 10—A three-color lens, designed to bring the primary colors to sharp focus at same distance from object. This lens is certified by the United States Bureau of Standards.

these objections is valid when applied to properly proved document photographs. They can be made correctly, this fact can be shown, and thus all objections are disposed of. Photographs are now rarely excluded.

The making of document photographs, particularly enlargements, is a rather unusual task, and some technical directions may be of assistance. It is not to be supposed that the average photographer is prepared to make the great variety of photographs required for the most effective illustration of all the diverse phases of the subject. Many of the photographs described here, however, can be made almost anywhere where ordinary photographs are made, and even some of the more unusual work can be done by ordinary operators who will give careful attention to the task.

The various parts of a document are reproduced in exact natural size or enlarged or reduced in exact proportions when the object, the lens and the photographic plate are in parallel planes. This position of the lens should be mechanically provided for in the camera, and the plate and object should be brought into parallel relations to each other and to

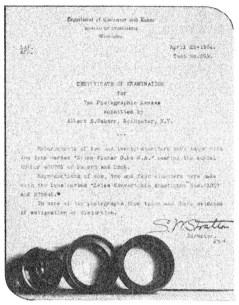

Fig. 11—United States Bureau of Standards lens certificate.

the lens.   In a regular document camera these conditions are all secured by mechanical means, but if such an instrument is not available the desired conditions can be secured by giving careful attention to these particulars as described.

It is very difficult to enlarge several diameters to a definite scale and at the same time to get the object in perfect focus unless the object-board is connected with the camera itself, but such an enlargement can be made without a special camera if adequate time is taken and proper care is exercised.

Since it is often desirable to make photographs on very short notice and in unusual places, a portable document camera is almost indispensable for such special work. Instruments such as are illustrated here show certain attachments and adjustments that make them more useful for this work.

FIG. 12—Portable Document Camera with detachable aluminum foot, special object board and extension tube for short focus lens.

Any kind of ordinary photographic plate may be used for document photographs, but the best results can usually be obtained by using a slow plate. Exposure should be ample and development carried well along until detail is brought out in the writing line or stroke itself. Care should be taken not to make negatives too strong in contrast, but more contrast is desirable than in a portrait negative. Negatives ought not to be retouched in any manner, but may be intensified or reduced if necessary.

Prints should be made as carefully as the negatives.

They should not be printed so dark that detail in the pen stroke itself is lost and care should be taken that the paper be in contact with the entire surface of the negative. Many kinds of photographic papers may be used for this purpose, but if the utmost detail is desired the glossy papers are necessary. For most purposes the excellent modern developing papers are entirely suitable. Papers with rough surface should not be used.

For court use photographs mounted only on backing paper are preferable in many ways. They lie flat, take up little room and are convenient to handle and they do not warp or buckle. Large prints may be hinged in the middle with binding tape. Even if prints are to be pasted in an exhibit book it is desirable that they first be mounted on backing paper so that they will lie perfectly flat. An excellent way to arrange photographs for use in court is to print them all the same size, no matter what size the negatives may be, and hinge them at one end and bind them in loose-leaf binders which can easily be taken apart if necessary.

Varying conditions call for photographs in great variety and they should be made in such a way as best shows the particular fact that they are intended to illustrate. Careful study should always be made of the particular case in hand in order that photographs may be as effective as possible. Those most frequently required are here described and some suggestions made regarding their preparation. In addition to the necessary technical knowledge and skill required for such work considerable ingenuity and mechanical ability are necessary if suitable photographs are to be provided for all the varied phases of the subject of questioned documents.

Fig. 13—Tilting Camera Stand in position for side window lighting.

For reasons already given a disputed document should, as a rule, be photographed complete in natural size. Many questions may arise in the course of an inquiry that will render such a photograph very useful. In making a comparison of classified parts, a natural size photograph may be used to cut apart as conditions require; for this purpose, however, it is generally preferable to use a photograph of the original document and of the standards enlarged from twenty-five to fifty per cent. When such slightly enlarged photographs are made it is not always necessary also to photograph the documents in natural size, but this should be done in important inquiries.

After such classified, illustrative exhibits are made up they can then be enlarged two to four diameters, depending upon the size or delicacy of

Fig. 14—Tilting Camera Stand in position for transmitted light photographs.

the characteristics illustrated. These final photographs are usually offered and marked as exhibits, but may be admitted simply as illustrations of the testimony given and employed in the same capacity as a blackboard or chart. They are graphic representations, however, from which the personal equation of the illustrator has been eliminated and are simply testimony of an ocular nature. If conditions permit and circumstances warrant every case should be illustrated in this manner.

Enlarged photographs are desirable in nearly every case. The fraudulent character of a signature is sometimes effectively shown by simply making an enlargement of it of from two to eight diameters. When such a photograph is compared with genuine signatures, similarly enlarged, it is in some cases most convincing proof of forgery. If a signature is unnaturally and slowly drawn or is patched and retouched, or shows hesitation and stops at unusual places, these facts are shown with startling clearness in such an enlarged photograph[1].

In a critical examination of questioned typewriting it may be impossible to show actual similarities or differences without putting the separate specimens for comparison close together in enlarged form. When this side by side comparison can be made many significant differing or identical characteristics are immediately apparent, as in a comparison of handwriting.

[1]The sensational method of illustrating a forgery case by the use of lantern slides, a projection lantern and the wall of the court room as a screen, as graphically described by J. G. Holland in his charming story of "Sevenoaks," has actually been employed. Circumstances might arise where such a method would be desirable, but the facts most appropriately illustrated by such a method can usually be more effectively shown by direct photographic enlargements that can be put into the hands of the jury.—"Sevenoaks," p. 404 (1875).

Enlargements should be made directly on the plate from the object itself. This can be done by the use of lenses of proper focal length and a camera with adequate extension of bellows. Direct enlargements exhibit every detail and can be made so as to show even the minutest characteristics of the original. An enlargement by the bromide process from a small negative, as ordinarily made in portrait photography, although sometimes useful, is never so clear and distinct as a direct enlargement.

Enlargements above ten diameters are necessary only when that which is to be shown is of a microscopic character, and these reproductions are usually described as photo-micrographs. They are often very effective illustrations. In crossed line inquiries, and questions regarding retouching, line quality, writing over folds in paper and certain classes of erasures and changes, they are really essential if the facts are to be clearly shown.

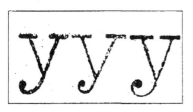

Fig. 15—Remington, Smith-Premier and Underwood small y's. Enlarged seven diameters, showing three distinctly different designs of letters.

Ordinary photographic apparatus will not permit these enlargements of ten diameters or more to be made directly on the plate for the reason that they require special short-focus lenses unless a very long bellows is available.

For all the different kinds of work required a document camera should be fitted with at least four lenses of approximately the following focal lengths: one inch, five inches, ten inches and twenty inches. Photo-microscopic lenses, designed especially for use with an ordinary camera, are made of as short a focus as three-fourths of an inch, permitting enlargements to be made up to fifty diameters with the usual document camera bellows extension. In order to avoid the shadow of the camera front it is necessary to mount such short focus lenses on a special extension tube as illustrated in Figs. 12 and 17.

In making an enlargement of ten diameters or more the object should be illuminated by direct sunlight or intense artificial light in order that the enlarged image on the ground-glass may be accurately focused. By the use of one or two ordinary small mirrors sunlight can be thrown on the object when it is not possible to get the camera itself in the direct light. The light should not come too much from one side and care should be taken that there are no strong shadows and no reflections.

Fig. 16—Transparent fields on ground-glass screen of Document Camera.

For document photography of any kind, and especially for such enlargements as have just been described, it is very helpful to have certain portions of the ground-glass screen made entirely transparent so that by the use of a focusing glass the image may be brought to a

microscopically sharp focus.   These transparent fields
can be easily produced in permanent form on the
ground-glass by attaching with Canada balsam narrow
strips of ordinary glass to the ground side.   One who

Fig. 17—Four inch and one and three-eighths inch focus Micro-Photographic
Lenses and Special Mounting Tube.   Both lenses certified
by United States Bureau of Standards.

has not employed such transparent fields for fine focusing cannot realize what a great help this simple device
is in accurate work.

In making such photographs it is almost imperative
that the object-board be connected with the camera itself and that the plate, the lens and the object-board all
be actuated by rack and pinion if enlargements are to
be made to a definite scale.   With the type of instrument just described photographs of this unusual character can be made almost as easily as ordinary photographs and with these enlargements made directly on
the plate it is possible to produce as many exact duplicate prints as may be desired, and if necessary the plate
itself can be submitted in court for verification.

Fɪɢ. 18—Removable Object Board for Document Camera.
Actuated by rack and pinion and having vertical, horizontal and oscillating movements, and controlled .
by operator from back of instrument.

Fɪɢ. 19—Object Carrier for transmitted light photography.
Adjustable horizontally and vertically.

A focusing glass (Fig. 21), enlarging about ten diameters and made so as to exclude all side light, is also very useful and for the finest work is almost indispensable.

An excellent method of determining the degree of enlargement and also of making a permanent record of it is to provide an accurately divided scale, printed on

Fig. 20—Photographic Enlargement Measure, graduated in 64ths of an inch, to be photographed with the object to serve as a permanent record of the degree of enlargement.

thin paper, which is placed on the object-board close to or upon the document and photographed with it. By the use of a suitable measure the degree of enlargement desired can be determined by measuring the image of the scale on the ground-glass. This image becomes a permanent part of the negative and can appear, if it is desired, at one side of the print itself as is shown in numerous illustrations in this book.

For measuring the image on the ground-glass beam dividers (Fig. 21), or those with the points parallel, will be found very convenient, and a steel rule carrying various divisions of an inch is useful in making an enlargement to a definite scale.

Fig. 21—Focusing Glasses, Beam Dividers and Steel Rule.

As a means of determining accurately whether the utmost detail of the original is reproduced in the negative and shown in the print, a gray test scale may be provided to be photographed at one side of the plate. This consists of narrow graduated shades of gray, numbered from one to five, the lightest shade being so delicate as to be almost pure white. If the photograph shows the numbered shades of the scale then it is certain that all the detail of the object photographed is faithfully reproduced. The photographed scale is particularly useful as a guide in making the print of proper depth. The gray scale is not essential in photographing ordinary objects.

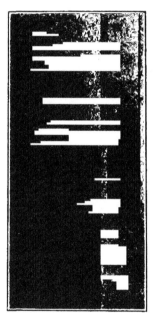

FIG. 22—A "Gray Scale" in natural size and with portion enlarged.

For document photographs, especially photographs of signatures, a series of dark paper cut-outs, arranged to go in the back of the camera just in front of the plate, are often very useful. They render it possible to make two or more exposures on the same plate which may be very desirable in certain comparisons, or when it is difficult to determine just the proper time of exposure required to show certain conditions. By this method several exposures of different lengths of time can be made on the same plate of the same object or comparisons of different objects can be made as exposed, developed and printed from the same plate.

In signature inquiries it is always desirable to photograph the original and the standards together in order of date. This can be readily done unless the original documents are too bulky. The dates and amounts necessary to identify the several papers can be written in condensed form and placed opposite the several signatures; this can be photographed and will appear on the prints as a

Fig. 23—Back of camera removed, showing cutouts in position for making one of three exposures on same plate.

description of the signatures. It may be desirable to write this descriptive matter not on the original documents but on a separate paper.

For the purpose of showing form characteristics it is not usually advisable to enlarge pencil writing as much as ink writing, because under great magnification the line may become so thin as to be indistinct, but to show retouching, disconnections, and a slow drawing movement considerable enlargement may be necessary. In photographing pencil writing it is particularly important that the object be focused with the greatest care in order to secure the finest possible definition.

In making a photograph of an unevenness, like a

pencil indentation without color, a seal impression on white paper, or any similar object, the illumination must be so arranged that the light and the shadow show the outline of the object. The space between the lens and the object should be partly covered and light should be admitted mainly or entirely from one side and should fall on the object at just the proper angle to obtain a perfect outline. For this work it may be necessary to admit light through a slit only a fraction of an inch in width.

Fig. 24—Post Mark and Embossed Impression, without color, on enclosed letter, photographed by side light admitted through narrow slit. See page 432.

To show lack of continuity or an unnatural order of pen writing several negatives of the matter in question should be made of different lengths of exposure by both direct and transmitted light. If three negatives are made the first should be given one-half, the second normal exposure and the third about twice normal exposure. Prints of varying degrees of depth from all three negatives should be made, some of which will show any unnatural order or lack of continuity in the writing.

This same fact may perhaps be more clearly shown by a series of prints of varying depths from a carefully

FIG. 25—Enlarged Photograph of impressed seal on white paper, taken by side light. Case of Hunt v. Peshtigo Lumber Co., Grand Rapids, Wisconsin, 1903.

timed negative. Several prints should be made under different lengths of exposure from one-fourth of normal up to full exposure. It is desirable to make several exposures in both processes as the distinction may be very slight between the parts to be compared, and it is necessary to secure just the right density or depth of printing to show the contrast.

These methods may also show differences in pencil writing that are not readily seen by the unaided eye.

Transmitted light photographs of varying depths of printing sometimes will illustrate the character and density of pencil strokes more effectively than can be done in any other manner.

In photographing folded and uneven papers it is sometimes difficult to get them all flat and level and on the same plane without putting a glass over them. Clean and clear glass should be selected and for some purposes glass without color should be used. Common glass has a green color the effect of which in a photograph is to accentuate slightly certain tints, but for ordinary photographs the effect is very slight and sometimes may actually improve the result. Where colors are being differentiated or color screens are used for special purposes, only colorless glass should be placed over papers that are being photographed.

It may be desirable in certain special cases to reverse a photograph and make the print white on black instead of black on white as it appears in the original. A photograph of this character may be useful when it becomes necessary to reproduce a standard writing in ink for comparison with pencil, chalk or slate pencil writing. Such a reversed photograph does not change the form in any way but simply reverses the contrast. This result is obtained by reversing the plate in the plate holder, then from the resulting negative a positive is made, either by contact or in the camera, and from the positive the print is made. By reversing the first negative as described the final print is made to read correctly from left to right. Some interesting results are obtained by this process.

Appropriate color screens or ray filters are necessary

in photographing certain colors and under some conditions no suitable photographs whatever can be made without them. The two principal colors which require

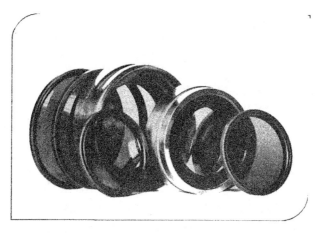

Fig. 26—Color Screens and Ray Filters of varying depths and tints.

the use of screens are blue and violet, and sometimes the color of the paper or background is such that a color screen is desirable even with black ink. Manila, orange, yellow and certain other colored papers, especially when photographed with white papers, require a color screen in order to make the background more nearly uniform. In some instances a color screen is useful in order to reduce or eliminate surrounding lines, strokes or words that tend to obscure the writing in dispute.

Orange and yellow screens are most frequently needed and two or three different depths should be provided which will increase normal exposure approximately five to ten times. In making enlargements or in making any photographs where the utmost detail is necessary it is sometimes desirable to use a large color screen or plate directly over the object photographed.

Under very high magnification ordinary color screens or filters used on the lens may interfere somewhat with the optical qualities of even the highest type of lenses.

Fig. 27—Photographs of the same matter without and with an appropriate color screen. See also Fig. 147.

This disturbance may be minimized or entirely eliminated when the color screen is put in actual contact with the object photographed. The use of the screen in this way is, of course, only possible with objects on the same plane, as in document photography, and with those of not too great area.

It has been suggested that colored light of the proper tint might be projected upon the object so that it could be easily modified and controlled and made to cover a large field; and no doubt for certain copying work this method would have advantages[1].

[1]As in so many other fields of scientific investigation, the German contribution to this application of photography to the investigation of documents exceeds that of all other nations and an exhaustive study of the subject must include the German works. A very full list of these books and pamphlets is given in the bibliography of this book.

CHAPTER V.

THE MICROSCOPE AND QUESTIONED DOCUMENTS

Controverted questions of fact which become the subject of testimony are finally presented to those called upon to decide the issue either through the sense of hearing alone or through the sense of hearing and sight. It is too often assumed that all who hear testimony understand it, which may be far from the fact, and those with the most experience know best that the presentation of visible evidence may be vastly more effective than an appeal to the sense of hearing alone. When it is feasible, therefore, it becomes important that testimony be made visible in every way possible. Fortunately this result can often be attained in disputed document cases, and inquiries of this kind are by this means brought into a distinctly different class from those investigations in which an intangible question becomes the subjcet of exclusively oral testimony.

As is well known the instrument which makes it possible to see physical evidence that otherwise might be invisible is the microscope, but its application to the investigation of documents is not so well understood. Objection is also always made to the use of the instrument in court and the necessity for its employment must be briefly considered, although it would seem that no extended argument should be required on so obvious a proposition.

---

[1]This chapter, in slightly different form, was first printed in Vol. VI, No. 12 of the Journal of Applied Microscopy and Laboratory Methods, Mr. L. B. Elliott, editor, and is reprinted here by permission. The files of that valuable publication, which are to be found in all leading technical libraries, contain many practical articles on the general subject of microscopy.

The incalculable value of the microscope in many fields of scientific investigation and particularly in the field of medicine, is well understood, and the great value of the instrument for the purposes herein described is at once recognized when the questions to be investigated are merely stated.

It is difficult for us to appreciate fully, although the fact is known even to school children, that the two well known instruments that come to the aid of sight, the telescope and the microscope, each actually introduces us into a new world. We know but do not quite fully understand how by one sight is vastly lengthened; by the other, marvelously intensified.

The average unaided, or so-called naked eye, can distinguish separate lines up to a fineness of only about two hundred, or two hundred and fifty, to the inch, lines finer than this appearing as a solid shade or tint[1]. Considering this fact it is easy to understand how far beyond unaided human sight are the individual red corpuscles in the blood when we know that about three thousand of them laid side by side extend only an inch. They are as far from unassisted vision as the beautiful rings of Saturn were before the invention of the telescope.

---

[1] The normal eye can distinguish from 200 to 250 lines to the inch and in a microscope such magnifying power should be used as will apparently bring the structure which is sought after at least up to this figure. To illustrate, take a ¼ inch objective of 0.77 N. A. and a 2 inch eyepiece. An objective of this kind, properly corrected, resolves the test-object Pleurosigna angulatum, in which the lines average 60,000 to the inch. With the above eyepiece it is utterly impossible to see them, while if it is replaced by a ¾ inch or ½ inch eyepiece, they can easily be distinguished. This is not owing to any peculiar quality of the eyepiece, but merely to the fact that by increasing the magnifying power, the dimensions of the object have been increased to such an extent that the lines have apparently been separated and become visible to the eye.—Manipulation of the Microscope. Edward Bausch, pp. 109-110.

In law inanimate things may become instruments of evidence and speak for themselves, and the ends of justice are always served when means are provided to show the facts more clearly. The microscope provides such means, and is simply indispensable if the facts in certain disputed document investigations are to be clearly shown; and a great variety of questions which it alone can answer arise in connection with a study of the various phases of forgery. In many instances its evidence is conclusive, and without such assistance as it gives we may indeed have eyes and see not.

In this special work, as in other fields, the instrument is necessary because it enables the observer to see clearly what otherwise is actually invisible or can only be seen indistinctly; and in this connection it should always be emphasized that physical facts are not less significant, if they actually exist, simply because the unaided eye cannot see them. It surely is good sense as well as good law that this useful instrument have a place in court whenever it will thus assist in pointing the way to truth. This it will often do.

The use of the instrument in a court of law is, however, still somewhat of a novelty because for so long a time a juryman was not deemed able to see things for himself, but was simply expected to listen to reports of observations made by others. If the observers disagreed he was often helpless, as he still is regarding things disputed which he cannot see and understand. If modern improved methods of investigation are employed, as is now possible in many cases, a judge, a competent referee, or an intelligent juryman cannot easily be misled by those who bear false witness, or by a client and his attorney who are opposed to the fact.

Many of the conditions calling for the use of the microscope are those which make certain photographs very useful, and photography and microscopy effectively supplement each other in many inquiries. The microscope serves to discover and show the physical fact by direct view of the thing itself, while the photograph, especially in enlarged form, makes examination and study easy that otherwise might be difficult or even impossible for some observers.

The following brief description of some of the more important of the various uses of the microscope in the examination of documents will direct attention to phases of such an investigation that otherwise might be overlooked, and will also afford opportunity of describing and illustrating the special apparatus useful in this work.

Forged signatures in many cases are not really written, but carefully and laboriously drawn from a model with frequent liftings of the pen and occasional stopping of its motion even when not lifted. With the microscope arranged for transmitted light observation the lapping of lines and uneven ink distribution are seen with astonishing clearness.

A document or part of a document is sometimes proved to be fraudulent if it can be conclusively shown that a part of the writing preceded and a part followed the folding of the paper. An ink line crossing a fold has certain definite characteristics, but such a line may not be more than one one-hundredth of an inch in width, and the unaided eye may not be able to see the physical evidence of the fact which under the microscope is so plain that it cannot be denied. A tiny portion of the ink in such a case may actually have gone through the paper

Fig. 28—Ink lines made over fold at the top and below a fold made across
an ink line.   Natural size and enlarged x 27.

to the opposite side, and under the microscope this fact
is unmistakable.

Fraudulent documents are frequently brought forward purporting to be several years of age which in
fact are only a few days or weeks old.   Such documents
may contain iron-nutgall ink which still has the distinct,
fresh, blue color of recent use and has not nearly reached
its ultimate degree of blackness.   The magnified image
of such a writing in good daylight shows its exact tint
and may be made a matter of record by the use of the
color microscope.   By this means the ink color as first
seen can be compared with itself a few weeks later when
it will have so changed and blackened as to show con-

Fig. 29—Crossed lines in raised note case, showing that upper line "Twenty" was written last. Nigrosin ink, original lines, $\frac{1}{100}$ inch wide. Case of People vs. Walker, Warsaw, N. Y.

clusively that the document could not be several years old; and practically this is final proof that such a document is fraudulent.

Fraudulent additions and interlineations in documents often touch the original writing, and the sequence or order of writing is ascertained by showing which of the crossed lines or strokes was last written. This obscure and delicate fact the microscope will often show with surprising distinctness.

Many other inquiries arise regarding ink in which the microscope is necessary if the truth is to be known. For example it may be shown that two writings are made with different inks because in one a microscopic sediment or precipitate is present which is not in the other. The

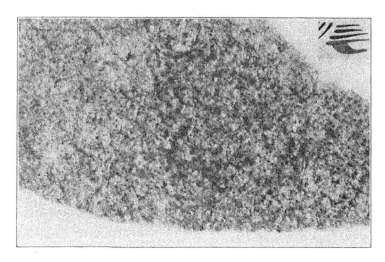

FIG. 30—Illustration of sediment in ink. Actual size
and enlarged x 22.

precipitate appears in the form of very fine specks or
black particles, darker in color than the main body of the
ink and entirely invisible without the microscope.

FIG. 31—An erasure by abrasion photographed by side light. Example of "9"
changed to "90" after erasure of end of stroke under
the two ciphers. Enlarged x 27.

Many erasures and changes of a fraudulent character are made in documents which would entirely escape detection if examined only with the unaided eye, but when examined under the magnification of a good microscope they appear so plainly that anyone can see them.

Forged signatures are frequently first outlined in pencil and then carefully inked over. In such forgeries the pencil marks not covered, indentations, and in some cases the graphite caught in the ink film, may be shown by the microscope with such clearness that the method by which the signatures were made is unmistakable.

In the examination of typewriting the microscope is

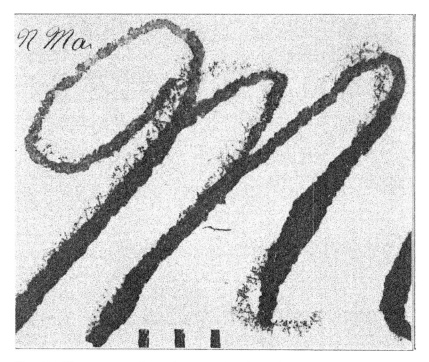

Fig. 32—Illustration made to show pencil outline of letter covered and partly covered with ink. Actual size and enlarged x 13.

necessary to show numerous conditions bearing on the questions of genuineness and identity. Numerous other uses are found for the microscope in the investigation of the many questions that arise regarding documents. In many instances, in fact, it is the only means that will lead unerringly to the truth.

High power magnification in these various examinations is usually neither required nor desirable and may actually render the microscope useless as a means of showing the fact. It is a common fallacy to suppose that the greatest possible magnification is always desirable, the fact not being understood that the field of view is diminished in proportion to the degree of magnification[1]. The process of microscopic examination is comparatively simple, and with suitable instruments and proper assistance, judge and jury, or any unskilled observer, can see what is pointed out and verify all testimony based upon the microscope. Testimony thus enforced becomes not a mere statement of opinion, but

---

[1]Beginners as a rule are apt to use too much magnification or amplification, and often attempt to view a large surface with an objective which will show but a small part of it. It must not be forgotten that the apparent field of view is decreased as higher powers are used and that a low power will give a better impression of a large, coarse object and its relative parts, because it makes a larger surface visible.

The following table will probably be of assistance to the beginner. After he has become better acquainted with his instrument his judgment will dictate to him what to do.

A power of 25 diameters will show a surface of about 1-5 inch diameter.

A power of 50 diameters will show a surface of about 1-10 inch diameter.

A power of 100 diameters will show a surface of about 1-20 inch diameter.

A power of 500 diameters will show a surface of about 1-100 inch diameter.

A power of 1000 diameters will show a surface of about 1-200 inch diameter.

This table is approximately correct with a Huyghenian eyepiece.— Manipulation of the Microscope, Edward Bausch, pp. 110-111.

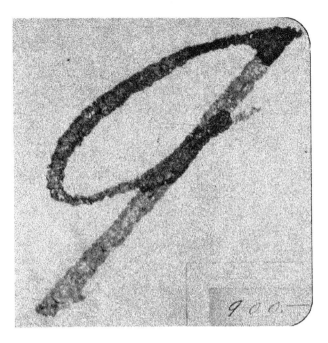

F<small>IG</small>.33—Photo-Micrograph (x 18), showing "100" changed
to "900" by addition of top to figure 1. Size of
original shown in small illustration in corner.

simply a recital of significant facts which can then be
interpreted by court and jury.

As briefly described in the previous chapter, photo-
micrographs, made by the aid of the microscope or with
microscopic lenses, are frequently very useful and in
some instances are absolutely conclusive. They supplement the ordinary use of the microscope in a very
forcible way. The enlargement shows plainly in permanent form what can otherwise be seen with the microscope only temporarily by one observer at a time, and,
as such illustrations are easily verified by comparison
with the actual image as seen in the instrument, no valid
objections can be raised against them.

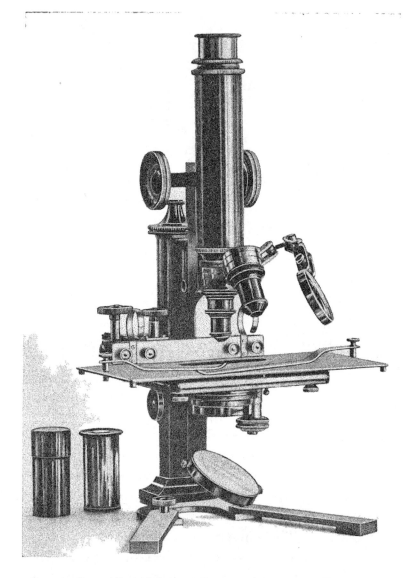

Fig. 34—Special Bausch & Lomb Document Microscope. The instrument illustrated has extra large special mechanical stage with two rack and pinion movements, ring document holders back of stage, bull's-eye condenser for direct illumination, Abbe substage condenser, special long spring clips for holding papers, and light, broad, detachable base.

Instruments especially designed for examination of documents should have a special large stage with ample room behind the objective; a microscope is also greatly improved for the purpose if provided with a large mechanical stage with rack and pinion movements. A sub-stage condenser, for certain transmitted light examinations, and a condenser on a movable arm for throwing additional light on opaque objects from above should also be included. A document microscope should be fitted with several eyepieces and with a variety of objectives. A one-sixth objective is as high a power as is likely ever to be needed, and this is but seldom required.

The document microscope is better adapted for certain uses if provided with rings having openings on the lower side and placed back of the stage; these rings will hold a large document when it is rolled and will allow the edge or any part to be drawn out under the objective for observation. This will obviate the necessity of folding, creasing or injuring the paper in any way and permit it to be reversed so that the image appears right side up.

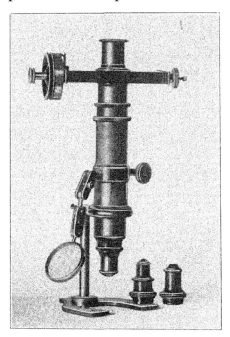

Fig. 35—Microscope with Filar Micrometer, mounted on special horseshoe foot.

One of the indispensable accessories of a document microscope is the filar-micrometer, which is illustrated in Fig. 35. As has already been seen this device is very useful in many instances for making accurate measurements and comparisons, and its value is increased because but little skill is required in its manipulation.

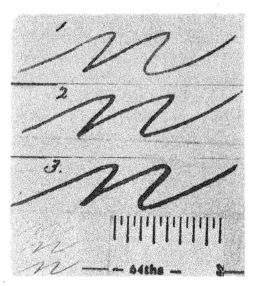

Fig. 36—Widths of pen strokes made with different pens, measured with Filar Micrometer. Upward strokes of No. 1 $\frac{1}{151}$ inch, No. 2 $\frac{1}{121}$ inch, No. 3 $\frac{1}{56}$ inch[1].

For the examination of large papers, matter on the pages of books, and all documents which should not be folded, it is desirable that the microscope be mounted on a special foot without a stage and with an open field directly under the objective, as shown in Fig. 35. The stereoscopic microscope, described later, as regularly constructed has an auxiliary horse-shoe foot of this

[1]Measurement of pen strokes—shown in Fig. 36—was made with the Filar Micrometer with two-thirds inch objective, 160 mm. tube length and the regular one-inch Filar Micrometer eyepiece. With this equipment 525 points on the toothed indicator and the micrometer graduated wheel equal 1-100 inch, which fact is determined by measuring with the instrument the actual graduation of 1-100 inch on the Stage Micrometer. The measurements of the upward strokes of the letter were: No. 1, 350 points; No. 2, 430 points; No. 3, 548 points, which in decimal fractions represent parts of an inch as follows: No. 1, .0066; No. 2, .0081; No. 3, 0104, which represented in common fractions are the widths shown under the illustration.

kind. This style of in-
strument permits the
middle or any part of a
large surface to be ex-
amined, which otherwise
might be impossible on
the small stage of the
ordinary microscope.

A camera-lucida at-
tachment, with which
drawings may be made
directly from the micro-
scopic image, is occas-
ionally useful and af-
fords a ready means for
making large illustra-
tions and outlines, par-
ticularly of matter which
may be introduced so

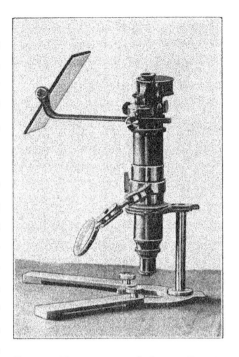

Fig. 37—Microscope with Camera Lucida
attachment and special foot.

late in a trial as to prevent its being photographed.
Drawings of this character are sometimes excluded, but,
if properly proved, are usually admitted as illustrations
of testimony. (See Fig. 57.)

When making a microscopic examination those unfamiliar with the microscope should be explicitly informed exactly as to what they are looking at and how
much of it they are seeing. It is not generally understood by the inexperienced that the image is inverted
and that the field of vision is restricted in proportion
to the magnification. Many observers when looking
into a microscope expect to see the whole page of a

document greatly enlarged instead of a small portion of one letter or word.

During such examinations observers should usually be seated and should not be hurried. Time enough should be taken to get the eye just at the proper point[1]. Many look in a microscope and see nothing because of embarrassment, haste, or improper assistance. This need not be the result if the examination is properly conducted.

If the examination does not require the determination of tints and shades of color, artificial light may be provided; court room light is frequently very dim and a good artificial light placed in proper relation to the microscope often assists greatly.

A special opaque eye-shade, attached to the top of the microscope tube, to shield the eye not used for observation, will be of assistance to those who are not accustomed to microscopic observations. To accommodate varying eyes it is also well to advise each observer to vary the focus slightly by the fine adjustment until the object is perfectly distinct.

The amount of magnification required obviously depends upon the question to be determined and, as stated above, high magnification is not usually desirable. For examination of crossed lines, traces of pencil marks,

---

[1]There is one point over the lens called the eye-point at which the rays cross within the smallest compass and this is the proper position for the eye, as the largest number of rays enter it. When above or below this point the size of field will be rather reduced, or shadows or colors will appear in it. In low power eyepieces the eye-point is farther than the lens; in high powers, quite close—in fact, in some so close that the eyelashes may rest upon the lens and may sometimes appear to be in the field as dark bars. Generally speaking the best point is where the entire field is seen and its margin (diaphragm) sharply defined.—Manipulation of the Microscope, Edward Bausch, p. 131.

line edges, paper fiber, retouching, and certain ink conditions high magnification is sometimes useful, but for many purposes a magnification of only from twenty to one hundred diameters gives the best results[1].

It is not often that objection is made to the ordinary magnifying glass, but the appearance of a microscope in court is usually the cause of a storm of protest; the objections to the use of the instrument usually being

[1]The Magnification Table printed below, prepared and published by the Bausch & Lomb Optical Co., of Rochester, N. Y., will be found convenient for reference. The objectives and eyepieces are designated in inches and also in millimeters. With a known tube length the degree of magnification reached by any combination is read off at the intersection of the lines.

Tube length 160 mm.	EYEPIECES					Tube length 6.3 in.
OBJECTIVES	2 in. 50 mm.	1½ in. 38 mm.	1 in. 25 mm.	¾ in. 18 mm.	½ in. 12 mm.	OBJECTIVES
3 in.	9	12	16	23	31	75 mm.
2 in.	14	19	26	36	47	50 mm.
1½ in.	18	25	34	48	63	37 mm.
1 in.	34	48	63	90	118	25 mm.
⅔ in.	41	60	87	110	146	17 mm.
½ in.	62	91	121	176	228	12.5 mm.
¼ in.	145	220	285	420	550	6.3 mm.
1/5 in.	180	260	340	495	640	5 mm.
1/6 in.	205	290	385	550	720	4.2 mm.
1/8 in.	270	415	530	760	975	3.2 mm.
1/10 in.	340	510	670	970	1290	2.5 mm.
1/12 in.	470	675	700	1300	1675	2.1 mm.
1/16 in.	640	875	1125	1575	2075	1.6 mm.

It is evident that a lens magnifies an object equally in all directions; this is said to be in areas, and is the square of the linear, so that if an object is magnified four times in the linear, it is sixteen times in area. The commonly accepted term to express magnifying power of simple, as well as compound microscopes, is in diameters (linear). A single lens of 1 inch focus magnifies about ten diameters; one of 2 inch focus, about five diameters; one of ½ inch focus, twenty diameters and so on. In a lens of high magnifying power, the focus is ordinarily about twice the diameter, so that if a lens is ½ inch diameter its focus is about 1 inch.—Manipulation of the Microscope, Edward Bausch, pp. 39-40 (1897).

based upon the somewhat natural but erroneous idea that if a thing exists that is really significant it can be seen by unaided vision.

It seems to be overlooked by those who object that ordinary spectacles are simply lenses placed between the eye and the object looked at and are merely a means by which sight is corrected and improved, and that the most elaborate and complicated microscope is nothing more than an extension of this same principle. To be consistent one who objects to the use of the microscope should also insist that judge and jury should be compelled to remove spectacles before examining a document that is questioned in a court of law.[1]

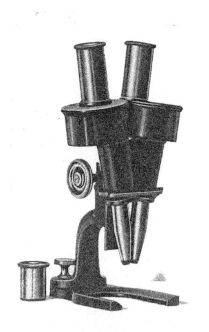

In certain inquiries the principle employed in stereoscopic photography, or what is known as binocular vision, is useful as applied to the microscope and such an instrument (Fig. 38) is now available. This microscope differs radically from the ordinary double eye-piece instrument and consists of two complete microscopes so ar-

FIG. 38—Stereoscopic Microscope with hard rubber special foot.

[1]Supplying the jury with magnifying glass, with the permission of the court, was no just cause of complaint. Many jurors are re-

ranged that they focus on exactly the same image; the combined two-eye view gives the true steroscopic effect, and in certain kinds of cases is of very great assistance in showing the exact facts.

Such a microscope is particularly useful in studying

---

quired by age or defect of sight, to use glasses to enable them to read the evidence submitted to them or to read the instructions of the court. If one of such jurors should lose his spectacles it would be rather a rigid sort of practice which would preclude the court from allowing glasses to be handed to him to enable him to examine such writings as his duty requires him to examine. We cannot see that allowing the jurors to use the magnifying glass was any departure from proper practice in the trial of causes.—Barker vs. The Town of Perry, Iowa 67, 146 (1885).

With the aid of the camera lucida he has made drawings of the disputed signature . . . . so as to make apparent to ordinary observation any singularity of formation, feature or proportion that may serve to distinguish or identify either of them.—Sharon vs. Hill, 26 Fed. Rep. 358 (1885).

When the jury were about retiring to consider of their verdict in this case, the defendant below, by his counsel, asked permission of the court to furnish the jury magnifying glasses, that they might examine the writings admitted to be genuine and compare the same with the note in controversy, which the court refused, but said to the jury that they might use their own spectacles. Why a jury should not be allowed the use of means to aid them in the examination and comparison of handwriting submitted to them to be examined and compared, which have been found by the experience of bankers and business men of the highest utility for such purpose, we are unable to understand. There is no more mystery in such a glass than in ordinary spectacles in daily use. An unlearned man, other things being equal, can see through such glasses quite as well as the most learned. For these reasons we think the Circuit Judge erred in his ruling on this point, and we reverse the judgment and remand the case for a new trial.—Kannon vs. Galloway, 49 Tenn. 230 (1872).

The microscope is exceedingly valuable in detecting erasures or other changes, in revealing the actual sequence or order of writing of additions and interlineations which touch a signature or writing above which they are placed, and in the examination of crossed lines, traces of pencil marks, line edges, paper fibre, retouching, and ink conditions.—Moore on Facts, Vol. I. Sec. 662 (1908).

As to photographs which were so enlarged as to make the proportions plainer we see no valid objection. Magnifying glasses and microscopes have always been used and parties are entitled to use them.— Howard v. Illinois Tr. & Sav. Bank. 189 Ill. 579 (1901).

The minute features of the writing—particularly those which indicate an erasure or a tracing—are often in their full detail invisible to the naked eye, and hence are unavailable in the liberal sense of the term; the case is in effect the same as that of an illegible document, which it is conceded may be proved by copy.—Wigmore on Evidence. Vol. I, Sec. 797 (1904).

any question in which depth or the third dimension must be considered, such as writing over folds, crossed line inquiries, questions regarding seals or any impressed characters, or erasures by abrasion. On account of its slight depth of focus the ordinary microscope may be less useful in these inquiries, and in such cases the stereoscopic instrument often will demonstrate clearly what otherwise cannot be proven.

CHAPTER VI.

INSTRUMENTS AND APPLIANCES[1]

Even those having but little legal experience know that the usual trial of an issue in a court of law is not exactly a proceeding where all co-operate to discover and show the existing fact, but rather that such a contest often resolves itself into a fierce controversy between those who seek to show the truth and those who endeavor to hide or distort it. Under these conditions it is desirable that testimony be illustrated and enforced by every possible means. In disputed document cases certain instruments may in this connection render valuable assistance in promoting the ends of justice.

Unlike many subjects calling for expert testimony the investigation of documents presents problems which in the main are to be solved by the study, comparison and interpretation of that which in some form is actually present before the court. The problem in many instances is the discovery and proof of a physical fact and in order that the discovery may be certain and the proof convincing every instrument and appliance should be employed that will assist in any way. That technical testimony which is based upon what the witness alone knows and sees is not usually of much value and for this reason every means should be used that will help the court and jury to see and to understand.

---

[1]Portions of this chapter were first printed in the Journal of Weights and Measures, Vol. I., No. 4, of February, 1909, and these portions are reprinted here by permission of the publishers of that valuable journal.

In the old days inquiries regarding documents were surrounded by all sorts of legal restrictions, but more and more the procedure in a court of justice not only permits but encourages the clearest exposition of the physical basis of all testimony. As already briefly suggested in the introduction of this book, this practice just so far removes such evidence from the bare statement of an opinion, and furnishes the facts by which means it becomes possible for judge and jury better to determine which of two conflicting contentions is the correct one.

The photographic camera and the microscope most frequently render assistance in such cases, and a presumptuous forgery may succeed in the absence of these useful instruments. Their various uses have already been outlined and these descriptions will suggest when they may be employed to advantage. Like all complicated tools, they may be of but little use in the hands of the unskilled, but properly used they enable even the untrained to see, interpret and understand that which otherwise might be effectively hidden.

It is important in a case in which visual testimony is a vital factor that microscopes and magnifying glasses of varying powers be provided so that each observer may get just the assistance that he requires. The ability to see clearly differs greatly in different individuals, and it may happen that a referee, who alone considers the testimony and decides a case, or a juryman whose intelligence gives great weight to his opinion, may have peculiar vision and may need special aid. Most persons are somewhat sensitive about defective vision, or may actually be unconscious of such defect, and sometimes will say that they see when they do not see well; the fullest opportunity should, therefore, be given to each observer to use the magnifying glass that is best suited to his eye, that he may be sure to get just the assistance that he needs.

Ordinary hand magnifiers, or simple microscopes, as adjuncts of the compound microscope are often of great

FIG. 39—Box of hand magnifiers or "simple microscopes" with powers ranging from two to forty diameters.

assistance and should always be at hand in a court inquiry; by their use the compound microscope can be dispensed with in many investigations. It often occurs also that some member of a jury, as already suggested, may receive no assistance from a compound microscope, and with such an observer an appropriate hand magnifier may show effectively what is to be proved.

A series of glasses, as illustrated in Fig. 39, varying in power from two to twenty diameters, will afford valuable assistance in nearly every inquiry. Those advanced in years usually do best with glasses mounted on a fixed stand, by which means the focal distance is mechanically provided for, while others with steady nerves can hold a glass in the hand and thus perhaps get a better light on the object examined. When delicate color values are under examination it is desirable to use glasses in which the chromatic aberration has been corrected. Magnifiers of this class usually consist of two or more lenses mounted together and show no prismatic or incorrect color effects even at the margins of the field; the more powerful ones are made as small as of a one-fourth inch focus with a magnifying power of about forty diameters, but it is very difficult for one without experience to use such a glass.

The ordinary tripod-stand glasses, or the so-called linen testers, if of good quality, often are very useful. When both hands are to be employed, or it is desirable to shut out side light as in transmitted light examinations, a watchmaker's eyeglass or a photographer's focusing glass can be used to advantage; but for general purposes the average observer can use to best advantage a hand magnifier with a focus of about one inch.

Accurate measurements that can be proved to be accurate are of vital importance in connection with the investigation of certain phases of the subject of questioned documents. A great variety of questions in such cases require that numerous kinds of measurements be made as a definite basis for certain conclusions; and to avoid possible error and to strengthen testimony it is desirable in all instances that measurements be made so that they can be reviewed and verified by judge, referee, or jury. In order that this may be possible the most suitable instruments must be provided.

In alleged traced forgeries it often becomes necessary to investigate the question of identity in size, proportions and position of the various parts of an alleged model signature and of one or more traced imitations. Particularly as part of the initial investigation in such a case, or for final use for illustrating testimony, it is very important to make definite measurements of the various parts to be compared in order to show certain exact identities which may in combination be very strong evidence of forgery.

For all such surface measurements finely graduated glass rules are best; with them more accurate measurements can be made because the graduations can be

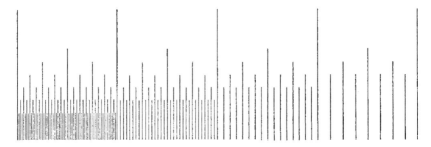

Fig. 40—Four inch transparent glass rule graduated to 64ths, 32nds, 16ths, and 8ths of one inch.

brought into actual contact with the parts to be measured as cannot be done with the ordinary opaque rule. A convenient and accurate form of this kind of measure is illustrated in Fig. 40. This, it will be seen, is a four inch rule graduated in 8ths, 16ths, 32nds, and 64ths of an inch. This arrangement permits measurement from any point up to four inches into the finely graduated field and for many purposes is more convenient than a scale marked throughout with the finest graduations. With a scale such as that shown it is possible for any-

Fig. 41—One-half-inch rule on glass graduated in 256ths of inch.

one with average eyesight to measure accurately up to its finest graduations and the great advantage of a glass rule over an ordinary measure can only be appreciated by actual comparison of the two.

Figure 41 shows a very small scale on glass, one-half inch in length, graduated throughout in 256ths, and Fig. 42 shows the same measure photographed over

Fig. 42 – Smith-Premier and Remington small r's photographed under Fig. 41 rule to show differences in size. Both enlarged thirteen and one-half diameters.

two typewritten characters. This measure is very useful in typewriting inquiries or any investigation in which it becomes necessary to show actual but minute differences or similarities. The scale can be placed over the letter or part under investigation and photographed in enlarged form as shown. In the illustration the difference in height of the small letters on the Remington and Smith-Premier typewriters is clearly seen. The actual difference in the height of these letters is only one one-hundredth of an inch.

For somewhat longer measurements which are occasionally necessary there is shown in Fig. 43 a steel rule which is graduated in fourths of an inch except that at one end a fourth inch space is graduated in hundredths of an inch. This design makes it possible to measure from any graduation up to six inches into the finely graduated space, as with the glass rule. By the use of needle pointed parallel dividers very accurate

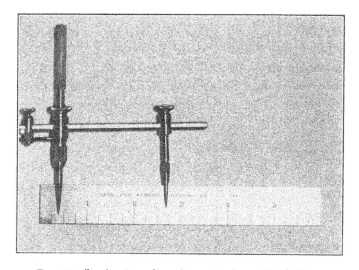

Fig. 43—Steel rule and needle pointed parallel dividers.

measurements can be made with this scale and for some purposes it is very useful. That illustrated has every graduation throughout its whole length certified by the United States Bureau of Standards to be accurate within one thousandth of an inch. Experienced operators will, of course, understand the necessity of using with the utmost care any needle-pointed dividers on a disputed document, and unskilled observers should not, under any circumstances, be permitted to use such an instrument on a valuable paper that is under investigation.

For the easy measurement of line widths, shadings, pen strokes, and for some other occasional uses, the measure illustrated in Fig. 44 is useful. This measure, as will be seen, shows numbered lines of gradually increasing width which, when printed up to the edge of a sheet of paper, permit the various lines to be placed directly over other lines or parts which are to be compared or measured. By the use of a hand magnifier very close measurements or accurate comparisons can thus be very quickly made. The printed measurements of the widths of the numbered lines as shown in the illustration reading in ten-thousandths of an inch, were made with the Filar Micrometer which is hereafter described. The measurements were made of the lines as printed on enameled paper, and one-eighth of an inch from the right end of the strokes where the lines are supposed to be cut at the edge of the sheet.

A convenient measure of a somewhat different character is illustrated in Fig. 45. This measure shows successive graduations on glass inscribing spaces each of which from the smallest is one one-hundredth of an inch wider than the preceding one. With such an instrument it is possible to make a very quick comparison of the outside measurements of two typewritten or printed

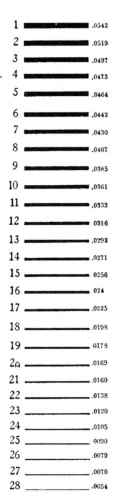

1	.0542
2	.0519
3	.0497
4	.0473
5	.0464
6	.0442
7	.0430
8	.0407
9	.0385
10	.0361
11	.0333
12	0316
13	.0292
14	.0271
15	0256
16	024
17	.0225
18	.0198
19	0178
20	.0169
21	.0160
22	.0138
23	.0120
24	.0105
25	0090
26	.0079
27	.0070
28	.0054

Fig. 44—Line measure with measurements as made with Filar micrometer.

Fig. 46—Micrometer Caliper with illustration of ratchet stop.

Fig. 45—Outside measure on glass. Each division $\frac{1}{100}$ inch wider than preceding one.

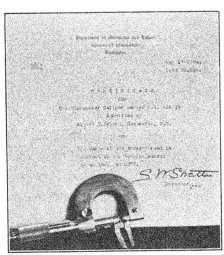

Fig. 47—Special Micrometer Caliper and reduced fac-simile of U. S. Bureau of Standards certificate.

characters or of a line or any small object within the field of the graduations.

These various instruments are each best adapted for certain uses and are also useful for the purpose of checking each other in all such inquiries. This last illustration here shown (Fig. 45), as in the case with the others printed herewith, is intended to be correct in size, but it is very difficult, in fact almost impossible, by the ordinary processes of reproduction and printing to secure absolute accuracy in such illustrations.

For some paper examinations and comparisons the micrometer caliper, shown in Fig. 46, is very useful. The instrument best adapted for such use is actuated by a ratchet stop, in order that uniform pressure may be mechanically insured, and it should also carry a vernier reading up to ten-thousandths of an inch. With an instrument of this character very accurate measurements of thickness can be made and it is usually possible to assort papers that are actually different by the thickness test alone.

Papers range in thickness all the way from the thinnest calendered tissue, which is in thickness about .0009 of an inch, up to heavy note paper which is about .007 of an inch in thickness. This makes a range of thicknesses, if measured in thousandths, of about sixty.

There is shown in Fig. 47 a special micrometer caliper, made by Brown & Sharpe from a special design, which carries two parallel knife-edge jaws neither of which revolves. This instrument measures surface distances within its field with great accuracy and convenience and also serves to prove or check measurements made in other ways. In a critical comparison of

typewriting this in-
strument is very use-
ful, serving to meas-
ure the impression
as well as the type
itself. It can readily
be seen that the
ordinary caliper with
one round revolving
point of contact, can-
not be used conveni-
ently for such sur-
face measurements.
The screw thread of

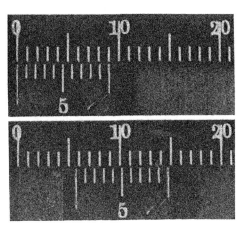

Fig. 48 – Illustration of Vernier set at naught
and the same moved five and seven-
tenths divisions.

this instrument as well as of that shown in Fig. 46 has
been certified by the United States Bureau of Standards to be correct to one ten-thousandth of an inch. The
vernier on these and other instruments described in this
chapter is illustrated in Fig. 48 and explained in the
footnote.

For the finest measurements, such as are required in
critical examinations of line widths, as may be necessary

---

[1]The Vernier is an instrument, or method of graduating instruments of many kinds, named from its inventor, Pierre Vernier, a native
of France. The device is designed to measure a fractional part of
one of the equal divisions of a graduated scale. The vernier scale,
as shown in the above illustration, divides nine of the primary or regular divisions into ten equal parts so that each line of the vernier, after
the first set at zero, is 1-10 of a division shorter or narrower than the
primary divisions. The advantage of the vernier consists in the fact
that any part or proportion of one of the primary divisions is read off
by simply observing which division of the vernier after the first exactly coincides with one of the divisions on the regular scale. In the
illustration it will be seen that the seventh division of the vernier is
in line with one of the divisions of the primary or main scale.

The primary scale on the Micrometer Calipers, illustrated herewith,
represents one thousandth of an inch, so that the reading in the illustration would be five thousandths and seven ten-thousandths of an
inch.

FIG. 49—Filar Micrometer, showing graduated indicator wheel.

in examining an alleged fraudulent interlineation, and also for pen comparisons, or for any very fine and accurate measurement, the microscope fitted with the filar micrometer is indispensable. The instrument, as illustrated in Fig. 49, easily measures to a fineness of ten thousandths of an inch so that even an unskilled and inexperienced observer can see and verify the measurement.

Comparative measurements can be made with the instrument by simply reading off the number of divisions indicated on the graduated wheel, but to reduce the measurements to fractions of an inch or fractions of a meter it is necessary to employ a stage micrometer, which is a glass ruled accurately in hundredths and thousandths of an inch or in fractions of a meter. These graduations are examined in the microscope and it is observed how many points on the graduated wheel of the filar micrometer are required to move the spider web line over one of the graduated spaces on the stage micrometer, as described more fully in footnote on page 82. Under high magnification a greater number of revolutions are, of course, necessary than under low magnification and for this reason the stage micrometer is necessary when it is desirable to make the measurements definite. Stage micrometers are also certified by the Bureau of Standards.

Illustrated in the chapter treating of slant in writing is shown a special protractor designed for the easy and accurate measuring of the slant of writing. This instrument is also made on glass so that the graduations can be brought into actual contact with the line measured and photographed with it if this is desirable. It is a tedious and difficult process to read the slant of the short fine lines of writing, with the ordinary commercial protractor. The instrument illustrated easily reads to one-half of a degree.

Another protractor which is sometimes useful is illustrated in the chapter on typewriting and is designed to show the slight abnormal slant of certain letters in typewriting. This delicate but fixed divergence in slant is one of the numerous individualities in typewritten work which in sufficient combination identify a piece of typewriting with absolute certainty. This protractor which reads five degrees each side of the vertical is on glass so that it can be put over the letters and both photographed together in enlarged form.

Another test instrument for typewriting examinations is also illustrated in the typewriting chapter and consists of a glass carrying accurately ruled squares and rectangles, ten to the inch, the spacing of ordinary typewriting, so that it can be placed over the typewriting to discover and illustrate abnormal alignment, which is always one of the significant individual peculiarities of typewriting.

Another test glass useful in the examination of alleged traced forgeries is shown in Fig. 50. This is a glass with uniform squares that can be placed over an alleged forgery and a model from which it was traced, or over two alleged tracings from the same original,

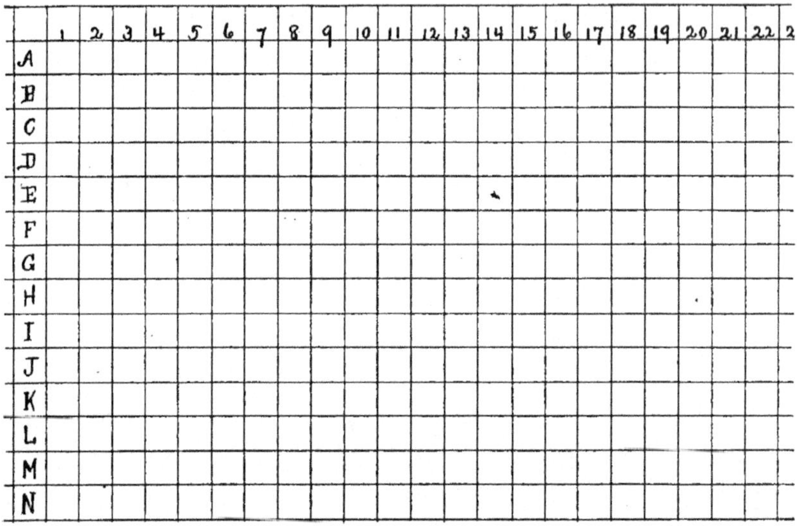

	1	2	3	4	5	6	7	8	9	10	11	12	13	14	15	16	17	18	19	20	21	22	23
A																							
B																							
C																							
D																							
E																							
F																							
G																							
H																							
I																							
J																							
K																							
L																							
M																							
N																							

Fig. 50—Illustration of ruled squares for comparison of alleged traced forgeries.

to show suspicious identities that may exist. Any part of either signature can be compared with a corresponding part of the other signature by observing where the line cuts the square. This glass can also be photographed over the signatures to make a permanent illustration as shown in Fig. 51.

Still another instrument useful in many document investigations is the color microscope, an instrument designed for the comparison, measurement and recording in fixed terms of color sensations. Many occasions arise in the examination of questioned documents for

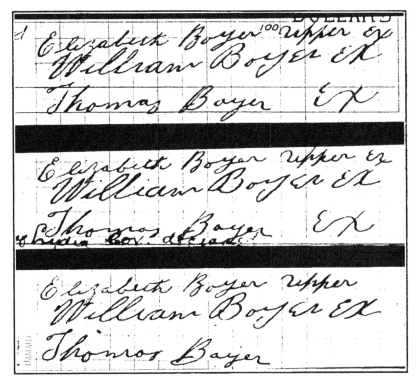

Fig. 51—Three sets of three each of traced forgeries photographed with ruled squares to show identities in size, spacing, position and shape of letters. From case of Fidelity Trust Co. (Buffalo, N. Y.) vs. Executors Lydia Cox Estate.

the use of such an instrument and without it the facts in some cases cannot be clearly shown. The instrument is useful in all ink investigations, and, as briefly outlined in the previous chapter, is useful in the early examination of a fraudulent document purporting to be some years of age, which in fact has been recently written and on which the ink has not yet matured and reached its ultimate intensity of color. If such a document is promptly examined and a definite record is made of the exact tint and shade of the ink, as may be seen and verified by competent observers, comparisons can then be made later and any change in the ink can be clearly seen and noted.

A decided change and blackening within a period of a few weeks of an ordinary iron-nutgall ink on a document purporting to be several years of age, indicates unmistakably that such a document is not as old as it purports to be. This test alone, if promptly and properly made and verified, is sufficient in many cases to prove that a document is fraudulent. The color microscope is illustrated and more fully described in the chapter on ink.

Beam dividers (Fig. 21) carrying parallel points are very useful for general measurements as well as in determining the degree of photographic enlargement by measuring the ground-glass image as already illustrated. More accurate measurements for any purpose can be made with parallel pointed dividers than with the ordinary jointed compasses.

In the chapter on photography are described numerous appliances, useful in connection with that special work, which may also become useful in connection with certain other phases of questioned document investigations.

CHAPTER VII.

In this and the chapters immediately following the more important features of handwriting are discussed somewhat in detail with a view of describing and classifying those that in the main constitute handwriting individuality and have most value in a handwriting investigation. Every element or quality of handwriting may have some value as a means of identifying it and the recognition, comparison and correct interpretation of all these various qualities are what constitute the theory and practice of scientific handwriting examination.

If we may use the broad definition of the word characteristic as "that which distinguishes or helps to distinguish," then we may describe the varying constituents of a handwriting as its characteristics. A handwriting characteristic, then, is anything about it that serves to identify it in any way or in any degree. These constituents of handwriting may vary greatly in significance, the gradations ranging from those common to all writing in the same language up through the various steps to the unique, individual characteristics of a particular writer.

As is well known handwriting shows great variety in speed and muscular skill, ranging all the way from the clumsy hesitation of the illiterate and the palsied feebleness of age up to the skillful dash and grace of the adept. Modern writing in all its great variety is, there-

[105]

fore, far from being a mere dead combination of outlines of conventional forms, like carved inscriptions on
a monument, but always has about it that which points
to the manner in which it was produced. There are as
wide differences in manner of writing as in the form[1].

Writing is in reality the track or visible record of a
movement and necessarily is greatly changed when produced in a different manner, and a thorough study of
any writing must necessarily give attention to this
fundamental question. As a rule fraudulent writing
is very defective in this matter of movement because
such writing is mainly an imitation of certain forms,
without due consideration of the manner by which they
were actually produced.

Free, natural writing is the almost unconscious visible
expression of firmly established muscular habits based
on fixed mental impressions of certain forms or outlines.
These muscular habits, as well as the mental patterns,
differ in a marked manner in different individuals and
this variation radically affects the visible result. The
forger usually acts on the false assumption that all writings are produced in the same manner and differ only
in design of letters.

The principal so-called movements in writing are
described as the finger movement, the hand movement,
the forearm movement, the whole-arm movement and
their various combinations. These movements are em-

---

[1]The way in which one writes will be determined in a measure by
the materials which he uses and by the strength and shape of his
muscles. But these are very secondary factors. The chief consideration is the nervous organization which controls the co-ordination of
the muscles. In other words, one's individual writing is the expression
of his individual habit of movement.—Prof. Charles Hubbard Judd,
of University of Chicago, in Genetic Psychology, Chapter VI., p. 169.

ployed at greatly differing degrees of speed and skill by different writers and make all together a great variety of movement habits.

The finger movement is that method of writing in which the letters are made almost entirely by the action of the thumb and the first and second fingers, the actual motion extending to the second and slightly to the third joints. This is the movement employed by children and illiterates and generally by those with whom writing is an unfamiliar process. Most of the new "vertical writing" is produced by this movement. The finger movement gives but little freedom of any kind and especially but very slight lateral freedom, and when such writing is hurried it degenerates into the very poorest kind of writing. Finger movement writing shows lack of clear-cut, smooth strokes and contains numerous broad curves, but is marked by somewhat irregular connections between letters and parts of letters and is usually slow and labored. It is the movement nearly always employed in forged writing.

Hand movement writing is that produced in most part by the action of the hand as a whole with the wrist as a center of action, but with slight action of the fingers. Much of the illegible, scratchy, angular writing written by women is produced by the hand movement. With this movement the paper is often held in such a position that the lateral or side to side movement of the hand is in a direct line with the slant of the letters. With this position and this movement the connections at the tops and bottoms of letters are very narrow or angular and the writing is often very illegible although it may be very rapid. The alignment of writing of this kind is very uneven and many words have an upward tendency.

What is known as the forearm or muscular movement really comes from the shoulder, but is the movement of the hand and arm with the arm supported by the desk on the muscular portion of the forearm with the elbow as the center of lateral motion. It is possible to write entirely with the forearm movement without any separate action of the hand and fingers, and many superior penmen write in this manner, but the easiest, most rapid and most perfect writing is that produced with the forearm movement used in connection with a slight action of the hand and fingers by which the small parts of the writing are produced.

Forearm movement writing shows smooth, clearcut, rapid strokes and is the style of writing that is forged with greatest difficulty for the reason that the method by which it is produced is the farthest removed from that slow, drawing motion employed in carefully following a copy. Forearm movement writing usually shows a uniform base line and gives great command of hand and the most complete lateral freedom.

The whole-arm movement in writing is the action of the entire arm without rest. In the forearm movement it is obvious that the motion and its source are nearly the same as in the whole-arm movement, but the forearm rests on a support of desk or table. This rest restricts somewhat the extent of the movement but with such support the movement is under much better control. The whole-arm movement is employed in very large writing, in ornamental penmanship, in blackboard writing and by a few writers in making all the capital letters.

The distinguishing difference between writing and printing is that in writing the letters in words are connected with each other. Originally writings were mostly what would now be called pen-printing, all the characters being made separately, but as writing became more common and the necessity for ease and speed increased the characters were connected. This manner of writing made a new requirement in the process, that of locomotion, or the ability to move the hand along as the letters were made in succession. In this manner the slope of writing to the right was developed and there arose the necessity for developing what are described as writing movements as compared with the printing movement used to make detached letters.

Finger movement writing, especially as taught in the new vertical writing, is essentially a printing movement which permits of the formation of but a few characters without a readjustment of the arm and a new start. Hand movement gives somewhat more lateral freedom while forearm movement carries the hand along from letter to letter, keeping the hand, arm and fingers in the same relation to each other and permitting the use of the fingers and hand for the formation of the small parts of the letters, and allowing that freedom, ease and force which are always characteristics of the best writing.

The various movements already described are each employed with a great variation in skill by different writers and a general classification may assist in making an analysis of this particular phase of the writing process. Under this head (Fig. 52) five classes can readily be distinguished: (1) clumsy, illiterate and halting; (2) hesitating and painful through weakness or disease; (3) nervous and irregular; (4) strong, heavy, forceful; (5) smooth, easy, flowing and rapid.

Under the head of speed alone four divisions can also be made: (1) slow and drawn; (2) deliberate; (3) average; (4) rapid. It is obvious that the fourth division under speed might accompany the third division under movement. These descriptions are necessarily of a very general character, but are of value in so far as they assist in calling attention to every element of the writing habit.

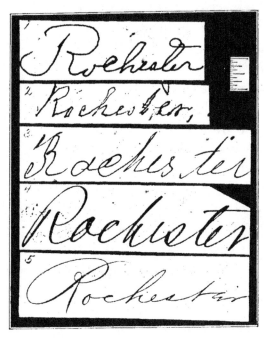

Fig. 52—Five examples of movement. All taken from business envelope addresses.

The degree of skill shown in one writing may be so superior to that shown in another that the difference is as irreconcilable as the most radical differences in form. This question must be studied with especial care at the beginning of all anonymous letter inquiries or in any investigation in which a writing is examined primarily as a means of identifying some person. It is obvious that a disguised hand would not show greater writing ability than the natural hand of the same writer nor a freehand forgery show more skill with the pen than the alleged forger possesses.

The different movements employed affect writing in different ways and change or modify the smoothness, directness, uniformity and continuity of the strokes and also notably modify the connecting turns or curves between letters and parts of letters. Unskillful writing is produced by a disconnected and broken movement and to produce practically the same form requires many more disconnected or interrupted motions or movement impulses than skillful writing. In the writing of a single signature one writer may actually make fifty distinct movement impulses (Fig. 53), which can

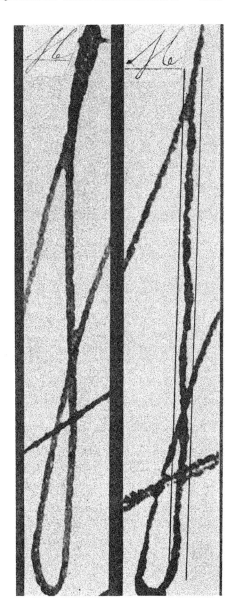

Fig. 53—Part of genuine letter and similar part of a traced signature. From Rice-Patrick case, New York.

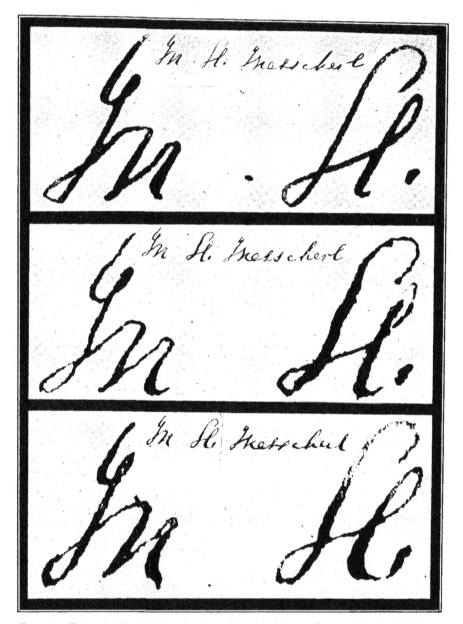

Fig. 54—Two genuine letters from model signature and two traced imitations, showing slow, hesitating, drawing movement. See especially top of last capital H. From exhibits in case of Essenhower vs. Messchert Estate, Reading, Pa. (1907).

be counted in the written result, while another writer in producing the same letters with the same number of pen-lifts, may make only twenty-five distinct motions. This marks a distinction in two writings even more funda-mental than divergences in form.

Fig. 55—Natural tremor, most pronounced on downward strokes and absent from some upward strokes and from final flourish.

A free uninterrupted stroke or motion makes a smooth, continuous curved or straight line while a change of direction, tremor, or unevenness in the inter-mediate part of what ordinarily is a single stroke in-dictates a hesitation or changing movement impulse[1]. Study of the strokes or separated pen lines themselves in a writing will show with what speed and force it was

[1]An excellent example of hesitating, changing movement impulses is shown in the enlargement of the downward stroke of one of the capital "M's" from one of the court exhibits of the Rice-Patrick (New York) case will signature (Fig. 53). A straight line is drawn each side of the stroke to show more clearly its character. The four forged signatures in the case were undoubtedly traced from one model and contained many strokes like that shown. Hold the book with the paper nearly flat so that it is possible to look lengthwise of the illustration when it will be seen that this line from one of the signatures could only have been produced by a slow, hesitating, drawing movement. This same condition is shown in numerous parts of the two traced imi-tations shown in Fig. 54, taken from exhibits in a similar case. If the lines are followed through with a dry pen it will be seen how from the lines themselves the manner of writing is unmistakably shown.

Fig. 56—Simulated tremor and blunt ended strokes showing slow drawing movement[1]. From exhibit in case of Newcomb vs. Burbank, (1909) New York City.

written. A straight line is not only the shortest distance between two points but also the quickest distance, and the line quality of writing always indicates the speed, force and freedom with which it was produced.

The connecting upward strokes are especially significant for the comparison of movement impulses, as such strokes show the propulsive power of the writer. In genuine writing the upward strokes, or some of them at least, are usually produced with more smoothness and freedom than the downward strokes, and just the opposite condition may be found in fraudulent writing.

[1]The tables of enlarged terminals and "t" crossings taken from the admitted writings of the parties, show a very marked difference; those of the defendant being blunt or clubbed at the latter end while those of the plaintiff are generally lighter and invariably pointed or tapering at the termination.—Sharon vs. Hill, 26 Fed. Rep. 358 (1885).

When a word is completed in free natural writing the pen is usually raised from the paper while in motion, and with many writers the motion also slightly precedes the putting of the pen on the paper at the beginning, so that the strokes at the beginning and ends of words gradually diminish or taper to a vanishing point.

. In simulated writing produced by a slow, drawing motion with the attention almost entirely directed to the matter of form, the lines will often

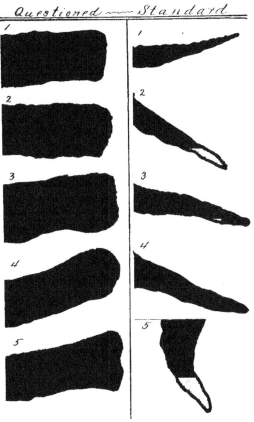

Fig. 57—Ten diameter Camera Lucida enlargements of first five word terminals of Fig. 56. Divergence in *direction* as well as form of finish is shown.

have blunt, stubbed ends (Figs. 56, 57), showing the stopping of the motion with the stroke itself and then the raising of the pen. The questioned and standard writing in any case should always be carefully examined under considerable magnification with this point in mind.

In genuine writing there are certain natural places

for the pen to hesitate or even stop, but in forged or fraudulent writing, which is usually produced by a drawing movement, such movement may show disconnection or hesitation at any point on upward or downward strokes or even in the middle of what are naturally continuous strokes.

In examining a questioned signature the separate movements or impulses required to produce the genuine and questioned writing should, as already suggested, be carefully counted and compared, and the exact points or places in the two writings where stops or hesitation is shown should be examined with the utmost care and thoroughness. A drawn signature will almost inevitably show significant divergences and inconsistencies, and also stops and joinings in unnatural places. Greatly enlarged photographs showing the utmost detail of the original writing are almost indispensable for thorough examinations of this character.

Genuine writing, even when showing much tremor, will usually show some free strokes made by the momentum of the hand, while drawn fraudulent writing, even though quite perfect in general form, may show but little if any such freedom and will often show hesitation at the wrong places and tremor wrongly placed. When, however, the writing imitated is excessively weak and hesitating the imitation may in some parts exaggerate the tremor and in other parts show an inconsistent strength and firmness that indicate that the writing is not genuine.

Line quality in writing is dependent upon the writing instrument, the writing surface, the relation of the writing instrument to the writing surface, the muscular skill or hand control of the writer and the manner of writing or movement employed. Deviations from uniform strokes, ordinarily called tremors, which are apparent without magnification, may be due to lack of skill on the part of the writer, self-consciousness of the writing process, or the hesitation which is the result of copying or imitating. Lack of smoothness or tremor may be due to uncontrollable nervousness on the part of the writer, or, in illiterate writing, to clumsiness or hesitation due to a lack of a clear mental impression of the form which is being made. Tremor of age, of illiteracy and of weakness are not always distinguishable from each other, but can usually be distinguished from tremor of fraud.

If standard writing is smooth and strong and shows no tremulous strokes then, of course, the presence of any tremor whatever in an alleged forgery is very suspicious in itself and such tremor may be very strong evidence of forgery.

The characteristics of tremor of fraud as distinguished from other tremor are inequality in movement at any place in a stroke or line, with lines too strong and vigorous combined with weak hesitating strokes; also frequent interruptions in movement, unequal distribution of ink on upward as well as downward strokes, and especially the varying pen pressure due to change in speed and interruptions in movement which may occur in the middle of direct curves or even straight lines. Such forged writing may lack the necessary uniformity with itself and thus contains evidences of unnaturalness that indicate a lack of genuineness without compari-

son with any other writing whatever. This result is
often particularly apparent where the forger attempts
to simulate tremor of weakness.

Two very significant parts of a signature or any
writing are the first and last strokes of words and separate capital letters. If evidences of attention to the

Fig. 58—Terminal of questioned signature showing changing pressure, significant
hesitation on last stroke and also blunt ending.

process of writing and inequalities in pen pressure and
movement continue to the very end of the last unimportant stroke of the word (Fig. 58) or letter this
usually indicates a self-consciousness of the writing
process which may be a strong indication of forgery,
and if the very beginning of the signature also shows
hesitation and changes of direction inconsistent with
the standard signatures, such unnatural condition is
strong evidence of a drawing movement instead of a
writing movement.

Characteristic tremor of age or extreme weakness
usually shows unusual and erratic departures of the line
from its intended course, abrupt recovery, and a general
indication of weakness or of movements beyond the con-

trol of the writer, particularly in downward strokes. Such writing frequently shows awkward digressions or distortions, which may be due to imperfect sight, and general irregularity caused by involuntary tremors, and it is often characterized by abbreviations or even omissions of letters or parts of letters.

FIG. 59—Portion of forged siguature showing two suspicious joinings, before and after small "n," and obtuse angles in final curve after small "r."

Signatures showing tremor of age often show very uneven alignment and may disregard entirely a line near which they are written, especially if such line is indistinct. Toward the end such signatures sometimes show apparent impatience and the desire to complete what may be a disagreeable and perhaps a very painful act, and the concluding parts may be made with a nervous haste and may be much distorted. Even the most clumsy genuine signature will usually show occasional careless, unconscious strokes while a forgery is often most carefully drawn from beginning to end. Old age writing indicating a lack of muscular control does not usually show fine continuous hair lines, but many strokes are usually made with considerable pressure.

Natural tremor, being involuntary, is apt to be comparatively uniform on similar parts and a forger may fail in showing too many or too few tremors. A forged signature purporting to be written by an old man with a trembling hand sometimes contains delicate and unnecessary retouching and repairing of fine lines which mark it as undoubtedly spurious. Such delicate corrections are inconsistent with genuineness in any writing, and in some cases may be conclusive evidence of forgery because it would have been physically impossible for the aged writer with a feeble hand and poor sight to make the repairs which appear in the questioned signature. In his tense anxiety for a perfect result the forger is very apt to be dissatisfied with his work as first produced and often attempts to perfect it by careful overwriting and retouching, thus marking it as unquestionably fraudulent.

Tremor of extreme weakness and tremor of age have many similar characteristics, and cannot always be distinguished from each other, but even the most feeble genuine writing usually has about it a certain carelessness or abandon that marks it as genuine, while tremor of fraud shows a painstaking and unnatural care throughout that indicates an effort to follow an unfamiliar copy[1].

---

[1] The signature, on its face, independent of any other consideration is, without any question, suspicious. Even when considering this signature in the most favorable light in connection with the other evidence in the case, tending to show that the decedent intended to make testamentary provision for the proponent, it nevertheless stands out as a silent, emphatic denial of genuineness. A person may write poorly at times, when his signature does not resemble his usual style of writing, perhaps, but there is a built up, mechanical appearance of this disputed signature which even a most liberal consideration cannot disregard.—Matter of Burtis, 43 Miscellaneous Reports, (N. Y.) (1904) (See Fig. 109).

In tremor of illiteracy the changes in direction are not apt to be as numerous as in tremor of age or of weakness, and in such writing omissions of parts of letters or strokes are not common, but, on the contrary, the writing may be clumsily overwritten, to make it conform to standard forms.   Illiterate tremor is characterized by a general irregularity that is due to hesitation because of uncertainty as to the form and to muscular clumsiness resulting from unfamiliarity with the whole writing process.

Illiterate writing, even on ruled paper, frequently shows a pronounced irregularity in alignment, some of it being above the line and some through the line, or the words may each go up from the line so that the end of each word is higher than the beginning, this characteristic being due to the fact that the arm is held so that the center of motion is so far to the right that as the hand moves along it is inevitably raised above the general line of writing.   On unruled paper this position naturally has a tendency to make the writing go up-hill across the whole sheet or page.

Disconnections or pen-lifts between letters in words may be due to lack of movement control.   With those who write clumsily or with difficulty the pen is raised frequently to get a new adjustment and make a fresh start, and words may be broken after almost any letter, depending somewhat upon where it is in the word.   With most writers, however, disconnections are more closely related to design of letters than with movement, and the habits controlling this characteristic were acquired when writing was first learned.

Many are taught when learning to write to take up

the pen before the letters a, c, d, g, q and t, and the design of certain styles of these small letters requires that the pen be raised. Similarities in these particulars would not therefore be very significant as showing identity of two writings, except in combination with other characteristics, but pronounced dissimilarities in these characteristics would be strong evidence of a lack of identity.

Many peculiar distinctively individual habits are developed in this matter of raising the pen before certain

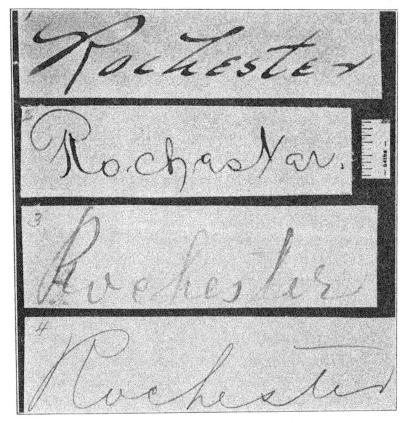

Fig. 60—Illustration of divergent pen-lift habits, showing eight pen-lifts in first word and none in last.

strokes or following certain letters, and this character- istic should receive careful attention in examining a handwriting. It is one of those inconspicuous and un- conscious habits that are usually entirely disregarded in a simulated writing, and its careful consideration is of special importance in examining anonymous letters or documents of any kind which contain a considerable quantity of writing. This matter of joinings and pen lifts is a subject requiring special attention in examining writings that may have been written by writers that originally learned different systems of writing. Forged writing often shows too many pen lifts (Fig. 59).

Alignment in writing as in printing is the relation of the several characters of a word, or signature or line of writing, to an actual or imaginary base line. Differ- ences and deviations in alignment conditions are due mainly to differences in movement, in position and in design of letters. In many writings alignment is a char- acteristic of much significance and shows many uncon- scious, individual habits, and should always be consid- ered in examining a writing.

Those who write with the elbow as the center of lateral motion and hold the arm at right angles to the line of writing often write words almost perfectly aligned and straight across the page even on wide unruled paper. Those who write with the wrist as the center of motion may write lines of writing made up of short arcs of a circle, representing the reach of the hand with the wrist at rest when moved around to the right as far as the hand will reach. The most uneven alignment is pro- duced when the arm is too far around to the right or the paper too far to the left so that lateral motions of the hand to the right extend above the base line of the writing. Writing produced with freedom in this position will show very uneven alignment.

Deviation from alignment in individual letters is often the result of defective or distorted designs of letters and like many other individual peculiarities was acquired when writing was first learned, or such a deviation may be a gradual and unconscious evolution from an original form. Some writers will habitually make certain letters too high and others too low, and many extraordinary peculiarities will be found in connection with this characteristic. There are writers who will always make the sharp intermediate angles of h, k, m, n and the German t too long so that they extend below the line of the other letters, while others make them too short.

Other writers will invariably make the small s too low while others again always make it too high. In some writing the alignment of certain letters is always affected when they precede or follow certain other letters, making a combined characteristic that may have much force as showing a particular writer, since this is a peculiarity in general writing that might not be shown in the model writing imitated by the forger even though the model contained all the letters imitated but in a different order. The alignment of capital letters with many writers is abnormal and, especially in anonymous letter investigations, should be carefully observed.

Some of these peculiarities are not conspicuous, and for that reason are the more significant as individualities, and they may be overlooked if writing is not enlarged somewhat for the purpose of examination. Fine lines should be drawn at the bottom and top of the minimum letters as they appear on an enlarged photograph; in this way persistent peculiarities may be discovered and shown that otherwise will not be properly interpreted.

In any examination it is well to make a definite list of all the things to consider and take them up in order and then nothing will be omitted. One who attempts to see all things at once will not see some things clearly

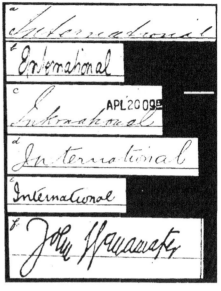

Fig. 60-a.   Six examples of alignment,
1 Uniform, 2 Irregular, 3 Curved,
4 Upward, 5 Downward,
6 Freakish.

and may omit entirely some important part of the process.

It is also well always to avoid hasty judgment even on what at first may seem to be a comparatively unimportant inquiry. It is better to have a reputation for accuracy than for celerity.

CHAPTER VIII.

The manner of holding the pen is one of the most fixed of writing habits, but varies greatly with different writers, so that it becomes necessary to consider the question in every writing investigation. The form of a writing is often very well simulated, yet this may be done with a pen position and a manner of writing utterly inconsistent with the habits shown in the writing imitated.

Pen positions differ widely and are of great variety, but vary in three principal ways; first, in the angle of the pen to the surface of the paper, second, in the angle of the pen to the line or direction of the writing, and, third, in the uniformity of pressure of the two nibs of the pen.

The pen is held by different writers at an angle with the surface of the paper varying all the way from almost vertical down to only fifteen to twenty degrees from the horizontal. The position of the pen in relation to the line of writing varies as much as ninety degrees, ranging from a position in which the penholder points directly toward the writer and parallel with the downward strokes of slanted writing, to a position with the pen swung round to the right nearly parallel with the line of writing. The relation of the nibs of the pen to the paper, or the third point already mentioned, varies all the way from almost exclusive pressure on the left nib to similar pressure on the right. All these divergent

[126]

conditions must necessarily affect the writing in distinctive ways entirely aside from that of general form or outline of letters.

A pen held in nearly a vertical position will make a fine line of about the same width throughout without pronounced shading and often with a tendency to a broken or a scratchy effect.   Such writing, as a rule, is produced almost entirely with the finger movement. With a pen held in the opposite position, or down nearly horizontal to the paper, a broader stroke with a similar pen will be made; the ink will follow the pen back at the angles or narrow turns and tend to fill up such parts; loops will often be filled in at the top where the strokes go to the left, and the lower edges of such strokes, as shown by the microscope, will be very rough. With the pen held very low frequent shading is very common

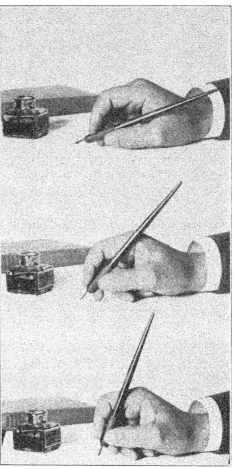

Fig. 61—Pen Position in relation to surface of paper.

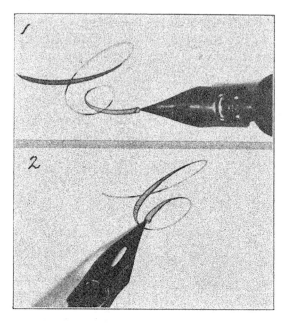

F IG. 62—Location of shading showing pen position.

and this position is often that assumed by one using the free arm movement. This position of the pen is inconsistent with finger movement writing.

As is well understood, what is spoken of as the point of an ordinary pen is really two points formed by two pieces of metal called nibs lying close together and making one mark when a stroke is made without pressure. Pressure separates the nibs producing shading and the pressure necessary to separate the two nibs has a tendency to indent, or disturb the fiber of the paper more or less, making the ink line heavier in their direct track at the edges of the stroke. It is impossible to hold the pen in any one position so that strokes at right angles to each other can be smoothly shaded and both show the distinct and equal track of both pen nibs; from this fact the pen position of a writing can be determined by the location of the emphasis or shading.

If the pen is held parallel with the downward strokes and pointing toward the writer, such strokes under pressure will show shading and the nibs of the pen will separate and leave parallel tracks on strokes made in line with the pen (Fig. 62), but will gradually approach each other as the stroke swings around to the right until the two nibs follow each other in making the single line. Thus lateral strokes with the pen in this position are made across the nibs and would not show separate and parallel tracks even if pressure is made at such point.

With a pen inclined around to the right, towards a position parallel with the written line, it will be seen that lateral strokes made from left to right will under pressure show shading and the parallel nib marks of the pen, and on downward strokes with the pen in this position one nib will nearly if not quite follow in the track of the other. This fact is well illustrated by making shaded circles with a pen; it will be seen that

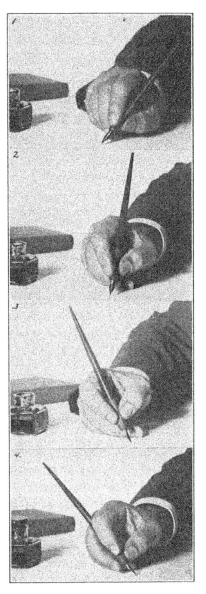

Fig. 63—Pen position in relation to the line of writing.

in such forms the location of the shading and the parallel

nib marks will be governed entirely by the pen position.

With a stub pen held in the usual position in which such pens are held, inclined somewhat around to the right, the writing strokes will show the full width of the pen point not only on the lateral strokes from left to right but also on those from right to left or at the tops or bottoms of letters (see Ex. h, Fig. 65), because at these points the width of the pen point is brought to a position at right angles to the strokes and makes a mark the full width of the point. This increasing width of strokes made from the right back to the left at the tops of letters is the typical mark of stub pen writing. This is not really shading in the ordinary sense because it is produced without any increase of pressure whatever and may not show any nib marks. Most stub pen writers hold the pen well around to the right and many such pens have a point cut not straight across but diagonally, requiring this position as described in order to write smoothly.

Pen pressure on the nibs of the pen is varied in three principal ways. Some writers put greater pressure on the right nib, others on the left, while others write with uniform pressure on both nibs. These three habits are shown by the general quality of the stroke and particularly by the comparative smoothness or roughness of the right and left margins.

With the pen otherwise in normal position and pressure on the left nib, up strokes may be slightly heavier than unshaded down strokes and the right side of the line will be rougher and more indented and ragged as seen under magnification, and the left nib track on shaded strokes will be more pronounced and deeper as viewed by the microscope.

With pressure on the right nib these results are partly reversed with no increase in width on up strokes. With equal pressure on both nibs the line margins are uniform with each other and the line or stroke on smooth paper appears clear-cut and smooth if written with a free movement. A divergent habit of pen holding as shown in a disputed writing is often very strong evidence pointing to a differcut writer, and, like movement or manner of writing, may be much more significant than certain minor changes in form characteristics.

When viewed by the microscope under even low magnification, the edges of an ink line appear indented and rough. This roughness is accentuated by certain pen positions which bring the writing instrument in such relation to the uneven surface of writing paper that one side of the line is made more uneven than the other even when the line is made with no tremor whatever. The character of the microscopic edges of the lines in a general way puts all writers into one of three classes, those who make the majority of pen strokes rougher on the left, on the right, or those whose strokes show uniformity.

On account of the position of the pen in relation to a majority of the strokes, right slant writing more frequently shows an excess of roughness on the right and lower side of pen strokes, making this class of writers much larger than either of the other two. This line edge characteristic may be very significant as showing divergence in two writings, but shows identity of two writings only so far as it puts them both into what must necessarily be a very large class. The character and extent of the roughness of the line edges are greatly changed by changes in the character of the surface of the paper, in its sizing, and in the materials of which it is made. The result is also affected by the character and condition of the ink used and by the rapidity, direction and weight of the stroke.

One of the most personal but somewhat hidden characteristics of writing is that which for want of a better term is described as pen pressure. The weight of hand, gradation of pressure, and placing of emphasis radically change the appearance of a writing as a whole without changing the form in any way. These are the delicate characteristics that almost baffle simulation and when properly exemplified are always among the strongest evidences of genuineness.

The pen of certain writers (1) dances over the paper with a springy, rhythmic motion that leaves a characteristic record; in other hands (2) the writing instrument moves in a stately way that suggests strength but not speed, while as guided by other writers a pen (3) leaves an irregular, broken line that is the record of a

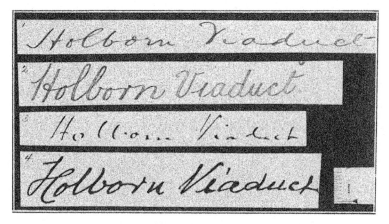

FIG. 64—Four divergent examples of pen pressure.

rapid, nervous movement. The record of the pen of still another class of writers (4) leaves a heavy, uneven, ragged line due to lack of skill and constant variation in pen pressure (Fig. 64). It is easy to understand how difficult it would be for a writer of the fourth class, specified above, to imitate successfully the writing of the first or second class.

Pen pressure, perhaps, more than anything else in certain writing shows that freedom and unconsciousness of the writing process that points to genuineness; or on the contrary shows that halting, studied, hesitating stroke that is characteristic of forgery. A genuine writing does not often suggest that the writer is thinking of what he is doing with his pen, while a dishonest writing when examined with care often shows quite conclusively that the writer was thinking of nothing else. The main features of this pen pressure characteristic are not consciously acquired and not intentionally put into a writing and therefore are all the more significant and personal and should always be most carefully considered in examining a questioned writing.

Lack of muscular skill with the pen, or what is usually described as tremor, is shown by lack of uniformity of speed in the making of pen strokes and by involuntary horizontal and vertical movements. Such uncontrolled horizontal movements produce a line with abrupt changes of direction, of a more or less zigzag character, and the involuntary vertical movements produce a line of varying width or intensity (Fig. 53) as the pressure is suddenly increased or diminished. This latter characteristic, which may not always be recognized as tremor, is in fact involuntary pen pressure or vertical tremor, and may be of great significance in identifying a handwriting. This varying pressure on light strokes is often the result of the slow drawing movement required to produce a traced forgery.

No very definite ' distinction can be drawn between pen pressure and shading in writing. The distinction made in the present discussion is that pen pressure refers more especially to the involuntary placing of emphasis, smoothness of stroke and quality of line in writing, as distinguished from that deliberate and voluntary emphasis that is ordinarily described as shading. This last named important quality or feature of writing, acquired at first by study and careful imitation, also becomes an unconscious, involuntary habit and is a characteristic that should always be most carefully considered. The shading impulse with some writers is a habit more fixed than that of form, and even when writing with a pen so stiff that the nibs will not spread the increased pressure on the strokes ordinarily shaded is perfectly apparent by the intensified line that may be but little if any broader than the other strokes. .

Shading should be studied with especial attention to its (1) form, (2) its intensity, (3) its frequency, and (4) its exact location. In many instances faulty shading is one of the first and strongest evidences of fraudulent handwriting.

Shading habits in writing can be classified in a general way as follows:

(a) Persistent or continuous as on nearly every downward stroke; (b) rare, unintentional or accidental; (c) graduated, controlled, smooth and artistic, as shown by gradual increase and decrease of pressure; (d) impulsive, nervous, bunchy or the result of sudden and violent pressure; (e) freakish or peculiar, as only on certain parts of words or occasional letters; (f) rough or scratchy as across pen points; (g) lateral or mainly on strokes from left to right; (h) stub pen shading or on strokes made back to left, particularly at tops of letters (Fig. 65). Some of these habits are closely related to pen position and must be studied in connection with that subject.

Because of exclusive attention to form, a forged imitation of a shaded signature often is first written without proper shading and the lines are afterwards strengthened by a careful retouching. This evidence of patching and fixing is usually unmistakable under the microscope or in a properly made enlarged photograph, and often is very convincing

Fig. 65—Eight examples of shading from business envelopes.

evidence of fraud. A careless and perfectly evident patching of a broken line, due to a defective pen or where the ink failed, is readily distinguished from delicate changes in a signature not necessary to its completion or legibility.

Defects of the character just described are most likely to appear in forgeries made to imitate the writing of old people who write the old round-hand. With many writers one of the fixed characteristics of this old writing, originally written with quill pens, is the shading of every downward stroke, a habit which with a mature writer is almost uncontrollable and is usually apparent in every letter. Simulation of this writing by one who habitually writes an unshaded system often omits or distorts this important feature in whole or in part.

The attempt is sometimes made to explain lack of proper shading by the supposition that a stiff pen was used when even the disputed writing itself actually contains some shaded parts which, however, are in the wrong places, thus showing the fraudulent character of the writing because the shading is omitted where it should appear and is placed where it does not belong. A shaded line may be only slightly heavier than a normal or unshaded line, or may, with a flexible pen, be from four to ten times as wide. In a careful study and analysis of this question it is important that actual measurements of strokes be made.

A traced forgery is an attempt to reproduce the exact lines of a model, while a simulated or copied forgery is a copy or imitation of the general form of the original. The method required in either case is almost certain to lead to divergences in pen position, pen pressure and

shading. Both of these classes of forgery are almost invariably slowly and carefully made with but little if any
attention to anything but the form. As ordinarily produced, they also both require frequent stops to look at
the copy or inspect the result, or to change the position
of the hand, and as a rule show a line with an unequal
distribution of ink, frequent breaks and interruptions
and distinct variations in pressure, all tending to produce a total result differing radically from a genuine
writing in line quality, pen pressure, and shading.

These tracing and simulating processes require a firm
position of the hand in order to draw with even approximate accuracy the lines of the model, and this firmness of
position is most readily secured by holding the hand
down on the side, which necessarily inclines the pen somewhat over to the right. This position naturally tends
to make of maximum width those portions of the strokes
which are at the bottom of the letters or on the strokes
made from left to right. This characteristic shading is
very often found in fraudulent writing.

In producing a tracing or simulation of a writing the
pen may be held over to the right for the further reason
that the track of the pen as the stroke is made can thus
be more readily seen by the writer. This is especially
apt to be true in case the forgery is traced over a faint
image as seen through the paper or over a very light
line first drawn. The location of the shading or maximum pressure thus becomes of vital importance for two
reasons; the position of the shading may show that the
pen must have been held far over to the right, and, if
the locations of the shaded places differ from the model
or genuine writing, it is doubly significant, as it not only

shows a difference in the writing itself, but suggests the possible method by which the forgery was produced. Such a divergence from the genuine writing is particularly strong evidence of forgery if the writing imitated is by one whose fixed habit it is to hold the pen inclined somewhat to the left or nearly parallel with the downward strokes as is the case with those who shade all downward strokes.

As we have already seen, shading itself is varied in many significant ways and shows numerous peculiar and unaccountable peculiarities that may be properly classed as the curiosities or idiosyncrasies of writing. A thorough examination of a writing in dispute should, as stated, give the most careful attention to this matter of location, character, and frequency of shading and it is sometimes helpful if the results of the examination are systematically tabulated. It will be found that some writers shade slightly the beginning of every word or letter, and others, without any reason, will shade only the concluding stroke at the very tip. Some writers will shade a few letters every time they occur but no others whatever, while other writers shade only certain parts of words whatever the letters may be. There are those who persistently try to shade lateral strokes with the pen in such position that such a stroke is across the point, the result being a ragged, heavy line in which the pen nibs nearly follow each other and scratch the paper, the result necessarily being an uneven, rough line (Fig. 66).

Some writers cross the "t" with a stroke beginning with pressure and ending with a light line, while others begin with a light line but end with a heavy shading

showing exactly the op-
posite characteristic.
Other writers will shade
the middle of the stroke
and some may make the
stroke a very light line
throughout its whole
length, and others
shade it heavily from
end to end. A wonder-
ful variety of shadings
is shown in the illustra-
tions in the chapter
treating of variety of
form. Attention is par-
ticularly directed to
the illustration of "t"
crossings. A high de-
gree of skill is required
to make and place ac-
curately the many vari-
ations of shaded strokes
shown on all the capital
and small letters, and
they are not likely to
be successfully imitated
except by an adept;
and fortunately the
forger is not usually

Fig. 66—Examples of shading: 1, light
line; 2, every down stroke; 3, stub
pen; 4, bunchy; 5, final stroke;
6, lateral strokes.

one who possesses extraordinary skill.

There is a close relation between shading and movement because shading necessarily interferes somewhat

with speed, although not with continuity and smoothness. Clear-cut smooth shades, especially on curves, show a free and well controlled movement and simulated or traced writing is nearly always defective in this particular feature. Being self-conscious and hesitating it usually lacks the smoothness and directness that are characteristic of genuineness.

On account of the necessity of seeing clearly what he is doing the forger may put the paper on which the writing is being done directly in front of him as a book is held in reading, and not slightly around to the right as is the usual position in writing. This front position of the paper, with the arm around to the right approaching a position parallel with the line of writing, often produces the result of writing slightly up-hill, as described in the chapter on movements, especially if effort is being made to reproduce a copy whose forms and proportions are somewhat unfamiliar. Thus it is often found that a forgery of this class inclines upward and may thus differ in another particular from the genuine writing imitated.

CHAPTER IX.

Writing habits are the result of many and varied causes; some are the direct outgrowth of definite teaching, many are the result of unconscious imitation, while others are due to some accidental condition or circumstance, and all are in some degree the expression of certain mental and physical traits of the writer as affected by environment and occupation. Habits of arrangement of the various parts of a writing are especially of this complex character, and a study of such habits is particularly necessary and important in the examination of disputed letters or of any document containing considerable matter.

The habits of arrangement of the parts of a writing are undoubtedly largely governed by the artistic ability or sense of proportion of the writer, and, like all significant writing habits, are, for the most part, developed and grown into rather than consciously acquired. Without actual examination but very few writers can specify even the most conspicuous of their own habits in this matter of arrangement, any more than they can tell how they carry their hands as they walk or what gestures they make during conversation, or do the thousand and one other things which make up individuality. It is inevitable that in producing simulated or fraudulent writing these unconscious characteristics of the writer himself are given no consideration, and similar characteristics in the writing imitated are misunderstood and misinterpreted.

The main features for consideration under the general head of arrangement are: (1) the general placing of writing on a sheet or page and its artistic and balanced arrangement of parts or its unbalanced and inartistic appearance; (2) the wide, narrow, mixed or uniform spacing between lines, between words, between separate capitals, between capitals and small letters in the same words; (3) placing or locating of words with reference to an imaginary or actual base line, i. e., on the line, above the line, below the line, or partly above and partly below; (4) presence or absence, character and uniformity of margins at left, at right, at top and bottom of sheet; (5) position of signature in relation to writing it follows; (6) horizontal, uphill, downhill, curved or mixed direction of signature on line of writing; (7) parallelism and width of space between lines of writing on envelope addresses or unruled paper; (8) arrangement of headings[1], introductions and conclusions of letters and their relation to each other and to body of writing; (9) paragraphing and its frequency or omission and average depth of indentation at beginning of paragraphs; (10) arrangement of figures and abbreviations, dollar and cents signs, etc., to line of writing and to preceding or following writing; (11) interlineations

---

[1]In every letter which we have seen from the pen of Mrs. Gaines the date thereof and the name of the place whence written are placed on the extreme right edge of the paper, so close thereto, as to leave barely enough space to write the necessary words. In the confidential letter, the words "Washington, D. C" are placed near the middle of the line, more to the left of the paper; and in the spurious will the words "New Orleans" are located on the extreme left edge of the paper. —Succession of Gaines, 38 La. 135 (1886).

and their character, position and frequency; (12) envelope addresses and their style, position and arrangement; (13) connections or unbroken pen strokes between words; (14) number of words to a line as in telegraphers' writing; (15) location of punctuation marks with relation to base line and to the words which they follow; (16) underscoring and its location.

Investigation shows that every writer has habits in these directions most of which are entirely unconscious and all of which are repeated with remarkable regularity. All frequent acts tend to become automatic, habit supplanting mental direction, and this is a conspicuous fact in all phases of the writing process. The writing act as normally performed follows the smooth grooves of habit until most writing is actually performed without even the assistance of the sense of sight except as directed to the process in general[1]. The majority of the numerous arrangement habits named above with many writers have never received conscious attention at any time, and the results have been developed by the requirements and external conditions surrounding the individual. It is well known that the condensed style of ancient writings

---

[1] Developed writing movements depend, then, on the existence of a group of brain-cells which are interconnected and interrelated in a most complex way. The growth of this series of interconnections between the cells was a process that required time and practice. At the beginning of this practice each cell acted in a large measure apart from its fellows, and there was no well-organized co-operation, or muscular co-ordination as we have learned to call it.—Charles Hubbard Judd, Ph. D., Genetic Psychology, Chapter VI., p. 166.

The laws of motor habit in the lower centres of the nervous system are disputed by no one. A series of movements repeated in a certain order tend to unroll themselves with peculiar ease in that order forever afterward. Number one awakens number two, and that awakens number three, and so on till the last is produced. A habit of this kind once become inveterate may go on automatically.—William James, Principles of Psychology, Vol. I., p. 554.

was due in part to the cost and scarcity of the materials upon which writing was placed, and certain habits of many writers are due in a measure to accidental external conditions which surrounded them at some time.

Bookkeepers and others who write much with fine

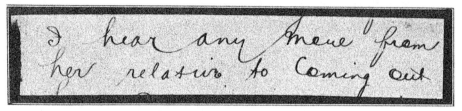

Fig. 67—Telegrapher's writing from letter. Five words to line, typical word connections and circle small "o's."

pens on narrow ruled books acquire a concise and definite style that is of a distinct but somewhat effeminate character, while in contrast with this the railroad clerk whose work requires boldness, strength, speed and legibility, develops a style that requires much room and is just the opposite of effeminate. The telegraph operator becomes so accustomed to writing five words to a line on telegraph blanks that he must resist his natural impulse or in any writing his hand will count off five words to a line.

The attempt to disguise a handwriting almost inevitably shows conspicuous evidences of the fixed and unconscious character of these various habits; that is disguised which is general and superficial, and that which is individual and specific is entirely overlooked. Illiterate writers especially are apt to incorporate into such writing some distinctly individual idiosyncrasies. The writer of the distinctive angular woman's hand, which is usually coarse and heavy and often of a sprawling, awkward, unwomanly character, with abnormally wide spacing between words and between lines and with horizontal concluding strokes to words, will almost certainly carry some of these habits into a disguised document whatever the manner or method of the disguise adopted.

Habits of arrangement in writing and general habits of neatness undoubtedly reflect certain individual characteristics which are likely to be shown in whatever is done; the writer who is methodical, definite, matter of fact and practical does not produce that with his hand which is slovenly and uncertain; neither do the bungler and the sloven produce a page of writing that is graceful, balanced and finished without excess. Certainly to the extent here specified, graphology points in the right direction although many of its deductions seem to be based on foundations too slender for scientific accuracy.

Size in writing is a characteristic that is somewhat divergent under varying conditions and may have but little significance when applied to only one example or to a small quantity of writing like a signature unless the divergence is very pronounced. But if a number of signatures alleged to have been produced at different times are in question, or even two or three are under suspicion and they are like each other in the matter of size, in which they differ from all admitted standards, then this divergence at once becomes significant in proportion to its extent, the number of divergent examples and the number of standards. This is also true of all divergencies in writing, which in one instance may have little force but in combination may point conclusively to a different hand.

The various parts of an ordinary signature when carefully measured bear a certain proportion to each other that with most writers is found to be surprisingly uniform. There is a natural divergence, however, within certain limits, and an occasional exceptional part, and this fact makes it dangerous to base a conclusion as to genuineness entirely upon a few measurements of size or proportions. Divergencies or similarities that can be clearly shown may, however, strongly confirm other indications of genuineness or forgery.

When a considerable amount of writing is in question and an adequate amount of standard writing is supplied for comparison, a system of measurements covering a sufficient number of features and examples may be very forceful evidence. In a large number of items the disturbing effect of an occasional exception is neutralized and does not seriously affect the general result. Any system of averages, to be reliable, must be based on an adequate number of separate examples.

Genuine writing or genuine signatures show a certain definite and fixed proportion of height of letters to length of words. This is one of the distinctive ways in which the general appearance of a page of writing is changed by a different system of writing; this change is, however, in many instances, very slight, although in combination it changes the general appearance of writing in a striking manner. Evidence based on the very great number of minute measurements necessary to show a very slight divergence is not usually of much weight in this or any similar inquiry, because it is practically impossible for court and jury to review and verify the basis of such an opinion. If the difference is apparent by inspection, then the measurements are of value in making definite what is apparently a fact without such proof.

Testimony of this character which cannot be reviewed by court, jury and opposing counsel, belongs in that class of expert testimony that is of slight value when conflicting testimony is given by a witness who is apparently as well qualified. Not much time should be spent in preparing testimony regarding a questioned writing that a judge or a juryman cannot see, understand and verify. A conflict of testimony in such a case nullifies it, which is not true

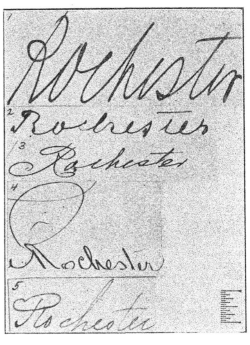

Fig. 68—Size and proportions. Words from business envelopes.

when proper illustrations are prepared and cogent reasons are given.

The different systems of writing differ from each other in size and proportions in certain definite and distinct ways, and such system characteristics and fundamental divergencies or similarities may be of great force in differentiating or connecting two writings. The presence or absence of these fixed system characteristics is of force and value in examining even one signature if an adequate number of standards is supplied with which it may be compared.

The modern vertical writing copy books and models make the highest of the small letter alphabet only twice as high as the shortest letters, and the longest letters extend below the line only one space or the same distance the minimum letters extend above the line, the whole field of writing covering three equal spaces, two above and one below the base line. The immediately preceding style of writing, or so-called Spencerian,

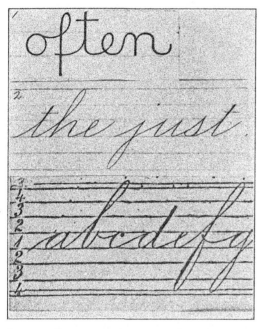

Fig. 69—Proportions in writing, from three systems, modern vertical, Spencerian, and an early American hand.

was arranged on a scale of fifths, three above and two below the base line, the longest letters being three spaces high and the minimum letters one-third as high, and the lower loop letters extending two spaces below the base line. Some of the older style of writing made loop letters four times as high as the short letters and small t's and d's the same height as the loop letters, differing radically from the Spencerian style which supplanted this old writing. The small "ᴾ" in the early style of this old writing was made like the printed form only slightly, if any, higher than the shortest letters, but as long below the line as the loop letters. This is still a characteristic of much English writing and is also one of the

Fig. 70—Examples of spacing habits, from recent business writing.

characteristics of the awkward modern vertical writing.

The spacing of writing is mainly changed by the slant of the upward or connecting strokes. Different systems of writing vary in the proportion of height to width of letters. The old round-hand or early American writing was written more compactly than the later writing which supplanted it, and in this particular the modern vertical is similar to the old style. This compactness was secured by making upward connecting strokes more nearly vertical, which brought the letters and parts of letters closer together, the result being that the small or minimum letters were higher in proportion to width of letters and length of words than in the later writing and all angles were retraced farther (Fig. 79) at the base of such small letters as "n" and "m."

This spacing characteristic often becomes very significant when one who writes the Spencerian system simulates the old round-hand style of writing and does not understand this radical and significant difference in the systems. The new vertical writing is in spacing nearly like the old round-hand, and a writer of this system in simulating the earlier or Spencerian hand would be likely to fail in just the opposite way from the Spencerian writer who attempts to copy the old round-hand.

Slant in writing is a characteristic that becomes high-

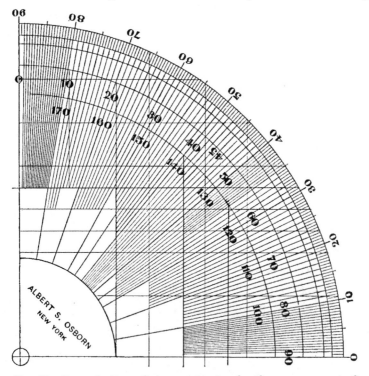

Fig. 71—Reproduction of glass protractor for the measurement of writing slant. The protractor reads to one-half degree and can be used to measure slant to the right or the left of vertical.

ly significant under certain conditions and with many writers is one of the most fixed of habits. The slight divergence in the few strokes of a single signature may be very strong evidence of lack of genuineness when such divergence is part of a combination of charac-teristics pointing to a writer of a different system of writing from that imitated. The old round-hand system slanted the straight down-ward strokes from about fifty-six to nearly sixty degrees from the horizontal. The early copy books of the systems of writing that final-ly entirely sup-planted the old round-hand var-

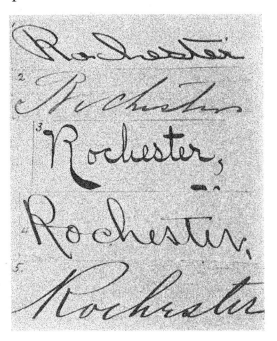

Fig. 72—Examples of slant ranging from 35 degrees above horizontal to the right to 56 degrees to the left of vertical. These specimens all taken from business envelopes.

ied in slant from forty-five to fifty-five degrees from the horizontal, but the copies of the new writing which from about 1860 to 1870 came to be taught in practical-ly all American public schools were, after the first edi-tions, all engraved on the slant of fifty-two degrees for the downward strokes and about thirty degrees for the upward strokes.

This change of slant gives a very different appearance to a page or any considerable quantity of writing and is a matter that should be investigated in a document inquiry especially in anonymous letter cases or any investigation involving a considerable amount of writing. The simulating process has a tendency to produce formal, stiff writing, and a fraudulent signature of this class will frequently diverge from the genuine writing imitated by being written with less slant. This may be one of the numerous features, each not necessarily very pronounced, but all together of great force, that may lead to the conclusion that a signature is not genuine. It is unusual for a forged writing to slant less than the genuine unless the imitation is made by a writer who writes a slant hand

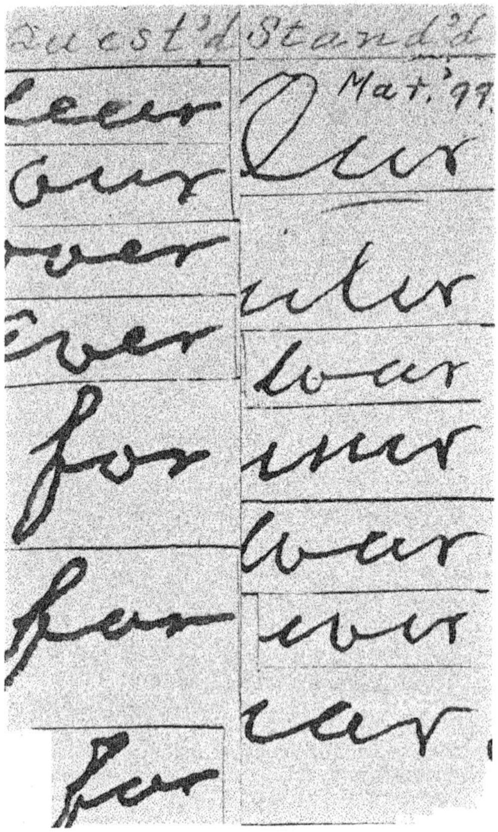

Fig. 73—Example of repeated divergence in slant of final letter, from exhibits in case of Newcomb vs. Burbank, New York City, 1909.

and attempts to imitate a more vertical writing such as the old round-hand style or the modern vertical system.

Slant would, of course, have little or no significance in connection with a traced forgery inquiry. It is obvious that even a clumsy forgery of this kind would approximate the slant of a model unless in the case of a part that in the model was very lightly written and that could not be distinctly seen through the paper. In the forgery of a whole document slight but repeated divergence in slant of the same letter as compared with the writing imitated may be a strong indication of a lack of genuineness as illustrated in Fig. 73.

An effective illustration showing divergence in slant is made by photographing the questioned signature or writing and the standards with superimposed glass carrying parallel lines, perhaps one-fourth of an inch apart, arranged parallel with the downward strokes of the standard writing. This effectively assists the eye to see and measure the difference between the two slants.

A glass protractor, like that shown in Fig. 70, will be found very useful in all slant examinations. The use of this instrument makes definite any general statements on the subject. It will be observed that by using as base lines those now shown in a vertical position the instrument also measures slant to the left of vertical.

CHAPTER X.

The effect of the writing instrument upon writing as a means of identifying it may have an important bearing as evidence in a case of disputed writing. It is often alleged that writing was produced in a certain manner or in a certain position and with a particular pen or pencil, or with the writing instrument in a particular condition, and since it is sometimes known with what instrument and under what conditions the writing was done if it is genuine, it is important to consider the intrinsic evidence in the writing itself pointing to the instrument or the conditions under which it was produced.

In a preceding chapter attention was called to the well known fact that an ordinary pen point is in reality two points which make one stroke or line of writing.

Fig. 74—Enlargement of pen points; broad stub, Falcon, Gillott's 604, crow quill.

[154]

Upon close examination nearly all writing with such a pen will show at some place the marks of these two points. As a pen becomes old or is injured the nibs become separated or of unequal length or width and the pen "scratches" or sticks into the paper and may in

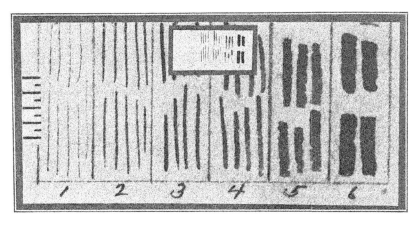

Fig. 75—Width of pen strokes, actual size and enlarged nearly five diameters. No. 1, crow quill, width, $\frac{1}{300}$ inch; No. 3, Falcon pen, average width, $\frac{1}{115}$ inch; No. 6, broad stub, width, $\frac{1}{32}$ inch.

rare cases show a double line even on unshaded strokes.

The nib marks show as two darkened tracks where more ink has been absorbed than at the middle of the stroke (Fig. 62), and are caused by the abrasion of the hard pen points upon the paper, making it more porous along the tracks. Such marks are particularly apparent if a blotter has been applied on a shaded stroke before the ink was dry.

Measured across both nibs where they begin to round off, the tips of pens range in width from about one-twenty-fifth (1-25) of an inch, the width of a very broad stub pen, to about one-three hundredth (1-300) of an inch, the width of the finest "crow quill" or the "No.

1000" steel pen. The broad pen without pressure and with ink in an average condition of fluidity, makes a normal stroke about one-thirtieth (1-30) of an inch in width and the crow quill pen makes a stroke of about one-three hundred and thirtieth (1-330) of an inch in width

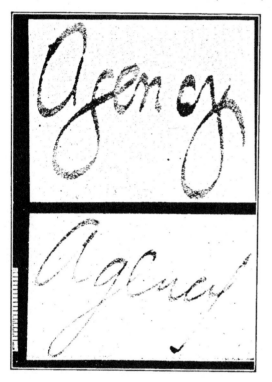

(Fig. 75). The common Falcon pen, which is considered a coarse pen, has a point only about one-o n e hundredth (1-100) of an inch wide and makes a normal minimum stroke not quite so wide. The surprising narrowness of such strokes is more fully appreciated when only dots are examined.

The ordinary writing pen i s sometimes made with the left nib

Fig. 76—Characteristic stub pen writing with shading on strokes to left.

slightly longer than the right to compensate for the common custom of holding the pen with the nibs pressing evenly on the paper but somewhat inclined to the right in the direction of the line of writing. Stub pens are made in just the opposite manner, the left nib being the shorter of the two (Fig. 74) to allow the pen to be turned with the bottom or concave side toward the right, or in the direction of the writing, in which position the right nib, as looked at from above, must be longer in order to reach the paper. Stub pens are designed especially for those whose habit it is to hold the pen far over to the right or between the first and second fingers. The stub pen, as we have already seen, makes a stroke the width of the point when the direction of the stroke is at right angles to the wide point and this is the result whether the stroke is to the left, right, upward or downward (Fig. 76). Any considerable quantity of stub pen writing and usually even a small signature written with such a pen will show this characteristic.

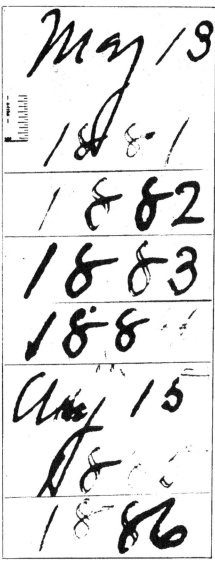

Fig. 77—Pen marks and date of writing. Six entries alleged to have been made one each year covering a period of six years. All written with the same old pen and thick ink, and undoubtedly all at one time.

Fig. 78—Comparison of width of pen points. Gold pen with special point and old corroded steel pen. From exhibit in Matter of Fredcrick C. Hewitt will, Owego, N. Y. Photograph enlarged sixty diameters.

Pens of the same manufacturer's number and style resemble each other very closely but do not all make · strokes of just the same width, and careful measurements and tests often show easily observable differences. This question becomes important in the examination of questioned additions to documents where it is reasonable to assume that ordinary prudence would suggest that a similar pen should be used. It is sometimes found that such questioned writing shows throughout a different average width of stroke unless not only the same kind of a pen has been used for the added writing, but a pen in just the same condition. The strokes examined and compared should be those made without pressure, in the same direction, and showing the minimum average width. If a large number of measurements of such strokes is made a uniform and accurate average result can be obtained. The microscope is, of course, indispensable for such examination and the filar micrometer will permit the examination and measurements to be tested by judge and jury. When it is alleged that a certain pen was used it becomes necessary to compare in every way this pen with the work it is alleged to have done. In some cases it becomes necessary to compare two pens with each other and also to compare writings alleged to have been made with the two pens (Fig. 78). The difference in width of two lines of one one-hundredth (1-100) and one one-hundred and fiftieth (1-150) of an inch is not easily discernible with the naked eye (Fig. 36), but when measured as described is unmistakable.

The same pen may at a subsequent period make a very different stroke. As is well known an ordinary steel pen begins to deteriorate gradually from the time that it is first used until it is worn out or spoiled. The difference between the stroke of a new pen as first used, which usually is covered by a protecting varnish, and the stroke of the same pen after being used on only one or two occasions may be perfectly apparent if sufficient matter is available for examination. Unless a pen is carefully cleaned at once after being used, ordinary writing fluid attacks the metal and if the ink is allowed to dry on the pen it will not write again exactly as it did on the first occasion. When a pen finally becomes thickly coated with dried ink it will necessarily make a very different stroke from that made when it is new, and when it becomes rusted or corroded by the action of the acid, which all fluid ink contains, it is of course greatly changed. If a pen is held incorrectly its life is much shortened and its work may very soon show a decided difference in result. These questions are of special importance in the investigation of continuity of writing, interlineations and all similar inquiries. The work of a peculiar pen may be the means of identifying a writing or may show that it was written continuously (Fig. 77).

The so-called "stylographic pen" was very popular some years age, but has nearly been displaced by the improved fountain pens. The stylographic pen is a hollow cylinder or holder brought down to a point from which projects a short blunt needle or stopper which prevents the ink from running out. When the point is pressed on the paper the needle is pushed back allowing the ink to escape. Writing with this pen shows a broad line, practically of uniform width, no matter in what direction it is made, and with no nib marks, but is of uniform intensity throughout its whole width like a stroke made with a brush.

The pens used in ordinary fountain holders are made of gold tipped with iridosmine, described as a native alloy of two metals, iridium and osmium, and harder than steel. It can be soldered to gold and therefore supplies a tip for gold pens that is practically indestructible by ordinary wear. Writing done with a good gold pen cannot ordinarily be distinguished from writing done with a good steel pen, except under certain conditions. Some years ago a very frequent characteristic shown in the writing of fountain pens was a failure to write promptly when the pen was first applied to the paper and this may indicate that writing was probably done with a fountain pen. A poor or cheap fountain pen will sometimes show very plainly this characteristic failure to write promptly.

Many men now living learned to write with quill pens at a time when these pens were in almost universal use. Mending and making pens was a regular part of the school teacher's work in those days. Quills prepared for pen making can still be bought in many places but are not now in use in America except on the stage. In England quill pens are still in common use in the law courts. Some old people in America, no doubt partly in reverence for the past, continued to use quill pens for many years after steel pens were almost universally used.

In the examination of very old documents it is sometimes necessary to examine the characteristics of quill pen writing. The quill pen is much more flexible than a steel or metal pen of any kind and an absence of nib marks even on very heavy shadings is one of the first characteristic differences to consider. This softness and flexibility also almost necessitated a shading of the downward strokes, which is another characteristic of quill pen writing, as it was of the systems of writing used in the quill pen days. Quill pen writing also allows a variety of shaded strokes not possible with a steel pen. The wide shading of lateral flourished strokes especially at ends of letters or words was very common. A single capital letter made with a quill pen may show shadings nearly at right angles to each other which were evidently made without changing the position of the pen, the flexibility of the points permitting the variation. It is thus impossible to reproduce certain engraved plates of old penmanship with a metal pen without changing the position of the pen on certain letters. Quill pens were also very frail, and it was frequently necessary to repair them and this often made a decided change in the appearance of parts of the same document.

Pencils are used for so many different purposes that it is inevitable that pencil writing should often be questioned, and it is necessary to consider its characteristics. As is well known ordinary pencil writing is produced by wearing off a continuous succession of small particles of graphite or plumbago which cling to or become imbedded in the fiber of the paper. Such a line differs greatly from a pen line and has certain well defined characteristics. Magnification of a stroke shows its peculiar construction; it is seen not to be solid like a pen stroke but resembles a line that might be formed by grouping small particles of coal or black stones on a white surface. The number of small particles making up the line is very great and it is almost impossible to remove them all by the use of an ordinary rubber eraser. The eraser removes at once the larger particles, but breaks them up somewhat and leaves imbedded and caught in the fibers of the paper hundreds of particles of graphite which can easily be seen with the microscope. All of a pencil mark can be removed by the ordinary eraser by actually wearing away the whole paper surface by abrasion, but this will show plainly a disturbance of the paper fibers and indicate that an erasure has been made. It is usually possible to distinguish the remnants of a pencil mark from ordinary dirt or finger marks.

Because of the manner in which a pencil line is produced it is sometimes possible to determine in which direction the stroke was made by the location and arrangement of the particles of graphite as seen under the microscope. This fact may have an important bearing on the investigation of a pencil writing. If a black line is drawn on a rough surface like matting with a very large crayon the particles making the line will be pressed against the sides of the obstructions on the side from which the stroke is made and this is also true with pencil strokes on paper; the collections of particles will tend to form a straight line next to the ridges against which they are pressed.

More pressure is ordinarily required to produce pencil writing than pen writing and it is sometimes sufficient to indent the paper so that it shows on the opposite side of the sheet. Indentations are sometimes present in traced forgeries and should always be looked for. Illiterate pencil writing is usually produced with much pressure and may show plainly the habit of frequently wetting the pencil. In attempted disguises of pencil writing changes are sometimes made and the first writing as partly erased may be legible from the indentations that still remain after the lines have been nearly removed. The indentations, or any unevenness of any kind, can be plainly seen by the aid of the stereoscopic microscope, or may be seen or photographed by lighting the document all from one side with the angle of light almost parallel with the surface of the paper, when a shadow will appear in the indentations. It is not usually advisable in photographing pencil writing for a better study of the form, to enlarge it as much as pen and ink writing may be enlarged because under great magnification the pencil line may become so thin as to be somewhat illegible.

An inquiry sometimes arises as to whether two writings were produced by the same ordinary lead pencil. This question can be answered only and so far as the difference in the hardness, due to the proportion of clay to graphite, may affect the width, character and indentation of the strokes. The attempt to analyze an ordinary pencil stroke for the purpose of showing identity or difference in two writings, as in the case of an ink line, is an unprecedented operation.

It is sometimes possible to show lack of continuity in writing claimed to be continuous, by the differences in line quality, width and character of stroke; or a striking and unnatural uniformity may be apparent in a number of pencil book entries or other writings which it is claimed were all written at different times on the dates they bear, but which show identical conditions as to width, indentation, depth of color, luster, care and speed.

Without a reasonable explanation the fact that a disputed document which is the basis of a claim of any considerable importance is written in pencil is a suspicious circumstance in itself[1]. There are cases, however, where a plausible explanation is offered for the use of a pencil, in which case it becomes necessary

---

[1] No prudent scrivener will write a will in pencil, unless under extreme circumstances. Whenever [thus] written, any appearance of alteration should be carefully scrutinized. Yet inasmuch as the statute is silent on the question, we cannot say the mere fact that it is written or signed in pencil, thereby makes its invalid.—Myers vs. Vanderbilt, 84 Penn. St. Rep. 510 (1877).

to determine whether a pencil writing is genuine or fraudulent.

Without doubt it is much easier to produce a forgery with a pencil than with pen and ink. Pencil writing does not show halting, tremor, lack of continuity, pen-lifts, pen position, retouching and overwriting as distinctly as pen writing shows these conditions, and differences in color and weight of line are not nearly so plainly seen in pencil as in pen writing. In pen writing, as we have seen, the relation of the mark of the two nibs of the pen to the direction of the stroke shows how the pen is held in relation to the paper, and is often a means of showing very divergent habits in two writings, but in pencil writing the position of the pencil cannot be thus determined from an examination of the strokes. These facts must all be considered in examining a questioned pencil writing.

The fact, however, that pencil writing is more easily retouched and perfected apparently has an almost uncontrollable tendency to lead the fabricator of the writing to excess in this direction, and such a document often is so laboriously overwritten and perfected in every detail that its fraudulent character is thus conclusively shown. Convincing evidences of genuineness in all kinds of written documents are indications of carelessness and disregard of minor and unimportant details in connection with close adherence to form designs, and the opposite characteristics are always suspicious. Reserve and self-control are rare qualities in the forger and the very act itself, with attention necessarily fixed on the process, leads to excessive perfection of details, and this is particularly true of pencil writing.

Every part of every stroke of a disputed pencil writing should be carefully examined with the microscope, under various magnifications and with a good light, to see, if possible, whether the various strokes are the result of one continuous motion or whether they are made up of several patches or disconnected movement impulses. It is also very important to study the composition of the strokes themselves, to observe the degree of uniformity in the distribution of the particles of graphite making up the strokes, and, as far as possible, to determine the direction of the various strokes. The stereoscopic microscope will be found very useful for these purposes.

Carefully made photographs enlarged from three to five diameters will sometimes be found very effective in showing retouching and lack of continuity in pencil writing. The photographs should be made so as to show the utmost detail in the line itself and care should be taken that they are not overprinted. An actual size photograph of a well executed pencil forgery may not show suspicious conditions that would be clearly shown by good enlarged photographs or that are apparent when a careful examination of the original writing is made. In a preliminary inquiry based on photographs of pencil writing opinions must always be qualified by the statement that it is assumed that the photograph is a faithful and adequate reproduction of the original. An opinion based enirely on photographs of any kind of writing should always be thus qualified, but it is particularly important that this be done in a pencil writing inquiry.

Pencil writing may, like pen writing, be very defective in design, as compared with the standard writing which it is made to imitate, and the standard and disputed writing should both be carefully analyzed and then compared in every particular. It is naturally desirable in such cases that some of the standards of comparison should be in pencil, especially if pencil writings of importance and similar in character to the writing in question can be found. It may be that pencil standards are all careless and unimportant writings of a distinctly different class from the writing in question, and it is clearly important under such conditions that some formal pen writings should also be used as standards. The fact, however, that no important pencil writings can be found makes it all the more imperative that an adequate explanation be given why an important document was written with a pencil.

Writings produced with ordinary copying pencils may, like ink writing, show perfectly evident differences in color, and such pencil writings under chemical reactions may show identities or differences in a more pronounced manner. Alleged old book entries and records made with aniline copying pencils have been shown to be false because they bore a date before such pencils came into use.

CHAPTER XI.

American handwriting shows more frequent and more radical changes during our comparatively short history than the handwriting of any other people during any period of time of the same length. This is not a fact of mere general interest, but has an important bearing upon the investigation of many disputed writings. These many changes have undoubtedly made it easier to identify and prove American handwriting than that of any other nation. The periods covered so overlap each other that there are now living writers of all the varied types; there are definite dates when many styles and forms were actually invented and adopted, and naturally the great majority of writers of each class are not fully aware of these various fundamental distinctions. To be entirely successful the forger must, in many instances, have some historical knowledge of American writing.

The framework or general character of the handwriting of the average writer is of the style or design acquired in youth and in general use during the formative period of life[1]. This style is afterwards greatly modi-

---

[1]For although each person (not a professed scribe), in practising the art of writing, has invariably had a style marked by certain individual characters, yet each example is stamped with the general impress of the age in which the writers lived; and thus, though different in detail, all private handwriting, of the fifteenth century, for instance, has, overlying the individual peculiarities, a general character belonging to the age; and the same may be said of the sixteenth century and subsequent periods.—The Origin and Progress of the Art of Writing, by Henry Noel Humphreys, London, 1854.

fied by individual taste, physical characteristics, and environment, but through all these changes the original system will visibly protrude as a foreign accent will show in speech. The forger may approximate the general form of a writing in an imitation, but will often omit the significant "accent" that gives the unmistakable touch of genuineness. It will thus be seen how important it is in the identification of a handwriting, first, if possible, to classify it by putting it into its proper general division as to date, system, and nationality.

Certain writing features point conclusively to foreign influences and others to a definite period of time. Some of these apparent peculiarities in two handwritings may be simply the traces of the former style or "accent" still appearing, and, where writing is being used to identify an individual, the unskilled observer may conclude that these peculiarities are personal individualities. Absence of these characteristics may be very forcible evidence in proving a handwriting not to be genuine, but are not alone sufficient to prove that two writings are necessarily by the same writer. One who attempts to give an opinion as to the identity of two writings should be able to give fundamental reasons and not depend merely upon superficial resemblances or differences.

The foreigner who has learned to speak and write his mother tongue brings with him into any new country his accent and his style of writing and it is seldom indeed that in either he discards entirely the fixed habits of his youth. There are, in fact, many striking analogies between writing and speech, two of these being the persistence with which habits acquired in youth are retained and the partial or total unconsciousness of them. Whatever he says, as soon as he speaks a man begins to tell where he was born and what his education and environment have been, and by his writing he does much the same thing.

Habits of speech and writing become so automatic and unconscious that even by the most strenuous effort it is almost impossible to change them. This is well known regarding speech and is also shown to be as true of writing when a careful study is made of it.

Not only may the speech and writing of any particular nationality be distinguished, of one who has afterwards learned the American language, but, as has been suggested, American writing itself, as shown by many historical characteristics, can be separated into distinct dated periods of time. The handwritings of Magna Charta, the Declaration of Independence, and the Letters of Junius date those documents, and the writing of our grandfathers, like their cravats and their trousers, connects them with the past and with that period of our history when English and American writing were almost identical. Handwriting can be put into its date class, within a certain definite period, as a skilled philologist can classify speech, and the different periods in this country of changes cover only a comparatively short time[1].

There are four main divisions in American writing. The writing of most writers who learned to write in this

---

[1]A true connoisseur in these studies will rather agree in opinion with Mr. Casley, who, in his preface to the catalogue of the Royal library (p. 6) has the following words: "I have studied that point so much, and have so often compared manuscripts without date, with those that happen to have a date, that I have little doubt as to that particular." And he observes, that "he can judge of the age of a manuscript as well as the age of a man."—The Origin and Progress of Writing, by Thomas Astle, London, 1784.

country before about 1830 to 1840 differs in many particulars from the writing of those who learned to write during the period from about 1840 to 1865; another and more radical change was made during the years from about 1865 to 1890, and a later and very radical change, the fourth, came between 1890 and 1900. The nineteenth century alone thus shows these four distinct classes of writing.

The first division, or that of the early part of the century, retained the old English round hand characteristics, and in numerous ways resembles some of the English writing of to-day. This old style (Figs. 79, 80) is still written by many old people in America.

The second division is a modified round hand (Figs.

FIG. 79—English hands from Bickham's "Universal Penman," London, 1743. The "Round Hand" and "Italian Hand" show only slight differences and are both usually described as Round Hand, although both were developed from an early Italian style.

81 to 84) and includes, among others, the early editions of the Spencerian and the Payson, Dunton and Scribner copy-books. This division began quite early in the century until the *systematizing* of the new copy-books had developed an entire new American handwriting.

The third division, or what is commonly called Spencerian, brought forward an entirely new alphabet of letter forms (Figs. 85, 86) and many other distinct and entirely new features. It came about through the de-

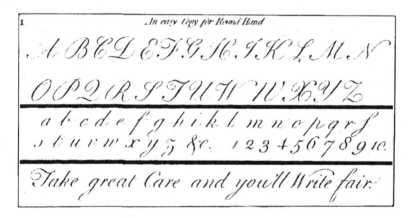

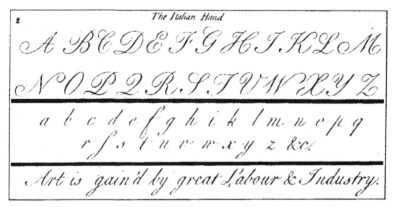

Fig. 80—American Round Hand and Italian Hand from "The Young Man's Best Companion," by George Fisher, Philadelphia, 1737.

development and modification of the two leading copy-book systems in the direction of simplicity, by the omission of extra strokes and flourishes, and a general tendency toward plain letters.

The fourth and last division of the century covers the development during the last few years of modern vertical writing (Fig. 89), an entirely new style, which will affect the handwriting of this country with more or less force for the next seventy-five years.

The angular style of writing taught to and written by many women during all the last century is entirely distinct from these four classes just described; and the many foreign hands which have been brought into America during the same time have necessarily affected writing in this country to some extent.

Distinctions in all these different classes of handwriting of one nation at different periods or of different nationalities are not, as many suppose, simply in a few forms or patterns of letters, which it is assumed may be fleeting and easily modified; but, as a matter of fact, many of the changes are much more fundamental, and affect writing in a more distinct way. Among these pronounced differences in general features are the proportions of letters to each other, turns and angles or relations of downward and upward strokes, spacing of letters in words, shading, slant, ornamentation or grace lines, habits of lifting the pen or pen stops, and manner of writing or movement. Even the unskilled observer is easily able to recognize the fact that even a small piece of writing is of a foreign character or of an ancient style, and the specialist must analyze these distinctions and show exactly from what causes they arise.

Until about the end of the eighteenth century, the handwriting of America was practically identical with that of England. The relations of the two countries were so close that handwriting, like speech, had little opportunity for individual development. After the American revolution, however, there was a noticeable tendency in this country toward individual development in every direction, and this included to some extent the subject of handwriting.

During the close of the eighteenth century and the beginning of the nineteenth, numerous American works on the subject of writing were published. These at first were practically the same as the old English publications, but some originality began gradually to appear until there was finally developed a quite distinctive modified round hand style. It was not, however, till many years later than an entirely new American handwriting was fully developed. This came about through a number of contributing causes.

Improvement in the methods of reproducing and printing copperplate engraving by lithography was undoubtedly one of the principal factors in this development. This improvement led to the publication of copybooks with a printed copy at the top of each page[1]. Be-

---

[1] No attempt is here made to write a history of American handwriting except as it has a bearing on questioned documents, or to revive the old copy-book controversies. The various systems of modern writing came finally to be described as a whole as Spencerian. This no doubt was due to the superiority of the system and, in large measure, to its able and energetic authors and advocates, several of whom are still living.

The earliest Spencerian publication was a series of copy slips published in 1848, three years before the first publication of P. D. & S., but to the latter belongs the distinction of issuing in 1851 the first modern copy-books, the improvement of which in both systems revolutionized American handwriting.

fore this time part of the regular work of the schoolmaster was to "set copies" for his pupils; this practice made
it impossible for any wide-spread revolution to be made
in the system of writing taught and practiced because

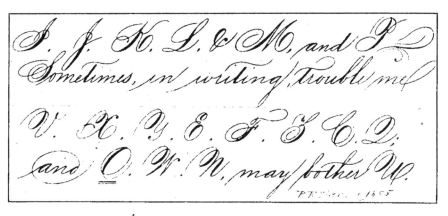

FIG. 81—Spencerian writing of 1855. A comparison of this writing with that shown
in Fig. 85 will show what a change was made between 1855
and 1874 in Spencerian writing.

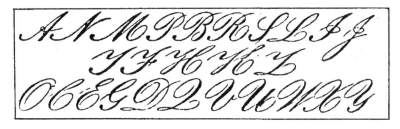

FIG. 82—Modified Round Hand. Potter & Hammond System, 1858.

FIG. 83—American Writing, Second Division, published by "Spencerian,"
1864. Double beginning ovals, (½ size).

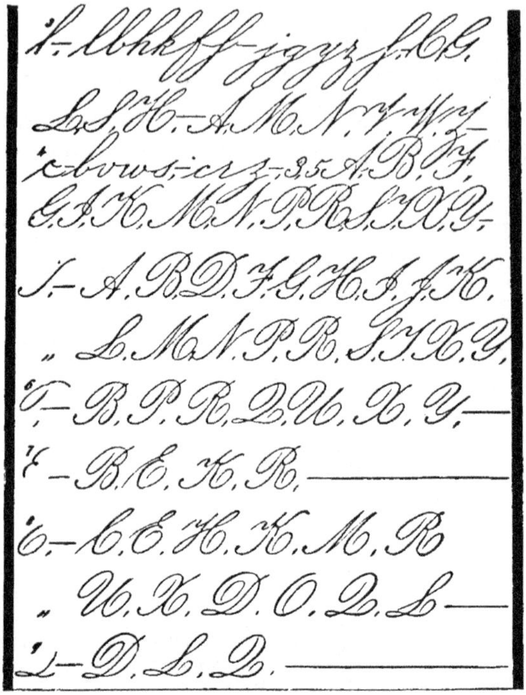

Fig. 84—American Writing (2d Division), published by "P. D. & S.," 1857. See beginning ovals and ending flourish on capital letters, ($\frac{2}{3}$ size).

it was all in the hands of the individual school teachers. But after the general adoption of copy-books as a means of teaching the forms of letters, the style of the writing of the schools of the land was determined by authors, engravers and publishers and not by schoolmasters. This condition still continues.

Between 1850 and 1860 two competing systems of copy-books were published in America and were so industriously promoted that before 1870 their adoption in America was almost universal. These two systems were the Spencerian and the Payson, Dunton and Scribner. Each claimed priority and superiority, but apparently they copied from each other continuously, and certainly both became radically different from what they were at the beginning (Figs. 83, 84) and more and more like each other and finally came to be practically identical as far as forms and systems were concerned. Together they formed a distinctive, new American handwriting.

The first editions of these copy-books were but little changed from much of the old writing taught in America during the first half of the

FIG. 85—The Spencerian letters, showing proportions (1874).

century. This old writing was much shaded, had large and flourished capitals, which varied greatly in proportions and size as compared with each other, and loops of small letters were very long and the writing was not systematized as the new writing soon came

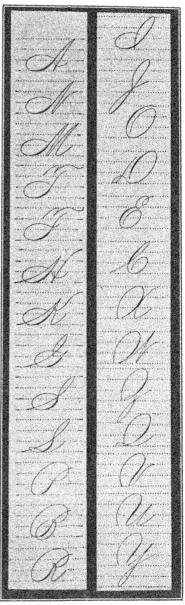

FIG. 86—The "P. D. & S." capital letters showing proportions (1890). Note similarity of Spencerian and P. D. & S.

to be. This intermediate stage is here described as the second division of American handwriting or the new modified round hand (Figs. 82, 84).

Competition of the two new systems was very fierce and a constant effort was made toward making the new writing systematic and uniform with itself and gradually but finally the old forms were all swept away and an entirely new style of writing was made, which differed in nearly all particulars from the old hand it dis-

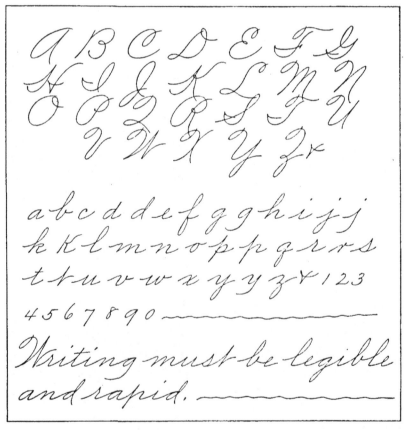

Fig. 87—Modern American Writing, engraved from pen and ink copy by E. C. Mills, Penman, Rochester, N. Y. (1909).

placed, especially the early old round hand, so that American handwriting was completely revolutionized.

The new writing as finally perfected was in certain features intermediate between two previous styles, the round hand which was legible but slow, and the angular hand, which was more rapid but difficult to read. The distinguishing characteristic of the new writing, as compared with the early round hand, was the narrow turns or angles of the connecting lines due to the straightening of the connecting strokes. The theory developed in the new writing was that connecting turns were to be made nearly angular but sufficiently rounded to enable the pen to make a continuous motion, it being maintained with good reason that the roundness would give the legibility of the round hand, and the narrowness of the turns (Fig. 85) would make nearly a direct

Fig. 88—Modern American shaded capitals of the general style of letters taught in American commercial schools from about 1885.

stroke which would make possible the speed desirable for rapid writing.

The new writing slanted fifty-two degrees from the horizontal, was finally constructed on a scale of fifths, three above and two below the line, had but little shading on the small letters, furnished a new set of capital letters, and was written more open or with wider spaces between all small letters than the old writing; in all of these particulars it distinctly differed,

Aztecs. ar Napoleon
Bay of B Ozone is
Cocoa Potatoes
Defoe wr Quito is
Elephan Rainbou
Frigid Spenser
Gold is u The Faeri
Helena Ulysses
Iceland Via mear
Jamesto Why is
Kingstor Xerxes wa
Llan Yokohar
Maine Zanzi
$12345 67890 $

Fig. 89—Vertical Writing.   Published 1893-7.
Used in American schools about ten years.

tinctly differed, not only from the old round hand, but also from the immediately preceding style which it displaced and which in the main was simply a modified round hand.

Out of the late Spencerian and P. D. & S. styles there has since been developed, from approximately about 1880, the modern commercial hand (Figs. 87, 88), which has certain distinctive characteristics. This style of writing was perfected and popularized through the excellent work of the American commercial schools that for years have given special emphasis to rapid business writing. An essential element of this writing has been a free movement, in which the arm is brought into use in the writing process, and the forms adopted have been those best suited to easy, rapid writing.

Another and the last great revolution in American handwriting began in the last decade of the nineteenth century, and was the adoption of vertical writing (Fig. 89) by the American schools. This revolution is in fact a reversion to the old systems of slow but legible writing. The new writing with its round, drawn letters is a kind of printing, as the old writing had been, and has been taught with almost no attention to movement and speed.

This last revolution, the adoption of vertical writing, is even more radical than the first because it affects form, movement and position, and has brought about a change in American handwriting which will be apparent for many years no matter what influences or changes may occur in the immediate future. The old round hand writing[1] went out with the old stage coach, and for the

---

[1]The modified round hand style among other things differs from the old round hand in proportions of small letters and numerous capital letter designs. This modified hand as written by many made the small loop letters four times as high as the short letters and the flourished oval finish of capitals N, H, R, K, L, U and X (see illustrations) was a pronounced characteristic of this writing. The capitals T and F were also very different from the regular round hand and were made with a peculiar top with an acute angle out at the right.

same reason, and the strange but brief revival of its leading characteristics in the American schools in the new vertical writing will be looked back upon as one of the most curious incidents in the history of education.

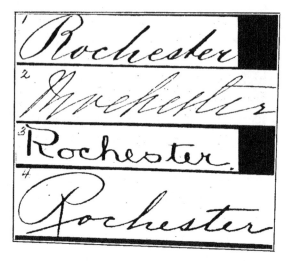

FIG. 90—Examples of four different systems of writing ; Round Hand, Angular, Vertical, Modern Spencerian. These specimens all taken from recent business letters.

Early writing was not what we call script, but what we now describe as pen printing, and the distinguishing difference between pen writing and pen printing, that is, the connecting of the characters as they are made, was not developed till rather late in the history of writing. As writing came into more common use its speed was increased, and the result of this in all languages was the tendency to slant letters in the direction of the writing and connect them with each other, which necessarily somewhat decreased the legibility, but made the writing more rapid and practical.

As we have already seen a very large proportion of all writing points unmistakably to the style on which it was based (Figs. 90, 92) and the time when it was written. What is left of the early style may be a mere trace of the original characteristics, but may yet be of the utmost significance in a writing inquiry, and, if not understood by a forger, may be omitted entirely or incorrectly reproduced, especially if the attempt is made to imitate a writing of a different system, class, or nationality from that of the writer. An accidental divergence in the writing imitated may be ridiculously exaggerated and repeated again and again in an imitation, and fixed system characteristics may be entirely omitted.

It is comparatively easy to procure examples of a system of writing or of any foreign writing the characteristics of which may enter into an inquiry, and such specimens should, if possible, always be obtained. It is, of course, not feasible to illustrate in this chapter the characteristics of all the varying systems, but illustrations of a few are shown.

There are occasionally found what may properly be described as original hands, which may be almost entirely unconventional, but in most cases they are but partly original and often are a combination of two other styles. Some apparently original hands are peculiar in but one way which, however, gives them a singular and striking appearance. A hand showing a few marked peculiarities is, as a rule, imitated more easily than an ordinary hand. An imitation of a fantastic and peculiar signature at once appears genuine if one or two of its leading and most striking features are reproduced.

It is rare indeed that any handwriting is a slavish reproduction of a system and almost certainly it will diverge in a great many ways. It is so improbable that the directions and extent of these divergences will be exactly duplicated in two individuals that such a coincidence becomes practically impossible, and this multitude

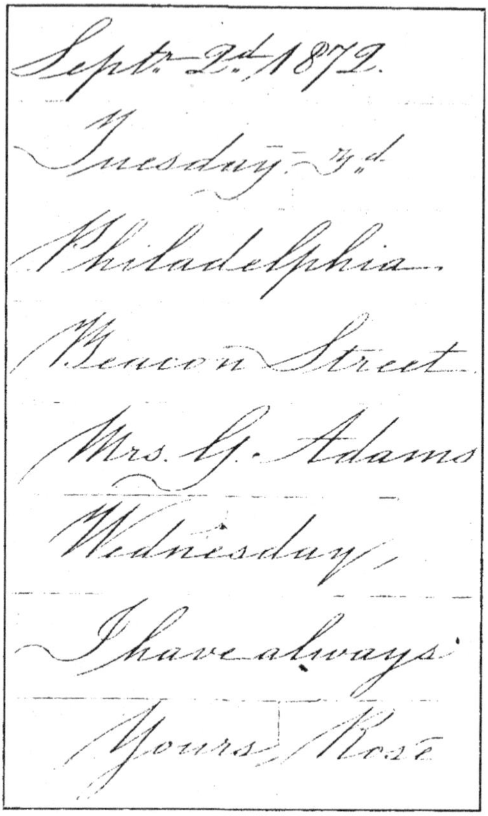

Fig. 91—The Angular Hand. Taught in America
mainly in Ladies' Seminaries. Popularized
among women in England and Canada
by having been written beauti-
fully by their much loved sov-
ereign, Queen Victoria.

of possible varia-
tions when com-
bined is what con-
stitutes individual-
ity in handwriting.

There are certain
types of writing de-
veloped in various
occupations that
have well known
characteristics. One
of these hands is
that used by the
telegraph operator,
already shown in
the chapter on ar-
rangement of writ-
ing. This distinc-
tive style is largely
the result of condi-
tions, but it is no
doubt also partly
the result of con-
scious and uncon-
scious imitation.

The manipulation of the telegraphers' key develops a
certain muscular action and skill which, no doubt, affects the writing process, and the necessity for continuity, speed and legibility, and the natural desire to
copy the style of those already expert all lead to the
result shown. The literary hand, the railroad style and
the writing of the business clerk or bookkeeper each have

certain well defined characteristics which are partly developed by the conditions and in a measure are also the result of imitation.

The distinctive and often large and awkward angular hand (Fig.91) taught in certain schools and seminaries for women, is one of the most certain and fixed sex indications in writing. The presence of such system features is very significant in some anonymous letter cases in relieving from suspicion men who may have been suspected or accused. System, class and nationality characteristics are especially important in identifying anonymous letter writers or in any inquiry in which a considerable quantity of writing is under investigation.

It is easy to understand how the writer of any distinctive system has difficulty in laying aside his own style and taking up another when he does not understand just how the systems differ. A few of the many ways in which system features of the Spencerian and old round hand enter into the identification of writing are here briefly outlined. They are numbered so that ready reference can be made to the accompanying illustration, Fig. 93.

Fig. 92—Old style writing, 1820 to 1850.

In a recent case (1) two capital "E's" appeared in a disputed document, each made with a loop in the

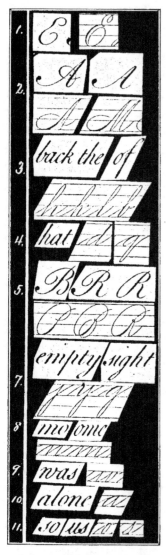

Fig. 93—Comparisons of old Round Hand and Spencerian characteristics.

center. Among scores of standard "E's" in the case made by an aged writer of the round hand system not one had a loop. Many old round hand models made this letter without a loop while the later systems all make the "E's" with a loop between the upper and lower parts. The presence of these two little loops thus became of very great significance.

In another case it was claimed that a certain writing, not disguised in any way, identified a man suspected of a murder on other evidence. Among some other foreign characteristics the writing contained several "M's" and "A's" made from the bottom and continuous (2) as in the old round hand and in some foreign hands. The suspected writer, a young American, among other divergences made the same forms of letters but always in *just the opposite direction* as they are taught in the Spencerian system which he learned. The suspected man clearly could not have been the writer and was at once given his liberty.

Many old round hand writers make (3) the small h, k, l and b without a loop in the top but do put a loop in the f as several of the systems taught. An imitation of this writing made loops in all the long letters as the later system teaches.

Other old round hand writers always raise the pen before (4) small a and d and g as the system taught, and in an imitation

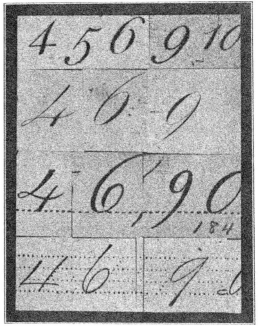

Fig. 94—Figures of 1783-7, 1821, 1848, 1864-88.

of this writing, composed of several lines, more than a dozen of these letters were made continuously, following the style of the later systems.

Another difficulty that imitators of this old style find is in (5) the capital B and R made without the loop in the middle of the letter and with the angle at the connection inclined upward. The later systems made a loop and inclined it downward to the right.

The old figures, particularly the 4, 6 and 9, have helped to prove many forgeries. The figure 4 was made with a sharp top or with the strokes distinctly inclined toward each other and the first part higher than the last, very different from the modern character. Many writ-

ers of the old system made the six from the bottom upwards, in just the opposite direction from that in which
the later form was made, and the six and nine were both
made with a distinctly curved staff instead of straight
as in modern characters. These figures and the modern
forms are shown in Fig. 94.

The lower loop letters (7) g, j, y show in the typical
old round hand a peculiar and decided shading beginning at the top but not continued to the base and the
lower part of the letter is thrown slightly back toward
the left. This form is also found in the capitals J and
Y when made below the line. Writers of the later style,
in which these strokes are straight and not shaded, find it
very difficult (see Fig. 107) to get this old round hand
effect in these letters.

The decided retracing of the sharp angles, as at the
bottom of (8) the small m and many similar letters, has
been a serious stumbling block to writers of fraudulent
documents and the continuous uniform shading has
caused many a forger's downfall.

The small letter w in many of the old round hand
alphabets (9) is so divergent from the modern form
(Fig. 80) that an imitator to whom it is unknown,
especially in making a whole document, will often fail
to make it correctly. In the old writing (10) the small
o, a, g, d, q at the beginning of words, were made with
no upward introductory stroke; the later systems put a
stroke on all these letters. The presence of these little
strokes in an imitation of this old writing thus may be
a matter of very great importance. The (11) small o
and s in the old writing at the end of words in sentences
usually omitted the short finishing stroke and all the late

systems, up to but not including modern vertical, made it; thus a few small o's and s's with these little strokes may be very damaging to a disputed document.

Some influence in America during the latter part of the eighteenth and the beginning of the nineteenth centuries, established the fashion that no capital letter should go below the line of writing, as shown in Fig. 80. This did not affect the legibility of the G, Y and Z, but did make it impossible to distinguish I and J[1]. Early English writing used the I and J form interchangeably, either form being used for I (Figs. 80, 97); many English alphabets in the eighteenth century show both forms (Fig. 79), but for many years in America John and James, and all similar proper names, were usually

---

[1] In this alphabet, the letter J has been restored to its long required situation and value. It is much to be regretted that it has been ejected from the good society of its former associates, by teachers of the past and present generations of men, who have instructed their pupils, that Iohn is the correct way for writing John, Ioshua for Joshua, etc.; and so extensive has been the effect of it, that but few penmen at the present day know how to form a J, for any particular required purpose. This has continued to be the case throughout one generation at least of mankind. The ruthless hand of fashion has rejected the useful J, because it passes below the line on which the other capital letters are written; but the errors, losses, and mistakes, which have been engendered by that violation on the alphabet, in many other important instances than those here enumerated, sufficient to amount to a little fortune monthly, if it could be registered throughout Christendom, has become of sufficient consequence in the business concerns of every one, to restore the J to its legitimately assigned and useful place in the alphabet.—American Text Book for Letters. Nath'i Dearborn, Boston, 1846.

You will recollect that on a preceding page of this book the capital J, in the word Judge, was placed on the line with the small and short letters; but in the word Jeffersonite, on the same page, it was carried below the line as far as the bottom of the g, y, etc., would extend, in the same sized writing. The author decidedly prefers the last method. The two forms are again exhibited on this page.

Were all persons to make this distinction between the I and J, there could be no mistaking the letter designed by the writer, as is now often done, and will be so long as only minor differences exist between them. This makes it a universal rule to carry the J below the line.—Badlam's System of Writing, by C. G. Badlam, New York (1850).

written with a capital I. This old fashion has often been misunderstood and misinterpreted by the forger.

Many of the old round hand system forms can still be seen in sign painter's and engraver's script. The streets of almost any city show many examples of the style of writing that formerly was written with pen and pencil. Every capital letter and every small letter in the old writing is very different from the later writing that displaced it, and pitfalls are on every side of the inexperienced forger who attempts to write, especially with freedom, that which he really does not see and often cannot understand.

It should not be understood that it is possible to look at every piece of writing, however small, and tell the system on which it is based or the age of the writer, but it can easily be understood what an important bearing the date value of written forms may have, particularly in examining a long disputed document. These almost hidden characteristics may be of great force as proof of genuineness or, if misunderstood and misinterpreted, may be almost conclusive proof of forgery. Neither should it be inferred that comparison of a disputed document is to be made only with the model writing of a system, but if such suspected writing diverges from the genuine standard writing in the case in the manner in which two systems differ from each other, then the reason for the divergence is explained and its force as evidence is greatly increased.

The shape of the beginning ovals of the group of capital letters of the U, V and W class has a definite date value. The old round hand shows a beginning loop or oval of two strokes in which the lines do not cross;

(Figs. 80, 82, 84) the later modified round hand shows a complete double oval (Fig. 83) beginning with an upward stroke; the later Spencerian and P. D. & S. systems begin this part at the base line (Figs. 85, 86) and make no loop or oval at the top, while the later American commercial hand goes back to the old round hand form except that the strokes *cross at the top* of the letters (Figs. 87, 88), and the modern vertical makes no loop whatever (Fig. 89). A study of these forms will show clearly the steps described.

The modern form of the capital J with the round top did not come into common use till about 1873. Before that time the model letter in the copy-books was pointed at the top and often was made with an oval at the center as in Fig. 82. Many old round hand writers made the letter with two separate downward strokes beginning at the same point as is clearly shown by the shading on both strokes. All late systems of writing make the J with a round top. Reference to footnote[1] with valuable

---

[1] Principally through the efforts of O. H. Bowler the old form of the seven capitals of the V, U, and Y class were changed to the simple reversed oval made from the base of the letter. These letters first appeared in copy books in one book, the "No. 12" of the P. D. & S. series, in 1867, and they were put into the regular numbers of the Spencerian books in 1873. They had already all appeared in the Eclectic system in 1870. They were not put in as regular standards in the P. D. & S. books until 1881.

The modern capitals C and D of the type of the Roman printed letters, were put into the regular Spencerian books in 1873; the same letters had already appeared in one number of the P. D. & S. series but were not both included in their regular series till some years later. Their general use, however, may be said to begin about 1873.

The pointed top I and J seem to have been changed to the round top form principally through the influence of Professor Hurlburt, of Lockport, N. Y., who in his "Boston Long Wharf" penmanship published and popularized this form but he did not publish copy books. These letters first appeared in copy books as regular standards in the Spencerian series in 1873. They were adopted as standard letters in the P. D. & S. books in 1876.—By Mr. George H. Shattuck, of Medina, N. Y., one of the "Spencerian" authors.

information regarding the adoption of numerous letters forms will show that capitals C and D also have an interesting copy book history.

It is plain to see that system characteristics may enter, not simply into questions as described above, but into any inquiry in which a writer attempts to imitate writing of a system differing from his own. Questions involving angular writing often arise and the new vertical writing, although now only a few years of age, is already entering into questioned document inquiries.

The facts regarding the dates and features of systems of writing have a particularly important bearing upon the question of the authenticity of ancient documents of any kind. Many questions have arisen involving the history of the development of English handwriting[1] and audacious forgeries purporting to be hundreds of years of age have been produced ranging in importance from alleged letters of the immortal Shakespeare to writing of kings and queens. Hundreds of thousands of dollars have been paid for forged writing of noted persons. The most ridiculous credulity is shown by those who on other subjects seem sane and sensible. No one should buy an autograph except from a reputable

---

[1]Upon the invention of printing in Germany, the letters made use of were naturally these old Gothic or German, but when the new art passed into Italy the Roman characters were substituted, and soon proved their greater suitability through their greater simplicity. That our modern round hand is merely an adaptation from the Roman letters no one can well doubt, they being at the same time made more freely running. One might have been inclined to believe that the MS. modern hand had been directly taken from the printed forms, although it is now understood that the earliest printing was in imitation of MS,. the sheet being placed upon the block and afterwards engraved; and the block impression having been ironed out of the back of the sheet, two of these were pasted together so as exactly to resemble and pass for MS.—"According to Cocker," by W. Anderson Smith, London, 1887.

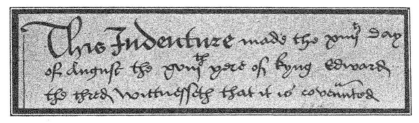

Fig. 95—Old English Gothic hand showing Roman notation, "XIIIIth day of August" and "XVIIIth yere of Kyng Edward the thred" (1347). From The Origin and Progress of Writing, by Thomas Astle, Keeper of the Records in the Tower of London (1784).

Fig. 96—The Shakespeare hand, English Gothic, from a school book, published in London in 1581, now in the Library of Congress, Washington, D. C.

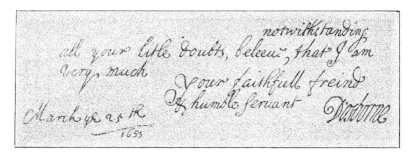

Fig. 97—Seventeenth century English writing. The change from the old Gothic script was made during the close of the sixteenth and the beginning of the seventeenth centuries.

dealer who can furnish an authenticated history of the document[1].

The study of palaeography[2] was at one time a very live subject in Europe and now and then some question still arises regarding some ancient charter or deed. Although these questions may be of the utmost importance they are not sufficiently frequent at this day to warrant

[1]What was ever more absurd than the readiness with which the public accepted the fabrications of young Ireland? What could possibly be more ridiculous than the sight of dear, clever, old Boswell reverently kissing, on his bended knees, the pseudo-Shakespeare writings which the young clerk had just manufactured, while he ecstatically uttered the Nunc Dimittis! No forgery was ever more clumsily done. The writing not only bore no resemblance to Shakespeare's, but was unlike any style of writing whatever, and would never have deceived anyone who had calmly examined it. But who could exercise cool judgment whilst gazing at what he believed to be the newly discovered autographs of Shakespeare? The very name of Shakespeare is a spell to cast glamour over the senses of Englishmen, and to get any further particulars concerning that genius, of whom we know so little, what would not be sacrificed? The very thought of seeing those lines, traced by Shakespeare's hand, would make the hearts of enthusiasts palpitate, and their brains reel with rapture; and thus men lost their reason, were incapable of reflection, and accepted whatever Ireland offered them. Old Boswell's extravagant action was only the outward and visible display of what many felt. It was in vain that a few persons of sober judgment pointed out, by the clearest evidence, that the writing could not possibly be Shakespeare's, for such heresy was not listened to with patience by those who were eager to believe.

Who, for instance, could be induced to believe that any human being in his senses would spend a fortune in purchasing autograph letters of Julius Caesar, Alexander the Great, Judas Iscariot, Mary Magdalene, etc., written in modern French, on paper bearing the fleur-de-lys water mark, which showed it had been recently manufactured at Angouleme? What then must be thought when we find an autograph collector of thirty years' experience, who, moreover, was a member of the French Academy, and bore a European reputation as a profound mathematician, doing this? After such a fact need one be astonished at anything?—Historical Documents, etc., by Scott & Davey, London, 1891., pp. 91, 92.

[2]"For some time after the invention of printing, as both compositor and scholar were familiar with the mediaeval script, no need of palaeographic study was felt; but, as the old contractions disappeared from printed books and the new Italian hand crowded out the crabbed monastic writing, the manuscripts grew unintelligible. At the same time the exposure of such forgeries as the Constantinian Donation and the Pseudo-Isidorian decretals threw doubt on the genuineness of all ancient documents. In their eagerness to save the true at the cost of the false, Catholic scholars went almost further than

exhaustive discussion in this work and space is taken for only a few footnote references to the subject and a few illustrations. Dr. Scott and Samuel Davey, in their interesting book, "Historical Documents, Literary Manuscripts, Autograph Letters, etc.," give much valuable information regarding the investigation of ancient

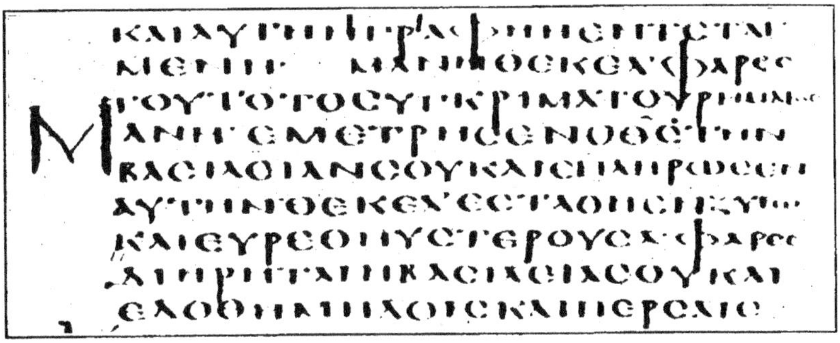

FIG. 98—Uncial Greek of the Fifth Century A. D. from the Codex Alexandrinus. (Daniel V. 25, 26, 27, 28.) Reproduced from a photographic copy of the original manuscript in the British Museum.

documents of all kinds. A valuable illustrated article on the general subject of palaeography is printed in the Encyclopaedia Britannica, and Mabillon's great work, referred to in the footnote, can be seen in the leading libraries. The many photographic reproductions of ancient documents now available are a great aid to thorough study of the subject.

Protestants in their skepticism, and in 1675 the learned Jesuit Papebroch, editor of the Bollandist Acta Sanctorum, made a sweeping assault on all charters claiming early Frankish origin. These charters were almost wholly in the hands of the one ancient monastic order of the West, the Benedictines, and the ablest of its scholars, Mabillon, came to the rescue of the questioned documents by the publication in 1681 of his De re diplomatica. It created at one stroke a new science. With the sure hand of a master he laid down the criteria and rules for the determination of the age of MSS., illustrating and proving from the ample materials at his hand. Even his Jesuit opponent was convinced, and Mabillon's book remains the foremost in the literature of its subject."—Prof. G. L. Burr, of Cornell University, in Universal Cyclopaedia, under "Palaeography."

CHAPTER XII.

VARIATION IN GENUINE WRITING

Arguments are sometimes made in good faith to the effect that because handwriting varies therefore it does not afford a reliable basis for any opinion whatever as to its identity. Unfortunately there are those whose interests strongly impel them to make this claim and in certain cases of wide interest much misinformation on the subject has been supplied to the public by those arrayed against the facts. It is true that genuine writing by the same writer does vary, and in an examination of questioned writing this phase of the subject should receive careful attention. The arm, hand and fingers under the direction of the brain do not constitute an absolutely accurate reproducing machine, like an engraved plate or a printing press, and certain natural divergencies are inevitable. If such divergencies were fundamental and applied to the whole process of writing then the identification of a handwriting would be an impossibility and forgery would be a very simple process.

Writing varies as speech varies; it may be large or small as speech is low or loud; it may be careful or careless, like speech, but both methods of human expression finally come to be habits of the individual acquired by thousands of repetitions of the same act. As well might one think that on one occasion a man would speak English with a strong German flavor and at another time drop accidentally into an Irish accent, as to think, for example, that a writer would to-day write the modern vertical hand of the school boy or the old round-hand of Revolutionary days, and to-morrow, without intention or premeditation, write the distinctive angular hand written by many women. His writing, like his speech, is part of his very flesh and bones.

It is true that speech and writing may both be disguised and unnatural, and may imitate a style very different from that usually followed, but average unconscious writing varies no more than average unconscious speech, since both finally are simply unconscious habits. If speech with all its quirks and mannerisms were actually visible how positively it would identify an individual! Writing is practically visible speech, or the "talking paper," as the Indian says, and, by all its thousands of peculiarities in combination, is the most personal and individual thing that a man does which leaves a record that can be seen and studied.

The variation of any particular handwriting is a matter, however, that must always be taken into account and given proper consideration. The characteristics of a handwriting are of various degrees of force and value as affecting judgment in regard to identity or difference of two writings, depending upon their character and permanency. As was outlined in the chapter on standards of comparison, the characteristics or features and elements of a particular writing as carefully analyzed and classified are (1) permanent or invariable, (2) habitual or usual, (3) occasional, and (4) exceptional or rare. Characteristics in one handwriting may have special significance which in another may have but little force, all depending upon the writing habits of the one whose writing is under examination, and the facts in each case must be made to apply only to that case. It is a matter of common knowledge that genuine signatures written by the same writer differ from each other within certain well defined limits, and certain normal divergencies in size, lateral position and proportions actually indicate genuineness. This fact is shown in an examination of traced forgeries which may be too nearly like each other or too nearly like a common model to be genuine.

Variations in genuine writing are ordinarily in superficial parts, and in size, proportions and the degree of care given to the act. Writing as a whole process is very much more fixed than it is generally thought to be, and, as stated, is in fact one of the most permanent and unconscious of human habits. This is clearly shown in any collection of genuine writings produced at different times, with different pens or pencils and under a great variety of conditions, but which when brought together and carefully examined show running through them a marked, unmistakable uniformity and individuality. When one says his writing is never twice alike, meaning that its primary characteristics differ, it is clear that such a penman is not qualified to speak with authority on the subject, and it is found, in almost every case, that he refers only to certain superficial form characteristics. Divergencies are of different degrees with different writers, but are seldom so pronounced as it is thought by many that they are. The signature of the halting, careless, changeable, unskillful writer is of course forged with less difficulty than that of the more skillful and uniform writer, and it is entirely possible that a skillful forgery could not be picked out from a mixed collection of signatures by such a writer. Each case, as suggested, must be acted upon and decided by itself, and circumstances are sometimes of a character that make it impossible for the most competent examiner to reach a positive conclusion.

Writing is sometimes questioned that it is alleged was written with the writer lying in bed seriously ill, or written soon after the writer had suffered from apoplexy, and it is easy to understand that such writing may be so broken, distorted and unusual that no one can speak confidently as to its genuineness by comparison with standard writing produced under normal conditions of health. Writing is sometimes disputed that was written while standing and in a book held in the hand, and questions have arisen regarding writing produced on a railroad train while in motion. The main difficulty about a comparison of writings under these conditions is that there are no available standards written under similar conditions and the difficulty of the problem is to reach a conclusion with no standard writing. In some inquiries sixty years separate a questioned and a standard writing, making it difficult to give any opinion whatever.

The examiner who claims to be able to determine with certainty whether a writing is genuine or spurious, no matter how unfavorable the conditions imposed upon the examiner, assumes to do that which cannot always be done. There are cases involving questioned handwriting the merits of which must be determined from circumstances outside of the writing itself. Such cases, however, are usually those in which only a very small

quantity of writing is in question or in which the standards supplied are either of an unsuitable character or
too few in number.

Investigation proves that forged writing usually
shows characteristics exactly opposite to those resulting
from unfavorable surroundings or from abnormal conditions in the writer, which conditions always tend to
produce distorted, erratic, incomplete results. Fraudulent writing is very seldom of this character, but shows
painful attention to details and a studied effort to produce a certain definite form and outline. In order to
explain extraordinary features in fraudulent writing,
unusual external conditions are frequently invented, and
many times, when attention is called to it, the incon-
gruity between the supposed conditions and the written
result is perfectly apparent, and it can be easily shown
not only that the conditions described are in themselves
improbable but that the writing in question does not
show the natural effect of such conditions.

A change of pen may apparently transform a handwriting and make it quite different throughout, but a
very brief investigation will usually show that the
change is merely superficial. A change in pen will affect
writing by changing the strength or width of line, and
a stub pen may change the location of the apparent
shadings, which, however, as illustrated in the chapter
on writing instruments, are not due to increased pressure but to the relation of the stroke to the width of the
point of the pen. A stub pen thus changes the appearance of the writing very materially although not in any
really fundamental manner. A pen of any kind may
be in such poor condition that it will hardly write at

all, but the work of such a pen is easily recognized.

A change of slant in a writing, which is the most common form of disguise, changes its general appearance in a striking manner, but if this is the only disguise it is easily shown to be perfectly transparent. A mere change in size of writing greatly changes its appearance, but this change is, of course, only superficial. Many writers think that their writing is very changeable and radically different at different times when in fact the change is only in a few characteristics; these changes, however, without analysis and careful examination seem very pronounced and fundamental. As a matter of fact two opposite writing habits do not coexist. Writing may be purposely disguised, but even then not often with success, and this being true it is not reasonable to suppose that unconscious, natural writing is likely to show fundamental conflicting habits.

Most writers really know but little about their own writing and would be incapable of describing it orally with no means at hand to illustrate it. The average person cannot even tell the style or design of many of the letters used, without making them, and would be totally unable to point out and describe the many personal peculiarities in his own writing as described in this book in the chapters on simulated forgeries and anonymous letters[1].

---

[1]We all of us have a definite routine manner of performing certain daily offices connected with the toilet, with the opening and shutting of familiar cupboards, and the like. Our lower centres know the order of these movements, and show their knowledge by their "surprise" if the objects are altered so as to oblige the movement to be made in a different way. But our higher thought-centres know hardly anything about the matter. Few men can tell off-hand which sock, shoe, or trouser-leg they put on first. They must first mentally rehearse the act; and even that is often insufficient—the act must be performed.— William James, Principles of Psychology, Vol. 1, Chap. IV., p. 115.

To ask one who has made no study of such a subject, to change offhand all these fixed and unconscious habits is like asking one who speaks broken English to drop his foreign accent at once. The thing cannot be done, because one cannot avoid that which he cannot see; he cannot omit that which he does not know he possesses, and cannot imitate that which he cannot properly interpret. Fundamental differences or changes in style or design of letters alone are sometimes wholly attributed to changed conditions entirely inconsistent with the result shown. For example, a carefully drawn signature showing retouching and the most careful attention to details, in one case was excused and apologized for by saying, "it was written with a broken pen on a rough surface with the writer seated in a rocking chair."

Many important questioned documents purport to have been executed by old people, and the question of eyesight must be considered. The attempt is sometimes made to explain away unusual features by saying that the light was poor or that spectacles were forgotten. And in these very cases the writing may show careful retracing or repairing of fine lines, perhaps not more than one one-hundredth of an inch in width, an act which would have been clearly impossible for the alleged writer to perform even with the aid of the absent spectacles.

Genuine signatures written under such conditions by one who could not see well will usually show unmistakable evidences of the fact; they will not usually be in just the right position and on the line, are often disconnected and broken and show a carelessness and unfinished condition that would never satisfy a forger. The erratic or the fixed character of a particular handwriting is a personal characteristic, however, that must always itself be considered and the same degree of divergence must be differently interpreted under different conditions, depending entirely upon the habits of the writer whose writing is in question.

This tendency to slight divergence, or with some writers pronounced divergence, in size, proportions and the degree of care given to certain frequently occurring words may be a most forcible and convincing means of showing that a whole document containing considerable matter is not genuine but a careful, studied, unnatural simulation. Such a document will almost certainly not contain the careless divergencies and modifications that are shown in genuine writings of any considerable length. Individual words may be imitated with considerable accuracy, but it is quite probable that several modified models for the same word will not be chosen, and the result often is that repeated words in such an imitation are in their uniformity similar to rubber stamp impressions. In comparing two documents of this character all the similar words from the document in question and the same words from the standards should be grouped (see Figs. 56, 110) in the order in which they occur and carefully compared.

Usually there is about genuine writing that which proclaims it as genuine, and one of the things that may be recognized by any examiner is that careless abandon and indifference that shows that the writing was the result of a habit and not the conscious following of a copy. Freedom, carelessness, speed and illegibility are always earmarks of genuineness.

The slow, drawn, unnatural and generally divergent

character of a forged signature is sometimes attributed
entirely to the fact that because the signature is attached to an important document it was written with
unusual care and deliberation which, it is urged, accounts for the divergence. Naturally those who seek
to profit by a fraudulent writing offer all kinds of ex-
cuses for its shortcomings and this is one of the most
popular. It is claimed that the importance of the document led the writer to write a signature differing in
fundamental ways from any other writing he ever
penned. The best answer to this contention is, of
course, the bringing forward of other signatures to important business documents as standards, but this is not
always possible, and it is necessary to consider this phase
of the question of disputed writing.

Investigation shows that with the average writer a
five dollar check or a five thousand dollar check carry
the same quality of signature but, as stated above, conditions may sometimes change the character of writing,
especially with those with whom writing is an unusual
act or who through age or disease write with great difficulty and hesitation. With those last named undue
attention to the writing process or intense realization
of the importance of doing it well may render it nearly
or quite impossible to write at all, and writing produced
under such conditions will necessarily be erratic and
broken and show more than the usual lack of muscular
control. These results, however, differ fundamentally
from the divergences from normal writing in the usual
forgery, which is not likely to be decrepit and incomplete but too careful, too perfect, too conventional and
not the natural product of an unskilled hand writing

with difficulty. The forger does not dare write so poorly and in so broken and distorted a manner as results when one who writes with difficulty writes also under strain or excitement[1].

---

[1]We are not always sure that our functions run best when we concentrate our effort on them and turn the full light of attention on the details. We may speak fluently, but the moment we begin to give attention to the special movements of our lips and of our tongue in speaking and make a special effort to produce the movements correctly, we are badly hampered.—Prof. Hugo Münsterberg, in "On the Witness Stand." 1908.

So long as the manner and degree of the conscious direction of our actions may vary, it follows that such direction may be wisely or unwisely, helpfully or disturbingly applied. And, as usual, the deviations from the normal status, particularly under the influence of emotional susceptibility, offer the most ready illustrations of this sensitive equilibrium. The most common of these is the irrelevant interference of the higher centre with the routine activity of the lower. * * * For it is true that, even where consciousness does not so decidedly impede the desired result, it modifies and makes unnatural activities which, when performed unawares, are performed the best.—The Subconscious, by Joseph Jastrow, 1906, p. 25.

CHAPTER XIII.

INDIVIDUAL AND GENERAL CHARACTERISTICS IN WRITING

Practically every one in this land of education will have some opinion about a disputed writing, and it is too often assumed that any one who can write is qualified to testify, and that any one who testifies is qualified to do so. With many such witnesses the slightest similarity is construed as identity, or, on the contrary, the most trivial difference may be interpreted as pointing to a different writer.

Errors in the identification of handwriting are perhaps most frequently made by mistaking certain general system or national features for individual characteristics and basing a conclusion thereon[1]. These general features may be very forcible as evidence pointing to a writer of a particular class, but not by them alone to an individual of that class; and this applies to all general characteristics indicating system, nationality, sex, or occupation.

---

[1]The illustration on the following page of a few German writing characteristics that sometimes appear in English writing will show how easily some of these peculiar forms in two handwritings might mislead an amateur examiner into thinking that both were written by the same writer. Among other things the illustration shows: (1) The peculiar top stroke to right on certain letters. (2) The peculiar small e like c. (3) The figure 7 with a cross stroke. (4) The small c connected at top. (5) The small a and o with top thrown far over to left. (6) The hyphen with two strokes and sometimes vertical. (7) The low finish of the small t. (8) The disconnected lower loop y. (9) The exclamation point after a salutation. (10) Capital I similar to English F or Y. (11) The small s with stroke at top.

Some of these forms are also found in other European hands, but all are found in the German. The presence of one or more of these characteristics in a writing may be of distinct assistance at the outset of an inquiry as a means of discovering a possible writer.

[206]

It is a fact, however, that in cases of forgery it is usually the failure to recognize and repro- duce these very charac- teristics that shows a writing to be a forgery, as the forger may omit a fixed system or national characteristic, which he does not see or does not understand, which may be as signifi- cant as the slanting eyes of the Chinaman, and he may put into a system of writing dif- fering radically from his own certain insis- tent but unconscious characteristics of his own style which mark the writing as spurious.

Errors are made in identifying writing of a foreign style because, as we have seen, the

FIG. 99 – German Writing Characteristics.

foreigner brings to his American writing that which marks it as distinctly as his face and accent show his nationality, and if a handwriting in dispute containing such a foreign flavor is being compared with writings by a different writer but of the same nationality it can

readily be seen how an uninformed examiner might conclude that these national characteristics show individual
identity and prove that both writings are by the same
hand. This same error may be made in identifying
the writing of those following a distinctive system of
writing, the general characteristics of which are not
known to the examiner.

Uninformed graphologists, who undertake to determine the most definite and detailed mental and moral
qualities from handwriting, make serious errors on this
very point by attributing, even in their printed books,
definite character significance to certain characteristics
which are distinct features of certain systems of writing. There are those who undertake to give opinions
on complicated and difficult handwriting questions who
know nothing whatever of the dates and features of the
various systems of American writing, or of the most
common characteristics of foreign writing, and with
such examiners testifying as to the identity of two
sets of writing the possibility of error is easily understood.

The important, fundamental fact to keep constantly in mind is that the genuineness or otherwise of a
writing is determined not alone by the number but by
the nature of the identical or differing characteristics,
and a positive opinion should not be given unless an
adequate amount of standard writing for comparison
is supplied, and then only after a careful consideration
of all the facts. As with any subject, superficial knowledge or hasty examination may lead to serious error.

It is also true that there are certain questions that
cannot be answered by anyone, and the honest and com-

petent man in any field does not hesitate to admit his limitations and the limitations of his subject. The charlatan and the pretender will make no such admissions, but stand ready to answer at once any question. ' Neither is the really qualified specialist in any subject inclined to give an unqualified off-hand opinion under any conditions. The data supplied in some cases may be entirely too limited or the time too limited to permit a proper examination, and under such conditions it is certainly better to reserve judgment than to jump to a conclusion.

As we have already seen in the chapter on movement, a writing characteristic is any element or quality that serves to identify a writing in any manner or degree; there are characteristics common to many nations, and others that are strictly national in character; there are those that mark a certain period of time, and others again that grow out of a certain system of writing or are the development of a particular occupation. In a thorough writing examination these varied characteristics must be discovered, analyzed and correctly interpreted.

The determination of the relative value and force of characteristics as evidence of genuineness or identity is the vital problem for the writing examiner to solve. It is impossible to illustrate and define all the thousands of actual and possible characteristics of writing and weigh and measure their comparative values, for the reason that such values differ with different writers and under varying conditions, and this tabulation is not so important as the discovery of some of the principles by which the force and significance of characteristics are to be measured. No set of infallible rules can be formulated, but some general principles can be stated that seem to apply in most cases.

One of the first is that those identifying or differentiating characteristics which are most divergent from the regular system or national features of a particular handwriting under examination are of the most force. The second important principle is that those characteristics should be first sought for and be given the most weight which are of an inconspicuous and unobtrusive character and are, therefore, likely to be so unconscious that they would not be omitted when the attempt is made to disguise, and would not be successfully copied from the writing of another when simulation is attempted. A third principle is that ordinary system or national characteristics are not alone sufficient on which to base a judgment of identity of two writings, although such characteristics necessarily have some value as evidence of identity if present in sufficient number and if confirmed by the presence of individual characteristics.

Any character in writing or any writing habit may be modified and individualized by different writers in different ways and varying degrees, and it is clear that the writing individuality of any particular writer is made up of all these common and uncommon characteristics and habits. As in a personal description it is the *combination of* particulars that identifies, and necessarily the more numerous and unusual the separate features are the more certain are we of the identity.

Two writings are identified as being by the same writer by the absence of fundamental divergences and by a combination of a sufficient number of the above described characteristics of both a common and uncommon nature to exclude the theory of accidental coincidence. As in the identification of a person by general description and by marks and scars, no fixed rule can be laid down as to the extent of proof necessary further than the appeal to ordinary common sense and intelligence. As two writings are connected by the fact that they contain a combination of similar characteristics and that there is an absence of significant divergencies, the process is a double one, positive and negative, and neither part of the process must be excluded or overlooked in reaching a conclusion. In order to reach the conclusion of identity of two sets of writings, there must not be present significant and unexplained divergencies[1].

---

[1] The principles which underlie all proof by comparison of handwritings are very simple, and, when distinctly enunciated, appear to be self-evident. To prove that two documents were written by the same hand, coincidences must be shown to exist in them which cannot be accidental. To prove that two documents were written by different hands, discrepancies must be pointed out in them which cannot be accounted for by accident or by disguise. These principles are easy to understand, but to exemplify them in observation is by no means always easy. It is not the merely having bodily eyes which enables any one to see in two documents either discrepancies or coincidences. In the words of Epicharmus, which are the motto of this work, "Mind sees, and Mind hears; all things else are deaf and blind." * * * * It is idle for an unpractised volunteer to look at two documents, and to suppose that he sees what is in them. He does not know what to observe. He may fancy that two handwritings are similar, when their essential differences are numerous; or he may pronounce them to be wholly unlike, when, radically, they are identical.

Finally it is to be remembered that the evidence of the identity of Junius and Francis as handwriters is cumulative; that is to say, the force of the evidence depends not on any one single coincidence, but on numerous coincidences varying materially in their individual strength, which, when viewed in connection, lead irresistibly to one inference alone, though each by itself may be inconclusive. A common fallacy in dealing with such evidence is to take each coincidence separately, and to show that a similar coincidence exists in some other writer. This would be a perfectly legitimate mode of reasoning, if any one coincidence so dealt with were adduced as in itself conclusive; but it fails to meet the requirements of the case, when the argument is based on the combination of many such coincidences collectively, and not on the separate existence of any one of them.—Handwriting of Junius, by the Honorable Edward Twistleton, pp. LXXV-LXXVII., London, 1871.

Two handwritings in the same language must inevitably have similarities, but, as we have seen, certain similarities show only that the writers belong to the same class or nationality. Although all writing in the same language is bound to be somewhat similar, like men of the same race, from this fact it does not logically follow that individuality cannot be distinguished. It would be as absurd to say that because Americans can easily be distinguished from Chinamen that therefore all Americans are alike. As a matter of fact they are alike in certain race features, but individuality is shown by a combination of variations of individual and general characteristics. Writing is individualized in precisely the same manner.

Writing that we often see has about it that which we instantly recognize as something that gives it a personality and a character which it may be difficult or impossible for the inexperienced to describe and analyze. It is not the form alone nor any one feature but a combination of all that mainly appeals to us, and we name the writer without hesitation. This individuality, which is recognized even by the untrained, results from the combination and proportion of all the varied elements which make it up, and irrespective of individual peculiar forms, may strongly affect judgment as to identity. The undisguised handwriting of a friend thus becomes to us almost as recognizable as the friend's face, and this general appearance or pictorial affect is always of assistance in identifying a writing, but, it must be added, is also the means of leading many into error who are not able to distinguish general from personal characteristics.

This instant recognition of a writing simply by intuition the careful examiner not only does not attempt but, on the contrary, studiously avoids; he reserves judgment until the characteristics of the writing have all been observed, compared and carefully weighed[1].

A forged or simulated handwriting must naturally resemble somewhat that which it is intended to resemble, and a disguised writing will inevitably diverge in some degree from a genuine writing and, as stated above, the whole problem is to determine and show what characteristics are of controlling force as a basis for an opinion[2]. A signature may be unusual in a number of particulars and yet contain undoubted evidence of genuineness, and again a signature may, in general appearance and superficial characteristics, bear strong resemblance to

---

[1] The specialist of every class is constantly tempted to do more or attempt to do more than he is able to do and thus become a kind of fakir. Many succumb to the temptation and bring discredit upon themselves and upon their specialty by the effort to reach conclusions by other than scientific methods. Those who dabble in graphology seem especially inclined toward reliance upon inspiration and occult power. The competent Mr. Keene, in "The Mystery of Handwriting," is led to say: "This insight, this seer faculty, is not so rare as might be supposed, and under proper and controlling restrictions is, I am confident, one of the highest qualities of which the soul is capable. It is the supreme manifestation of intelligence, and perceives clearly a flash of the Eternal Truth. Through the everyday senses we see as through a glass darkly, but this trained and developed intuition gives times of illumination both precious and exalting."

The scientific man will continue to "see as through a glass darkly" by the use of his reason and his senses or run the risk of getting into that condition of mind in which he is unable to realize how ridiculous he appears to the entirely sane.

[2] The unfortunate rule laid down by Justice Coleridge in the controlling English case, followed until 1854, refusing to admit standards (Mudd vs. Suckermore), already discussed in the previous chapter on standards of comparison, says, "The test of genuineness ought to be the general resemblance * * to the general character of the writing." This is just the way not to do it and is the method usually followed by the inexperienced and the uninformed. "General character" in a writing may simply point to the old round hand system, or the angular system, or the modern vertical style, or to a German writer, and it is easy to see how fallacious such a "test of genuineness" may be.

the writing it imitates and yet upon closer examination be positively shown to be a forgery.

As was considered in the preceding chapter some writers write a fixed and uniform hand that diverges but little from a normal type, while others are extremely erratic, and these facts must always be taken into consideration in forming a judgment in such a case and each inquiry must be weighed and measured by itself by examination of the standard writing in the case. The fact must be carefully investigated and considered as to the manner and degree in which writing is affected by changes in conditions, and this matter must always be given due consideration and weight whether the conditions under which the writing was done are known or not.

That a questioned and a genuine handwriting resemble each other in that they were written on a slant of about fifty-two degrees from the horizontal would alone be of little significance as showing identity, except that they belong to the same general class, for the reason that up to a recent date this has been the normal slant, nor would it be significant as showing identity that the downward strokes all slanted alike, because this is the standard form. If, however, in such a handwriting it is shown that certain letters repeatedly depart from normal forms in slant and for no apparent cause, then such characteristics at once become significant. As we have seen there is but little significance in a few of these similarities in standard copy book forms, excepting in combination with other forms, because these are to be expected in a writing of that class or system; but just in proportion as such forms are distorted or modified they become individualized and personal, and therefore it always becomes necessary to comparé a questioned writing, not only with the genuine writing of the alleged writer, but also with the normal original writing on which it was based. To know whether a characteristic is general or personal it is necessary to know what the normal forms are; the examiner, therefore, should know what the writer originally aimed to do.

Many writers have various forms of certain letters under command and make any one of two or even three normal styles under different circumstances and conditions, and a few such divergencies as these will not alone be sufficient to differentiate two writings. An entirely different design of letter may not so conclusively indicate a different writer as a persistent and peculiar modification or distortion of a minor part of the same general type of letter. In one case the writer writes from an entirely different mental pattern, as though he were to make an entirely different letter of the alphabet, while in the other case a slight but persistent divergence may be very strong evidence pointing to a different writer. This is a point that requires the most careful attention.

Some systems of writing, in the proportion of the long and short letters and the parts of letters above the line, are arranged on a scale of one to two, others in one to three, and others in one to four or five; thus the smallest letter above the line would be one space high and a loop letter two, three, four or five times as high, according to the system. When a person is taught a certain proportion until his writing has become a fixed habit he finds it very difficult to change this proportion in a definite way, and persistent uniform divergence through

a considerable amount of writing in such a characteristic would be strong evidence of a lack of identity.

In every handwriting examination the alleged date of
the writing in question and the actual date of the standard writing should be known. The standards should include all that are available, within a certain definite
period including the time when it is claimed the disputed
writing was written. If it is alleged that either set of
writings was produced under unusual surroundings of
any kind this fact should be known by the examiner. If
the writer was subject to unusual changes in physical or
mental condition, due to age, disease or through any
cause, this also should be known. The competent examiner, however, must know to what extent and in what
manner writing is affected, changed or modified by
varying conditions and must give due attention to this
phase of the question whether he has any information
on the subject or not.

CHAPTER XIV.

VARIETY OF FORMS IN HANDWRITING AND MATHEMATICAL CALCULATIONS APPLIED TO QUESTIONED HANDWRITING

It hardly seems possible that there could be so many ways of doing simple things as are shown in the illustrations in this chapter of some of the variations of a few of the letters. There are shown sixty-three divergent capital I's, forty-seven differing specimens of the abbreviation Co., twenty-five divergent examples of the abbreviation N. Y., fifteen varieties of the capital E, and thirty-six different methods of crossing the t! The various specimens are examples of actual business writing, not one letter being written for the purpose of illustration. These few illustrations do something toward showing in graphic manner the marvelous variation in handwriting, especially when all the characters are taken into consideration.

Only a small proportion of the vast variety of forms in writing can be accounted for by tracing them back to a parent system. This curious and unaccountable variation is, of course, what gives to handwriting its individuality, and it is undoubtedly true that every mature handwriting shows peculiarities which in combination of all the characters can not be exactly duplicated in the writing of any other person. It is like the mysterious variation in human personality in which a slight variation in features, proportions, complexion and size, individualizes the millions of members of the human family. Look at a vast crowd; all similar yet all different!

It requires much study and analysis to discover how it is possible for all this variety in handwriting to be produced, especially when we consider the fact that variety is not sought for by the average writer; he writes as he does simply because that is his way of doing it.

In examining a collection of specimens of handwriting certain conspicuous variations at once attract our attention. Some of these are: (1) design, (2) size, (3) proportions, (4) slant, (5) shading, (6) vigor, (7) artistic finish. When we observe the bewildering variety in design of a group of letters; the awkward and artistic, the legible and illegible, the fanciful and the prosaic, the wide and the narrow, the long and the short, the round and the angular, the big and the little, it seems impossible that another variation could be made, and then we come upon still another one different from all the rest! We look at a peculiar form and are inclined to wonder why anyone would make a letter like that and others look at ours and think the same thing[1]. Examine the examples of t crossings and the capital I's and try to imagine what the varied conditions were that produced the curious results there shown. In a study of design of any of the letters illustrated it is interesting first to see if our own letter appears in the collection.

A study of the t crossings is of particular interest. They should be examined with special reference to design, direction, position, length, and shading. Compare one and thirty with two and thirty-three; one with five, and seven with twenty-one; nineteen and twenty-two,

---

[1]As the good old Quaker lady said to her husband, "Everybody is queer but me and thee and sometimes, dear, thee is a little queer."

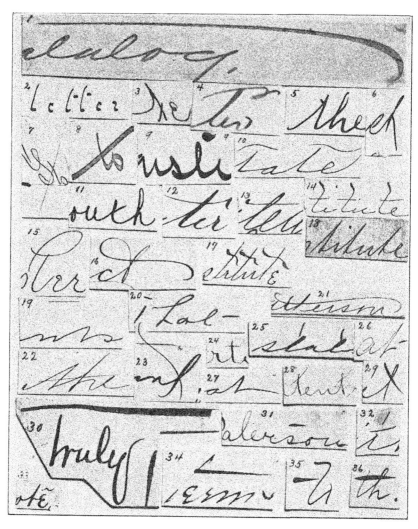

Fig. 100—Thirty-six examples of t crossings, all taken from actual business writing.

and twelve and thirteen; eight and seventeen and ten and thirty. Observe the curiosities, numbered two, three, eleven, seventeen, twenty-five and thirty-two. Probably no stroke in writing is so clear an index of vigor and some other personal qualities as the t crossing, and if every element of writing were as eloquent graphology would have a more definite and accurate story to tell.

In the capital I, in addition to the seven special points specified above, observe the different *places* and *directions* of the beginning and finishing strokes, also the width of the letter in proportion to its height and the width of the top compared with the bottom. In comparing the capital I's in artistic quality the attention is attracted to nineteen, with a dot over it, and to six with its clear-cut outline, and four in contrast with twelve. On the question of vigor compare fifty-six with twenty-four and twelve with fifty-nine; in shading observe twenty-one and forty-six, forty-eight, twenty and fifty; in size compare fifty-one, fifty-three, eight and thirty-two. See the two capital I's with dots. nineteen and fifty-six, and among the freaks, those numbered two, four, seven, nine, ten, eleven, thirty-four, forty-two and forty-five.

The differences in size, proportions, slant and shading in the capital E's at once attract attention, and the shape, size and direction of the connecting loop, between the upper and lower parts of the letter, show peculiar variations.

The illustration Co. affords an excellent opportunity to compare all the seven variations specified above and many others. In proportions compare twenty-five and forty-five, both taken from envelope addresses, as all the

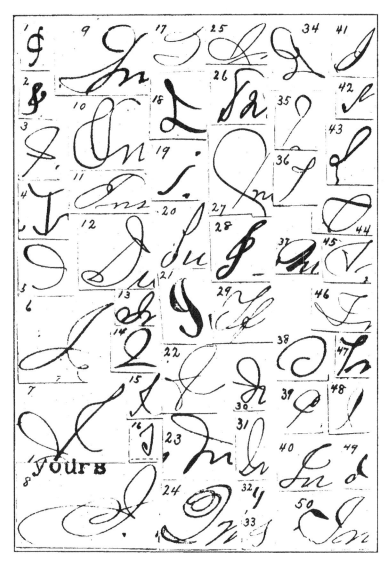

Fig. 101—Variations of the capital I as made by different writers.   All from recent American writing.

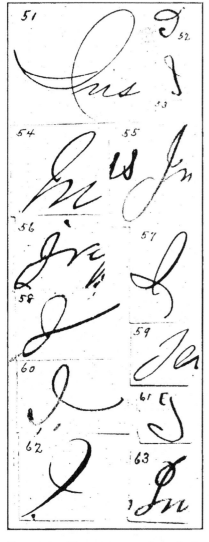

Fig. 102—Thirteen examples of the capital I.

others were; in artistic finish compare thirty-eight with twenty-six or eleven with twenty-three; in size compare one with fourteen and thirty-seven with forty-seven; in slant compare thirty-three and forty-seven; in shading compare thirty-one and forty-two and thirty and forty-four.

In the abbreviation N. Y. we see the ancient and the modern style, the big and the little, the plain and the flourished, the light and the shaded, the artistic and the awkward, and yet each the natural handwriting of some one. In view of the peculiar and divergent habits shown in these illustrations, which include only a few writing characters, it is easy to understand why it is so difficult for these various writers to duplicate each other's work and at the same time exclude their own individualities.

Another fundamental variation that deserves special

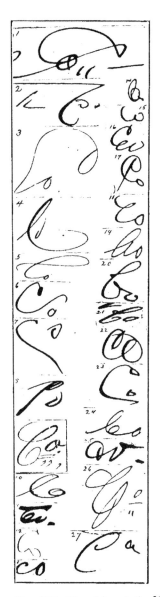

Fɪɢ. 103—The abbreviation Co. from envelope addresses of business letters. As with many of the other illustrations much detail is lost in the half-tone reproductions compared with the originals or with the photographs.

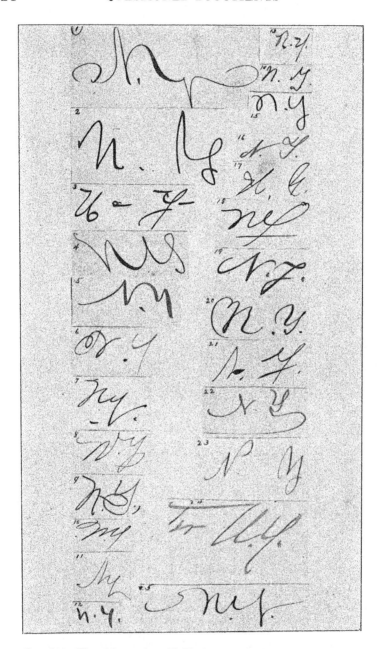

FIG. 104—The abbreviation N. Y. from recent business envelopes.

Fig. 105—Varieties of the capital E.

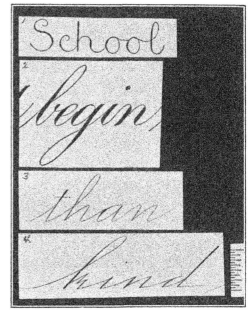

Fig. 106—Illustrations of connections between strokes. 1, Modern vertical. 2, Round hand. 3, Spencerian. 4, Angular hand.

attention in an analysis of writing is that of angularity or roundness, especially in the small letters. The connections between the various strokes in writing vary from very acute angles to broad curved connections that represent arcs of circles.

There are shown in Fig. 106 four different systems of writing which illustrate the wide variation in this matter of connections between strokes. The first is the modern vertical; the second, the old round hand; third, the Spencerian, or what was at first called 'the semi-angular system;" and fourth, the angular system. Any considerable collection of American writing will show examples of all four styles. From the character of these connections alone writing can be classified into at least three well defined divisions; (1) circular, (2) oblong, or elliptical, (3) angular. A very slight change in the nature of these angles changes the whole appearance of a writing in a very pronounced way; the spacing and compactness are at once changed and the speed is also in a measure governed by the width of the angles between the strokes. Slow writing usually shows rounded connections, while speed always tends to narrow the width of angles. Many of these varied characteristics are as unknown to the average writer as the number of ridges on the bottom of the feet, and it is such features of writing that most successfully baffle disguise and expose forgery, for the reason that we cannot easily discard that which we do not know we possess, nor imitate successfully that which we do not see.

The principle underlying the identification of a handwriting is the same as that by which anything with a great many possible variations is identified as belonging to that class or being that particular thing. It is first necessary to establish the standard, and then identity or difference is shown by a careful comparison of all elements, features or characteristics which all together constitute the basis for a conclusion. The force of the conclusion is naturally governed by the number and significance of the points under consideration, ranging from a mere conjecture up to what amounts to moral certainty.

There are many close analogies between the identification of an individual by bodily characteristics and the identification of a handwriting by examination of its various elements. As we know in some instances identification is practically certain, but in others only probable, or there may not be sufficient basis for any opinion. If an individual is sought for who is definitely described as follows: (1) exactly five feet eleven and one-fourth inches in height, (2) blue eyes, (3) brown hair, and in addition has (4) lost his left thumb, and the (5) lower part of his right ear, and has (6) a mole on his left temple one-half inch in diameter, and (7) a tattooed anchor on the back of his left hand, and a (8) narrow scar five inches long on his right forearm, and an individual is found who exactly matches these eight points of identity, we say without hesitation that we have undoubtedly found the man decribed. We promptly conclude on these eight points alone that this man differs from all the other millions of men on the earth. Theoretically there may be other such men but we say confidently that it is so strongly against common sense and all experience to expect it that it is practically impossible.

This problem is capable of a mathematical solution if we first agree on the basis for the calculation. It is possible to show mathematically how vastly improbable it would be for these eight separate points of identity to coincide in two individuals. We must first determine how often, or rather how seldom, each feature will be found separately and then, by a mathematical formula, as fixed as the multiplication table, we determine how often coincidence of all the features may be expected. This formula, as given by Professor Simon Newcomb, is as follows: "The probability of concurrence of all the events is equal to the continued product of the probabilities of all the separate events." If one thing will occur once in twenty times and another once in twenty the probability of the two occurring in conjunction is represented by the fraction which is the product of one-twentieth and one-twentieth or one four-hundredth[1].

---

[1]Calculus of Probabilities: the application of mathematical reasoning to the art of judging in cases where only probable evidence can be obtained. . . The mathematical solution of problems in probabilities consists, first, in dividing the possible processes or results into elementary and equally probable cases; and, secondly, in finding how many of these cases favor the proposed event. . . It cannot be doubted that an understanding of this calculus would afford a very material aid to judgment in weighing and estimating the probabilities of events in the affairs of life; for, although these events, or the causes which give rise to them, cannot generally be made the subject of mathematical calculation, yet the examination and enumeration of the various combinations of circumstances which give rise to an event affords our only means of judging of its probability. The longer a man's experience of worldly affairs and the sounder his judgment, the more nearly he will conform to the rules and methods of the mathematical calculus in estimating probabilities. An eminent writer happily described the calculus of probabilities as common sense expressed in numbers. . . If the concurrence of a large number of circumstances is necessary to the production of an event, each of these circumstances may be, in itself, very probable, and yet their concurrence, and consequently the event itself, very improbable. The mathematical rule for determining probability in such a case is that the probability of the concurrence of all the events is equal to the continued product of the probabilities of all the separate events. . .

One of the principal marks of the practical wisdom of age and experience is the ability to recognize this principle, and there are plenty of proverbs which are really founded on it.

Professor Simon Newcomb, formerly Professor of Mathematics and Astronomy, Johns Hopkins University, in The Universal Cyclopaedia.

For the purpose of showing the practical impossibility of these eight personal features all being exactly duplicated in two individuals we can make so small the fraction representing how frequently each point may be found that it is certainly within the fact and will be promptly granted.   For number one, the exact height, we will say that in every ten men we shall find one who exactly measures as therein described, of the second or eye color one in three, of the third one in four, of the remaining five points we will say that out of every two hundred men one will be found precisely answering one of each of the peculiar descriptions specified, although for some of these accidental and unusual features more than one in ten thousand would certainly be too many to expect.

We now have our separate events represented by eight fractions, one-third, one-fourth, one-tenth and five fractions each of one-two-hundredth.   Now, assuming that our problem is to determine how frequently all these peculiarities and elements that have accidentally combined in this one individual would be likely to be exactly duplicated in another individual, we find by applying Professor Newcomb's rule that the continued product or the mathematical probability is one in thirty-eight trillions and four hundred billions, (38,400,000,000,000), or more than thirty thousand times the total population of the globe, and we naturally conclude if we find an individual who answers the description that we have found the man and that there is not another man who has had the same things happen to him.

To say that such remote, improbable and shadowy events as that represented by the fraction named are practically impossible conveys a more accurate impression to the mind than to say that they are remotely probable. Mathematically speaking such a fraction is certainly a "negligible quantity." Any one of ten thousand different things may happen to one individual, and thus he becomes the definite combination of a few of the thousands of things that might have marked him. The improbability of a definite combination arises from a specification of the certain few that are to occur and the exclusion of all the others that might have occurred.

It is well understood that certain personal characteristics are vastly more significant than others as indicating identity and the same is true of handwriting characteristics. Naturally those things most abnormal and accidental are more significant than those that are general and usual, although here again the large number of the separate "events" of a low fraction may render it exceedingly improbable that they will all unite at one time. Scars and deformities in personal features are exactly paralleled in handwriting by mutilations, abbreviations and personal inventions and peculiarities, which in number in all their possible combinations go up into the thousands.

It is sometimes contended, by those whose interests make such contention necessary, not only that two handwritings might be exactly alike, but that such an event would not be at all unusual or unexpected. It is plausibly argued that thousands learn the same system and that the natural result is identity. Without investigation this may seem to be true but the facts show that it is not. If those taught were all identical then the result might be uniform.

Any system of writing, as we have seen, puts its impress upon a class or nation of writers, but such impress does not by any means produce a slavish uniformity as any one knows who examines the subject even in a superficial manner. Variation begins as soon as writing begins and continues till each writer writes in the way that seems best and·easiest to him. Only young school children write with comparative uniformity, because they have never used writing in a practical way, but even they do not write exactly alike. Even in school as soon as writing begins to be used for any other purpose than to learn it, variation at once begins and any teacher knows how impossible it is to get an adult class, even when they are attempting to do so, to write all alike. The failure in the new vertical system began when the writing came to be used outside of school in a practical way.

What we find in the examination of actual writing is the result shown in the illustrations in this chapter; that is, a pronounced and unaccountable variation. We see at·once that identity in two complete adult writings is so remote a possibility as to be practically impossible. The amount of writing must necessarily always be considered, but total coincidence is so remote that even identity of a small amount of writing is very improbable.

Let us see just what a proposition it is to expect complete identity in two handwritings. We must imagine groups of the variations of each of the eighty or more characters in English script with from a dozen to a hundred or more variations in each group. Now, we take one of the capital I's from that group, one t crossing, one Co. and one N. Y. and so on through the eighty characters until we have a complete set. Then we must select a group of occasional letters and variations until we have exemplified a complete handwriting. The proposition now is to go out and find a writer who will duplicate in his writing every one of these selected characteristics. The improbability is simply ridiculous and we say at once it cannot be ·done. Even if the probability of making a particular form in each group were as low as one-fifth, to have this combined on the same ratio with a particular form in all the other groups would make a probability represented by a fraction with one for a numerator and the eightieth power of five as a denominator. The number is too stupendous even to write.

The same problem may be stated in another way. We will say that movement or manner of writing will be represented by the fraction one-half; that is to say that all writers write in one of only two possible styles of movement, and let pen position, slant, shading, size and alignment each be represented by the fraction one-half. The various letters, characters, abbreviations and pen marks in English writing are more than eighty in number, with scores of variations and modifications of each style which, when taken all together in the great variety of handwritings, are numbered by the thousand. We will assume that all characters except forty will be made exactly alike and that those forty will each have but one possible modification of one kind in one direction instead of many as is the fact. We now have as representing our separate "events" forty-six fractions each of one-half and the question to determine is how frequently will this or any other particular selected group of varying forms and habits all combine in another handwriting. Applying the rule again we find that even on this low basis the mathematical probability of two complete handwritings being identical is one in something more than sixty-eight trillions (68,000,000,000,000).

It is, of course, true that hardly in any investigation will all the characters of a handwriting enter into any inquiry, but by reference to the particulars enumerated for examination in the chapters on simulated forgeries and anonymous letters it will readily appear what an extended basis for calculation there is in connection with the examination of the various elements, features and characteristics of even a single signature[1].

Fraudulent and questioned writing may be roughly divided into two general classes, first forged or simulated writing in which the attempt is made to discard one's own writing habits and assume the writing personality of another, and second that class of writings that are disguised in which the writer simply seeks to hide his own personality. Mathematical calculations may be employed with either class of writings to show difference

---

[1] It is a surprise to most people to know that in the Bertillon system of measurements by means of which criminals are identified, only eleven measurements are made. By these few measurements accurately made and a general description of the individual any one of hundreds of thousands can be positively identified. Experience has shown that the probability of these few characteristics exactly combining in two individuals is so remote that it is perfectly safe to assume that it is impossible. A necessary part of the system is the classification of the measurements and descriptions so that out of thousands on file it is possible to find the measurements of an individual under suspicion who has already been measured.

The measurements are: (1) height, (2) stretch from finger tips to finger tips, (3) trunk or height sitting, (4) head length, (5) head width, (6) cheek width, (7) right ear length, (8) left foot length, (9) left middle finger length, (10) left little finger length, (11) left cubit or forearm.

or identity, whichever the fact may be. A forger who seeks simply to abandon his own writing personality, which is exceedingly difficult if not impossible, and at the same time assume that of another, which is still more difficult, will almost certainly fall short of perfection by errors in both these particulars. Errors of commission consist in putting in what is not usual and habitual, and even though it may be possible to find in a sufficient amount of standard writing separate approximate examples of every unusual characteristic appearing in a questioned signature, those individual characteristics may be so rare that the combination of all of them in one signature would be so improbable as to amount to very strong evidence of forgery[1].

If among other indications of a lack of genuineness we find six unusual form characteristics in a single signature each of which it is claimed appears partly exemplified once in fifty genuine signatures, but never with two in the same signature, what is the mathematical likelihood on this basis of all of them appearing in one signature? We have as the separate events six fractions

---

[1] There are at least two distinct causes which we can see at work whenever experience improves discrimination:

First, the terms whose difference comes to be felt contract disparate associates and these help to drag them apart.

Second, the difference reminds us of larger differences of the same sort, and these help us to notice it.

Let us study the first cause first, and begin by supposing two compounds, of ten elements apiece. Suppose no one element of either compound to differ from the corresponding element of the other compound enough to be distinguished from it if the two are compared alone, and let the amount of this imperceptible difference be called equal to 1. The compounds will differ from each other, however, in ten different ways; and, although each difference by itself might pass unperceived, the total difference, equal to 10, may very well be sufficient to strike the sense. In a word, increasing the number of "points" involved in a difference may excite our discrimination as effectually as increasing the amount of difference at any one point.— Principles of Psychology, by William James, Vol. 1, p. 510.

of one-fiftieth and we find on this basis that the mathematical probability of just these unusual characteristics all appearing together in one signature is only once in several hundreds of millions.

Assuming that the premises are correct, such improbability is certainly strong evidence on this question. The proper answer to the inquiry whether the production of two such signatures on the same day or even in succession is possible would be that it would be practically impossible although theoretically it might be remotely possible. Those on the wrong side of a case may be obliged to base a hope on fractions as small as one one-hundred millionth.

Mathematical calculations may be employed with much force in the examination of traced forgeries where the model signature is found or where companion forgeries are produced which were made from the same model. This question is further discussed in the chapter on Traced Forgeries.

CHAPTER XV.

As the name clearly signifies, a simulated forgery is a simulation or imitation of a genuine writing. A forgery of this class is produced by a method similar to that employed by a pupil in following a copy. It is not always possible to tell by what method a fraudulent writing was made but it throws some light on the investigation of the subject to consider briefly some of the inevitable conditions surrounding the act of forgery.

In the first place it is important to remember that the act is a crime and is performed with the knowledge that while success may perhaps bring a great reward, failure may bring punishment and disgrace. The crime necessarily is always one of secrecy around which must be grouped corroborating circumstances of time and place and conditions. These are carefully planned and then, with preparations all made, the door locked and the curtains drawn, the act is stealthily performed.

It is of interest to consider what preparation the fabricator may have had for his difficult undertaking. The history of such crimes shows that in most cases he is a beginner, a tyro in such a role, who not only has had no experience, but has made no special preparation whatever for such a task and does not realize its difficulty. This being true it is easy to anticipate what the result will be; the work is not likely to be well done. It is indeed fortunate that the rare one or two in every community who might do such an act well are seldom inclined to commit forgery and that he who attempts it is not usually an adept.

To return to him who sets out on the way of the transgressor, let us consider what effect the conditions we have outlined may have upon the forger himself. It is well known that even with those possessing the requisite skill, foolish errors of omission or commission in the production of a forged paper often prove so conclusively that the writing is a forgery that, in this as in many other crimes, the truth seems to proclaim itself. The explanation of these errors undoubtedly is that the mind is so riveted on certain details of the act that other matters of importance are entirely overlooked[1]. Realization of the fact that forgery is a criminal act, the fear of discovery, and the painful anxiety to do the work well, all combine to bring about a mental and muscular condition that make it very difficult if not altogether impossible to do the work in a skillful manner, and an actual criminal forgery undoubtedly always is a much poorer piece of work than could be executed by the same writer merely as an exhibition of skill. This intense fixing of the attention on the matter and process of writing

---

[1]The fact that it is more difficult to produce a criminal forgery than to make an imitation as a test of skill has an important bearing on certain so-called tests that are sometimes applied to those who undertake to distinguish a forged writing. It sometimes seems to be assumed that if any one can imitate any writing by anybody so that it cannot at once be recognized as an imitation then this proves that one who can not at once recognize it as an imitation is not qualified to testify on the subject. The unfair and unscientific character of such a test is apparent on its face. If a test is parallel to the main inquiry then it is right and proper; otherwise it is not.

If any one assumes to have such ability then by all means the test should be applied. As described in the chapter on standards of comparison there are those who through presumption or through ignorance will undertake to do what the most experienced and competent will not attempt.

makes it extremely difficult to write even one's own hand in a free and natural manner, and under such conditions to be required to imitate sucessfully the writing of another is a task of the very greatest difficulty.

Forgeries nearly always show plainly the natural results of such strained conditions; too much attention is given to unimportant details and a drawn, hesitating, and unnatural appearance is shown in the writing, even if it is a quite accurate copy of the main features of the genuine writing imitated[1]. It usually is not a good imitation of form characteristics and thus fails even in the elementary part of the process.

To forge a writing with entire success one must first be able to see, and then must have the muscular skill necessary to reproduce the significant characteristics of the writing of another and, at the same time, eliminate the characteristics of his own writing. The result usually shows failure in both directions because the forger does not determine, and is not able to determine, what the most significant characteristics are in the writing which is being imitated, and even less does he recognize and interpret the controlling characteristics of his own writing so that he may not unconsciously include them in the forgery. As we have seen, simulation in almost every case gives attention to the conspicuous features of form only and the many other elements entering into the task receive no attention whatever.

It is very much more difficult to simulate an unfamiliar movement than an unfamiliar form, and to copy unfamiliar forms and at the same time write freely in an

---

[1]Examples of movements in writing inconsistent with genuineness are shown in Figs. 53, 54. The illustrations show that these writings must have been produced in a halting, slow, drawing manner.

unusual manner is simply impossible. Writing, naturally unconscious and automatic, follows the fixed grooves
of habit, but as soon as attention is given to it it necessarily becomes strained and unnatural. Self-consciousness of a familiar act always tends to produce unnaturalness, and as fraudulent writing is inevitably written with
the attention fixed on the process of writing, this is one
of the main reasons why it is not well executed[1].

It is important that the writing process itself be examined with some care for the purpose of determining
what bearing it may have on the forger's undertaking.
Writing is the result of a very complicated series of acts,
being as a whole a combination of certain forms which
are the visible result of mental and muscular habits
acquired by long continued, painstaking effort. That
which is seen as writing is the end aimed at, but this is

---

[1]We note how, accordingly, the quality of a performance will vary
and take its tone from the mental conditions of its execution. Rivalry
excites our latent powers and sharpens the edge of our endeavors;
yet the very presence of a considerable stake may act to upset the
nicer poise of our exertions through over-anxiety. . . . There are
relatively few players who do quite as well at tournaments and at the
critical moments of play as upon less momentous occasions; and the
anxiety of the performer makes itself felt, and complexly, in the report of his own consciousness. Over-guidance by the higher centres
thus cripples the efficiency of the work of the lower. . . .

Walking, talking, writing, dressing, drawing, sewing, using a typewriter, playing upon a piano or violin, riding a bicycle, handling a
tool, a tennis racquet, or a golf club may all serve as illustrations of
the path of progress of such acquisitions, involving various and vari-
ously complex co-ordinations of mental, sensory, and motor factors.
In each case the several parts of the acquisition must be repeatedly
introduced to consciousness and held in the focus of attention, until
both senses and muscles appreciate their respective tasks. It will also
not escape observation that as the habit or accomplishment is acquired, the effort involved diminishes, the skill, that is, the nicety of
adjustment of impulse to the desired achievement, and the avoidance
of unnecessary or round-about exertion, increases, and facility becomes an expressing of the decreasing demand upon a directive attention. We can then do things well not only without half attending,
but also without half trying.—The Subconscious, by Joseph Jastrow,
Professor of Psychology, University of Wisconsin, pp. 28, 42. (1906.)

only the record of the more fundamental part of the process, which is a series of controlled movements growing out of the imitation of certain arbitrary forms. A written form is simply a record of a motion, and mature writing, by numberless repetitions, finally becomes what the psychologist calls an unconscious co-ordinated movement. We write as we repeat poetry "by heart," each part automatically suggesting that which is to follow. Many kinds of acquired skill become as automatic as walking or speech and are carried to the point where the operation not only requires no conscious direction but is actually almost beyond control of the mind and hand. Writing is a conspicuous example of such a habit and cannot be discarded or assumed at will[1].

The perfection of a forgery depends in a measure upon certain other conditions that it may be helpful to consider briefly. That writing is imitated with the greatest difficulty which is strong, smooth, free and rapid and that cannot be correctly reproduced by a slow, careful, copying movement, and, naturally, a hand that is slow and hesitating and that is itself produced by interrupted,

---

[1]Writing, which is essentially a co-ordinated movement, has to be developed through trial after trial, with consciousness directed, not upon the movement itself, but on the visual images which appear as results of the movement. What one is training is the movement; what one is thinking of is not movement at all, but visual images. When the movement becomes well enough trained so that one need not have any anxiety about its operating well, then attention is withdrawn in great measure from even the visual forms.

This automatic character of adult writing is one of its most interesting and significant characteristics. Because the habit is so thoroughly automatic, we do not recognize it in ordinary experience as a subject worthy of study. We come to think of it as we do of a hundred other automatic habits—as a natural endowment. Of course it is not a natural endowment. More than most of our highly developed habits, more than walking or talking, for example, writing has become automatic through individual practice.—Charles Hubbard Judd, Ph. D., Professor of Psychology, University of Chicago, in Genetic Psychology. Chapter VI., pp. 187, 188 (1903).

changing movement impulses is more easily imitated because its manner of production is similar to that of the imitating process. The perfection of a forgery also depends upon the amount of the writing involved and upon whether the nature of the document permits many attempts only the best of which it becomes necessary to bring forward.

Although the usual forgery is not a good piece of work it is well to know and to remember that there are adepts who can imitate certain classes of writing so well that no one can tell the imitation from the genuine, and certain kinds of awkward, unskillful signatures may be simulated so perfectly, even by those who are not adepts, that the fraudulent can not readily be distinguished from the genuine. Its importance seems to justify the repetition of the statement that not much weight should be given the opinion of one who pretends to be able to detect any forged or imitated writing, criminal or otherwise, produced by any writer, no matter how skillful, and under any conditions no matter how favorable to the operator.

A scientific study of writing must include consideration of all these mental and physical means by which it is produced and the evidences of the operations as shown in the writing itself. Thus the form of a letter is not simply an arbitrary outline, like an unfamiliar drawing, to be compared with a similar outline but, as already described, is the visible illustration of habits which are themselves to be studied and compared with the physical and mental habits in the writing brought forward for comparison.

Many of the important things to which attention

must be given have already been described in the preceding chapters, but it may be useful in this connection
briefly to review some of them and show their direct
application to a thorough handwriting comparison.

We have seen that the line or stroke itself shows the
speed and continuity of motion with which it is made,
the muscular skill employed in the operation, the relation of the pen to the surface of the paper, the nature
of the movement employed in making the stroke as
shown by its force and freedom, and the quality and
uniformity of the line as indicating continuity of motion
and uniformity of pressure of the writing instrument.
The edges of the stroke, the locations of the shadings in
relation to the line of writing, and particularly the tracks
of the nibs of the pen, show the angle of the writing
instrument to the strokes as made.   The design of the
letters themselves may point to the nationality of the
writer, to the system learned, to the date when the writing was acquired and to the influences that have surrounded the writer.   Here the value of historical knowledge of systems of writing becomes highly important,
and, as we have seen, there are many forms and styles
in writing that would be entirely inconsistent with
certain other forms and systems.

Considering these facts it will clearly appear how
superficial and unscientific is that examination of handwriting which gives attention only to conspicuous form
characteristics of letters, with no knowledge of their
history and no interpretation of their significance, and
it is evident how unreliable a conclusion may be if based
solely upon such comparison.   When all the varied elements are considered that enter into the process of writ-

ing it is seen how difficult, if not impossible, it is to imitate forms accurately and at the same time correctly exemplify all these other characteristics of a writing; and it becomes still more difficult for a forger, under the strain, fear, and anxiety surrounding the act, to assume all the writing characteristics of another and at the same time throw off all his own writing individuality. In most cases it cannot be done.

Evidence regarding handwriting may affect property, liberty, or even life, and prudence and justice demand that a final and definite conclusion on the subject should not be reached by witness, judge, referee or jury until the matter has been examined from all standpoints in a thorough and systematic manner; an offhand opinion on any such question of importance should never be given.

If it is feasible it is usually advisable that such an investigation should begin, not with an examination of the questioned writing itself, but by a careful study of the standard writing with which it is finally to be compared, and this study of the genuine writing should be made, if possible, before the questioned writing is seen by the examiner. The genuine writing should be gone over step by step, as outlined in the preceding chapters and in the condensed procedure at the conclusion of this chapter, and should be studied and, in some cases, tabulated, classified, averaged and measured, until the examiner actually begins to recognize, as it were, its complexion, features and characteristic individuality. It is also desirable in some cases that this preliminary examination of the genuine writing be made at two sittings with a few hours or a day intervening so that all the first steps may be carefully reviewed before any comparison is made with the disputed writing. This allows the mind after rest and attention to other matters to come back and renew acquaintance with that which at first was strange and unfamiliar.

The second stage of such an examination is the study of the questioned writing in the same manner as the genuine writing has been studied and, if the conditions permit, its careful tabulation and classification, and the third and final operation is an exhaustive comparison of the two writings. Too many times this order of examination as described is not only reversed on the first examination but almost all the time is unprofitably given to the questioned writing, and frequently, if not usually, an adequate amount of standard writing for comparison is not at first supplied.

The first test applied to a disputed writing by nearly every examiner is the test of general appearance or pictorial effect as compared with the genuine standard writing. This test is first because it is an almost uncontrollable operation of the mind and, unfortunately, many examiners go no further except to look for evidence to fortify a first impression. The danger of entire dependence upon this phase of writing has been pointed out in a previous chapter. It is true that there is in the combination of arbitrary characters, connected as written letters are connected, a certain proportion of parts, a particular average width of angle and turn by which letters are connected which, independent of designs of letters, give to writing a certain individual character as a whole.

It is this, in a measure, indefinable general appearance

or pictorial effect of writing, on which the bank clerk must mainly depend in paying checks, as it would be impossible under the circumstances to make a careful analysis and examination of all the characteristics of a writing at the paying teller's window. A careful and scientific examination of a handwriting always includes careful attention to this general appearance and analyzes and points out its features, but in arriving at a final conclusion does not by any means depend entirely upon it. As has been suggested the bare intuition, although often helpful and pointing the true way, is an unsafe guide, and, at the outset, should always be subordinated. At first glance a writing may seem to be genuine which upon careful analysis and examination is clearly seen to be a forgery, and again a writing may at first view look somewhat suspicious which will prove to be genuine when carefully examined.

Every questioned writing should also be examined with a view of determining whether by itself and without comparison with any writing it shows evidence of fraud as indicated by line quality, retouching, hesitation, pen lifts, interrupted movements, identity of forms with a model, or any evidences of unnatural, drawn writing.

A barefaced and bungling forgery may be detected at sight; the careful examiner, however, will not identify a writing as genuine at sight, nor give a final and positive opinion to that effect until he has examined it by good daylight; until he has examined it with the microscope under different magnifications by both direct and transmitted light; and, in some instances, no opinion should be given until enlarged transmitted light photographs of the writing have been made.

In submitting writings to an examiner for an opinion the procedure and order of presentation as outlined above should, if possible, be followed, and, if the questioned writing cannot be distinguished by other conditions than those in the writing itself, it is well to submit it to the examiner with the genuine writings without any information as to which document, paper or writing is suspected. In whatever way the question is presented no outside facts bearing on the question of genuineness should be given until after a definite opinion has been rendered.

In order that study and comparison of the two writings may include consideration of every feature, element and condition that may throw any light on the inquiry, the following detailed and numbered list of points for consideration is given. They do not all apply to every case, but if an examiner goes through the list the features of importance will receive attention.

General Features: (1) General appearance, or pictorial effect. (2) General style or system of writing; (a) old style round hand, (b) old Spencerian, (c) modern Spencerian, (d) foreign, (e) modern commercial, (f) angular, (g) new vertical, (h) telegraphers' hand, etc. (3) Slant; (a) of downward strokes, (b) upward strokes; average and exceptions tested by protractor. (4) Spacing of letters in words and words in sentences. (5) Size; of capitals, of small letters, uniformity of size. (6) Proportions of individual letters to each other, proportions of parts of the same word. (7) Pen lifts; general habits, before what letters and after what letters. (8) Connections of all letters with each other and of capitals with small letters. (9) Habitual, occasional and rare forms of all small letters tabulated. (10) Forms of all varieties of capitals tabulated in the same manner. (11) Forms of figures, punctuation marks, abbreviations, original characters or letters tabulated. (12) Individual or original form characteristics or idiosyncrasies. (13) Flourished, abbreviated or illiterate forms of letters and characters[1].

Movement or Manner of Writing: (14) Movement; Finger, Hand, Arm, or Combined, Free or Restricted. (15) Speed of writing as shown by line quality; (a) very slow, (b) slow, (c) medium, (d) rapid, (e) very rapid, (f) uniformity or consistency of speed. (16) Care and attention to the writing process; (a) utter abandon and carelessness, (b) normal average care, (c) delicate attention to every detail even to the end of unimportant strokes, (d) inconsistent attention. (17) Quality of line, its smoothness or roughness as a result of the manner of writing; on up strokes, on down strokes, on beginning and on finishing strokes. (18) Position of pen in hand and relation to paper as shown by location of shading and indentations on right or left of line. (19) Alignment or relation of parts of the whole line of writing, or the line of individual letters in words to base line, showing relation of arm to base line of writing. (20) Occasional letters high or low. (21) Movement impulse or motion beginning with or before beginning of stroke and continuing beyond or stopping with stroke as shown by blunt or sharp begin-

---

[1]Form characteristics are further discussed in the chapter on Anonymous and Disputed Letters and where applicable the procedure there outlined should also be carefully followed. Some of the directions regarding the examination of an alleged forgery of a whole document, given in the latter part of this chapter, also apply to some signature forgeries.

nings and ends of words. (22) Flourishes or extra strokes. (23) Abbreviations or deficient strokes.

Pen Pressure and Shading: (24) Shading; on all capitals, on all small letters, on figures. (25) Location of shading on letters; on main downward strokes, on lateral strokes, on diagonal strokes. (26) Line quality, smooth, rough, irregular. (27) Exact location of nib marks and maximum shades. (28) Pen strokes; heavy and strong or weak and light. (29) Tremor; of age, of illness, of weakness, of fraud. (30) Location, uniformity and extent of tremor. (31) Pen Pressure, delicate or heavy, uniform and consistent or varied and inconsistent. (32) Beginning of strokes with fine line or with pressure, ending stroke with fine line or with pressure or dead stop. (33) Marks of pen nibs; pressure uniform on both nibs, or heaviest on left or right nib. (34) Edges of Lines; clear cut or ragged; magnified indentations uniform on both edges; larger on left or on right. (35) Uniformity of Line, as affected by halting movement, stops or variations in speed showing whether letters are carefully drawn or freely written. (36) Final strokes; carefully drawn and finished, or free and unconscious. (37) Use of blotter; no blotting, immediate blotting or occasional blotting.

Special Features: (38) Erasures; by abrasion, by chemicals, by rubber. (39) Retouching; of light lines, shaded lines, of unimportant strokes. (40) Pen stops; at angles, at narrow turns, on curves at unnatural places, on first stroke, on last stroke. (41) "t" crossings and "i" dots; location, shape, direction and care. (42) Decreasing, increasing, irregular or uniform height of small letters in words. (43) Spacing or opening between capital letters, between words, between capital and first small letter of same word. (44) Relation of writing to ruled or imaginary base line, regular, irregular, all above the line, all on line, or all below. (45) Alignment or Inclination; all upwards continuously, each word upward, perfectly horizontal, each word downward, signature all downward, all in arc of circle, or zigzag up and down. (46) Indentation of paper shown on front or back, made by pen or by pencil. (47) Pencil marks under or in connection with pen marks.

Paper and Ink: (48) Surface of paper examined by transmitted light and by oblique lighting to observe disturbance of fiber, dulling of finish, or change of tint. (49) Folds across writing; before writing, after writing. (50) Ink, compared with that usually employed as to class, quality, condition, exact color examined by daylight in shaded portions, light portions, when blotted, when not blotted, tested and recorded by color microscope. (51) Color or tint at edges and extremity of strokes. (52) Age of writing as shown by condition of ink. (53) Uniformity of ink throughout writing. (54) Retouching indications examined by transmitted light to show presence of double or overlapping ink films; frequency and exact locations of retouched strokes.

Writing Instrument: (55) Kind and quality of pen used; fine, coarse, stiff, or elastic, old or new. (56) Fountain, stylographic, gold, steel, or quill pen. (57) Width of shaded and fine lines. (58) Pencil; ordinary or copying, hard or soft, sharp or blunt, light or heavy pressure, wet or dry pencil mark.

Reproduction of Document: A helpful operation in

an exhaustive preliminary examination of a questioned writing or document is its reproduction in as nearly as possible the exact manner in which it is claimed to have been produced and also in the manner in which it was probably produced. For this reproduction every physical circumstance, as far as possible, should be the same as surrounded the production of the document in question, pen, ink and paper should, if possible, be the same and every detail in a document of folding, endorsing, mailing, filing, copying, etc., should be repeated. If typewritten the same machine should be used and signatures should be affixed following as closely as possible the disputed or questioned paper. If a disguised or feigned hand has been employed the writing should be reproduced imitating in every way as nearly as possible the writing or pen-printing of the document in question. This careful reproduction of a questioned document or writing often leads to more accurate conclusions in some particulars than would otherwise be reached and in this way attention may be directed to important matters that might be overlooked.

Simulation of a Whole Document.

As the amount of forged writing is increased naturally the difficulty of forgery is greatly increased and some new difficulties arise that deserve consideration in this connection. Daring forgeries of this class are occasionally produced by operators who, as a rule, have no conception of the great difficulty of the undertaking. When looked at as a whole such documents may appear to be strikingly like the writing they were made to imitate and many are inclined to say offhand that they must be genuine because it is assumed that no one would undertake so difficult a task. The principal difficulty in examining such a paper is to look at one thing at a time instead of depending on the "general character" of the writing. A thorough examination of such a paper will sometimes show to a moral certainty that it can not be genuine.

A comparatively brief examination of the question will show that the successful forgery of a whole document is a task of extreme difficulty and requires intelligent attention to many particulars and details that do not enter into the task of fabricating only a signature. If such a document is of any considerable length it is almost certain to differ in many ways from the genuine writing of which it is an imitation.

On the question of writing habits such a paper must not only exemplify the ordinary and usual letter forms of the one whose writing is imitated, but it must also show the natural variation in design, proportions, size and spacing, that any considerable quantity of genuine writing always shows. It must also exemplify habits of pen position and movement and, what is the most difficult of all to attain, must in its various parts show that careless abandon, disregard of details and inattention to the writing process that is always one of the most forcible indications of genuineness. At the same time such a paper must show that evidence of continuity and consistency with itself that points to a continuous natural writing. If such a complete fraudulent document shows close conformity to design, outlines and variations of letters it will almost certainly show slow, painful movement and a painstaking attention to details which are inconsistent with free, honest writing, and, if it is written freely, it is almost certain to be defective in design and will not exemplify the significant form characteristics of the writing imitated. It is almost inevitable that a fraudulent document of any considerable length will show defects in both directions.

A complete document of this kind usually shows by mere inspection that it is not a free, natural writing, and as a rule such a writing is more defective in manner of production or movement than in designs of individual letters. As with a signature imitation the simulation of a movement or manner of writing is much more difficult than the copying of the outlines of letter or word forms, and, as in signature forgeries, the principal if not the only thought in the mind of the forger seems to be the thought of form. The process of forgery involving a brief signature, as we have seen, naturally induces a constrained, fixed and nervous attention to the process of writing, that is almost certain to show in the result, and this applies with greatly added force when a whole document is forged; letters are drawn, rather than written, and inequalities in strokes, interrupted movements, pen lifts, retouching and a general painstaking attention to details are almost certain to be the result of such an effort.

The conditions surrounding the production of a complete fraudulent document of this character are similar to those under which a disguised anonymous letter is written. The successful production of such a complete paper, however, is a task of much greater difficulty than the hiding of personality in an anonymous letter because the successful simulation of a complete document involves the double process of discarding the writer's own writing characteristics and at the same time the adoption of the characteristics of another.

At the very beginning of such an inquiry regarding a document in which all the writing is in question it is well to go over carefully the preliminary steps outlined in the preceding part of this chapter and also the parts of the chapter on anonymous letters relating to inconspicuous characteristics. Examination should, of course, be made of the general appearance of the whole paper, but much time is lost in such examinations and no definite result is reached by looking all the time at the questioned paper as a whole instead of examining in order and in detail its constituent parts. In some methods of examination of a document it seems to be expected that if one will only look at the whole thing intently enough and long enough that a message from somewhere will be flashed out, saying, "This is a forgery," or "This is a genuine writing."

The principal points to consider in the examination are: 1st. Normal form characteristics of every character as previously outlined. 2d. Variations in genuine forms under varying conditions in design, size, completeness, abbreviation. 3d. Arrangement of matter on page, including spacing between lines and words, margins at left, right, top and bottom. 4th. Continuity and consistency, abrupt and unnatural changes in size, slant, or rapidity of writing. 5th. Undue attention to unimportant details as shown by labored production of first and last strokes of words, careful and uniform "t" crossings, accurately placed "i" dots, carefully drawn flourishes, grace lines or any unnecessary strokes. 6th.

Pen lifts at unnatural places or in what should be free strokes, on curves and ovals, the careful joining of the ends of fine strokes at unusual places, unnatural stops in the middle of letters. 7th. Patching, repairing, retouching, and added shadings to letters first made without shading. 8th. Tremor on what should be free strokes, excessive tremor, inconsistent tremor, tremor on finishing strokes, omissions of natural tremor. 9th. Character of line or stroke; changing pressure producing bunches and unevenness especially on upward strokes, unevenness due to changed position of pen or pencil. Hesitating strokes made up of a combination of short, nearly straight, controlled movement impulses resulting from a copying or simulating process. 10th. Close similarity or exact identity in repeated words or combinations of letters, indicating that one model was used from which to imitate or trace several parts. 11th. Character, frequency and exact location of all shadings. 12th. Alignment of words and whole lines.

At some stage of an inquiry regarding the genuineness of a complete document attention should be given, as in an anonymous letter inquiry, to the general question of materials, including paper, pen, pencil, ink; also to composition, subject matter, style, idioms, grammar, spelling, use of capitals, punctuation, division of words, titles, use of numerals or words to express numbers, corrections, erasures, interlineations, abbreviations, folding, creases, worn portions of paper, machine cut, hand cut or torn edges of paper, size and shape of paper and water-marks.

It is very important that such a document be photographed with extreme care at several different degrees of enlargement. Exposure and development should be exactly timed so that the utmost detail is shown in the lines or strokes themselves. In some cases such photographs alone, if properly made, are sufficient to show the fraudulent character of a complete forged paper.

It should of course be understood that correct exemplification of these various characteristics as described is proof of genuineness, and that the process of examination and illustration is just the same for the proof of genuineness as for the proof of forgery. The scientific examiner starts with no presumption, and looks, not for facts to bolster up a preconceived theory, but for facts upon which to base a final conclusion.

Questioned Figures.

Other characters than script letters may be questioned and in such inquiries the same general procedure should be followed as has been outlined. The conventional forms of figures are modified in many different ways by different writers, and combinations of these modifications, as shown in a sufficient number of figures, will often point very conclusively to a particular writer. As with ordinary writing the significance and force of such characteristics increase in geometrical ratio so that the probability of exact coincidence in a combination of numerous peculiar characteristics by two different writers is very remote. If figures are few in number or conventional in form it may be impossible to determine their identity with any great degree of certainty.

In an inquiry as to the genuineness of figures or when it is desired to discover the actual writer of a series or group of figures the steps as outlined in a questioned

writing inquiry should be followed, but especial attention should be given to the following points: (1) Exact
form, (2) direction, form and size of beginnings and
endings of all figures, (3) size and proportion of figures
to each other and of parts of individual figures, (4)
slant of figures and of parts, (5) alignment of figures
to each other and to base line, and horizontal relation
of figures to each other in groups on unruled paper,
(6) shading and location of greatest and least pen pressure, (7) method of writing cents in amounts of money,
(8) manner of writing fractions, (9) method of writing
figures in dates, (10) use of numerals instead of words
in sentences.

In connection with the study of form of figures,
particular attention should be given to (a) shape of
beginning stroke or loop and the length, direction and
horizontal position of last stroke of figure 2, (b) shape
of beginning loop or stroke and proportion of upper
and lower parts and direction and length of last stroke
of figure 3, (c) comparative height of two upper parts
of figure 4 and also comparative slants of various parts
of this figure and the degree of elevation of horizontal
stroke above base line of writing, (d) length, connection
or disconnection, and angle to base line of upper horizontal stroke of figure 5 and looped, pointed or obtuse
connection of strokes at center of figure, and direction
of last stroke, (e) degree of curvature and height of
first stroke of figure 6 and size and width of opening of
concluding portion, (f) beginning impulse upward or
downward, compound curve or straight top of figure 7,
also length of top compared with length of figure,
straightness or curvature of downward stroke and pro-

portion of whole figure to portion extending below the line, (g) figure 8 made like capital S or in opposite direction, proportion of upper and lower parts, length and curvature of beginning stroke and of concluding stroke, (h) proportions of width to length and direction of beginning stroke of "a" form at top of figure 9, closed or open top, length and curvature or straightness of concluding stroke and degree of extension below base line, (i) size of naught in proportion to figures, circular or elliptical form, open or closed top, finished with loop, with acute angle connection or with stroke back to left at top or to the right.

Comparison of Writings.

A general discussion of the question of "giving the grounds of belief" in connection with testimony regarding documents is included in a later chapter dealing with several questions regarding a handwriting case in court, but it seems appropriate to consider the question briefly at this place in connection with the subject of comparison.

In the investigation of any questioned handwriting the final and important part of the process is that of comparison, and this is not the simple operation that at first it may appear to be. As the psychologists put it, likeness and difference co-exist in things not utterly unlike, so that comparison for the purpose of classification, must include analysis and reasoning[1]. The like-

---

[1] We go through the world, carrying on the two functions abreast, discovering differences in the like, and likenesses in the different. To abstract the ground of either difference or likeness (where it is not ultimate) demands an analysis of the given objects into their parts. So that all that was said of the dependence of analysis upon a preliminary separate acquaintance with the character to be abstracted,

ness may be general and simply indicate the class or genus, or the difference may be merely superficial that does not differentiate. Two American writings are strikingly alike when compared with Arabic or Chinese writing but the two American writings may be fundamentally different if compared to see if they had a common origin.

This matter of analysis and reasoning assumes special importance in connection with arguments in favor of certain restrictions of expert testimony when it is asked that the ruling be made that, "The witness be allowed to point out the similarities or dissimilarities but make no comment thereon." Such procedure tends to put all testimony, good and bad, on one dead level and suppresses the vital element in comparison which is rational interpretation of likenesses and differences[1]. The sensible discussion of this subject by Professor Wigmore

---

and upon its having varied concomitants, finds a place in the psychology of resemblance as well as in that of difference.

The perception of likeness is practically very much bound up with that of difference. That is to say, the only differences we note as differences, and estimate quantitatively, and arrange along a scale, are those comparatively limited differences which we find between members of a common genus.

The same things, then, which arouse the perception of difference usually arouse that of resemblance also. And the analysis of them, so as to define wherein the difference and wherein the resemblance respectively consists, is called comparison.—Principles of Psychology, William James, 1890; Vol. 1, pp. 528, 529.

[1]Mr. Justice Ward, of the United States Circuit Court, in the case of Newcomb vs. Burbank, tried in New York City, October, 1908, discussed the same question as follows:

"The second class of witnesses are the experts, and my own judgment is that their testimony is extremely important. The ordinary man cannot tell in looking at documents whether they are genuine or not genuine with anything like the degree of skill of an expert who is trained in this business to detect the characteristics of a writer. I do not think that the witnesses, the experts on one side or the other differ very much about the process. It is a question of reasoning altogether. . . . Now, you have got to give weight to these experts in proportion as you think the reasons they give for their opinions are good reasons or bad reasons."

deserves special emphasis. He says: "On the direct examination, the witness may and, if required must point out his grounds for belief in the identity of the handwriting, on the principle already considered. Without such re-enforcement of testimony the opinion of experts would usually involve little more than a counting of the numbers on either side."—Wigmore on Evidence, Vol. III., Sec. 2014 (1904).

As we have already seen in a previous chapter, to reach the conclusion that two writings are by the same hand we must find present class characteristics and individual characteristics in sufficient quantity to exclude the theory of accidental coincidence; to reach the conclusion that writings are by different hands we may find likeness in class characteristics and divergence in individual characteristics or divergence in both, and the divergence must be something more than mere superficial or accidental difference.

Some of the old discussions of this subject contain utterly fallacious arguments to the effect that similarities and differences have equal weight, which would amount to saying that an individual is proved to be a certain person if certain *similarities* could be shown without regard to certain existing fundamental differences. Such an argument is, of course, absurd. A handwriting is identified exactly as a person is identified by a comparison of general characteristics that, in the case of a person, point to a general class or race, and *in addition* the identification must include that which is not general but distinctly individual and personal, as, for example, in a person scars, deformities, finger prints, or a series of accurate measurements.

The study of identity and difference, then, or what may be called scientific comparison, is observation combined with reasoning. It is not enough simply to see with bodily eyes, but it is necessary also to understand and show the real significance of the thing seen. As Twistleton well says[1]: "The case is very different in the comparison of documents presented to the eyes of those who are to judge respecting them. Here they know both the terms of the comparison. Ultimately, their conclusions need not rest upon authority at all. One skilled in handwriting may point out coincidences in documents which a volunteer would not have observed, if the documents had been in his possession during a long series of years; but those coincidences are outward objective facts, the common property of experts and of volunteers. If the expert has skill in analyzing his own impressions, he can go through the proofs of everything which he asserts and can make others see what he sees. If he makes a mistake, his error admits of proof. Hence the case with which he deals, however complicated, becomes merely one of reasoning, in which internal circumstantial evidence is applied to demonstrate a disputed fact."

Illustrations of Simulated Forgeries.

Nearly all the preceding chapters of this book, it will readily be seen, are really introductory to the present chapter on simulated forgeries and the two following chapters on traced forgeries and anonymous letters. Naturally the questions discussed in these three chapters

---

[1] Handwriting of Junius, by Charles Chabot and Hon. Edward Twistleton, John Murray, London, 1871. With two hundred pages of text and two hundred and sixty-seven pages of fac-similes.

should be studied in connection with the illustrations and all of the discussions on the preceding pages.

A large proportion of the photographs desirable for the adequate illustration of these various questions are of large size, ranging in most cases from 8 by 10 to 11 by 14 inches. They must be made so as to show the utmost detail of every part, and it is impracticable to illustrate the various questions in the most effective manner on the small pages of this book by any available process. The accompanying illustrations in this and other chapters only suggest what is possible when space and method are not restricted.

Fig. 107 illustrates the extreme difficulty of imitating an unfamiliar style of writing. The two genuine signatures, the first and third, were the two signatures nearest in date to the disputed signature.

The middle signature of Fig. 108 is an alleged signature of a man who at the date of the disputed writing had great difficulty in writing as the two genuine signatures nearest in date clearly indicate. The disputed signature shows many divergencies, among others that of pen position which is shown by the shading. In hesitation, changing pen pressure and delicate tremor, extending to its very extremity, the disputed signature shows every characteristic of a drawing movement. A part of this signature is illustrated in the chapter on movement in Fig. 58.

The first signature in Fig. 109 is a typical example of suspicious line quality. The second signature is the nearest in point of time after the date of the disputed signature and shows the freedom and force which are always characteristic of genuineness. The disputed signature was probably produced by a combination of the copying and tracing processes and a brief examination even of the small half-tone cut will disclose the basis for the emphatic finding of the court that: "A mere inspection of this signature will satisfy the most careless observer that it needs an explanation and when the signature is analyzed and the proper tests applied this explanation becomes imperative." In an able decision, Matter of Burtis, 43 (N. Y.) Miscellaneous Reports, the court decided the signature to be a forgery.

Figs. 110 and 111 are illustrations of the cumulative force of repeated examples of similar minor divergencies. These illustrations, like Fig. 56, show the extreme difficulty of simulating a whole document with the natural variation of genuine writing.

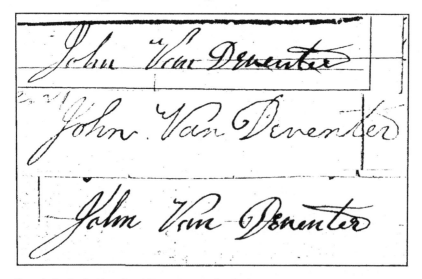

Fig. 107—Imitation (middle signature) of the old Round Hand writing. Observe divergence in shading, angularity and spacing, and also in curvature of capital J. Part of the signature showed a very suspicious pencil underwriting. Matter of Van Deventer Estate, Penn Yan, N. Y. Part of this disputed signature is shown in Fig. 59.

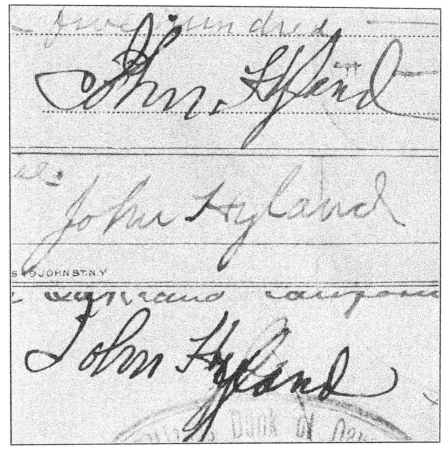

F_{IG}. 108—Two genuine signatures and a disputed signature in the Matter of the John Hyland Estate, Dansville, N. Y.

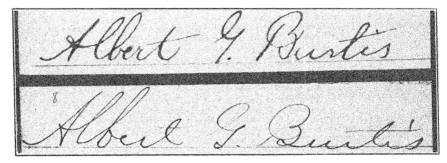

F_{IG}. 109—Disputed and genuine signatures in Matter of Burtis, Auburn, N. Y.

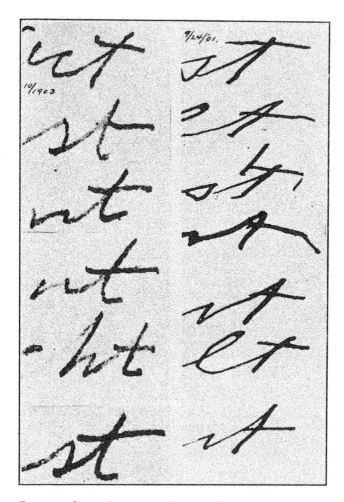

Fig. 110—Concluding letters from words in a disputed document on the left and a genuine letter on the right taken
in order as they appear. Observe differences in
design, slant, position, variation, and care.
From exhibit in case of W. D. Parr
vs. Executors of D. G. Parr Estate, Louisville, Ky., (1908).

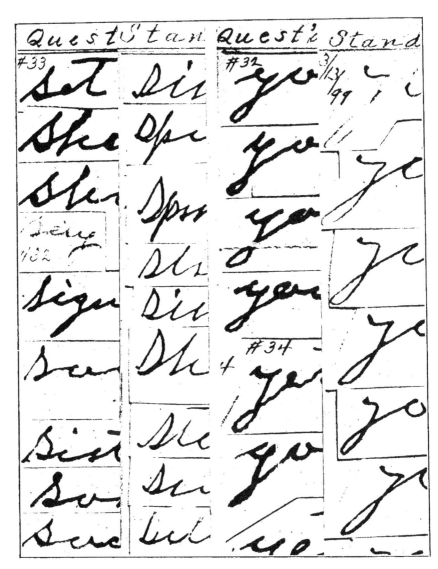

Fig. 111—Disputed and standard initial letters juxtaposed to illustrate the cumulative force of repeated slight divergence. Observe curvature in down stroke of s and beginning and shape of y. From exhibit in case of Newcomb vs. Burbank (1909), New York City.

CHAPTER XVI.

A traced forgery is the result of an attempt to transfer to a fraudulent document an exact fac-simile of a genuine writing by some tracing process. A forged writing of this kind is usually a poor piece of work and of the various classes of forgery is one of the easiest to detect. The selection of the tracing method seems to be a confession by the operator that he does not possess the skill necessary to write an imitation and employs this process only as a makeshift. As we have seen, a simulated forgery is an imitation of the general features of a genuine writing but does not aim to be an exact duplicate in size and proportions, while a traced forgery is intended to reproduce not only the form but also the size, proportions and relations of all parts of the original, the exact detail of each line, stroke, and dot being followed as closely as the method employed and the skill of the operator will permit[1].

No positive line of distinction that will apply in all cases can be drawn between these two classes of forgery. Many of the defects of simulated writing are the same as those in traced writing, and a tracing, through lack of skill or care, may diverge more from the model than

---

[1] In numerous ways the method of procedure is the same in the examination of alleged traced forgeries, of alleged simulated forgeries, and of anonymous letters. It has seemed best to treat the three subjects separately, but the three chapters should all be consulted in connection with the investigation of any one of the three subjects.

a skillful freehand simulation. The only positive evidence that a writing is a tracing is the discovery of the actual model from which it was made, or the discovery of two or more identical companion forgeries which could only have been made from one original. Numerous divergencies in form are evidence that a disputed writing was not produced by the tracing process.

Traced forgeries usually show hesitation, abnormal changes of direction, inconsistent pen pressure and unnatural movement interruptions in a more pronounced manner than simulated forgeries, but this again depends upon the specific process employed and the skill of the operator. It is natural that the model from which a traced forgery was actually made should not be discovered, and the true character of such a disputed signature must ordinarily be determined by an examination of the signature itself and by a comparison of it with genuine signatures. Strange as it may seem, however, in many important cases the model writing is actually put in the case to prove the forged writing to be genuine by means of it. The reason for such strange action seems to be the thought that a genuine writing so like the disputed signature will undoubtedly prove the disputed signature to be genuine. Traced forgeries are often passed as genuine by those who depend alone on form or, as it is vaguely described, on the "general character" of the writing. It is reasonable to suppose that in a tracing the outlines of the letters will conform quite closely to the particular genuine writing imitated and it is also evident that the spurious character of the writing must be mainly determined by other than divergence in form characteristics.

A traced forgery will probably be defective in one or more of the following named particulars: 1, Natural movement, freedom and speed of writing. 2, Quality of line or stroke. 3, Pen lifts, retouching and shading. 4, Selection and date of model writing. 5, Pencil outlines or indentations pointing to a tracing process. 6, Identity of the writing with a genuine model or identity of two or more disputed writings.

A brief examination of the tracing process will show that it is impossible by this method to produce a writing with a natural writing movement. If an accurate imitation of a writing could thus be executed no one could detect it as not genuine because it would be practically the writing imitated. A successful forgery, however, must reproduce not only the form—which is the only imitation usually attempted—but also in some reasonable degree must follow the style of movement employed, the speed, pen position, pen pressure, and other characteristic habits of the writer whose writing is being imitated, and on some of these vital points the traced forgery is almost certain to fail; in short, natural, free, unconscious writing cannot be produced by the tracing process[1]. It is very difficult if not impossible to trace

---

[1] In forgeries perpetrated by the aid of tracing, the internal evidence is more or less conclusive according to the skill of the forger. In the perpetration of a forgery the mind, instead of being occupied in the usual function of supplying matter to be recorded, devotes its special attention to the superintendence of the hand, directing its movements, so that the hand no longer glides naturally and automatically over the paper, but moves slowly with a halting, vacillating motion, as the eye passes to and from the copy to the pen, moving under the specific control of the will. Evidence of such a forgery is manifest in the formal, broken, nervous lines, the uneven flow of the ink, and the often retouched lines and shades. These evidences are unmistakable when studied with the aid of the microscope.—Criminal Investigation, by Dr. Hans Gross, (Berlin) Trans. by J. and J. C. Adam, p. 246 (1906).

even one's own signature and produce a good result for the reason that the method itself necessarily interferes with the natural writing movement. In tracing a genuine writing which contains numerous free and smooth strokes there undoubtedly will be shown in the result a hesitation inconsistent with genuineness; and a tracing by a strong hand of a very weak and decrepit original will undoubtedly be inconsistent with it in many ways.

The line quality of a traced forgery, the second point to be considered, is almost certain to be defective. A fraudulent tracing may conform with great accuracy to the particular model from which it was made but usually its unnatural line quality alone (see Figs. 53, 54) is sufficient to mark it as not genuine. In many cases this conclusion can even be reached without comparison with any genuine writing whatever and simply from a study of the questioned writing itself, especially when shown in an enlarged photograph. The question of line quality and movement as affected by an unnatural method of writing is discussed more at length in preceding chapters devoted to these questions to which reference is made.

Under the third division of probable defects in traced forgeries, or that of pen lifts, retouching and defective shading, it is necessary to discuss somewhat at length certain important phases of the subject relating not only to traced forgeries but to simulated forgeries as well. Experience shows that by whatever method a fraudulent writing is produced it is not as a rule entirely satisfactory in every particular as first written, and effort is made to improve it by patching and strengthening various parts. The nervous anxiety to do the work well and the unnatural concentration of the mind on the act of tracing a criminal forgery seem to make it almost impossible to let the fraudulent thing alone after it is once written. The tracing process necessarily gives attention almost exclusively to the form, and often shows conspicuous hesitation and tremulousness in the finer lines and may entirely omit strong, characteristic shadings which are afterwards carefully added. Pen lifts may be covered up, wavering lines strengthened, gaps filled in, unimportant strokes extended, and even flourishes carefully added to a signature which as first written may have been good enough to pass as genuine.

It may be very difficult to show the fraudulent character of a small amount of pencil writing produced by the tracing process if the tracing was skillfully made and was not afterwards retouched. This is true for the reason that pencil writing does not show line quality, hesitation, pen lifts and disconnections as clearly as pen writing. Experience shows, however, that fraudulent pencil writing is usually retouched and overwritten in such a suspicious manner that its true character may thus be conclusively shown. The ease with which such corrections are made in pencil writing seems to create the temptation to do too much. Comparatively few important disputed documents are pencil-written, however, for the reason that such a writing is suspicious in itself and calls for an adequate explanation.

For various reasons genuine writing is sometimes retouched, and with a few writers retouching is a peculiar habit, and thus it becomes necessary to distinguish that which is genuine from that which is fraudulent. Natural retouching is usually done for the perfectly evident purpose of correcting a palpable defect or supplying a part necessary to the form and legibility; such retouching is usually perfectly apparent and is made with one or two free, bold strokes. Fraudulent retouching, however, is more delicately and carefully done and often shows the evident intention of concealing the operation, and it may be the result of many delicate touches of the pen to the paper at different points. This condition in a writing, to say the least, is very suspicious and must be interpreted in a different manner from the plain open correction or remaking of a stroke where the ink was exhausted and the pen failed to write, or where it is perfectly evident that a part or the whole of a wrong letter was first made and the correct letter or stroke was afterwards made over it[1].

The location of the retouching on a writing is a matter that should always be carefully considered and may indicate its suspicious character; the attempt to improve unimportant parts is always suspicious but particularly so if such parts are not necessary to the legibility. The

---

[1]Ink will sometimes flow back on a stroke from a shaded to an unshaded portion, giving the appearance of two ink films, the lower one apparently much lighter than the upper and the stroke showing a distinct contrast where the two parts come together. The inexperienced may conclude that this phenomenon shows a retouching of the writing. The condition as described is most frequently shown at the tops of strokes where a lighter film of ink apparently extends out beyond the main heavy stroke. Logwood ink that has slightly gelatinized and some kinds of thin ink will show this peculiar characteristic. Such a flowing back of ink on a stroke will not be mistaken for a retouching if carefully examined. The ink flows back because attracted by the still damp but unshaded line immediately preceding the heavier deposit of ink and always covers the exact width of the lighter line, showing a smoothness and uniformity of distribution that distinguishes it from a retouching. A natural flow-back also appears in connection with a shading or heavier deposit of ink immediately following a lighter line, and never in the middle of a stroke. A retouching may appear anywhere and almost certainly will show under proper magnification certain ragged irregularities or violent contrasts that are unmistakable.

last stroke of the signature and the last stroke of each of the separated parts of the signature should be examined with special care. A retouching of an unimportant final stroke, an unnecessary flourish or a "t" crossing is sometimes very strong evidence of fraud. Retouched writing may sometimes show apparent shadings even on upward strokes (see Fig. 54) where such shading would be impossible in natural, genuine writing.

Another thing to be considered in making an examination of retouched writing is the fact that if ordinary fluid ink were used such retouching may be much more apparent after a lapse of time than when first made. By reason of the darkening of the ink, retouching may eventually become so perfectly apparent that it may seem unreasonable that it would have been made in the first place, but it should be remembered that with the strokes of the color and strength as shown when first made such changes could not then have been seen by ordinary observation. If, as sometimes occurs, the retouching is actually done with ink different in kind but similar in color to the ink of the first writing, but which changes and grows black by age while the original writing does not change, then such changes are, as they finally appear, still more suspicious because this condition would indicate that at some time after a first writing was originally written an effort was made to improve and perfect it.

Suspicious pen lifts or disconnections should always be looked for in a writing that may have been produced by either the simulating or tracing method. The necessity of looking at the copy in a simulated writing or of clearly seeing the dim outline in a traced forgery may make it necessary to take off the pen. This may be done at any point and not where the pen would naturally be raised. It is particularly important that broken lines of this character should be looked for in a suspected pencil writing, and any forgery may show stops and disconnections where they should not appear[1].

The fourth defect possible in a traced forgery, as outlined above, is in the choice of a model. Many writers are not aware of the fact that even a few years, especially with those of advanced age, may make a great change in a handwriting and one who sets about making a tracing may select a model writing of the wrong date. It is often assumed that any genuine writing is good enough and a model may be taken that was written twenty years or more before or after the date of the questioned writing. In every case of this kind a chronological study should be made of the standard writing, any changes should be carefully noted and their application to the investigation in hand carefully considered.

The fifth possible defect in a traced forgery is any condition in the alleged traced writing or the alleged model that points to the tracing process. The model or the tracing, when clean and fresh as first brought forward, may show indentations resulting from the making of an outline with a sharp instrument of some kind; the tracing may show suspicious remains of a pencil outline, or the ink of the suspected writing may be rubbed or worn away by the erasure of a previously made pencil

[1]Retouched writing and pen lifts should be examined under different degrees of magnification by both direct and transmitted light and should be accurately photographed in enlarged form. Transmitted light photographs enlarged from two to four diameters or direct light photographs enlarged from three to ten diameters, as the conditions require, will usually show retouching so plainly that it cannot be denied.

or carbon outline. The possible existence of conditions of this kind shows the importance of an early and thorough examination of such a writing by a competent examiner before it is handled, soiled or experimented with in such a way as permanently to impair its evidential value in these particulars. In the case of Day vs. Cole, referred to in a footnote and illustrated on a following page, an indentation on the model writing had a very important bearing on the investigation. In the Boyer case (Fig. 51) parts of the ink strokes had been carried away in erasing the pencil outline.

The sixth possible basis of attack upon a traced forgery, and perhaps the most important of all, is its identity with a model present in the case, or the suspicious similarity of two or more questioned signatures. The underlying principle upon which identity is considered an indication of forgery is that a large number of rare events will not all accidentally coincide and if they are actually combined then such result must be due to design and not to accident[1]. In an argument of counsel in an important case, a picturesque illustration of the

---

[1]The courts have spoken but few times on the subject of identity as proof of forgery and it is interesting to examine a few brief excerpts. One of the latest utterances is in the celebrated Rice-Patrick will case, New York City (Matter of Rice, 81 Appellate Division, (N. Y.) 223, 1903, in which the Honorable Surrogate, the Appellate Division and the New York Court of Appeals were unanimous in the finding of forgery. Whatever the merits of Patrick's appeal on the murder charge these courts all practically convicted him of forgery by declaring his will was not genuine. The Appellate court in this case said:

"Upon a critical examination óf these four signatures it will be found that they correspond almost exactly,—a coincidence which could not possibly happen in the case of four genuine signatures of a person upward of eighty years of age. . . In other words, each signature will, when superimposed, show a similarity which does not appear in the concededly genuine signatures introduced in evidence, and which, from the very nature of things, could not occur. This fact taken in connection with the other evidence bearing upon the subject, is of such a character as to irresistibly lead to the conclusion that had the

principle was given as follows: "It has been said that
if a person meet in a waste place three trees growing in
a row, he thinks they were so planted by man; should
he find the distances equal, he is convinced. Such accidental situation of thirty trees would not exceed in
strangeness a coincidence like the one in this case."[2]

A brief examination of the writing process clearly
shows that every time even one short name is written
there is possibility of slight divergence and variation in
every direction of every part of every stroke in size,
position, proportions and relations of all parts, and a few
simple experiments will demonstrate how impossible it

testimony which was stricken out remained in, the Surrogate's conclusion would have been the same. . ."

In Matter of Burtis, 43 Misc. (N. Y.) Reports, 437, (1904), the
Court says:

"I refer to the physical evidence furnished by the disputed signature itself. A mere inspection of this signature will satisfy the most
careless observer that it needs an explanation, and when the signature
is analyzed and the proper tests applied this explanation becomes imperative. . . True, there are slight departures occasionally from the
model but these variations are only in the detail of certain lines—the
whole of the disputed signature being structurally the same as the
other and occupying the same physical field. Indeed it may fairly be
said that these very departures tend to indicate the process which
has produced the signature, for it will be noticed that after each
departure, the line of the disputed signature immediately returns to
the line of the model,—showing conclusively, as I think, that there
was a model which was steadily operating as a guide to the writer's
hand. This coincidence of a disputed signature with a genuine one
when superimposed against the light has long been held by the courts
to be proof of simulation."

The learned Surrogate in Matter of Koch, 33 (N. Y.) Misc. Reports, 153, (1900) N. Y., says: "There is not the slightest deviation
except such as might and naturally would occur if both signatures
were tracings from the same standard.

The opinion in Hunt vs. Lawless, 7 Abbott's New Cases, 113 (1879),
puts the matter as follows: "Where two or more supposed signatures
are found to be counterparts I think the simulation is detected by
that circumstance. Genuine signatures will not lap with perfect similarity over one another. . . But a close examination shows that

[2]From an argument by T. M. Stetson, Esq., counsel for Respondents
in Robinson vs. Mandell (Sylvia Ann Howland Case), New Bedford,
Mass., 1867.

is to write two signatures precisely alike so that the path of the pen throughout is exactly identical in both cases. A line, as we have learned, is the path of a moving point, and exact repetition would require that at the second writing the pen should exactly hit a thousand or more selected but invisible points. The degree of similarity in writing will naturally depend upon the skill of the writer, the length of the signature, the number of detached parts it contains, the width of the strokes and some other possible conditions. By comparing a great

the signature of Exhibit 9 is identical with that to the above named receipt and with those to Schedules A and B. It would require a vast amount of credulity to suppose that those four signatures can all be genuine and yet all of them lap over another so that the whole are identical. One of them is probably genuine, the others traced; or, perhaps all four are traced. . . Did ever any man sign his name four times with such invariable uniformity? All experience testifies to the absurdity of the supposition that he did."

In the case of Day vs. Cole, 65 Mich. 129 (1887), the question is discussed as follows: "I am satisfied the signature is a forgery. All the facts seem to point in that direction; but the one thing that fastens conviction upon my mind above all others is this: These two signatures are too evenly alike to be both genuine. . . Such a perfect coincidence as in the case of these two signatures in this cause is at least highly improbable, and but barely possible, if attainable at all.

"There is in my mind but one explanation of this remarkable and striking similarity; and that is that, while Exhibit 128 was in the hands of Cole, this signature to the assignment was copied and manufactured therefrom by some one. And I am satisfied it was done by tracing and outlining so that virtually, with some slight inaccuracies, the signature upon 128 was transferred to the assignment. There is too much method shown in the latter signature, and this method has exposed, to my mind, that it is not the genuine signature of a business man, like Gardner, writing in a hurry, and without thought of the manner of making or the form of such signature, but the cunning imitation of a forger, whose cunning has yet been the means of detecting the forgery."

In the case of Fox vs. McDonogh's Succession, 18 La. 448 (1866), the opinion of the court says: "The remarkable and almost exact sameness of the size, form and position of each letter, line and flourish or dash in the space occupied by the signature to the propounded codicil; and that to the lease of November 1st, 1846, obtained from Fernandez, renders it not only possible, but probable, that the former was traced from the latter."

The editor of Abbott's Trial Brief, Second Edition, p. 400, in speaking of identity as proof of forgery says: "It seems that such proof is conclusive and would require instruction to the jury to that effect."

number of signatures of a free, skillful and uniform writer, there can be found some closely resembling each other, but even with such an exceptional writer exact identity is extremely improbable.

In the famous Howland case, illustrated herewith, Professor Benjamin Pierce, the celebrated mathematician of Harvard University, testified that the probability of identical coincidence of all the thirty downward strokes of the long "Sylvia Ann Howland" signature with the same strokes of a second signature must be represented by the fraction with one for a numerator and the thirtieth power of five for a denominator[1]. Exact coincidence in writing is enormously more improbable than it is generally thought to be. This phase of the subject of traced forgeries is governed by the same principles that were discussed in the chapter treat-

---

[1]This case has been incorrectly reported in nearly every reference to it in the decisions, the text-books and magazine articles even up to the year 1909. In the first place the thirtieth power of five is not as reported 2,666 followed by eighteen ciphers but is 931 followed by eighteen figures, or upwards of nine hundred and thirty-one quintillions (931,000,000,000,000,000,000). The difference in the numbers makes no practical difference, as the least is entirely beyond human comprehension. This strange error is in the original report of the case and has been repeated from that time. No doubt some change was made in the basis of the calculation without making the resulting change in the result.

Another error that has been repeated many times is the statement that Professor Pierce testified that "No two signatures will be identical, etc.," but his testimony applied only to the signatures "No. 1" and "No. 10" in this particular case. The magazine article, 4 American Law Review, printed shortly after the trial, is full of errors and apparently reflected the views of a partisan in the case. The testimony in full and a most interesting and valuable verbatim report of the arguments of counsel in the case and also photographs of the writings are on file at the Public Library at New Bedford, Mass.

This famous case was finally decided on a point of law and the facts were never passed upon by court and jury. Considerable interest is added to the case by a knowledge of the fact that the claimant, "Hetty Robinson," afterwards married a Mr. Green, of New York, and has been known for many years, especially to the financial world, as "Hetty Green," of New York city.

ing of mathematical calculation applied to writing.

Although, as has been said, it is not necessary that a model writing or an identical companion forgery be found in every instance in order to show that a traced writing is undoubtedly spurious, the finding of such a model, showing marked and significant identities, or the discovery of two or more questioned signatures that resemble each other in a suspicious manner and at the same time bear in themselves the inherent evidences of fraud which writing shows when produced by a tracing method, affords the strongest kind of additional proof that the writing is a forgery. Close similarity of a suspected signature to a possible model in design, size, proportions and position is always a suspicious circumstance especially if the resemblance is very close, like a rubber stamp impression, or includes and reproduces accidental or unusual features in the model signature. Under these last named conditions the identity alone may be very strong evidence of forgery.

A fact that should always be considered in such an inquiry is that even a traced forgery will not be a mathematically exact reproduction of the model from which it is made. Even if the forger has the rare skill required to draw such a copy the natural tendency seems to be to attempt to improve the model more or less, which obviously would lead to divergence; and, in some rare instances, divergence in size or position is undoubtedly intentional. Ordinary unshaded pen marks are only from about one-fiftieth to one-two hundredth of an inch in width and under usual conditions it would be physically impossible to reproduce with absolute accuracy all these fine lines of a signature by the tracing process.

These divergencies are due to various causes, among which are nervous strain induced by a realization of the criminal act being performed and the intense desire to do it well, lack of muscular skill, and especially inability to see clearly the line of the model which is being followed, particularly if the tracing is being made by one operation direct from the model by following the lines as seen through the paper[1].

The tracing will also be likely to differ slightly from the model because of the almost uncontrollable tendency in imitating writing by any process, to incorporate even in a tracing some of one's own writing habits. Slight divergence may be due to the fact that the paper on which a forged writing is being traced was accidentally moved during the process, especially in case the signature is made up of several detached names or parts. A tracing may also differ slightly from the model because the traced lines of the copy may not quite reach the ends of strokes of the model or may go slightly beyond the extremities of the dim outlines which are being followed as seen through the paper.

Divergence from the model in a traced forgery as in a simulated forgery also tends to make the letters more formal and perfect in shape than the genuine writing

---

[1] When alleged forgeries are associated with a genuine signature from which they may have been traced, comparisons by transmitted light as to design, size, position, and proportions should properly be made of the alleged forgeries and the model with the tracing over the model as it was made if it is a tracing. Such forgeries may diverge more from each other than any one of the number differs from the model, for the reason that divergencies may be in opposite directions in different tracings. When the model is not found, therefore, a close resemblance in size, proportions and design in alleged forgeries that form a similar group is especially significant, as allowance must be made for divergencies from the original which may apparently make the imitations differ more from each other than any one would differ from the original.

imitated, and such writing, as in a simulated forgery, invariably lacks that appearance of carelessness and unconscious freedom which is always one of the strongest evidences of genuineness. Where a tracing diverges from the model in design of letters it will naturally tend to conform to the style of the operator so that the divergencies may in a very slight degree tend to identify the one who makes the tracing as belonging to a certain class of writers, although such resemblance is not often of much force as pointing to an individual.

A careful consideration of the process required to produce a traced forgery will show that divergencies of a certain character may actually point to the process of tracing. If in the tracing the general line of direction of each stroke is closely followed, with occasional slight departures in either direction which, however, are constantly corrected and do not affect all subsequent parts, such zigzag movements, beginning at the same place as the copy and coming out in the end at practically the same place, suggest that a model was being followed, and naturally this suggestion is still stronger if there are three or four such signatures in a group. A traced forgery may thus resemble the track of one attempting to follow an indistinct trail where the track of the one following may slightly diverge from time to time, but if it regularly returns to the original line of direction it shows that a track is being followed.

The most significant points of identity are the distinct beginning points of separated parts of the signature, the downward or shaded lines and especially the exact reproduction of unusual features in the model signature. As already suggested such a tracing may actually reproduce with the utmost care and fidelity a peculiarity of a letter or part of a model signature which can only be found in the model and the tracing. It is easily understood how such careful reproduction in a disputed signature of what may have been merely an accidental slip of the pen in the model is very convincing evidence of forgery[1].

As has been said, no two genuine signatures can be exactly alike, but such a statement should be understood to be true speaking microscopically, and not as the carpenter measures, because by examining a great number of genuine signatures of certain exceptional writers signatures can be found which are nearly identical. The degree of resemblance to be expected in any case is not based on any fixed principles but is a matter that depends altogether upon the writing habits of the one whose signature is in question. Some persons write with much greater uniformity than others, and similarities in such writing, in size and proportions, would, as a natural result, be more common than the same similarities in the writing of one who writes an erratic hand; the significance of identity, therefore, as bearing on the question of genuineness should be determined in every case by the actual circumstances of that case.

---

[1] Identity of position of an alleged forgery and a model, or between two or more alleged forgeries in relation to the edges of a document may be exceedingly forcible evidence of tracing. If the signatures in question are written on printed blank forms of exactly the same size, and it is found by placing the papers together with edges even that the signatures not only match in size and shape but also that they occupy exactly the same field on the document, this suggests at once that the forgery was traced from a model found on a similar form by placing one exactly over the other, and such identity of position is a very conclusive confirmation of other evidences of forgery. This relation of signature to the edges of the paper has been one of the evidences of tracing in several important cases.

The significance of unusual identity as evidence of forgery would naturally be strengthened by increasing the number of signatures in dispute. If one alleged forgery of one name closely resembles a certain possible model such resemblance in connection with other evidence may be very strong evidence of forgery, and it is naturally a more suspicious circumstance if two, three, or four such signatures closely resemble the model. In a recent important case a model signature and five duplicates were found, and in another famous case four traced signatures from the same model all appeared on different pages of the same will.

The question of identical signatures being produced in succession is also a matter that should be considered. As we have seen if comparison is made of all the thousands of signatures that certain uniform writers have written there can be found, by picking out the most favorable examples, some very similar to each other, but if the attempt is made to find two such similar signatures written in succession the search becomes still more difficult, and if three or four practically identical successive signatures are looked for, as for example on the same document or on the same series of papers, they can not be found.

A careful study of the tracing process and of the signatures in the reported traced forgery cases and numerous other similar cases shows that entire identity is practically impossible, unless produced by some mechanical process like engraving, lithography or a rubber stamp. Absolute identity of this character would obviously in itself show that such writing could not be genuine. In considering the force of identity as evidence of forgery, it must therefore be remembered, in the first place, that no traced imitation of a model will be an exact fac-simile of it, so that what is described as identity is really only approximate identity. It is easily possible to exaggerate the force of this identity alone as proof of forgery; some of the frequently quoted statements on the subject do exaggerate it. If it is contended that this identity, which it is to be understood is only approximate, is "impossible in any genuine signatures written by any one at any time," the natural and conclusive answer to such a challenge is the bringing forward of actual signatures by other writers that are as nearly identical as the disputed signature and the alleged model. *In some cases such signatures can be found.*

This may seem to prove that identity has no value whatever as evidence of forgery in any case but it does not by any means do so. Such similarity may be quite far removed from absolute identity and yet show conclusively that one signature was undoubtedly made from another or that two or more signatures were made from one model. Suspicious identity is that which suggests the tracing process and which is not inconsistent with the theory. If all beginning points distinctly diverge and distinct strokes do not coincide then numerous other identities would not necessarily point to tracing, while divergencies of fine lines at intermediate points, especially if such divergence returns to the line of the model, would not be inconsistent with the tracing theory, and finally, if the theory of tracing is to be maintained the line quality of the alleged tracing must in some degree indicate the tracing movement and not exactly conform to that shown in the genuine writing. Identity in the opinions quoted beginning on page 274 is described as "almost exactly," "slight departures," and "almost exact," all indicating a suspicious similarity which yet was not exact identity.

The significance of the identity in each case must also, as stated above, be considered as applying only to the one particular writer in that case. The degree and character of the identity must also be examined and properly interpreted by consideration of the length of name, the fineness of the strokes, the number of detached parts, and the number of separate signatures that are suspiciously alike. In one case a witness who had testified that identity had no significance except to prove genuineness, was on cross-examination led to say that fifty signatures might be just alike and all genuine, but he did reluctantly admit that a group of one hundred exact duplicates would attract his attention as peculiar.

In his charge to the jury in the case illustrated in Fig. 51 (Fidelity Trust Co. Buffalo, N. Y. vs. Executors of Lydia Cox estate), the late Justice Childs of the New York Supreme Court, after describing how it was alleged each of the three writers on three occasions had written so that the three groups of three names could all be practically superimposed, said in an impressive manner and with emphasis on "likely": "Gentlemen, it is for you to say whether such a thing is *likely* to happen." The jury decided that it was not likely to happen.

The most interesting and famous testimony on the subject that has been given is undoubtedly that of Professor Pierce, in the case referred to above. He was called as a witness to give testimony based on the calculus of probabilities, as to how frequently all the thirty downward strokes in a given signature would coincide. The basis of the calculation was the observed coincidences in the genuine signatures in the case. This testimony illustrates the application of mathematics to such a problem[1].

Illustrations of Traced Forgeries.

Illustrations are desirable in all kinds of disputed document investigations, but in traced forgery inquiries their use is sometimes imperative if the true character of a skillfully executed traced forgery is to be conclusively shown. To those who consider only the question of form

---

[1]Professor Pierce testified in part as follows: "I have carefully examined the signatures of 1 and 10 of Sylvia Ann Howland. I have placed them over each other, and have compared their magnified photographs. The coincidence is extraordinary and of such a kind as irresistibly to suggest design, and especially the tracing of 10 over 1. There are small differences in every portion of the signatures, so that no letter of the one is precisely identical with that of the other; but the differences are such as to strengthen the argument for design suggested by the coincidences. . . The mathematical discussion of this subject has never, to my knowledge, been proposed, but it is not difficult; and a numerical expression applicable to this problem, the correctness of which would be instantly recognized by all the mathematicians of the world, can be readily obtained. . .

"The relative frequency of coincidence expresses how often there is a coincidence in either of the characteristic lines; such as in line 1 for example. The product of the relative frequency into itself expresses how the coincidence of a characteristic line 1 is combined with that of line 2; the cube of the relative frequency of coincidence shows how often there will be the simultaneous combination of the coincidences of the three first lines, and so on.

"Finally, the relative frequency must be multiplied into itself as many times as there are characteristic lines to express how often there can be a complete coincidence in position of all the lines of the signature.

"In the case of Sylvia Ann Howland therefore, this phenomenon could occur only once in the number of times expressed by the thirtieth power of five [nine hundred and thirty-one quintillions of times—931,000,000,000,000,000,000]. This number far transcends human experience. So vast an improbability is practically an impossibility. Such evanescent shadows of probability cannot belong to actual life. They are unimaginably less than those least things which the law cares not for." (The signatures are shown on page 301.)

in a writing even a clumsy tracing is promptly passed as genuine, and, with such an examiner, it may be difficult to prove that a good tracing is not a genuine writing.

Illustrations are desirable for two principal purposes; first to show hesitation, tremor, inequalities in pen pressure, stops, retouching, and that line quality in general which points to a drawing instead of a writing movement, as is well illustrated in Figs. 53 and 54. With large and accurate photographs showing these conditions the true character of a traced signature can usually be clearly seen. The second purpose to be served by photographs is to show suspicious identity, or approximate identity, of a disputed signature and an alleged model, or to show identity of several disputed signatures.

The first condition, or that of suspicious line quality, can be shown most clearly by photographic enlargements by both direct and transmitted light. Experimental photographs of various degrees of enlargement should be made and those used that show best the actual conditions. When practicable it is advisable to make enlargements of two and also of four diameters, and in some cases enlargements of from about eight to twelve diameters should be made.

It is not usually helpful to make single illustrations larger than can be seen all at once, or nearly all at once, at about the ordinary reading distance. As is well understood, when an object is removed in distance it is in effect reduced in size, and, except to be used as a chart so that all can see at once, a photograph larger than about eleven by fourteen inches is not necessary, as this size is about as large as can be seen at the ordinary reading distance. Many suggestions regarding photographs, applicable in such cases, are made in the chapter on photography.

The second class of illustrations require considerable care and ingenuity, if the evidence pointing to the tracing method is to be shown effectively. The method desirable depends somewhat upon the conditions, but the same facts should always be shown in more than one way; what may appeal to one observer may not be so clearly seen by another.

Some of the methods employed are: (1) the photographing of the signatures on transparent films so that they may easily be superimposed; (2) the photographing of the signatures under glass carrying uniform ruled squares so that parts may be compared by inspection; (3) the photographing of the signatures as composites or one over the other with identical lines superimposed; (4) the photographic reproduction of the signatures with various lines drawn over them representing identical measurements; (5) the photographing of the signatures with a superimposed transparent rule showing exact measurements of positions of various parts and especially of beginning points; (6) the comparison with each other of pencil tracings of the signatures; (7) the illustration of identity by actual measurements of the originals from various points; (8) the cutting apart and matching together in various ways of parts of different photographed signatures showing the unnatural uniformity; (9) and, finally the superimposing of the originals over each other by transmitted light at the window or over an artificial light.

As far as practicable these various methods are illustrated here, and their desirability is briefly discussed.

It is impossible by the methods available on the restricted pages of this book to do more than suggest what can be done with large, clearly printed photographs.

The test of tracing that naturally is made first is that of superimposing the original writings by transmitted light. This method is useful, especially as a first step, but frequently is not practicable on account of the thickness of the papers or the fineness of the lines, and under these conditions it may be possible to find genuine signatures that apparently are as nearly alike as a disputed signature and an alleged model.

Composites made by photography for some reasons are also not the best illustrations as the signatures hide each other and tend to emphasize the dissimilarities which are clearly seen, while the identities tend to cover and hide each other; composites are, however, often desirable in connection with other illustrations, especially when the identity is very close.

It is obvious that pencil tracings may be objectionable because being made by hand the personal equation of the tracer can not be removed, and also because it is dangerous to allow anyone to make a tracing of a disputed signature that is suspected of being a tracing. A careless pencil tracing of a suspected signature may destroy important evidence of tracing in the disputed signature itself.

The objection to the method of drawing identical lines over two or more signatures that are suspiciously alike is that the lines tend to cover up the signatures if any considerable number are drawn and the personal equation again enters into the operation. Actual measurements of the signatures themselves should always be made and opportunity and assistance should always be given for court and jury to verify all measurements. For this purpose enlarged photographs are almost indispensable as a verification of testimony.

The photographing of the signatures under ruled squares is in numerous ways the most effective as well as the fairest way to illustrate suspicious identity; no lines are hidden and the divergencies as well as the similarities can be seen, neither signature is covered and suspicious hesitation, pen-lifts, or line quality can also be seen. There can be no valid objection to the method as it in effect is simply a method of measuring the signatures[1]. This method was first used in the Rice-Patrick case and has since been employed in numerous other important traced forgery cases[2].

---

[1] Nor did the fact that the photograph exhibited the signature on a back-ground of ruled squares destroy the admissibility of the offered picture. . . The photographs were taken by placing over them a glass upon which such lines were drawn forming uniform squares. The purpose was to exhibit the uniformity in the size and proportion of the letters in the two photographs. . .

No one, I think, will dispute that a glass, plain, or with magnifying powers, marked with lines so as to afford a measure of space and a standard of proportion, could have been put into the hands of the jury for the purpose of applying it to the signatures, whether of written size, or of magnified size. It would amount to no more than applying a measure to the signatures, and then viewing the measure and the signatures through a glass.

So we think there was no error in the admission of these photographs.—The State vs. Matthew J. Ready. New Jersey Supreme Court, 1909. (72 Atlantic Reporter, 495.)

[2] These cases are: The Rice-Patrick civil and criminal case in New York City; the Crawford-Schooley will case, at Scranton, Pa.; the Messchert-Essenhower will case, at Reading, Pa.; the Parr will case, at Louisville, Ky.; the Boyer-Lydia Cox Estate case, at Buffalo, N. Y.; the Burtis will case, at Auburn, N. Y.; the case of The State vs Matthew Ready, Newark, N. J., and the case of Pye vs. Pye, Rochester, N. Y. In the trial of all of these cases photographs of the signatures under ruled squares were admitted in evidence over objection, and in nearly if not all of the same cases transparent film photographs and composite photographs were also admitted.

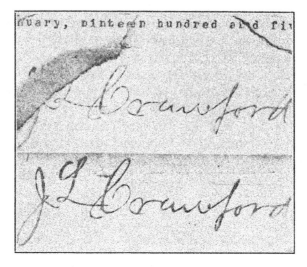

FIG. 113—The two disputed signatures in the Schooley-
Crawford case at Scranton, Pa.

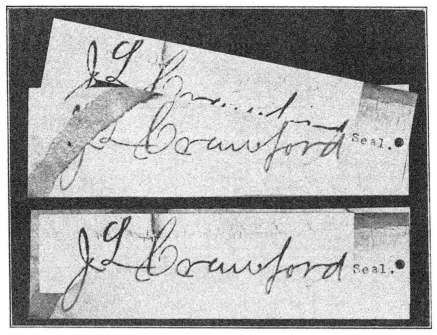

FIG. 114—Identity of signatures shown by matching upper part of one on to the
lower part of the other.

Fig. 115—Retouching on codicil signature in Schooley-Crawford case.

NOTES REGARDING ILLUSTRATIONS OF TRACED FORGERIES.

For use in this chapter diligent effort has been made to secure photographs of the signatures in all the traced forgery cases referred to in the decisions and in all other important cases tried but not appealed. In some of the cases, strange to say, no photographs were made and the original papers have been lost. The following pages show all that can now be obtained, and illustrate the leading features of the subject. Nearly all the illustrations were made from actual exhibits used in the trial of the cases but are necessarily much reduced in size.

Figures 113-115.

These illustrations are from the celebrated Schooley-Crawford will case at Scranton, Penn. A claim to an estate of more than a million dollars was based on the genuineness of these two signatures which were attached to an alleged will and codicil. The claimant discovered after making the document that it was a suspicious circumstance that the two signatures should be so nearly identical and before the case was brought into court the codicil it was claimed was accidentally torn to pieces and one small piece was lost. Enough remained, however, to show the extraordinary identity. The two signatures were actually made from a rubber stamp in some manner and one of them had been carefully retouched as is clearly shown in Fig. 115. The claim was vigorously pressed by a leading attorney but the will was declared a forgery by the prothonotary and later by a jury. The claimant, Schooley, and his two witnesses were indicted and, in March, 1908, at the beginning of the criminal trial, all of them came into court and pleaded guilty and were sent to the penitentiary. All of these illustrations are from exhibits in the case. The identity of the signatures was shown in numerous ways and the matchings of the cut signature over the other showed clearly "the piece that was lost."

Figures 116-120.

These illustrations are from a very similar case tried about the same time at Reading, Penn. In this case the claimant had one genuine letter from which he made a will bequeathing him "Ten thousand dollars and the estate in France." From the same genuine paper he also made standard writings to prove the will and all by the tracing process. In this case there was the model signature and five duplicates and it will be seen that not only the signatures but the words "Very truly yrs" also superimpose. "Ex. Z" is the model, " Ex. C" is the claim paper and "Ex. F" was one of the alleged "standards." The jury promptly decided that the will was a forgery. The illustrations show the various methods of showing suspicious identity. The very suspicious line quality of two of the disputed signatures in this case is shown in Fig. 54.

Figures 121-122.

These illustrations are from one of the noted Land Fraud Cases in Oregon and are from photographs made by Mr. J. Frank Shearman, Questioned Document Examiner, of Wichita, Kansas, who was a witness in the case. The composite shows the suspicious identity and the line quality in the enlarged photographs showed clearly the character of the writings. The defendants pleaded guilty.

Figure 123.

This illustration is from the alleged model for a disputed signature and the disputed signature itself photographed under glass with squares so that comparison of parts can be made by inspection. The writer followed the strange custom of preceding his signature with the figure of a hand as shown. The alleged model writing not only furnished a copy for the signature but the hand as well and, in addition, other parts of the claim paper. Another phase of this same case is illustrated in Fig. 108.

Figure 124.

The case illustrated in Fig. 124 was tried in 1887, but no photographs were made and those here shown were made for use in this connection. An interesting excerpt from the opinion in the case is printed on page 276. In the original writing in the case, not seen in the illustration, an identical outline was strong evidence of the method employed and as the opinion states, "There is too much method shown in the latter signature."

Figure 125.

This model and traced imitation are photographed to illustrate one method of showing identity. An enlarged photograph of this disputed signature showed retouching entirely inconsistent with genuineness and the identity showed the method employed in making the signature.

Figure 126.

This illustration is from other signatures in the case illustrated in Fig. 51. This is the case in which the presiding judge said, "Gentlemen, it is for you to determine whether such a thing is likely to happen." Mere inspection in this case shows that the signatures were drawn from a copy.

Figures 127-130.

In the celebrated Rice-Patrick will case (New York City) it happened that five genuine signatures were actually written on the same day that it was alleged the Patrick will was signed. Figures 127 and 128 show the four disputed signatures and the five genuine signatures and a comparison of them shows the extraordinary and significant similarity of the four and the characteristic variation in size, proportions and relation of parts of the genuine signatures.

Considering only the questions of shading, line quality and pen position the four signatures are clearly not genuine and these facts in connection with the significant identities constitute overwhelming proof of forgery. As the Appellate court said (Affirmed by Court of Appeals) "This fact [of identity] taken in connection with the other evidence bearing on the subject, is of such a character as to irresistibly lead to the conclusion" [of forgery]. A brief excerpt from the interesting opinion is printed on pages 274, 275.

Figures 127, 128, and 129 are from actual exhibits used at the trial. Figure 130 was made at the time but was not introduced in evidence.

There is shown in Fig 53, on page 111, a detail of traced signature No. 2 which shows the slow, painful, drawing movement employed to make certain parts of all four of the traced signatures.

Figures 131-133.

These are illustrations taken from the original exhibits in the case of the disputed signatures in the celebrated "Howland case." Signature No. 1 was the genuine will signature and signatures 10 and 15 were signatures to alleged codicils. Signatures 1 and 10 were those compared in the testimony of Professor Pierce, quoted on page 285. In addition to the wonderful identity shown in "1" and "10" these two signatures were also exactly the same distance from the edge of the paper. Signature 15 shows striking identities but the names were spaced differently due, it was alleged, to the moving of the paper during the operation of tracing. Figure 132, from signature 15, shows the slow, drawing movement employed in making the disputed signatures and Fig. 133 shows that signature 10 "covers" signature 1. The case is further discussed on page 277.

Figure 51.

In Fig. 51 on page 103 is shown another set of signatures from the case illustrated in Fig. 126. Notwithstanding the extraordinary identities in these signatures it was contended by three banks that they were genuine and the attorney adverse to the genuineness of the signatures waited nearly two years before bringing the case into court, he himself thinking the signatures were genuine. He submitted the checks independently to three handwriting specialists who all reported that eleven checks were forgeries by tracing. It was so conclusively shown that the signatures were not genuine that although three cases were pending only one was tried.

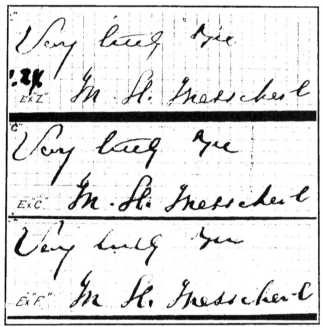

Fig. 116—Model "Very truly yrs" and signature, and two traced imitations photographed under ruled squares.

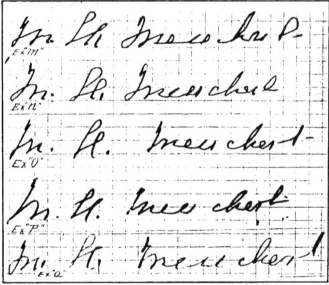

Fig. 117—Five genuine signatures showing natural variation in size, proportions and position.

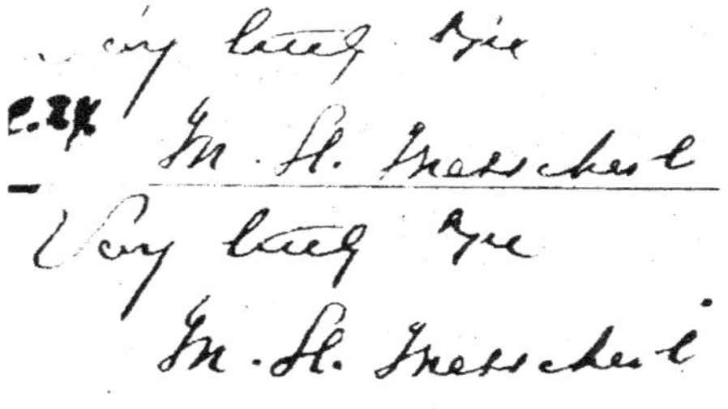

Fig. 118—Model and one traced imitation. Actual size.

Fig. 119—Transmitted light photograph of two films with signatures and "Very truly yrs" superimposed.

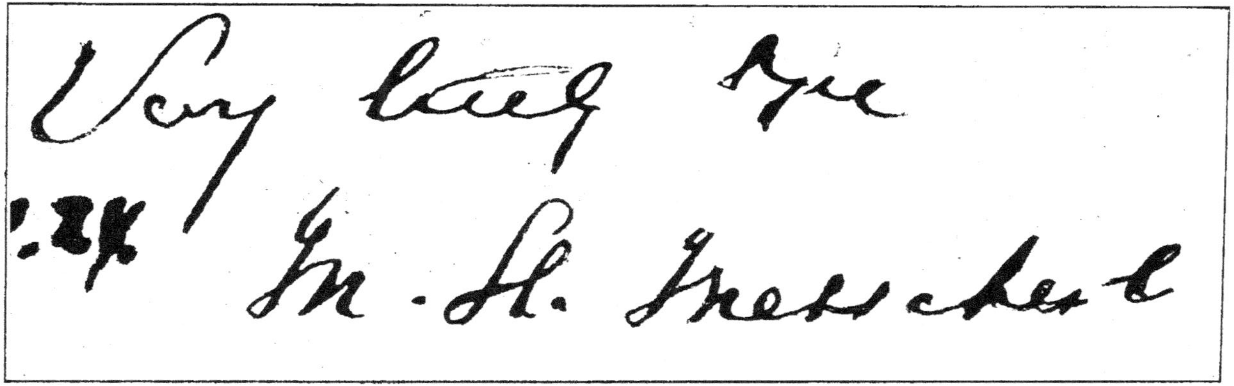

Fig. 120—Composite of signatures "Ex. C" over "Ex Z." From original photographic exhibit. This illustration shows the extraordinary identities of the six separated parts.

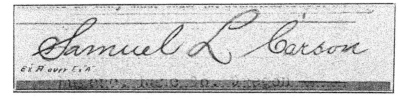

FIG. 121—Exhibits in one of the "Oregon Land Fraud" cases of two traced forgeries.

FIG. 122—Composite of the above signatures.

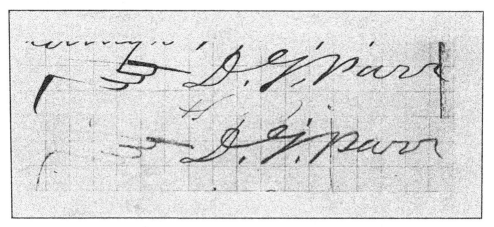

FIG. 123—Disputed signature and "hand" and alleged model in the Parr Will case at Louisville, Ky.

Fig. 124—The model and forged imitation in case of Day vs. Cole, 65 Mich. 129.

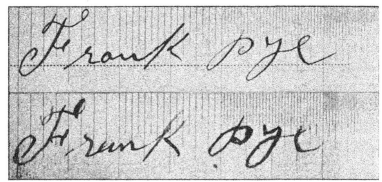

Fig. 125—Model and traced forgery with superimposed glass rule showing actual measurements and points of identity. The tracing was almost all retouched or overwritten. Case of Pye vs. Pye, Rochester, N.Y.

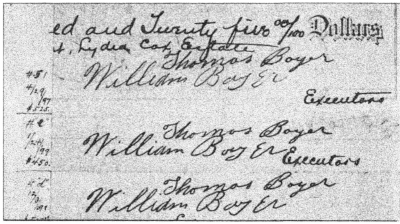

Fig. 126—A genuine signature, "No. 51," and two "traced" forgeries. The identities in size, proportions, spacing and alignment and many other particulars show by mere inspection that the signatures "e" and "d" were made from "51."

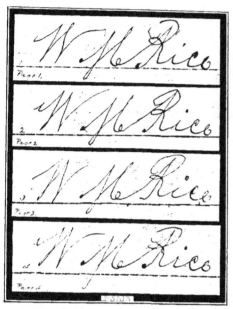

FIG. 127—The four disputed signatures in
the Rice-Patrick civil and
criminal case.

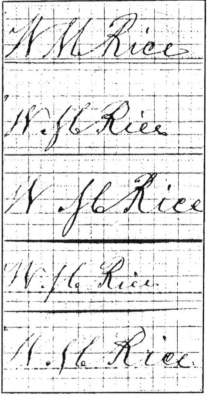

FIG. 128—Five genuine signatures of
the same date as the alleged
Patrick will.

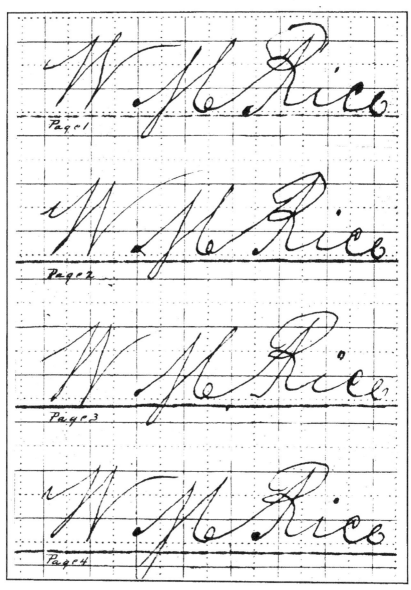

FIG. 129—The four disputed signatures in the Rice-Patrick case photographed with ruled squares showing identities in the signatures.

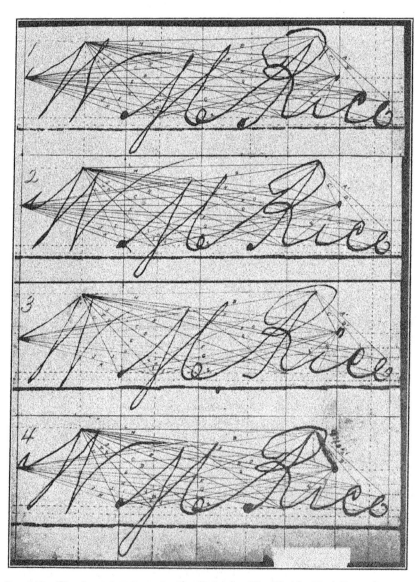

FIG. 130—The four signatures to the Patrick will with identical lines drawn from point to point.

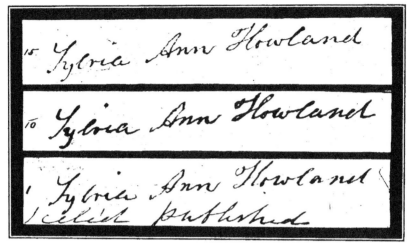

Fig. 131—The genuine will signature and the two disputed signatures, 10 and 15, in the Howland case.

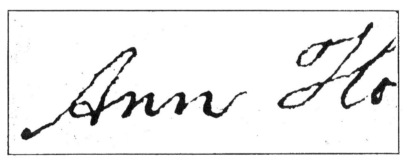

Fig. 132—Enlargement of portions of signature 15 showing line quality.

Fig. 133—Composite of signature 10 over signature 1 showing identity.

CHAPTER XVII.

ANONYMOUS AND DISPUTED LETTERS

Letters of various kinds are frequently offered as evidence if they are not the actual basis of an issue in a trial at law, and their correct identification is often a matter of very great importance. Spurious letters are sometimes manufactured expressly for the purpose of being used as evidence in a legal contention, and fraudulent or genuine letters may be brought forward in the midst of a trial when an immediate decision as to their genuineness is imperative. Disputed letters, however, in most cases are anonymous communications of an abusive or threatening character.

Anonymous letters occasionally are of a friendly nature but usually reflect with more or less severity upon the character or conduct of some one. It is important to know that in numerous instances the writing of such letters is one of the earliest manifestations of a mild sort of insanity which takes this peculiar form; in any case that certainly is a strange satisfaction which comes through saying disagreeable things in this manner. The number of anonymous communications written is very great, and they range in importance all the way from foolish practical jokes to threats of kidnapping, arson and murder. Whole communities are sometimes wrought up over a series of letters which may for a long time baffle detection. Anonymous letters usually receive but little attention, the majority of them going directly into

[302]

the waste basket, but sometimes they are of the most serious character, in many instances being important links in chains of evidence pointing to grave crimes. On account of the scurrilous and obscene nature of many anonymous letters it is illegal to send them by mail, and United States Commissioners are called upon to investigate great numbers of these peculiar missives.

There are some strange facts in connection with anonymous letter writing known to those frequently called upon to make such examinations. One of the first is that in many cases anonymous letter writing becomes chronic and frequently by patient waiting a whole series from the same source can be collected. They are apt to increase in frequency and vehemence until there is some positive indication that they have attracted attention and caused pain and annoyance. Another usual condition is that the disguise employed is apt to be partly disregarded or forgotten after the first few letters, which may be prepared with great care and are sometimes very effectively disguised.

Another peculiar fact of great importance in connection with the investigation of the authorship of such letters is that in a large proportion of cases, perhaps twenty per cent., the actual writer is also one of those who receive them and is supposed to be one of the victims of the work of some one else. On account of this fact one of the first steps to be taken in such an inquiry is to learn the name and get samples of the writing of every one who claims to have received similar letters. A further surprising fact is that in a large majority of cases the anonymous letter writer is a woman who may write what it does not seem possible she could write; but often the use of improper language is undoubtedly a part of the attempted disguise. It should also be stated for the protection of the innocent that often if not usually the one first suspected of writing anonymous letters is not the actual writer, and frequently the actual writer is one who for some time wholly escapes even suspicion.

At the outset of an inquiry of this kind it is important to realize the possibility of error unless every precaution is observed, and even then, as with any subject, questions arise that no one can answer with much certainty. In many cases conclusions are based upon so many elements and are so enforced and corroborated that they amount almost to a mathematical demonstration, while in others only a qualified opinion can be given. It is a fact that many errors are made by those who attempt to give opinions regarding disputed letters. Volunteers, with no appreciation of the difficulty of the problem, give offhand opinions on either side of the most important inquiries, their only qualification for the task apparently being that they themselves are able to write. The great majority of errors of this kind are due to the fact that inadequate or improper standards are used, or to the causes outlined in the preceding chapter on individual and general characteristics in writing. As there shown it is easy to understand how superficial knowledge or hasty judgment may lead to error. The principles outlined in the chapter just referred to should be applied to every disputed letter inquiry. Other preceding chapters also have a direct bearing on such investigations.

Another fact that should always be considered and given early attention in examining an anonymous writing for the purpose of discovering the author is that an unnatural or disguised hand cannot show greater writing ability or skill than the actual writer possesses. Disguised writing is usually slow and clumsy, but, whether good or bad, it is a fixed principle in determining its authorship that all possible candidates must at once be excluded whose best natural writing shows a lower order of skill than the anonymous writing. It is important in such an inquiry to make a thorough analysis of the disputed writing on this question of writing skill and the accuracy and perfection of design of every character. This procedure will often at once greatly reduce the number of possible writers, for the very good reason that no one will write better than he can write although sometimes he may write much worse.

Another important initial step in the inquiry is the careful analysis of such a communication with a view of determining the educational, literary and grammatical ability of the writer. The result of the analysis often is the prompt exclusion of certain candidates under suspicion whose ability in these particulars is clearly inferior to that shown in the anonymous writing.

Notwithstanding the apparent difficulties of the task the identification of anonymous letters in most cases is the simplest problem in connection with the investigation of disputed handwriting. The forger who attempts to simulate only a signature or who seeks to disguise even a small amount of his own handwriting assumes a task of great difficulty, but when the effort is made to write a complete letter or a series of such communications, the varied elements entering into the problem are so numerous that it requires an extraordinary degree of skill for the writer to hide his personality. It is important to know that an anonymous letter of any considerable length and particularly a series of anonymous letters can in most cases be positively identified if a sufficient quantity of genuine writing of the actual writer is produced for comparison.

It should not be understood that the claim is made that handwriting cannot be successfully disguised; but, as a rule, it is not. It is erroneously assumed, by the educated as well as the ignorant, that to disguise a writing is a very simple operation, and the subject is given no serious attention. The usual writer of such letters makes no study of the subject whatever and the disguises ordinarily adopted are so ineffective and transparent that it requires but little experience to see through them at a glance, and, in effect, the anonymous writer often unwittingly writes his own name on every page. Anonymous letters by their writing, materials used, composition and general form often indicate at once the sex of the writer, and frequently show nationality, age, education and occupation, and these facts, under the known conditions, often point to the probable author, whose writing in the form of letters should at once be obtained and compared with the anonymous letters[1].

---

[1] The general procedure should, if possible, be followed with disputed letters which is outlined in the chapter on simulated forgeries. The genuine writing should, if possible, be studied first, following the points there given, and in addition the special points referred to in this chapter should be carefully considered. The disputed letters should then be studied and finally the two sets of writing compared. The subjects discussed in numerous other chapters may have an important bearing on the identification of a disputed letter, especially the chapters on individual and general characteristics, arrangement of writing, divergencies in genuine writing and systems of writing. Many of the suggestions regarding the examination of what is alleged to be a complete simulated document (p. 250) apply as well to disputed letters and the procedure there outlined should be carefully followed.

The points for consideration in such an examination are all of the hundreds of writing characteristics which enter into any considerable quantity of writing as considered in a questioned signature alone, and in addition to this, careful attention should be given to the question of materials, composition, grammar, spelling[1], idioms, division of words, proportions of letters, shading, alignment, spacing, margins, watermarks, titles, corrections, erasures, punctuation, use of capital letters, underscoring, abbreviations, folding, superscriptions, typewriting and ink.

The writer, without study and without careful practice, who is successful in excluding all his natural habits in all these directions, and who at the same time can adopt and consistently maintain unnatural characteristics through a complete letter, and especially through a series of letters written at different times, is certainly a rare individual with a very high degree of natural ability. One of the chief difficulties under which an anonymous writer labors is that the different letters being written at different times the disguises adopted are not continuous and are not consistent with each other, so that a collection of such letters will usually indicate almost at a glance the natural habits of the writer and the assumed habits. The anonymous writer who makes and keeps carefully made duplicates of all such letters is certainly an exception and is the rare one who may perhaps be able to make a series of such letters consistent with each other.

Early in the investigation of anonymous writing care-

---

[1] And slightingly as counsel treat the identity of orthography, writing "hit" for "it" in both documents, [show that] "it" is a pretty decided hit after all.—Reid vs. The Sate, 20 Ga. 684 (1856).

ful examination should be made of the inconspicuous characteristics which in disguised writing often are of the most significance because they are given no attention whatever by the writer. In disguising a writing thought is naturally first given to the conspicuous features which may be much changed, while persistent but inconspicuous parts are not, as a rule, modified in any way. Two writings, one of which is disputed, may appear very different in general appearance but may contain so many small but peculiar and persistent characteristics that the conclusion of identity is irresistible, and again two writings may be very similar in certain general features but may differ in so many significant but inconspicuous particulars as to show that they were undoubtedly written by two different writers. A disguise in inconspicuous features alone would be very extraordinary if not altogether inconceivable, and could only be attained by the most complete knowledge of these minute details in combination with a very high degree of manual skill. When inconspicuous characteristics persistently and consistently diverge, the conclusion must be reached that two such writings are not by the same hand; when they coincide in sufficient number the conclusion is reached that they were by the same writer.

Some of these inconspicuous but highly important features to be first carefully compared are here described. They are numbered so that none will be omitted in making the comparison:

The shape, position, angle, size, slant and height of connections between the following small letters and the following letter in a word; (1) b, (2) f, (3) o, (4) p,

Fig. 135—Inconspicuous characteristics. A few examples of the great number of variations of the seventeen specified letters.

(5) s, (6) v, (7) w. Form of final small letters (8) w,
(9) r. The form, shading, crossing, and height of initial
small (10) t, and intermediate and final small (11) t.
The initial and intermediate small letter (12) a. The
form of initial and final small letter (13) o. The form
of initial and intermediate small letter (14) c. The
distance that sharp angles are retraced at base of letters
(15) m, (16) n, (17) h.

.The second group of inconspicuous characteristics, as
important perhaps as the first, are: (18) The length,
width and slant of the upper loop letters l, b, h, k, and f
compared with the shortest or one space letters and also
as compared with the lower loop letters g, j, y, z; (19)
the height of separation above the line of the two strokes
of the small letters b, l, h and t at the beginning and
also in the middle of words; (20) the distance that up
strokes are traced back at the sharp angles in the connections at the tops of letters a, g, i, j, s, w, u, y; (21)
the length, slant, direction and exact shape of beginning
strokes of all words; the same of (22) ending strokes of
all words; (23) exact location of shading on all loop
letters; (24) the ovals of small a and o and their connection with preceding letters; (25) position, form and size
of figures, all punctuation marks and the signs &, $,
and all abbreviations.

This preliminary procedure alone, if carefully followed out, is usually sufficient to lead to a very positive
conclusion as to the identity of two sets of writings. If
this method is followed in the comparison of two writings that resemble each other very closely but which are
actually by different writers it will very quickly be seen
that two writings by different writers will inevitably

differ in many of the particulars named. The questions of variety of forms in handwriting and of the mathematical probability of two complete handwritings being identical, as discussed in Chapter XIV., have a direct bearing on this phase of the study of anonymous letters.

The favorite disguises adopted in anonymous letters are, a change of slant, a different size and proportion of writing, the printing of the communication instead of putting it in script, the use of a different kind of pen from that ordinarily employed, and the invention of certain fantastic forms which may give a very different superficial appearance to a page of writing. As already observed the most significant characteristics are usually not disguised in the least for the simple reason that the average writer with his knowledge and study of the subject is unable to recognize the peculiar and significant characteristics in his own writing as compared with writing in general. It is rare indeed that the disguise adopted is more than merely superficial, and in most cases it covers only a small number of the characters employed and but few of the habits exemplified. A change in the slant and a change in a few of the forms of the capital letters are often the only disguises attempted, and, while such changes may affect the general appearance of writing in a striking manner, it is easily seen that the bulk of the writing of such a letter remains practically undisguised.

Writing is so automatic that the anonymous writer, particularly if he becomes excited and vehement and his attention is mainly directed to the matter of composition, forgets the effort to disguise and almost inevitably lapses into his natural hand. In a disguised letter cover-

ing two or more pages, it is almost certain that some
letters, words or parts will be written naturally, and
when even the greatest care seems to be taken, some
foolish, tell-tale thing is quite sure to be included that
points conclusively to the writer.

Few writers know their own general habits in such a
simple matter as the arrangement of words and lines
on a page, and have never compared their own practice
with that of others in the matter of leaving margins on
the left, right, top and bottom of the page, as to spacing
between words, or as to the change in such spacing when
punctuation points are inserted, or to the various other
important points enumerated in the chapter on arrangement of writing. The writer who uses a hyphen both at
the end of the line and at the beginning of the following line thinks this is a universal habit, and the writer
who makes quotation marks on the base line even with
the line of writing in the German style, thinks this is
the usual American custom, and the writer who begins
the paragraph in the middle or nearly at the right side
of the sheet instead of the left has no idea that this also
is not the usual practice. One who makes the interrogation point facing the wrong way and places the comma
and period up even with the tops of the small letters
instead of on the line thinks this is the way they are
made in the books, and one who omits punctuation entirely has the idea that but few writers use these unnecessary marks; and the one who has the strange notion
that a line is incomplete without some kind of a punctuation mark is under the impression that this also is according to rule.

The possible identity of pens, ink and paper in the

examination should always be considered. In more than one instance it has been shown that a disputed writing was actually written on a piece of paper torn from a sheet upon which a conceded writing was written, showing at least that the paper was once in the hands of the one who disputed the letter. Blotters or writing pads have been found in connection with such cases (Fig. 144) in the possession of suspected persons, showing the actual impression of a part of the writing in question, and the work of a peculiar pen or of unusual ink may in some cases point to a possible writer.

The latitude of possible variety in genuine handwriting differs greatly in different individuals, ranging from the illiterate writer who makes but one form of each letter—and sometimes does not even know how to make all the letters—to the ready writer who makes a variety of capital letter forms and frequently modifies many of the small letters, as they are written in the initial, intermediate, or final position in a word. The illiterate may not have a mental pattern of all the written characters, while the free writer may actually use fully twice or three times as many forms. The bearing of this fact is that anonymous writing by one who makes a variety of forms may be connected with genuine writing by identity in the varied as well as the normal forms, thus increasing the strength of the connection, while the illiterate by the deficiency of his knowledge of forms may thus show his connection with an anonymous writing. Questioned illiterate writing frequently consists of a combination of script forms and Roman capitals, or pen or pencil printing, and often such writing contains original or "freak" forms of letters, abbreviations, or punctuation marks that are individual creations and are of the utmost significance as indicating individuality. Pen printing may show striking individuality and this may be true even when standards of the kind are made by request. In such cases printed standard writing should, if possible, always be obtained.

Assumed illiteracy is a frequent disguise, and it is sometimes important to determine whether letters were actually written by an illiterate person or by a writer who is assuming illiteracy. On account of its fixed character and lack of skill it is usually easier positively to identify the handwriting of an illiterate person than the writing of one who writes much and easily. One of the common indications of illiteracy as shown by writing is the faulty arrangement of words, lines, paragraphs, and pages, proving general unfamiliarity with the whole writing process. Illiteracy is also shown in a measure by materials and by the manner of folding the document; errors in punctuation also in a measure indicate illiteracy, but in some of these matters illiteracy may be successfully simulated. An educated person in simulating illiterate writing may include glaring errors in spelling and use uncouth ungrammatical expressions, but may forget to disguise the arrangement, paragraphing and punctuation, which fact would unquestionably show that the writing was not by an illiterate person. The illiterate writer is of course entirely incapable of simulating the writing and style of an educated writer.

In connection with suspicions regarding the authorship of anonymous letters, or actual accusations that sometimes are prematurely made, it may be important to consider the question as to whether letters were written by a man or by a woman. Sex is often very clearly indicated in disputed letters by composition, by choice of words, and especially by certain peculiar expressions or idioms which are characteristic of one or the other of the sexes. Profanity or threats of personal violence naturally have a masculine significance, while expressions regarding the appearance of things, such as "horrid" or "awful scene," more frequently point to a feminine writer. When an anonymous letter is carefully analyzed and its words, its thought and its manner of expression are all considered, it will often appear very plainly whether it is the work of a man or a woman. Interjections, epithets and degree and manner of empha-

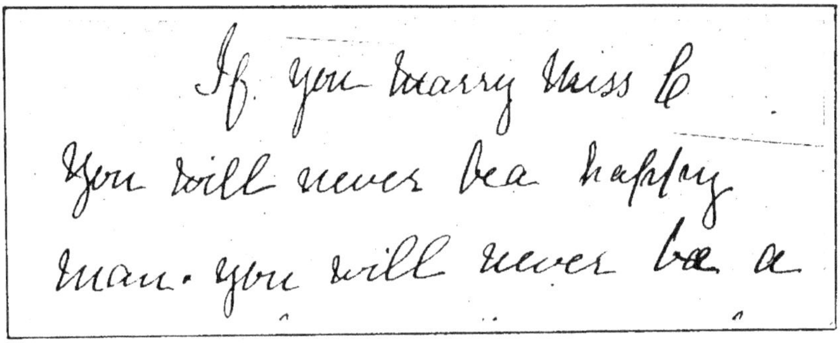

Fig. 136—Beginning of an anonymous letter which by its composition, subject matter and handwriting shows clearly it is the work of a woman.

sis are sometimes particularly significant as indicating sex. For the better study of the language alone it is an excellent plan to have made a typewritten copy of the whole letter with the sentences separated.

The sex indications in handwriting itself in some cases may be very clear, but these characteristics are not very numerous and in some instances may be somewhat misleading. This question of sex should, however, be carefully considered in every way possible and a systematic investigation is often fruitful, although many times a disputed writing contains no pronounced sex characteristics, or not a sufficient number on which to base a definite judgment.

The peculiar style of writing known as the "angular system," already described and illustrated, is a distinctive woman's hand and this writing, or distinct traces of it, almost certainly points to a woman writer. This is due to the fact that this style of writing is taught only to women, and there is no good reason why it should be imitated or acquired by men. It was formerly much in vogue and has long been a distinctive "society" hand. It is the style which has been taught for many years in certain church schools for girls, and in America is the exclusive style of writing taught in many ladies' seminaries. It has never been taught in the public schools and has not been taught directly to many writers, but, because it has been fashionable, it has been consciously and unconsciously imitated by thousands of women writers.

This style of writing, as we have seen, is strikingly distinctive, and if once learned is almost certain to leave its indelible impress upon a handwriting whatever other system or style may afterwards be acquired. It is usually unshaded and often is large and uncouth; it is sometimes very illegible and has many very peculiar capital letter designs. Many of its capital and small letters begin in the same unusual manner with an upward stroke made toward the left, which has the effect of apparently bending the beginning stroke of words around into the letter or word following. Many words in this writing are ended with a straight horizontal stroke often distinctly shaded, which is a peculiar and distinctive characteristic of the actual models of the system. In making an examination of disputed letters for the purpose of determining if they show characteristics of the angular hand or of any distinctive nationality or system, it is very helpful to have for comparison numerous specimens of such writing by different writers. Great care should be taken not to connect two sets of writings by different writers simply because they both show characteristics of the angular hand or of any other definite system or nationality.

Entirely outside of system characteristics there is undoubtedly in some writing a certain feminine quality that in some instances is very easily recognized, while in other writing distinctive masculine characteristics appear. These differences are due to many causes, among which are environment, the effect of business requirements and the influence of occupation, as well as the mental and physical differences in the sexes which no doubt in some degree affect writing. The writing of women as a whole is naturally more delicate than the writing of men and contains more little superfluous peculiarities and mannerisms; and as a rule it is more carefully finished in minor details. There are, of course, masculine women and feminine men, and the writing of such men and women may show characteristics that are misleading. The habit of putting shading on letters in little bunches, particularly at the ends of words or at the finishing parts of certain letters is a feminine trait, while the heavy shading of every downward stroke and especially vicious jabs of the pen that almost cut the paper, are distinctly masculine. The fact should always be considered that women are more apt to acquire the characteristics of men's writing than that men are likely to learn to write like women. This is due to the fact that more often women do the work of men than men do the work of women. The woman in business naturally acquires a business style of writing which may differ but little from that of her brothers similarly situated. M. Alfred Binet, a French psychologist, after a careful investigation of this subject, makes the statement that in French writing it is possible to determine accurately the sex of the writers in about seventy-five cases out of a hundred.

Graphology, or what is known as character reading from handwriting, would be of great assistance in identifying disputed handwriting if the so-called science were more certain in its results. This method of investigation, at least in its present state, seems to be of doubtful value as an aid in the discovery and proof of the facts in any kind of questioned document inquiry[1]. So many modify-

----

[1] The subject of graphology can hardly escape serious criticism as long as its advocates attempt to do too much, and its authors put into the books on the subject such silly stuff as is found in them. It would be much better if those who practice graphology did not attempt to find in handwriting indications of "disturbances in the functions of the bowels," or "altruism restricted to family," or "love of animals," or "sterility either in the male or female." The following quotations show to what lengths graphologists will go:

The sweep of the pen to the left is the graphic sign for defensiveness, and, when the stroke describes the segment of a circle, and sweeps in that direction, protectiveness and the love of the young or animals is surely indicated thereby.—Richard Dimsdale Stocker, in The Language of Handwriting, p. 93 (1901).

Briefly, then, I have noticed that a love of athletics is indicated by the small letters p, y, and g, having an abnormally long down-stroke commencing on a level with the other part of the letter. . . In cases where sterility, either in male or female, seemed indicated by lack of family in married life, I have frequently noticed an extreme lack of

ing and disturbing elements enter into the problem of determining from handwriting alone the higher attributes of human character that it seems dangerous to put much reliance upon it. This statement is made with full appreciation of the skill acquired by certain exponents of graphology, and also with some knowledge of their errors and limitations.. Discredit and ridicule are brought upon the subject by the tendency of its advocates of all grades, in their practice and their books, to carry their deductions to a ridiculous extreme.

Every one knows who has had even limited experience that through handwriting if not by it certain things regarding an individual are shown with more or less clearness. Is it not possible, however, that many, perhaps unconsciously, attribute to the handwriting what the message itself reveals? One sentence, spoken or written, may give a definite measure of the mental or even spiritual stature of a man. Excluding, however, the content or message, which the graphologist does not seem inclined to do when he insists on complete letters for examination, it is true that handwriting itself does

---

liaison between the letters of a word.—J. Harrington Keene, ("Grapho") in The Mystery of Handwriting, p. 17 (1896).

From a table of General and Particular Graphologic Signs: Words whose letters are not near together although they may be connected,—a person easy of access. Capitals joined to the letter following,—altruism. Capitals joined to the letter following after making a loop,—altruism restricted to family or to coterie. Small m and n in form of the u,—natural benevolence. Dots placed very high,—religious spirit. Capital M the first stroke lower then the second,—envious pride.—John Holt Schooling, in Handwriting and Expression (1892), a translation of "l'Ecriture et le Caractere," by M. Crepieux-Jamin, Paris.

The left-handed bending on right-handed main strokes, seems—if placed at the upper part of the stroke—to show disturbances in the functions of the bowels; at the intermediate and lower part of the stroke, it is indicative of different kinds of diseases of the stomach. The latter form is seemingly of graver significance than the former.— Magdaline Kintzel-Thumm, in Psychology and Pathology of Handwriting, p. 137 (1905).

show certain characteristics of the individual. The most pronounced of these are perhaps extremes of vigor and of weakness; education is shown in some measure, and illiteracy with more certainty by the bare forms themselves. Neatness and its opposite are also shown, as they would be by clothing or personal appearance; fussiness and its opposite can also no doubt be distinguished in some cases, and some other similar traits.

Those with the fullest scientific knowledge of the human brain put the least reliance upon what has been called the science of phrenology, which at one time was very popular, and of handwriting it also seems to be true that a thorough study of the subject, especially of its chronology and history, tends to weaken belief in what are described as the principles of graphology. It is one thing, through a thorough knowledge of the subject in its various phases and history, to discover and interpret the thousands of writing characteristics by which writing is identified and shown to be genuine or false, and an altogether different and more audacious thing to attempt to attach to all these characteristics a definite character value. In some foreign countries the word graphologist seems to be applied interchangeably to those who attempt to read character from handwriting and also to those who investigate disputed documents and testify in courts as experts as to the identity of handwriting, but in America and England a sharp distinction is drawn between the two classes. A graphologist rarely if ever testifies in court in America or England.

There are many devoted disciples of graphology throughout the world, and the science may be a true one as they firmly believe—and it is no doubt true in some measure—but many are of the opinion that it has not yet entirely proved itself. Two journals devoted to graphology are published in Europe and the subject seems to be most popular in Germany and France. Many books of widely varying quality have been written on the question and in many ways the study is a most fascinating one. It is but fair to say that the subject should always be judged by its ablest exponents and not by the many ignorant pretenders whose palpable blunders often make it ridiculous.

The finding of suitable standards of comparison in disputed letter cases is a matter of great importance and should receive the most careful attention. The subject is discussed in the chapter treating of standards of comparison and the suggestions there given should be carefully followed. By a systematic review of all the business, social and general interests of the one whose writing is sought ample standards are often found in cases where the effort at the outset is apparently hopeless. One of the frequent characteristics of the work of the amateur examiner is the acceptance and exclusive use of standards that may be not only too meager in quantity but entirely unsuitable in kind.

The peculiar, personal characteristics contained in a series of anonymous letters, which also appear in a series of standard letters, may be so numerous that the chance of two different writers employing all the same characters and showing all the same habits of omission and commission is entirely beyond any reasonable probability, and the only conclusion possible is that both series of letters are the production of the same mind and the same hand. An opinion in no case should be based upon a single characteristic, but upon mutually confirmatory characteristics which in combination can lead to but one conclusion. This topic is treated more fully in the chapter on individual and general characteristics.

In every case all unconscious, frequent characteristics should be carefully observed in both series of letters as outlined, and then carefully compared. Those things especially should always be looked for that even a clever disguise will not be likely to cover. Before reaching a final judgment as to identity or difference the weight and significance of the various characteristics must necessarily be carefully considered. As has heretofore been shown, some similarities and some differences have but little significance while others have great weight. It is just at this point that the limitations of the uninformed are shown. Of what avail is it for one who is ignorant of chemistry to observe a chemical reaction? It means no more to him than to an untaught child. In this same way similarities and differences in writing, especially in that which is disguised, are dim and shadowy unrealities to one who does not know what a handwriting characteristic is. With such an observer, who is unbiased and honest, an opinion is based only upon what he sees and understands which may be very little of that before him which is really important and significant. Too often he sees only what is pointed out to him and what he is expected to see.

Finally, as in any disputed document inquiry, illustrations should be made and reasons given for whatever opinion is advanced so that an intelligent man called upon to decide the question can see and understand and weigh the testimony. In this connection the court, with trained mind and ability in weighing testimony, by timely participation and pointed inquiry, kept entirely within the legal barriers, can greatly assist an earnest jury in reaching a correct conclusion. The interests of justice would undoubtedly be promoted by enlarging the powers of the presiding judge in American courts, and in this particular field he may greatly assist in finding and proving the fact.

Juxtaposition of Writings.

In many cases it is necessary that writings be grouped in proper form for comparison if the fact regarding their identity or difference is to be clearly seen and proved. If, as Professor Wigmore says (p. 41), the writings are to be presented to "instantaneous perception" the parts must be grouped close together. This can only be done by the aid of photography. The method is the same to prove identity or difference and only serves to assist the perception in arriving at the truth.

As outlined in the chapter on photography it is impossible for the average observer to carry form or color impressions even from the pages of one book to another, and to be compared things must be looked at side by side. In Fig. 138 and also in Fig. 142 it is easy to see the unmistakable connection between the writings when they are brought close together. Unmistakable difference may also be shown in the same manner as is well illustrated in Figs. 110 and 111. Slight differences or resemblances in separate instances may not be seen, but when grouped and looked at all together cannot be overlooked.

The underlying principle in this method of comparison, as clearly stated by Professor James and already quoted in a footnote (p. 234), is so important that it deserves a place in the regular text in this connection. He says, "Suppose no one element of either compound to differ from the corresponding element of the other compound enough to be distinguished from it if the two are compared alone. . . . Although each difference by itself might pass unperceived, the total difference . . . may very well·be sufficient to strike the sense. In a word, increasing the number of 'points' involved in a difference may excite our discrimination as effectually as increasing the amount of difference at any one point." Figures 3, 56, 73, 110, 111 are excellent illustrations of this important principle.

THE ILLUSTRATIONS.
Figure 137.

This is a typical "Black Hand" letter in a New York city case. To emphasize the demand in this instance the marble stairway on one of the floors of an apartment house was blown out by a bomb. Such a series of letters usually furnishes sufficient handwriting basis for a positive identification if the right person is suspected and his genuine writing supplied. In this case the writer was not found.

Figure 138.

In the case of People vs. A. J. Whiteman, the noted bank forger, tried at Buffalo, N. Y., in 1905, it was claimed that the accused was in various cities at the time certain forgeries were committed, but registered under an assumed name. This illustration shows a genuine registration and the alleged registrations from hotels in six different cities. The words "& wife," "Syracuse" and "New York" are peculiarly individual. See also connections between letters, pen position, and shading. The accused was convicted.

When these six hotel registrations are brought together by the aid of photography the connection between them is unmistakable. Exclusion of photography in cases of this kind is equivalent to the exclusion of competent and material testimony. Photographs are now rarely excluded, although always objected to, and in some jurisdictions it is now almost if not quite reversible error to exclude them. The tendency of all courts of all states is toward that procedure which assists in showing the facts. In at least ninety-nine cases out of a hundred photographs are now admitted and the most enlightened and progressive courts will hardly listen to objections to them.

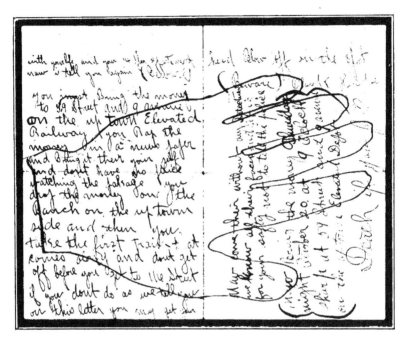

Fig. 137—A "Black Hand" Letter.

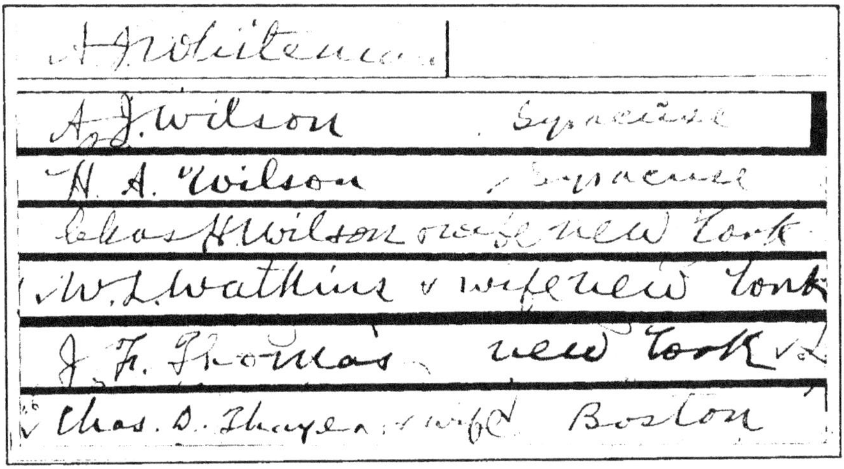

Fig. 138—A genuine signature and six "aliases" in six hotel registers in six different cities.

Figures 139, 140, 141.

These sad communications are all "suicide notes" and emphasize the necessity for handwriting examinations and the vital importance of such investigations. In the case of Fig. 139 the husband was accused and convicted of murder, but not on evidence based on the note as no evidence bearing on its authorship was presented by the prosecution. After conviction, however, realizing that the authorship of the note was the key to the whole case, the note and writing of the accused and the wife were submitted to specialists. It was then most conclusively shown by a number of enlarged and juxtaposed photographs that the wife undoubtedly wrote the note and as a result the convicted man was pardoned by the governor of the state on the advice of the prosecuting officer.

In the case illustrated in Fig. 140 (photographed by William J. Kinsley, Examiner and Photographer of Documents, New York), the note was written by the suicide as were also many others, and the final question to be determined was whether others aided and abetted her to commit suicide. · It was alleged that the copy for the notes was supplied by those who would profit by the death.

In the case illustrated in Fig. 141 there was suspicion that the death was not suicidal, but it was so clearly shown from the handwriting that the note was genuine that the inquiry was discontinued.

Figure 142.

This illustration shows clearly that the average writer is almost entirely unconscious of the fact that his own writing is full of peculiar individualities. The first part of the illustration shows the beginning lines of a most vicious anonymous letter. The suspected writer was asked at a preliminary examination to write the matter from dictation and the second part of the illustration was the astonishing result which amounted almost to an open confession.

Figure 143.

This illustration also shows how entirely unconscious many writing characteristics are. The first line is from an anonymous letter, the second and third are from standard writings by the alleged writer. This writer had the strange habit of beginning with a capital letter all words in which the small "o" was the first letter. Although the anonymous letter was written in backhand as a disguise every word beginning with "o" was distinctly capitalized.

Figure 144.

This illustration was made to show how a signature may be connected with a blotter impression. These impressions on a blotter are, of course, reversed and it may not appear until they read correctly from left to right how plain they are. In order to reverse the blotter impression when photographing it, the plate should be reversed in the plateholder, which will make the resulting print read the other way. In making such a photograph it is simply necessary after focusing to rack the camera forward the thickness of the plate and the result cannot be distinguished from a photograph made in the ordinary way. There are other occasions requiring reversed photographs and this method will apply in any case.

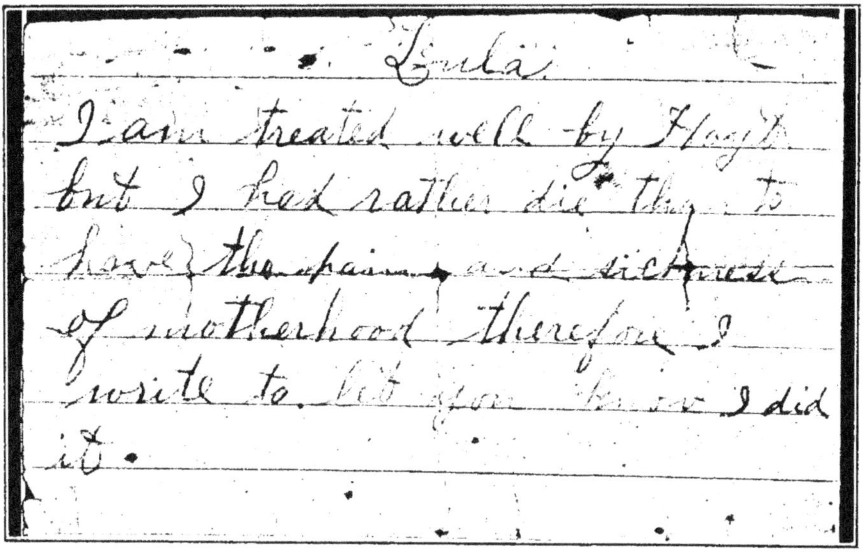

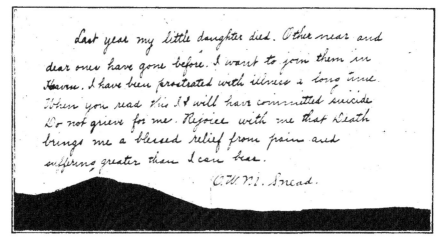

FIG. 139—A suicide note. If the woman wrote it she committed suicide, if she did not write it she was murdered.

FIG. 140—One of a series of suicide notes.

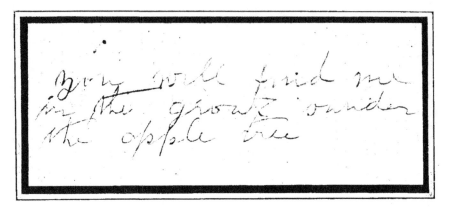

Fig. 141—A questioned suicide note.

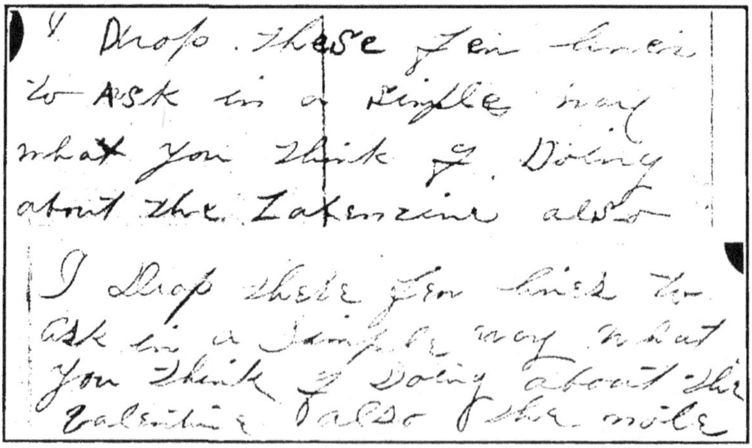

Fig. 142—Four lines of an anonymous letter and four lines of a "request" writing written from dictation.

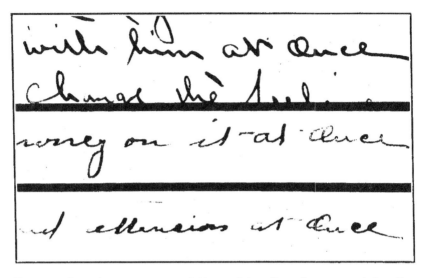

FIG. 143—Line from anonymous letter and two lines from suspected writer showing individuality in use of capital letters.

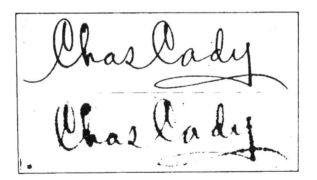

FIG. 144—A writing and a blotter impression of it photographed for comparison on reversed plate.

CHAPTER XVIII.

INK AND QUESTIONED DOCUMENTS[1]

Questions regarding ink frequently arise in connection with the investigation of disputed documents. An inquiry of this kind is sometimes merely collateral and may have only an indirect bearing on the investigation, or may be a matter of vital importance. Among the great variety of questions on the subject there are many that no competent man will attempt to answer with sufficient definiteness or certainty to make the answer of value as evidence; unfortunately, however, there are witnesses who undertake to answer any question, and this particular phase of questioned document investigations, perhaps more than any other, offers an opportunity to the pretender and the charlatan. It is therefore important to know what cannot be shown as well as what is a proper subject for investigation. Fortunately many of the questions regarding ink can be answered and illustrated in such manner that the answer is not a mere opinion, but evidence of the most convincing character.

One of the most frequent and most important questions is whether an ink is like or different in kind from ink on other parts of the same document or on other

[1]That portion of this chapter relating to the recording of ink colors and the description and use of the Color Microscope in the investigation of disputed documents was first printed in the Chicago Legal News, Vol. XI, No. 23 (Jan., 1908), and afterwards reprinted in the Criminal Law Journal of India, Vol. VII, No. 6, published at Lahore, India.

documents. This is a question that many times admits of the most positive and convincing answer. A second question of the same class is whether two writings made with the same kind of ink were made with the same ink or with inks of different qualities or in different conditions. A third question is whether documents of different dates, or a succession of differently dated book entries, show the natural variation in such writing or whether the result points to one continuous writing under identical conditions. The fourth inquiry, in some ways the most important of all, is as to the age of a writing as shown by the ink.

In considering the subject of ink in its relation to the investigation of documents it throws light on the inquiry to examine briefly the characteristics, qualities and differences in the inks in common use. Many different kinds of inks are known and made, but the three classes of black ink, now used almost exclusively in this country, are iron-nutgall ink, or so called writing fluid, logwood ink and nigrosine ink. Although they may look exactly alike these three inks differ from each other radically, and, even in the form of fine written lines on paper, one cannot be mistaken for either of the other two if properly tested. The downfall of the forger is often due to his lack of knowledge of the fact that black inks are not all alike.

The iron-nutgall ink is the most important of these three classes and has nearly supplanted all other kinds for writings of importance. Its use for general business purposes is almost universal and it is used almost exclusively in important books of record. It seems to be well established that this ink in its present form was first made commercially by Stephens in 1856. It differs from similar ink used before that time in that it is a true chemical solution as distinguished from a similar combination of ingredients with part of the coloring matter or precipitate held in suspension. Because of its extreme fluidity this ink of the modern type penetrates the fiber of the paper, where it blackens and thus actually makes its record partly in the body of the paper instead of simply on its surface, as is the case with inks that are not true solutions.

As is well known these iron-nutgall fluids are not immediately black when used but contain a temporary blue color which makes them legible until the sulphate of iron and gallic acid turn black, and the permanent and final color of the ink is formed, consisting of what is described as black tannate and gallate of iron. This lack of initial blackness is a defect in fluid inks that the most skilful chemists have not yet been able to remedy. Other objections to this ink are that the slight excess of acid it contains, in order to keep the iron in chemical solution, corrodes steel pens, and also that writing done with it is readily removed by the application of simple chemicals, thus rendering it easy fraudulently to change documents written with it. The characteristics of this ink that have made it popular are its excellent flowing quality, its ultimate blackness and permanent color imbedded in the paper fiber, and especially its excellent keeping qualities before being used.

Logwood ink of the potassium chromate type, it is said, was first produced commercially in 1848. This ink is a saturated solution of logwood to which a very small quantity of potassium-chromate is added forming a purple-black fluid which turns slightly darker on the paper. Logwood extract is sometimes combined with other ingredients to make other kinds of inks that are, however, but little used.

Nigrosine ink is made by dissolving in water a coal-tar product, called nigrosine, which makes a blue-black ink that flows freely but does not turn darker on the paper like iron-nutgall ink, and is easily smudged or affected by dampness even after it has been on the paper a long time. Nigrosine was first produced commercially in 1867 and writing with ink of this class dated before that time is either fraudulent or incorrectly dated.

The various kinds of ink in use each have desirable qualities. All carbon inks and inks of the India class, not heretofore described, are exceedingly permanent and very black and cannot be removed by chemicals, but being too thick and heavy to flow freely and thus undesirable for ordinary writing, are but little used. Logwood ink is inexpensive, does not corrode steel pens, will not wash off the paper even when fresh, flows freely and is nearly black when first written, but it does not keep well. Nigrosine ink does not corrode steel pens, is nearly black when first written and flows freely, but it never reaches the deep black color of good iron-nutgall ink and, as already stated, is easily affected by water or dampness at any time.

The composition of inks in writings on paper is determined by the application of various chemical reagents the color reactions of which are known as applied to different classes of inks. In this manner the question is answered whether two inks belong to the same class. Enough of the ingredients of an ink is not deposited on the paper in ordinary writing to permit a quantitative chemical analysis to be made, but the tests by reagents are conclusive within certain limits. If two inks give distinctly different reactions in response to the same test this indicates conclusively that the inks are not the same, though it cannot be definitely shown what all the ingredients of the inks actually are, and if two inks give the same response under several different reagents this shows that they belong to the same class even though it cannot be shown that they are necessarily identical in proportions of ingredients.

The two most useful reagents are chemically pure hydrochloric and oxalic acids in from five to fifteen per cent. solutions. They are easily obtained and only a small quantity is necessary. Logwood ink and iron-nutgall ink are conclusively differentiated by the hydrochloric test. Under this reagent iron-nutgall ink gives a distinct blue or blue-green reaction and logwood ink gives a distinct red or purple-red reaction, the results being so distinctively different (Fig. 145) that they are unmistakable.

Inks containing iron are also distinguished by the application of ferrocyanide of potash, which when applied to such inks instantly produces a characteristic bright blue reaction. Care should be taken to be sure that this reaction is from the ink and not from the paper.

Oxalic acid applied to iron-nutgall inks or logwood inks bleaches or removes them entirely, but this reagent has but little if any effect on nigrosine ink except to make its color somewhat brighter temporarily. By this test nigrosine ink and also carbon ink are conclusively differentiated from logwood inks and iron inks. Iron-nutgall ink and logwood ink are also differentiated from nigrosine ink by applying water or alcohol. Nigrosine ink, being merely a stain obtained from nigrosine dissolved in water, is easily dissolved again on the paper and the color runs or spreads out when any fluid is applied to it. Logwood ink is not affected even if water is applied to fresh writing, and iron inks are not thus

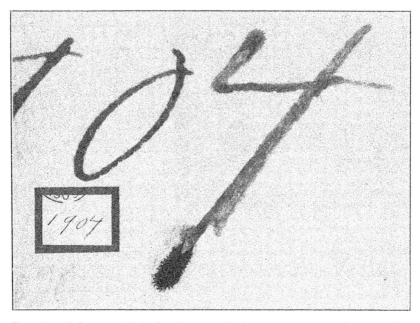

Fig. 145—Ink test with hydrochloric acid showing one part of overwritten figure was in logwood ink, and one in iron-nutgall ink. This illustration was made to show the facts in a case where it was claimed that a figure "7" was first made and a figure "4" made over it at once. The opposing party claimed the change was made long after for a fraudulent purpose.

affected after writing has been on the paper a short time.

Nigrosine ink is distinguished from carbon ink by the application of a bleaching agent, such as the ordinary ink eradicator, which bleaches nigrosine at once but does not affect carbon ink.

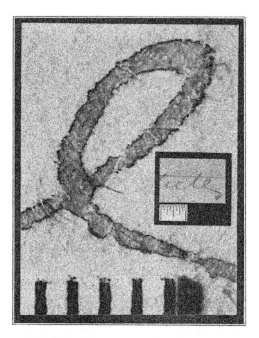

Fig. 146—A nigrosine ink line with microscopic black edges.   Actual size and enlarged x 21.

Nigrosine ink can often be quite positively identified as such by a microscopic examination. Ink lines made with this ink have peculiar dark microscopic edges like a very narrow black border, and this ink also sometimes has a peculiar metallic luster and secondary color when observed at a certain angle of light[1].

Iron-nutgall ink cannot ordinarily be differentiated from logwood ink by microscopic examination after both inks have reached their full depth of color, and some nigrosine inks cannot be so identified.

[1] An excellent article on the testing of inks, "Zur Methode der Chemischen Untersuchung von Tintenschrift," appeared in the September, 1908, (Band I. Nr. 3) of 'Archiv Gerichtliche Schriftuntersuchungen und verwandte Gebiete," a magazine, ably edited by Dr. George Meyer and Dr. Hans Schneickert of Berlin, and devoted to the discussion of subjects relating to questioned documents. The contribution on the subject of ink is by Richard Kynast, Chief Chemist of Edward Beyer's great Ink Works at Chemnitz, Germany, and is a condensed, clear statement of the leading facts on the subject with directions for making tests.

Another important paper on ink testing, "English Inks, Their Composition and Differentiation in Handwriting," was printed in Analyst, 33, 80-5 London, 1908, and is by C. A. Mitchell, one of the authors of the English book on the subject, entitled "Inks, Their Composition and Manufacture," London, 1904. On the question of qualities of various inks Mr. Mitchell finds: "In spite of probable

One who assumes to be able to recognize all the various kinds of ink by a microscopic examination alone is either ignorant or pretends to do what cannot be done.

The second question regarding ink, as outlined at the beginning of this chapter, is usually more difficult than the first. At the outset it should be understood that the writing fluids in general use cannot be actually identified and distinguished from each other by name after the ink has matured on the paper, although it may be possible to show clearly that the inks on several documents or on different parts of the same document are of a different quality or were in different conditions when the writing was done.

These fluid inks are composed of certain proportions of iron and nutgall chemical solutions with a very small addition of gum and a small amount of carbolic acid, or some other preserving agent, and an aniline blue

similarity in methods of preparation there are wide variations, the total solids varying from 1.89 to 7.94%, ash from 0.42 to 2.52%, and iron in iron gall inks from 0.18 to 1.09%."

The reagents most useful, according to Mr. Mitchell, are: (1) Hydrochloric acid (5%). (2) Oxalic acid (5%). (3) Stannous chloride (10%). (4) Nascent hydrogen (50% HCl with zinc). (5) Bromine (saturated aqueous solution). (6) Bleaching powder (saturated solution). (7) Titanous chloride (the impure commercial solution). (8) Potassium ferrocyanide (5% containing 1% HCl). Nos. (1) and (2) act mainly upon the iron tannate, and leave the provisional coloring matter. Nos. (3) and (4) bleach the iron tannate and reduce the provisional pigment, changing its color. Nos. (5) and (6) may act on both pigments, causing superficial bleaching. No. (7) is a powerful reducing agent towards both pigments, and No. (8) acts mainly upon the iron liberated from the iron tannate.

It would appear from certain discussions of this matter of ink testing in foreign periodicals that there is much greater variety in inks of the same class than in this country. No competent American ink chemist would undertake to do with American inks what, for example, Mr. Mitchell seems to have done with English inks. Chemist Kynast in the article referred to above voices the best American judgment on the matter when he says: "Ink manufacturers themselves would be unable to say, with certainty, whether a certain writing is written in an ink of their make."

temporary color. The differences between them are due to the methods of compounding and the care, skill and uniformity with which they are made, and the slight differences in proportions cannot be accurately determined from the small amount deposited on paper in actual writing. Some inks, generally speaking, may be very superior to others, in strength, in uniformity, in cleanliness, but with a comparatively small amount of writing in question it is almost certainly an unwarranted assumption to say positively that a writing was produced with a certain American fluid ink made by a particular manufacturer. The English inks, Stephens's and Arnold's, which have been much used in this country, are made with indigo as the temporary color and have a distinct greenish tint before maturity or under the hydrochloric test, and while they cannot ordinarily be distinguished from each other, they can sometimes be distinguished from fresh American inks of the same class[1].

While a chemical test is the most conclusive method of differentiating inks actually different in kind, it may be the most ineffective method of distinguishing from each other inks of the same class. A chemical test of two inks not identical but of the same class tends to show they are the same for the reason that the chemical reactions would be substantially alike. Two different inks of the same class and containing the same chemical ingredients may actually differ from each other in many ways as they appear in the form of writing on paper. The most common difference perhaps is that due to the

---

[1] A bottle of Stephens's ink bought during the preparation of this chapter shows the characteristic blue color of American inks indicating the use of aniline blue instead of indigo. The latest Arnold ink still shows the pale green color.

amount of water present or the thickness or thinness of the ink. This difference may be caused by the fact that the ink has more solid matter in it from the beginning, or water may have disappeared by evaporation, or, in some instances, may be added in excess by the user.

Different inks of the same class are distinguished from each other by differences; (1) in depth or strength of color, (2) in range of color or contrast between various parts, (3) by variation in tint of the ink as a whole due to chemical changes after the inks are compounded, (4) in secondary color by oblique reflected light, (5) in margin of the stroke whether clearcut or feathered, (6) in penetration or degree it is absorbed into or shows through the paper, (7) color of blotted strokes or smeared portions, (8) in amount of sediment or precipitate shown in thin strokes, (9) in gloss or sheen. Some of these conditions are related somewhat, but a careful detailed examination under these nine heads may show differences that are indisputable.

Depth and range of color should be compared by examination of the writing as a whole and then by comparing with each other the lightest, the medium, and the darkest portions in the two writings. It can often be shown that one of two inks of the same general tint has a much greater range of color either in the direction of lightness or darkness, a difference which is due to a slight difference in the consistency or fluidity of the two inks. Two inks may be the same in appearance except that one is never at any place of as deep a color as the other and one may show delicate tints on thin films of ink, especially on beginning strokes, that cannot be found in the other at any place.

These inks are intended to be true solutions, that is, without precipitate or suspended matter, but they often show marked differences in this regard depending upon the skill with which they were made, their age, and especially upon the kind of vessel in which they have been kept. By oxidation before use a fluid ink may develop a very perceptible sediment in the form of thousands of dark particles which are plainly shown in every thin ink line made with it as seen on the background of the light tint. Sediment may be dust that has fallen into the ink and become mixed with it, but usually comes from the ink itself. It is much more apparent if writings are made from ink kept in one of the plunger or patent ink wells in which each operation of dipping the pen stirs up the ink from the bottom of the well. These ink wells probably also tend to develop sediment by the constant operation of alternate wetting and drying of quite a large surface at the opening of the well and the continual washing of the dried portions of the ink back into the receptacle. The presence or absence of sediment is easily shown with the microscope under comparatively low magnification (see Fig. 30) and does not require that an observer shall be specially skilled in order to see these facts.

The great variation and range of color of ordinary iron-nutgall inks are partly due to the fact that the color of the ink gradually changes in the bottle before it is used from a bright blue to a green and then to a greenish yellow, these changes being governed by the method of compounding, the original proportions of ingredients, and the conditions under which the ink is kept. In perpetrating a fraud it thus often becomes difficult to match exactly the color of a previous writing and it is not the simple operation of finding a bottle with a similar label, even if it is well known what the ink is that is to be matched. As was said above, ordinary writing fluid is colored or given its initial blue color by the addition of aniline blue, and ink makers do not seem to be able to make ink of this kind that will remain indefinitely the same color before being used. Fresh ink will usually differ distinctly in initial color from ink that is two years old and in three years it may change in the bottle so that it looks like an entirely different ink.

In comparing inks examination should first be made with the naked eye in good daylight and then with hand magnifiers, and finally with the color microscope. A thorough examination of this kind sometimes requires that careful chemical tests be made of inks which are being compared. All such tests on a questioned document should be delicately and carefully made and the exact location, nature and the results of the tests should be recorded at the time. If proper methods are employed chemical reagents can be applied so that documents are not only not injured, defaced nor obliterated but so that without the microscope it cannot be observed that any tests have been made.

The reagents should be applied with finely pointed instruments made from quill or wood. When the test is made a microscope with low power objective or magnifying glass mounted on a stand should be focused on the spot to be tested so that a very small quantity of the reagent may be accurately applied to an unimportant and inconspicuous part of a pen stroke. An area larger than the size of a small pin-head should not be covered,

and a second application may be made to the same spot
if necessary until a definite color reaction is clearly
shown. A clean white blotter should be applied at the
conclusion of the test and it is usually well to apply a
small quantity of clean water several times to the portion tested, taking up the water each time by the immediate application of a clean blotter. If this is carefully done the chemical reagents can be almost entirely
removed from the paper and no perceptible discoloration
will follow.

Very minute tests can be made, by using the microscope as described above, so that the document shows
practically no effects of the tests. Tests should always
be made in good daylight, and the result should always
be observed under proper magnification, and usually
more than one portion should be tested. Especially in
signature inquiries even these very minute chemical
tests should not ordinarily be made on a document of the
adverse party without consent. Such a chemical test
might be misconstrued or might slightly change some
writing characteristic.

In making a visual comparison of the ink of two writings a superficial or hasty examination may easily lead
to a wrong conclusion. The exact tint of a small mass
of any substance is not easily recognizable by the unaided eye, and, as already seen, ink colors should always
be compared under proper magnification with a good
microscope. As it is difficult if not impossible for most
observers to carry in the eye a tint or shade even for a
very short space of time, two ink lines to be compared
should always be observed at the same time. This is
possible with the double objective color microscope,

described hereafter, or with an ordinary microscope the same purpose may be accomplished if it is possible to bring the two lines close together into the same field. Examination and comparison should always be made in good daylight but not in direct sunlight.

Care should always be taken not to decide hastily that two writings are with two different inks when one has been blotted and the other not. A blotted ink stroke looks very different from one made with the same ink and unblotted, although this does not make it impossible to say that the writings were or were not actually made with different inks. It is usually possible to tell whether a blotter was applied by comparing the first and last portions of the word, signature or line. The very last part of a blotted writing almost certainly will be lighter than the beginning part because ink is partly absorbed into ordinary paper in a few seconds, and more of the ink of the last part of the writing will quite certainly be taken up by the blotter than of the beginning portions. Where the blotter is applied somewhat slowly only the heavily shaded portions may show its effect. Blotted iron-nutgall ink shows yellow discoloration due to age much sooner than unblotted ink, and will fade and become illegible much earlier. A blotter should never be applied to important writing of any kind.

The apparent color and age of ink are changed by the color, condition and character of the paper upon which it is placed, and this point must be considered when the inks on different documents, written on differing papers, or ink on different parts of the same document, when the parts are in different conditions, are compared. Writing on old yellow paper may look distinctly aged and the appearance may be almost wholly due to the paper and not to the ink. An imitation of an old document may have an old look due almost entirely to the old paper used. If genuine old documents are compared with such a paper the difference in the actual condition of really old ink and fresh ink will usually be apparent at once.

The depth of color in an ink line is also governed in a measure by the amount applied at any point or the thickness of the ink film. In any considerable quantity of writing and usually in even a short signature three depths of color can be found and compared; first, the very thinnest lines as at the beginning and ends of strokes; second, the average unshaded normal strokes; third, the shaded strokes, or any portions where there is a thick ink film as at angles or loops where the wet ink from the pen has flowed back on the previous line just made. If the ink film is very thick it may be difficult to make an exact color reading of it. As colors approach black it becomes more difficult to differentiate them so that the medium and the thinner portions of ink lines may furnish a better basis for comparison of tints than the dense and darker portions.

Black inks may be very nearly identical except that one may have a slight blue tinge, another a purple tinge and a third a yellow, brown, or red tinge. In inquiries regarding interlineations or the continuity of writing it may be very important to differentiate these inks in the most positive and conclusive manner. This can sometimes be done by means of photography. A photographic analysis of these slightly varying colors sometimes will show conclusively what may be but a very slight difference in two inks. This is accomplished by measuring the comparative chemical effect of light of different colors by means of the sensitized photographic plate.

As is positively exemplified in the three color photographic process this analysis shows a difference in the colors as real as the chemical difference in two substances of any kind. Analysis is made by photographing the writings through color screens or light filters (Figs. 27, 147) which allow only certain colors to pass and to affect the sensitized plate. If it is desired to emphasize one of the slightly differing colors in two writings in the black and white reproduction on the resulting print, a filter is used which is complementary in color and does not allow that color to pass or allows it to pass only feebly; and to reduce a tint or to weaken a color a filter is employed of a color similar to that to be reduced, which allows the light to pass freely, so forming a thick deposit on the negative which will as a result make a light print. Both writings are photographed together on the same plate, developed together and printed together under exactly the same conditions, and if the two writings do actually differ in color this process will show it plainly. By the use of ordinary, orthochromatic, and panchromatic plates and appropriate light filters any desired photographic color comparison or analysis can be made. Each particular case of comparison must first be studied in good daylight and worked out by itself with the microscope[1].

[1]There are shown in Fig. 147 five photographs of standard colors from the beautiful Prang & Co. colored plate under "spectrum" in the Standard Dictionary. Some of the finer gradation of tint is lost in the half-tone but this illustration shows clearly what command of the situation the photographer has by a proper selection of plates and light filters. Plate No. 1 shows plainly why the ordinary photographer has

The third question regarding ink, or that of continuity, is sometimes of great importance and requires very careful consideration. The condition of the ink as it appears on suspected papers may be of distinct value as evidence showing whether two or more documents, purporting to have been written at different times, were not in fact all written at the same time. The condition, uniformity and age of ink must also be carefully considered in the examination of records, or book-entries, which are suspected of having been written fraudulently at one time instead of having been entered in due course of business on the several dates they bear. Such entries may show an unnatural uniformity when they purport to have been written on widely differing dates and necessarily under varying conditions, even when the same ink is admittedly used throughout. If numerous entries purporting to be written at different times and on widely divergent dates all show exactly the same ink color and condition this may be a very suspicious circumstance. This question is more fully discussed in a subsequent chapter treating of additions and interlineations.

---

difficulty in photographing blue or purple or any color on a red or orange paper or background. It will be seen that any of the standard colors can be reduced or intensified, thus making it possible to photograph any kind of questioned document written in any color of ink and on any color of paper.

In No. 1 it will be seen that red and orange are darkest and blue lightest, while in No. 2 blue is darkest and yellow is lightest. In No. 3 yellow is darkest and in No. 4 yellow and green are lightest while in No. 5 the opposite end of the spectrum is light as compared with No. 1, and blue is the darkest color as photographed.

Much valuable information on the subject of color photography may be found in "Three-Color Photography," by Von Hübl, (Vienna). English translation by Klein.—Penrose & Co., London, 1904.

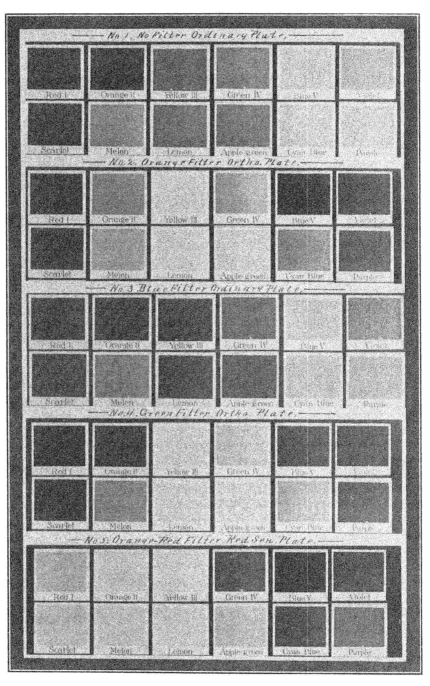

Fig. 147—Five photographs of the same colors with different plates and light filters.

[347]

The Age of Ink.

In discussing the fourth inquiry regarding ink as outlined at the beginning of this chapter, the question of its age, it may be best to consider first what cannot be done and what cannot be shown. After iron-nutgall ink has been on paper long enough to mature and reach its darkest color it is not possible by any method to ascertain with much accuracy how old it is until it begins to show evidence of the yellow discoloration which ordinarily indicates that it has been on the paper more than from seven to ten years. To say that one writing with this ink is three years old and another four and another five, judging from the ink alone, is almost certainly an unwarranted assumption, although it may be very clear that not one of these inks is as old as another ink that has been on a paper ten, fifteen, or twenty years. If iron-nutgall and logwood inks have been on the paper a long time they do not respond so quickly to chemical reagents as ink not so old, and comparative age may thus be determined in a general way but not very accurately. Definite statements as to comparative ages of writings based on such tests alone should be received with great caution unless the tests show that the inks are of very widely differing dates[1].

---

[1]Dr. Dennstedt, the celebrated chemist, director of the State Chemical Laboratory, at Hamburg, Germany, in his excellent treatise on "The Proof of Forged Manuscripts, etc." (Der Nachweis von Schriftfalschungen usw.), says (p. 97):

"The chemical examinations for the purpose of deciding the age of a manuscript according to our knowledge were first made use of by Sonnenschein. According to him the differences in time shown in responding to chemical applications, as measured by the stop watch, would indicate different ages. It is true very old ink responds less rapidly than younger ink to chemical application. The conclusion regarding the age is only then allowable and even then only conditionally if it is a question about the same ink. If the two inks are

If a writing was done with a purple, blue, or red ink or with a black nigrosine ink[1], it is not ordinarily possible to tell from the ink alone how old it is. But it may be possible to determine that a very recent writing with some of these inks was written after a very old writing with a similar ink, for the reason that in an investigation of

not identical any judgment is unreliable in spite of the scientific appearance of the method of using the stop watch.   One must therefore make use of this process very seldom and always with greatest care."

Fresh inks give a better copy than old inks and it has been proposed that a press copy be made to show whether one ink is older than another.   The method is a dangerous one and often entirely inconclusive.   If it is known positively that the two writings are with the same ink and that the ink will give a copy after it has been on the paper as long as the most recent writing has been written, and the conditions surrounding both writings were the same, then it may be advisable to try the copying test.

[1]Color readings of nigrosine black ink on bleached, white rag paper, covering four years' time, made with the Color Microscope described on pages following, show the following results   :

	Red	Yellow	Blue
Thirty minutes	1.6	.90	3.6
One year, one month	1.6	.90	3.6
Four years, six months	1.6	.90	3.6

The reading of a similar ink by a different manufacturer on December 30, 1903, was Red 1.6, Yellow 1, Blue 3.6, and after six years the reading is just the same.

The color reading of good logwood ink is very nearly like nigrosine but usually has a little more red so that the visual color is a deeper purple.   These inks can usually be recognized by these colors and can be distinguished from each other because the nigrosine ink has the peculiar, black microscopic margins.   An initial reading of a good logwood ink in good condition gives: Red 1.9, Yellow .90, Blue 3.4 and the same ink after three years gives: Red 1.8, Yellow 1.5, Blue 3. It will be observed that the nigrosine ink has not changed and the logwood only slightly, having grown somewhat darker in shade by an increase in the yellow.

In the readings tabulated only the constituent colors directly from the glasses are given.   The visual colors obviously are not the same as the constituent colors, as equal parts of blue and yellow would visually be green, and red and blue would be violet.

Three glasses of the same value give not a tint but a shade, so the lowest in a combination of three we read as neutral or black.   In a reading of Red 1., Yellow .90, Blue 5.60 there would be, for example, black .90 and .10 red excess to combine with the blue, giving a violet of .10, and leaving an excess of 4.60 blue above the sum of the two other visual constituents.   The predominant color is of course blue tinged with violet and shaded or damped with the .90 of yellow which does not appear as a tint.   The visual reading therefore is Black .90, Violet .10, Blue 4.60.

this kind other questions than color may enter into the inquiry. Old and recent writings with logwood ink can sometimes be differentiated, but this cannot always be done. Nigrosine ink writing an hour old does not differ materially in any way from writing with the same ink one, two or three years old. Nigrosine inks are not all of the same quality and, therefore, may differ from each other somewhat in appearance, but the ink does not change on the paper to a sufficient extent to warrant any opinion as to its age unless it be very old.

It is sometimes very important to determine the age of an ordinary lead pencil writing, or the comparative ages of two such writings, but unfortunately this cannot be done. One who undertakes to do it, or to say that one pencil writing is "more than a year old," and another "less than a year old," may safely be set down as a pretender and unworthy of belief.

Fortunately it is possible to answer definitely one inquiry of the most vital interest in connection with the age of ink and its bearing on the genuineness of a disputed document and that is whether it has yet matured and reached its fullest depth of color. In many cases it has been positively known that the ink on a disputed document purporting to be many years of age, has matured or "turned black" after the paper has been brought into court, but such a statement based on mere recollection is of little value as evidence. There has long been great need of some means by which ink colors under the above conditions could be accurately measured and recorded. In most cases it is a dangerous undertaking for anyone to make one examination of an ink and venture to say just how old it is, unless it is very recent or very old, but by recording the color as first seen any observer with good eyesight can answer the question whether an ink is still undergoing a change in color.

In the natural course of events a fraudulent document is manufactured only a short time before it is actually brought forward, and the conditions often require that such a paper be dated back many months or even many years. Fortunately the ink in most common use, iron-nutgall ink, goes through more changes on the paper than any other ink and is most affected by lapse of time, and these facts may be of great importance in the investigation of a suspected document. It is highly important to know that the color of the ink on such a document may be the means of showing that it is not genuine. If a writing of this kind purports to have been written long before and it can be conclusively shown that the ink has not yet matured, and that it actually goes through those changes that are characteristic of ink during the first few months of its history, it is only necessary to prove these facts to invalidate such a paper.

The fact that ordinary fluid ink changes color has naturally received some attention in the examination of questioned documents purporting to be written long before, but there has been no means of making an accurate and permanent record of the tint and shade of the ink for subsequent comparison with itself. The important fact is that the iron-nutgall inks in common use reach their fullest intensity of blackness by a continuous process of oxidation, and this chemical action cannot be entirely arrested to be resumed and completed at a remote period of time. The facts about the time required for these changes of color are not generally understood.

It is essential to know the rate of development of such changes and also when they are entirely completed.

The first steps in the darkening of these inks are much more rapid than the later ones. A good ink in summer

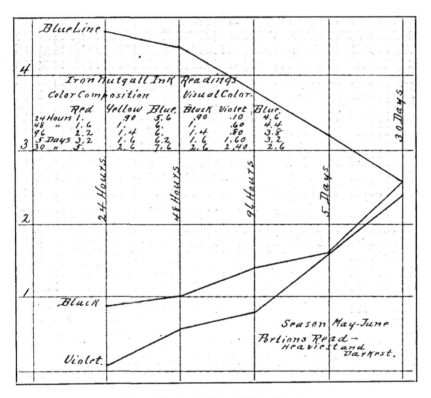

Fig. 148—Iron-Nutgall Ink Chart.

under ordinary view will appear to be black at the end of from one to two weeks and in winter this degree of blackness will be reached in from six to eighteen weeks, but in both cases the ink is then far from black and a very long way from its ultimate condition. This first apparent blackness is not blackness at all, but, under proper magnification and good daylight, is seen to be a rich blue-purple color at its densest portions, shading off into light blue in the thin places[1]. This blue gradually disappears and the purple gradually deepens until the ink finally reaches a neutral black without any purple or blue color whatever. This latter process is very slow and oftens covers many months, the time depending upon the surrounding conditions, the quality of the ink, and the kind of paper upon which it is placed.

The time required for fresh iron-nutgall ink of good quality to reach a neutral black is from about fourteen to twenty-four months. After this ink reaches its fullest intensity of color it remains in a practically fixed condition for some years, approximately six to ten, and then it begins to show slight yellow discoloration on the edges of the pen strokes. This discoloration is progressive until after a sufficient lapse of time, depending upon conditions, the ink finally all becomes a yellowish brown color. Iron-nutgall ink may be so old before being used that it has turned yellow in the bottle and writing with such ink may be a distinct yellow color in a short time.

As we have seen, iron-nutgall ink color develops much

---

[1]In January, 1910, color readings were made from nine different commercial iron-nutgall inks all purchased in the open market on the same day. It is true that some of these inks because of age may have degenerated in the bottle but most of them were apparently only a few months old.

The results of color readings of these inks on pure white paper after forty-eight hours are as follows:

	Red	Yellow	Blue
No. 1	.80	.70	5.8
No. 2	.40	.70	5.8
No. 3	.40	.44	5.
No. 4	.38	.50	4.8
No. 5	.40	.38	4.6
No. 7	.38	.44	4.4
No. 6	.38	.44	4.6
No. 8	.80	.90	4.6
No. 9	.60	1.20	3.6

slower in winter than in summer. The most rapid change is during the warm, humid months, the humidity undoubtedly affecting the change much more than the heat. In the months of July and August an iron-nutgall ink will reach a degree of blackness in ten days that will hardly be reached by the same ink on the same paper in ten weeks in winter in northern latitudes where artificial heat takes a large percentage of the humidity out of the air. This varying rapidity of development is a fact always to be taken into consideration in such an examination. If a fraudulent paper is made during the winter months there is a much longer interval during which a color examination of the ink may be useful in ascertaining the actual date of the document.

Even under conditions producing the very slowest development iron-nutgall inks lose most of their distinctive initial color in a few months and usually in a few weeks or even days. The blue or green tints do not fade, but are gradually extinguished by the development of the darker developed colors of the iron-nutgall solutions[1]. The first part of the process, the dulling or extinguishing of the distinctive bright blue color, is comparatively rapid, as we have seen, but the completion of the entire process covers a comparatively long time.

This astonishingly slow rate of development is not generally understood for the reason that opinions on the subject are usually based upon the ordinary view by unaided vision. Because of this slow development it is

---

[1]The distinct blue color of American iron-nutgall ink is produced, as we have seen, by the addition of aniline or coal-tar blue which serves the temporary purpose of making the ink legible when first put upon the paper. The iron-nutgall solution alone is a pale brown color and writing with it is almost illegible.

possible in many instances to make useful color comparisons of inks that have been on the paper for some time. The important fact is, as already said, that the process of oxidation is a continuous one until the ink has reached its fullest and final intensity of color. Even on the leaves of a tightly closed book ink oxidizes continuously until it reaches its ultimate color. If a book with writing in it is kept under great pressure and not opened, the air, with the moisture it always carries, may be sufficiently excluded to retard the oxidation slightly, but not to stop it.

In view of all these facts it is obvious that if a disputed writing, purporting to have been written some time before, is a distinct blue or green color when it is first shown *and then turns black in a short time,* it is only necessary to prove this fact in order to show that the ink has not been on the paper for a long time. To show and to prove this changing color it becomes necessary, as we have seen, to compare the ink with itself at successive examinations, and to do this a record must be made of the color as first seen. A new method of making such a record is here described.

The Color Microscope.

A color record of an ink can be made by means of a new instrument that may be described as a Color Microscope, which was especially designed for the comparison, measurement and recording in fixed terms of tints and shades of ink[1]. This special instrument brings the

[1]Many occasions arise in the examination of questioned documents when other uses can be made of such an instrument and without some such assistance as it gives the facts in certain cases cannot be clearly shown. It is useful in all ink investigations, but is especially useful for the purpose just outlined above.

magnified images of two objects or fields into one microscopic eyepiece so that they may be observed side by side. This is accomplished by means of two parallel tubes surmounted by inclosed reflecting prisms which bring the rays of light from the two objects in juxtaposition so that each image occupies one-half of the field as seen under one eyepiece. By the use of matched objectives the two fields of view are easily and accurately compared by being thus brought close together under suitable magnification. Most ink strokes are so narrow that they lack a sufficient mass of color to show tints and shades in natural size by unaided vision, but under proper magnification the most delicate distinctions, both in tint and depth of color, can readily be seen.

The Color Microscope was made to utilize the Lovibond tintometer glasses for the recording of ink colors. By interposing these delicately graduated red, yellow, and blue standard color glasses in one tube any color can be exactly matched as seen under the other tube and a definite record made of it, as the color value of each glass is etched upon it[1]. The observation is made through the glass standards against a standard white

---

[1] The first attempts were made with coloured liquids in test tubes of equal diameters, and by these means some useful information was obtained. The liquids, however, soon changed colour, requiring frequent renewals; and there was always a little uncertainty concerning their exact reproduction. . . Coloured glass was next tried, and long rectangular wedges in glass of different colours, with gradually graded tapers, were ground and polished for standards, whilst correspondingly tapered vessels were made for the liquids to be measured. These were arranged to work, at the end of the instrument, up and down at right angles before two apertures, side by side, with a fixed centre line to read off the thickness of each before the aperture when a colour match was made; but here also the difference of ratio between the thickness and colour depth of the different coloured glass and liquids proved fatal to the method.—Lovibond's Light and Colour, p. 14, George Gill & Sons, London.

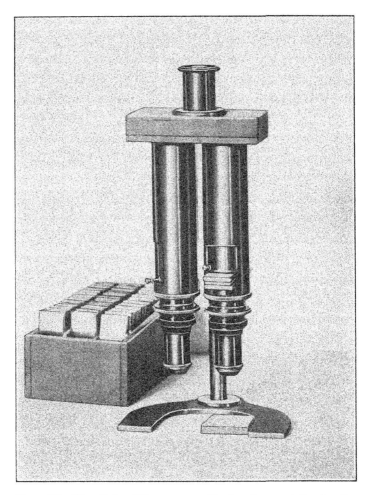

Fig. 149—The Color Microscope.   Designed especially for the
reading and recording of ink colors.

background, pure sulphate of lime under uniform pressure being used for this purpose as with the regular tintometer instrument. In this manner the exact constituents of the most delicate tints can be determined and recorded and comparisons can be made that otherwise it is absolutely impossible to make. The regular Lovibond tintometer is an instrument with which color readings are made without magnification and cannot be used for the purposes here described. Unless the color conditions are very distinct and pronounced, it is useless to attempt to make such comparisons without a suitable instrument.

Exact records should be made of the tint and shade of numerous parts of the writing on the first examination and color reading, which may be seen and verified by a number of observers if this seems desirable. Definite descriptions, illustrated by drawings, should also be made of the exact portions of the line examined, so that at the second and all subsequent examinations the instrument can be replaced and the glass standards introduced that exactly matched the ink color at the first reading when any change in the ink is at once apparent. If the ink has changed, then the standard glasses should be rearranged until the color is matched again and a second record made of the glasses required to match the color of the ink[1].

If at the first examination the ink is apparently very recent the second reading in summer should be made about ten days later and the third a month later. In

---

[1]It is advisable in using the Color Microscope to exclude all front and side light by the use of a small hood made of black paper, similar to that around the eyepiece of the ordinary stereoscope.

winter the second reading may be made two or three weeks or longer after the first reading. If, when first examined, the ink is several weeks old, the second reading may be made two or three months later.

The colors are matched by a combination of the red, yellow and blue standard glasses viewed by transmitted light. The most delicate differences in tint or shade can be shown[1]. With fifty of the accurately graduated glasses of each of the three colors, the number of pos-

---

[1] It is difficult to realize that a color seen as Blue, for instance, may really be a combination of the colors red and blue, or yellow and blue, or red, yellow and blue, only one of which we see. Few of the countless and beautiful colors surrounding us are simple, but are made up of combinations of various colors, one of which is visually predominant. Under "Spectrum" in the Standard Dictionary is printed an excellent color chart showing forty-eight type colors with an analysis of each. A few of the more familiar colors, with the proportions of constituents, are as follows:

	Black	White	Red	Orange	Yellow	Green	Blue
Robin's-Egg Blue..		38				41	21
Nile Green........		25				45	30
Gobelin Blue......	40	17				13	30
Turquoise		34				34	32
Sapphire Blue.....	12					18	70
Russet	40		24	20	6	10	
Olive Green.......	13	18	17		8	44	

Many, no doubt, will be surprised to know that Robin's-Egg Blue is more green than blue, and that the same is also true of Turquoise.

It is well known that proper mixtures of the three colors red, yellow and blue in the form of pigments or printers' colors will produce the three colors of the spectrum, green, orange and violet, and by changing the proportions of the colors first mentioned a great variety of tints and hues can be produced. The various colors of the spectrum can also be produced by the combination of the three colors red, yellow and blue as transmitted by colored glass. A colored glass, red for example, produces its color by absorption of the greater part of the other colors, so that only red is visible. It is a common error to suppose that a colored glass actually colors a beam of light. From the fact that colors by absorption are not simple, it becomes possible by the mixture of such lights to produce a marvelous number of tints by the use of graduated red, yellow and blue glasses.

It seems to be very well established that the three primary colors of the spectrum are not red, yellow and blue, as has long been taught, but red, green and violet; but for the use of the artist who works in pigments, or for the matching of tints by colored lights produced by absorption, the practical colors are red, yellow and blue.

sible combinations is very great. Each red standard can be combined with each blue standard, making twenty-five hundred combinations of these two. Each of these combinations can then be combined with each of the fifty yellow standards, making a total of one hundred and twenty-five thousand combinations. These do not all represent visible distinctions, as many of the lighter tints are extinguished by the heavier colors, but with this number of graduated standard glasses many thousands of actually visible tints can be matched. It is entirely possible to make more than a thousand visible blue tints and shades. This extremely fine gradation of tints and shades makes it possible to match an ink color with remarkable accuracy and detect the slightest change in it[1].

With the means at hand to make these delicate and accurate color tests it may appear that it ought to be possible to tell by the color alone after one examination how old an ink is. This could be done with accuracy if inks were all made alike in the first place, and then were all kept under the same conditions, and used only when they had reached a certain age, and finally, if the writings with them were put on the same kind and color of paper. These are the reasons why by any method

---

[1]From such data he (Aubert) calculated that in a solar spectrum at least a thousand distinguishable hues are visible. But we can still recognize these hues, when the light producing them is subjected to considerable variation in luminosity. Let us limit ourselves to 100 slight variations, which we can produce by gradually increasing the brightness of our spectrum, till it finally is five times as luminous as it originally was. This will furnish us with a hundred thousand hues, differing perceptibly from each other. If each of these hues is again varied twenty times, by the addition of different quantities of white light, it carries the number of tints we are able to distinguish up as high as two millions.—Rood's Text Book of Color, p. 40, D. Appleton and Company, New York.

F<small>IG</small>. 150—Red, Yellow and Blue pigments and mixtures of them producing the second series of colors, green, violet, and orange, and the combination of the three pigments producing black, and a representation in color of the Lovibond standard glasses.

it is difficult to say exactly how old an ink is by one examination[1].

In actual use it is possible during the summer months to match with the color microscope the changing color of an ordinary iron-nutgall ink on white paper at intervals of about four hours the first day; then every second or third day the change in the tint and in depth of color can be seen and recorded for about one week. Later a recognizable change can be recorded every second week for about four weeks. Then there is a difference that can usually be seen and matched between two months and four months and between four months and eight months, and the difference in color and shade between eight months and twenty-four months or more is, in most instances, readily seen and recorded.

The changes that take place in these iron-nutgall inks are so pronounced that they are unmistakable and cannot be denied. The change is so great between the color, for instance, of an ink after only a few days and after two months that any competent observer will say that

---

[1]Much valuable information and reference material can be obtained by a systematic series of color readings and records of the standard inks. It is possible to say that, if an ink under examination is a fresh, good standard ink, in one month, or three months, or a year, it will, on white paper, reach about a given color.

In the month of May iron-nutgall ink by four different manufacturers, on bleached white rag paper, showed the following color measurements after forty-eight hours:

	Red	Yellow	Blue
No. 1	1.	1.	5.2
No. 2	1.4	.70	5.2
No. 3	1.8	1.	5.6
No. 4	1.	.80	5.6

In these readings only the heavier parts of the ink strokes were observed. As has been said above, it is usually preferable, for the purposes of comparison, to examine also the thinner portions. The difference is not in tint but in depth of color and it is usually easier to observe changes in tints or colors not too dense.

it is not the same color at all. If at the second reading
the same glasses are replaced that matched the color at
the previous reading, and the surrounding conditions
are duplicated and exactly the same portion of line or
spot of ink is observed and compared with the color in
the opposite tube that at the previous reading was exactly the same color as the ink, and the colors are distinctly different and do not match, then the only conclusion possible is that the ink has changed in color. No
one can realize how distinct these changes actually are
without making the observations.

This method of examination takes the question out
of the field of opinion testimony and makes it one which
is simply the observation and interpretation of physical
facts that are within the view and understanding of any
one of average intelligence. The interests of justice are
always promoted when means are provided that in any
degree assist in discovering and showing the facts in a
court of law.

In order to ascertain the proportions of the black inks in common
use chemical tests were made of the ink on one hundred business
envelopes containing printed cards of business houses with the following results: Iron-nutgall 83; Logwood 10; Black Nigrosine 6; Blue
Nigrosine 1.

One hundred envelopes from individuals containing no printed
business card, mostly mailed from small towns, show by chemical test
the following kinds of ink: Logwood 45; Iron-nutgall 30; Black
Nigrosine 22; Blue Nigrosine 3.

Taken together these tests show the following averages: Iron-
nutgall 56½%, Logwood 27½%, Black Nigrosine 14%, Blue Nigrosine
2%.

The number of writers using logwood ink is surprisingly large, and,
as will be observed, more than twenty per cent. of the second class of
writers used nigrosine.

CHAPTER XIX.

Ordinary caution would seem to suggest that the paper on which a forged document is written should be carefully selected, but experience shows that in many cases no thought whatever seems to be given to the matter. A thorough investigation of a questioned document requires that the paper be thoroughly examined in every particular, and, if possible, traced to its source and positively identified, but in many cases only a superficial and hasty examination is made. As the result of a thorough examination the fraudulent character of documents many times has been conclusively shown by the paper alone. Many forged wills have been written on paper made years after the alleged dates of the documents and in some cases the paper has actually contained a dated water-mark (see Fig. 7) which anyone could see when it was held up to the light.

There are numerous ways in which the matter of paper may become important in connection with the study of documents. In the first place, as stated above, is the question of the actual age of the paper as compared with the date of the document. The question also may arise as to whether a paper is identical with or different from other paper the history of which is known. It also sometimes becomes important to determine if possible whether two sheets of paper of the same manufacture were made at the same time.

[363]

It has been conclusively shown that several questioned documents of widely different dates were all written on paper that originally formed one sheet, as was clearly proved by the matched indentations on the edges of the several pieces where they had been torn apart. The sheet of paper on which an anonymous letter has been written has been traced to a blank book from which it had been torn, and which had been in the possession of the one who was accused of writing the letter; and, it is sometimes shown, in cases of disputed or anonymous letters, that a letter was written on a sheet of paper which was part of the identical pad or package from which the paper of a standard or genuine letter was taken.

Identity or difference in paper is shown by its, (1) color, (2) thickness, (3) finish or surface, (4) watermark, (5) wove or laid style, (6) cutting, (7) size, (8) ruling, (9) padded or loose sheets, (10) wire marks, and (11) composition, or character of fibers used in its manufacture.

A quick test of identity of papers that externally seem to be identical can be made by micrometer calipers. As described in the chapter on instruments and appliances, the best instruments for this purpose are actuated by a spring rachet, which automatically governs the pressure exerted, and the instrument should also carry a vernier to read in ten-thousandths of an inch. Actual measurements of papers in fractions of an inch show wide variation in thickness as indicated by the following results: thin Japanese tissue, calendared .0009; ordinary tissue .0014; light typewriting .0027; heavy wedding note .0071; average visiting card .0182; forty-ply card .0763. By these accurate measurements ordinary writing paper can by the thickness test alone, as shown in the chapter on instruments, be put into about sixty classes when measured in thousandths of an inch.

When measured so accurately as in ten-thousandths of an inch there is some variation in the thickness of sheets in the same package, but with good paper, when several measurements are averaged, the variation is very slight. It is possible to mix up sheets of paper of very similar character but actually of different make and to sort them by the thickness test alone. Thin papers tested show an occasional variation of one ten-thousandth of an inch in a maximum thickness of twenty-three ten-thousandths, and thick paper shows an occasional variation of five ten-thousandths of an inch out of a maximum thickness of seventy-two ten-thousandths.

When questioned documents are written on printed forms it is very important to find when and where the forms were made. It has been shown that the printed blank forms on which disputed checks, notes, drafts and marriage certificates where written were printed long after the alleged dates of the documents. Investigation should not be stopped because it seems to promise no results; astonishing information has been secured in some instances after most discouraging initial efforts. In one important case it was positively shown that a diary containing a record of an alleged marriage was bought four years after the date of the diary and the entry.

If documents purporting to be old contain a blank date line with the year partly printed, this portion of the form should be scrutinized with especial care to see if erasures or changes have been made to make it conform to the century or division of the century desired. It is difficult, for example, in 1910 to find a blank form of the year 1890, and it may be necessary for the forger to make it partly by hand or to have it specially printed.

The question of the matching of paper and envelopes is sometimes of importance, especially the indentations on inclosures made by post-office dating stamps. It has been shown in this way that an alleged letter was not mailed in an envelope which it is claimed contained it.

Checks, drafts or other commercial paper torn from a stub at a perforated line can in some cases be matched

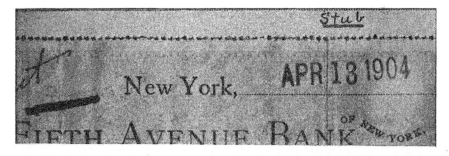

Fig. 151—Check Stub and part of Forged Check, showing, by the matching of torn perforated line, the unmistakable connection between the Forged Check and this Stub Book. The Stub Book was found on person of accused.

with the stub by the inequalities and variations in the torn parts, thus showing where the particular form came from. Such a task may seem hopeless at the outset, but it is astonishing how convincingly such apparently obscure facts can sometimes be shown.

The exact condition of the paper of a document as to cleanliness, folds, creases, etc., is also at times a matter of vital importance and should receive careful attention. Blots or offsets may show the original relation of two sheets of paper or envelopes and blots or offsets on the back of a genuine or standard letter may match the writing of the address of a disputed letter showing the contact of letters before the ink was dry and pointing to their common origin. Soiled places due to accident or design should be carefully studied and if possible interpreted. Finger prints if discernible in the slightest degree should be carefully examined and photographed. Marks or words may be made by accident or design on the side or edge of a pad or block of paper and by this means sheets of paper from this source can sometimes be identified.

The exact tint and shade of the paper in question should be ascertained in good daylight by the color microscope and its exact thickness measured by micrometer calipers, as described above. The exact size of the original sheet and whether it was cut by hand on one or more edges[1] should be ascertained; also whether it is note, letter, legal or foolscap and whether it was glued at top or side of the sheet in pad form. If the

---

[1] The next question whether the edges of the note were cut, or the ordinary foolscap edge, was competent for the same reason.—Dubois vs. Baker, 30 N. Y., 365 (1864).

paper was torn from a larger sheet the indentations should be carefully examined. The exact width, uniformity, location, and kind and color of ink of the ruling of the sheet should be observed and also the parallelism of the ruling with the upper and lower edges of the

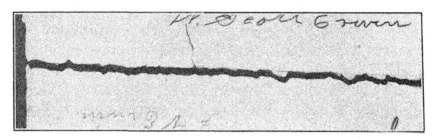

Fig. 152—Two examples of matching of torn edges of paper. The upper illustration shows the matched torn perforations of postage stamps. The lower illustration is of the torn edges of two disputed receipts of widely differing dates.

sheet. Any imperfections of any kind should be carefully noted and investigated. Some paper is not finished alike on both sides, and this is another matter that should receive attention.

At the first examination the whole surface of both sides of the paper ought to be carefully examined in good daylight with the sheet held at various angles allowing the light to strike the surface obliquely. If this is properly done any evidences of chemical or mechanical erasures, or disturbance of the paper fiber, or of dulling of the finish of the sheet by any means can usually be clearly seen. All folds and creases on both sides of the sheet should be carefully examined under proper magnification to see if the writing was done before or after the folding.

The discovery of the actual date of the making of a particular sheet of paper is not, of course, always possible but the fact that such paper must have been made before or after a certain definite date can sometimes be shown and this information alone may be sufficient to prove that a document could not have been made at the time it is claimed that it was made.

In some cases paper contains a dated watermark showing the year it was made and then again it can be proved that a certain water-

FIG. 153—Illustration of an accident to a watermark.

mark which contains no date was not used before a certain definite time. Paper on which important documents are written can frequently be traced to the mill where it was made and there the sheets can often be positively identified as of a certain particular run. Accidents, changes, repairs, new methods and different materials used, all affect the result and may indicate clearly when the paper was made. A careful study should be made of every part of the water-mark as well as of the wire gauze marking of the paper.

In the process of paper making the paper fiber is floated out on a moving gauze sheet through which a large part of the water runs at once, leaving the loose fiber which is carried under a revolving cylinder, also covered with wire gauze, and this packs the fiber together and squeezes out most of the water that has not already drained through the lower gauze. This gauze covered cylinder, called the dandy-roll, carries the water-mark which is formed of flexible wire soldered to the surface of this roll, forming a design with letters or figures. The pressure of these raised wires on the soft wet fiber presses aside a portion of it, making the paper more transparent and thus printing into the sheet the mark.

When the dandy-roll carries equidistant raised wires around the roll these mark the sheet lengthwise with parallel marks, in the same manner as the water-mark is made. Paper with these parallel water-marked lines is called "laid" and paper without such marks is called "wove." The "laid" paper has also a series of finer transparent lines running at right angles to the conspicuous water-marked lines.

Many things may occur that will indicate the date of the paper. One of the most common is regular changes in the water-mark in design, size, position, or arrangement of parts. These changes, the dates of which can usually be ascertained, indicate before or after what date the paper was made. When the water-mark contains an actual year date this is, of course, conclusive. As has been said the water-mark design is soldered on the dandy-roll and repairs are sometimes necessary as part of the design or letters may become loose, bent or broken. Such an accident may have marked in a peculiar manner a part of a certain definite run of paper, and, as samples are usually kept for future reference, such imperfect paper may be definitely identified and the date fixed. The dandy-roll or the gauze apron may be renewed or changed, which would also affect the result. As the water-marks are soldered on the dandy-roll by hand, no

F ɪɢ. 154—Dated water-marks in ordinary Government stamped envelopes of years '99, 1903 and 1907. A transmitted light photograph.

two of a series are likely to be exactly identical. In case of a change in diameter of the dandy-roll the water-marks in the sheet would be just so much nearer together or farther apart, and would thus identify and date every sheet of paper made in which two water-marks or parts of two water-marks appear.

Accidents may occur by which the wire cloth under the paper or the wire covering on the dandy-roll may be injured so as to mark every run of paper thereafter. The dandy-rolls for the different styles of paper, although carefully handled, are sometimes buckled or twisted, causing streaks to appear in the paper in exact relation to certain water-marks and this may mark the date of paper showing this characteristic. The date significance of some of these accidents may not be apparent to the mill foreman or manager until his attention is particularly called to them, and investigations should not be given up because discouragement is met with at the outset. It may be possible to discover conclusive evidence bearing on a case involving the distribution of an estate worth hundreds of times more than the value of the mill.

It is said that imitation water-marks or designs have been made with oil or grease or produced by pressure with a die after the paper is made. In these cases it would appear that there is as much fiber where the mark appears as elsewhere but the paper has been made more transparent either by the pressure or by the grease or oil. It is recommended in such a case that the wetting the sheet with a caustic solution or even with water will dim or obliterate such a design but will make a true water-mark more distinct[1].

Fig. 155—The earliest example of an English water-mark, 1363, as given by Scott & Davey in "Historical Documents, etc."

Questions of this nature are not likely to arise regarding forged commercial papers of any kind, but must sometimes be considered in connection with the investiga-

[1]Historical Documents, Literary Manuscripts and Autograph Letters, by Rev. Dr. Scott and Samuel Davey, London, 1891.

tion of alleged writing of celebrated persons and the examination of forged manuscripts of various kinds. In the celebrated Ireland-Shakespeare forgeries, entitled "Miscellaneous Papers and Legal Instruments," published in London in a beautiful folio edition in 1795, the fabricator was unable to find suitable water-marked paper for an extended writing[1].

The identity of paper may be determined by a microscopic examination of the materials of which it is composed, the different fibers having distinct peculiarities

---

[1] Into the manuscript of his presumptuous new version of "Kynge Leare," Ireland, the literary forger, put paper with "twenty different water-marks." Edmond Malone, in his scholarly book exposing the fraud, "An Inquiry into the Authenticity of Certain Papers and Instruments Attributed to Shakespeare, etc.," published in 1796, says on this point:

"The true and natural paper-warehouse for such a schemer to repair to is, the shop of a bookseller, where every folio and quarto of the age of Elizabeth and James would supply a couple of single leaves of white-brown paper, of the hue required." . . . What would an author naturally do when he sat down to write a play, at least such an author as Shakespeare, who at the time LEAR was produced was in the zenith of his reputation, and in affluent circumstances? Would he not purchase a paper-book, or at least a quire of paper, which would be sufficient for the longest piece he ever wrote, and could then be procured for five pence? But what would he do who sat down to write a play for him near two centuries after his death? He would pick up as well as he could such scraps of old paper as he could find, at various times, and in various places; he would, as in the present case, not be able to show any of his pretended originals except in the form of half or quarter sheets, and these single leaves having been collected from various quarters would exhibit more than twenty different paper-marks."

"As I trust, that the now unknown contriver of the present imposture will hereafter be discovered, and hope that he will have a due sense of the heinousness of his offense against society and the cause of letters, the following formulary of recantation and contrition, written for Lauder by Dr. Johnson, may very properly (mutatis mutandis) be recommended to him:" (pp. 311, 313, 355).

Strange to say nine years afterwards, in 1805, Ireland, the forger, apparently following Malone's advice, wrote his confessions which were published in book form, and on the question of paper, of interest in connection with Malone's surmise and our present discussion, said:

"I applied to a bookseller named Verey, in Great May's Buildings, St. Martin's Lane, who, for the sum of five shillings, suffered me to take from the folio and quarto volumes in his shop the fly-leaves which they contained." (p. 71.)

that can be positively identified. In questioned documents that purport to have been written many years before it may be possible to show that the paper actually contains wood fiber, a constituent not in use before a definite date. The first foundation patent in the sulphite process for preparing wood pulp was granted in 1867.

The fibers most commonly used in paper making are linen, cotton, straw, jute, hemp, manila, also bleached and unbleached sulphite preparation of spruce and poplar pulp, soda poplar pulp and ground or mechanical spruce and poplar pulp. These various fibers are identified by their shape and length, by their joints, thickenings, and markings of the cell walls, and by the presence of characteristic cells. These fibers are also identified by color characteristics upon being brought in contact with certain staining agents which show different results with different fibers. There are many tests for ground or mechanical wood which taken together are considered conclusive by those best qualified to speak on the subject.[1].

---

[1] A valuable article on the subject of paper composition by W. R. Whitney and A. G. Woodman of the Massachusetts Institute of Technology was published in the Technology Quarterly, Vol. XV. No. 3, Sept. 1902. This paper is elaborately illustrated and contains much important information on the subject of paper materials. All phases of paper making are discussed in the valuable "Text-Book of Paper Making," by C. T. Cross and E. J. Bevan, Third Edition, London. Two other important books on the subject are, "The Chemistry of Paper Making," by Griffin & Little, and a new work, "The Manufacture of Paper," by R. W. Sindail.

CHAPTER XX.

To show which of two pen strokes that cross each other was last made is sometimes a matter of great importance in the investigation of a questioned document. To one unfamiliar with the subject it may seem impossible that such a problem would ever furnish adequate physical evidence on which to base a positive conclusion, but a few simple experiments will show that under many conditions the sequence or order of crossed strokes can be shown with absolute certainty.

As with nearly all the special questions discussed on preceding pages it seems necessary to say plainly that while it is true that the problem treated in this chapter can sometimes be definitely solved, it is also important to remember that under some circumstances it is impossible for any one to tell which of two crossed lines was last made, and in every such inquiry the evidence upon which a positive opinion is based should be clear enough so that with proper assistance and instruments even an unskilled observer can see for himself. A few easy tests will expose the assumption of one who claims to be able to determine under any and all conditions which of two lines was last made. When one claims to see in a disputed document what, with the best assistance, judge, jury, or opposing counsel cannot see, it is safest to assume that that thing does not exist.

The necessity for an investigation of this question of

[375]

line crossings arises when it is alleged that an interlineation or qualifying statement is written in after a signature was attached to a document and the two writings
touch at some point, or it is desired for any reason to
learn which of two writings that touch was last written.
There are many occasions when to prove which stroke

Fig. 156—Exhibit in case of Kerr vs. Southwick. It was decided in the U. S.
Circuit Court, New York, that the interlineation followed
the writing of the signature.

is uppermost is to decide a case. It may be very important simply to show the order in which signatures
were attached to a document. Another related question
that sometimes arises in this connection is as to the length
of time intervening between two writings that touch
when there may be no dispute as to which was written
last.

If a distinct second ink line made with ordinary fluid
ink crosses a first after the first has been absorbed into
the paper *but is still slightly damp,* the ink at the crossing will run out on the first line in a pronounced and
unmistakable manner. Many examples of crossings of
this kind can be seen in pages of writing where the long
letters of the different lines touch each other. It re-

quires some minutes for a line to become absolutely dry, and under very humid conditions this pronounced running of the ink will continue for a considerable time.

The running or spreading of the ink into a preceding line or stroke is not merely the running of the ink from stroke to stroke but from the pen itself charged with ink when it touches the previous line. A light unshaded stroke contains but little ink and it would appear that there is not enough ink to run over upon a previous line, but it must be remembered that the line must have been made with a pen carrying more ink than was necessary to make the line up to that point.

It is important to know that this same spreading of the ink of the second line out on the first also continues,

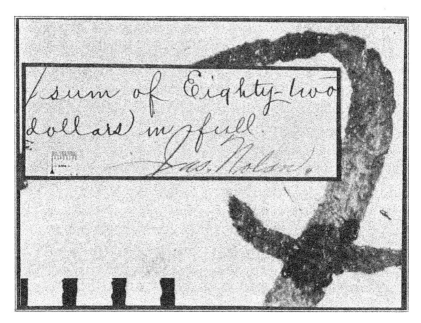

Fig. 157—An illustration made to show how clearly a delicate and obscure fact can be shown by an enlarged photograph. The enlargement (x 32) shows that "full" must have been written *after* the signature.

but in a less pronounced manner, after the first line is
entirely dry, the extent of the spreading depending upon
various conditions but especially upon the time intervening between the two writings.

The main cause of the widening of the last stroke at
the crossing seems to be that the paper and ink where
the first line was made, even when the ink is entirely
dry, have greater attraction for the fresh ink than the
paper where no ink has been applied. An ink line made
across a place on ordinary calendered paper, like ordinary foolscap, where simply a drop of water has been
applied and allowed to dry on the paper will be wider, as
compared with the same line made over other portions
of the same sheet. Another cause of the spreading of
the second stroke when two lines cross is the abrasion
of the paper under the first line by the nibs of the pen
which makes the paper more porous. The ink of a
crossing stroke will often run out in the furrows of
the pen nibs when it does not run out on the main part
of the line. The ink of a second line will also sometimes
run out into the abraded tracks of the nibs of the pen
in the first stroke even after the first, ink has become
completely oxidized and set and when the ink itself does
not attract the fresh ink of the second stroke.

It is of course understood that the swelling of the
line at the crossing is a microscopic fact, but it is none
the less a fact on that account, and can be easily seen
with the microscope by an ordinary observer and readily
measured with the filar micrometer; without the microscope the fact may be denied. The widening of the last
stroke can sometimes be seen by transmitted light even
with a hand magnifier under low magnification, but it

Fig. 158—Parts of two signatures in a legal controversy. One party claimed the lower signature was written first. The enlarged transmitted light photograph shows that the signatures were written in natural order.

Fig. 159—Vertical stroke crossed by upper horizontal after five minutes and by lower stroke after a few hours.

is most effectively shown by an enlarged transmitted light photo-micrograph of the crossing.

The physical result of the crossing of two ink lines is greatly changed if the last or upper line, made not too long after the first, is shaded and a blotter is applied at once. If the second line is made before the ink of the first line has oxidized and become fixed the fresh ink unites to some extent with the ink of the first line at the point of crossing, and the blotter takes up much of the ink of the line last made and also some of the ink of the first line at the crossing. The result of this blotting of the second line is that the first or under line is dimmed or lightened at the crossing and is not of uniform, continuous color, and the upper or last line is more uniform and shows continuous uniform margins.

If the first stroke was also shaded and then blotted at once and the second stroke also immediately blotted it may not be possible to determine which was last made unless, on two lines of equal width and made with the same pen, the continuous tracks of the pen nibs of the upper or last line show at the crossing more distinctly than the nib marks of the first stroke. If the first line was blotted and the second line made soon after was not, then the distinct and conspicuous widening of the last line at the crossing usually shows without any doubt which was last written.

The result produced by the application of the blotter is different if the second line is made a long time after the first line is written, unless the first line was written with ordinary nigrosine ink, in which case the lapse of time does not greatly change the result. If the ink in the first line is ordinary writing fluid of the iron-nutgall

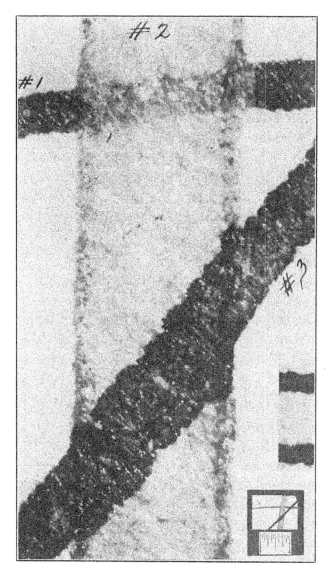

FIG. 160—The order of writing of three lines shown clearly
by enlarged photograph. Line No. 2 was blotted
at once and No. 3 was made before
No. 2 was entirely dry.

class and, as stated above, has become completely oxidized, a blotting of the second line will not dim the first
and it may be difficult to determine which was last made,
and at first sight the darker, unblotted first line may
appear to be over the other and lighter line last made.

Writing with the ordinary commercial iron inks when
fresh can be nearly all washed off the paper by simply
applying water. This is the reason why such ink lines
even when dry if not too old are partly taken up by a
blotter if crossed by a heavy line that is blotted at once.
A peculiarity of logwood ink is that it is not thus affected
by water, so that the ink in a first stroke, if dry, is not
thus taken up to the same extent by the process of
blotting.

In the natural course of events fraudulent additions
to documents are usually made soon after the document
is first written and sometimes immediately after and
with the same writing materials, and thus the sequence
of crossed lines can usually be shown whether blotted or
not. The indented tracks of the nibs of the pen in very
old writing are apt to become indistinct and may almost
entirely disappear, in which case a shaded stroke across
such old writing showing distinct pen furrows would
indicate a later writing.

As described in the chapter on ink, the extreme edges
of lines made with certain classes of ink show microscopic continuous dark borders several shades darker
than the main part of the stroke. These borders are
outside of the tracks of the pen nibs and on the extreme
edges of the strokes and are apparently due to a doub-
ling of the ink film or a gathering of the suspended
coloring matter at the rounded edges of the wet line

when it dries on the paper.   This peculiar margin is a pronounced characteristic of inks which are not true fluids but carry coloring matter in suspension.

Nigrosine ink and some colored aniline inks show such line margins very plainly and this effect is accentuated if the writing was blotted with the ordinary blotter.   When the same ink is used for both writings these dark margins alone are sufficient in many instances to show which of the two crossed lines was last made if one carefully observes on which line the margins are continuous, as is clearly shown in Fig. 29.   In some cases these margins and the nib marks are both continuous on one of the lines at the crossing, showing conclusively that this was the last line made.

Ink of the nigrosine class, which, as we have seen, is simply a coloring agent dissolved in water, does not run out on a crossed line to such an extent as fluid ink, although a fluid ink line will usually widen on a nigrosine line first made.   When a nigrosine ink line is crossed by an ink line of the same class the last or wet line has a tendency to dissolve the first at the point of crossing, no matter how old the first may be, and the margins of the last line plainly extend across the first, although the last line with this ink may not widen at the crossing.

If a wet or unabsorbed ink line is crossed by another line in the same condition the result does not usually show which was last made.   If a heavy and still wet shaded line is crossed by a similar line on very hard paper the nib marks of the last line at the crossing as observed by transmitted light will be much more pronounced than on the first line because the wet line first made has softened the paper at that point.   If a blotter is applied before the ink is dry, this increased density of the nib marks of the second line will often be shown quite plainly. When the second line is not at right angles to the first but crosses in a direction only a few degrees removed from the first the manner in which the ink runs across from one line to the other may show which was last made.

For examination of crossed lines a good hand magnifier or a compound microscope must be used, and examination should be made in good daylight after experiments with light on the document from various directions until just the proper angle is found that shows most clearly the existing facts. A certain particular angle of view will usually show conditions which otherwise may not be clearly seen. It is also advisable to remove the microscope tube and observe the crossing under magnification with the tube inclined at various degrees from horizontal up to vertical[1]. The two crossed lines should each be looked at lengthwise with the surface of the paper held nearly on a line with the eye and turned gradually around until each line has been looked at lengthwise in both directions. Such examination may show which line is continuous at the crossing.

None of these phenomena as a rule are plainly observable in fresh writing, and specimens for comparison, study, or tests, should be old enough so that fluid ink has reached its fullest intensity of color, if this is the condition of the writing in question. If the inquiry is

---

[1]Under certain conditions examination by "oblique vision," as described by Frazer in "Bibliotics or The Study of Documents," will show the sequence of crossed lines, but the method must be used with great caution or incorrect conclusions may be reached.

regarding a nigrosine ink specimens can be made and the phenomena observed as soon as the ink is dry.

As already stated, under certain conditions it is not possible to tell which of two crossed lines was last made. The conditions affecting the question are, the kind of pen used, the movement employed, the speed of the strokes in question, the kind or kinds of ink used and its condition, the character of the paper, the probable time between the writing of the parts in question, the number of crossed lines for examination, the use of blotter on one or both writings, the delicacy or lightness of the lines which cross, and the porosity or dryness of the paper.

Strokes made rapidly on rough paper with a fine pen crossed by similar strokes may not show which was last made, but fortunately fraudulent additions to a document are usually made deliberately and distinctly; often such writing is actually heavier than the regular writing, and the sequence of the crossing is always more clearly shown if a light stroke is crossed by a heavier and slower one than if this process is reversed.

If two inks of entirely different composition are used and the second writing does not follow soon after the first the second line may not widen at the crossing; but under such circumstances other things will be apt to show a different time of writing. Thick and heavy inks may not widen at a crossing, and inks may be so thin, pale and indistinct that the order of the crossing cannot be determined. One part of such an examination under some circumstances should be a chemical test of the ink of the two writings, and if the inks are different this will naturally show a different time of writing.

Special caution is .necessary in determining the sequence of lines of different width or different intensity of color. A heavy line at first sight always seems to be over a light line when they cross, and a pale line seems to run under a very black line at a crossing. Under such conditions it may be impossible to determine which was last made. A light line made rapidly may not to any appreciable extent run out on a heavy line, and it may be so thin and light that when it is crossed the second line does not run out on it as it does on a distinct strong line. If a light line is crossed at once while it is still damp by a heavy line the spreading of the second line on the first is unmistakable.

If a dark and heavy soluble ink, like nigrosine, is crossed by a decidedly lighter ink, or a colored ink, and the second strokes are full and strong a condition may be shown that may lead to an erroneous conclusion. If the first ink is sufficiently soluble the two lines may coalesce at the crossing and the stain of the first line may extend slightly out on the light or colored line, apparently showing that the dark line was made last. Careful examination under these conditions will show an indefinite edge to such a stain and a mixture of the two inks instead of the running out of one on the other.

Crossed lines in other parts of the same document should, if possible, always be compared with those in question if in the crossing in dispute it is probable that the second writing followed the first within a short time or while the first line was still slightly damp. Ordinary. commercial writing fluid, now in almost universal use in business, will dry very quickly or become absorbed and fixed in the paper in a few seconds so that a "t" crossing made across a letter at the beginning of a long word is frequently across a line entirely absorbed in the paper but still damp, and the result in such a case can be compared with the actual crossing in dispute on the same document if it is probable that it was made under similar conditions. Shaded lines three one hundred and twenty eighths of an inch in width, written with common fluid ink on ordinary calendered foolscap paper in the month of May, under average conditions of humidity, require sixty seconds to be entirely absorbed in the paper so no ink is taken up with a blotter. Nigrosine ink under similar conditions requires about twenty seconds longer to be absorbed. This time of absorption is of course much longer in well sized hard paper than in soft porous paper.

Where two ink lines are made with different inks a close direct examination of the crossing may show which line is continuous by the arrangement of the ink film or the condition and coloring of the disturbed paper fiber. If an ink line which has been made dull in color or dead black by the use of the blotter is crossed by a line showing a gloss or lustre, and the second line contains a considerable quantity of ink, the bright line will be continuous, and if the dull ink line is made last the first line may be dulled or dimmed at the point of intersection, although it is dangerous to base a positive judgment upon this fact alone since the combination of the two inks may show a result different from that which either alone would show.

It has been proposed in a discussion of this subject that a letter-press copy of crossed lines should be made in order to determine their sequence, but this should never be permitted. Such a test will rarely show any definite result whatever and will render it impossible to make any further intelligent examination of the conditions by any method. Comparison should be made with ink lines the sequence of which is known, and the larger the number of examples for comparison the better.

If the lines of writing are thick enough to be appreciable and stand up on the paper, the upper continuous line may plough through the first and thus show that it was last made, or possibly may show its additional height above the surface of the paper at the crossing. This may be observed under high magnification by holding the surface of the paper nearly on a line with the eye, as directed above, so as to look towards the side of the ink line. The paper should be held so that neither ink line will be at right angles to the line of vision but so that both are equally divergent. This position is important, as otherwise, especially when a high power objective is used, one line will be in focus and the other not, and the line in focus will appear to be the continuous line and apparently the last one made. As a matter of fact, however, few ink lines are heavy enough to show a thickness sufficient to render this method of examination practicable. If the first line is ploughed through by the pen in making the second, then thick ink may render it easier to determine which stroke was made last.

If the last line is actually higher at the crossing it will be necessary under direct view and very high magnification to change slightly the focus of the microscope to get first one and then the other line in sharp focus and, of course, the line farthest away will be the under line.

An ink line of good density if made over a pencil

stroke will usually cover the stroke in such manner that
the pen stroke will be seen to be the last made, but here
again the width and weight of the strokes greatly affect
the result. The sequence of two pencil strokes can be
determined if the strokes are made with considerable
pressure so as to indent the paper slightly. Indentations of this character, even if very slight, can be seen
with the stereoscopic microscope. The upper line will
show a continuous indentation across the lower, similar
to two crossed strokes on a piece of wax, and the upper
line in some instances will show, under just the proper
angle, distinct bright scratches or bright lines in the
stroke itself across the first or lower line.

A distinct pencil stroke over an ink line usually
shows, when examined from just the right angle, continuous un-
dimmed metallic
lustre which is
broken or dulled
at the crossing
when the ink line
is last made.

For nearly all
line crossing ex-
aminations, ink
as well as pencil,
the stereoscopic
microscope is pre-
ferable. This in-
strument shows
hills and furrows
and microscopic

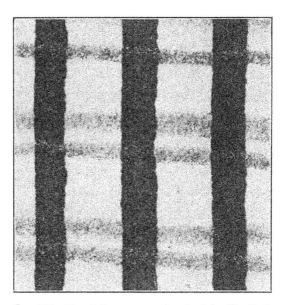

Fig. 161—Pencil lines over and under ink. The first,
third and fifth pencil lines it is clearly
seen are over the ink strokes.

indentations that cannot be seen with the ordinary micro-scope even if the highest power objective is used.   In such an examination the matter of proper lighting must be carefully considered, and it is sometimes highly im-portant that photo-micrographs be promptly made be-fore the microscopic conditions are accidentally or inten-tionally disturbed.   The facts in an apparently hopeless case may be so clearly shown by skillfully made illustra-tions that the case does not get into court.

Fluid ink writing over a fresh impression made by a rubber stamp inked with the ordinary ink pad, will

Fig. 162—Ink lines over typewriting.

run out slightly where it touches the rubber stamp impres-sion. If the stamp impression is allowed to dry thoroughly be-fore the writing is written over it the ink will not run out as it does on a damp ink line. Pen and ink written lines over typewritten letters do not run out and combine with the ink of the type impression as they do on a damp pen line or damp stamp impression. Ink strokes over typewriting are actually repelled when the lines touch as if written over a greasy paper and this condition will indicate that the writing followed the typewriting.

The matter of determining the comparative age of two writings by the line crossings is an inquiry quite dif-ferent from that of showing which was last made.   A dispute sometimes arises as to whether two writings were written within a few minutes of each other, within a few hours or a year or more apart. As we have seen, if an absorbed but still damp line is crossed by a well filled fresh line the ink will run out on the first line in a very pronounced manner and if this condition exists it is clear that the second writing followed soon after the first; and if the second line does not run out on the first in the slightest degree it is probable that the second writing was long enough after the first so that the first had become oxidized and set. From these facts it will be seen that it may be very evident that a second writing must have followed a first within a few minutes and other conditions will sometimes show that a second writing must have been added some considerable time later. As a rule, no very positive conclusion should be based on these phenomena unless the lines are clear and distinct. This is one of the subjects upon which the pretender may be led to give most positive testimony on the very slightest foundation.

As suggested above it is sometimes important in crossed line inquiries that the photo-micrographs should be made at the earliest opportunity; illustrations of this class are desirable in every such investigation and sometimes are essential if the facts are to be clearly shown. It is well to make such illustrations under various lightings and enlarged from ten to forty diameters. Great care should be exercised to get the sharpest possible focus and if possible different lengths of exposure should be given until just the proper degree of contrast is obtained. If properly made such photographs alone will sometimes decide a case.

The order of writing as shown by crossed strokes, even on very fine lines, is so unmistakable in some cases that when properly illustrated the fact must be admitted. But it does not by any means follow, as was suggested at the beginning of this chapter, that in every case the fact can be conclusively shown. In many instances it is impossible by any method to discover or show which of two crossed strokes was last made.

One who makes a serious study of the subject should

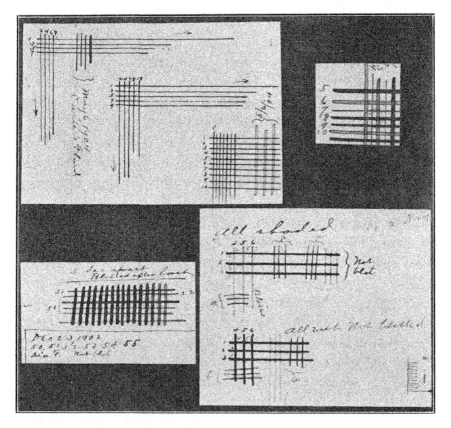

Fig. 163—A few examples of "crossed lines" of various dates with a variety of inks and on various papers.

make specimens for comparison and study with all kinds, classes and conditions of ink, on all kinds of papers, with light, heavy and blotted strokes made slowly and rapidly and at intervals of a few seconds up to several years. With such a collection of actual examples for comparison regarding which the facts are known, the possibility of error is much reduced.

No matter how well qualified as a scientist or microscopist a witness may apparently be, unless he has made and carefully studied such actual examples of known crossed lines his opinion on the subject should be received with much caution[1].

---

[1]Certain witnesses, apparently having especial experience, and seeming to have especial knowledge, have testified that the addresses were written after the cancellation stamps, or the impressions of the postoffices, were placed upon the envelopes, and that some of these stamps or impressions, as well as certain of the receiving and back stamps on the envelopes, were made by dies not in use in the postoffice department, or by authorized dies, which in the detail of dates and otherwise, have been tampered with and are not genuine imprints made by postoffice employees.   .   .   .

The specialists for the respondents testified that the appearance of superposition of inks of different ingredients and of varying densities, after the writing and stamping had been done, was deceptive and entirely misleading, and that, in many instances, which was above the other, or last applied, could not be determined by any method, inspection or examination.   Finally a postoffice employee, bringing into court an official stamp, appeared as a witness, and by actual experiment demonstrated to the satisfaction of the court that the contention of the respondents was correct.   It appeared that the heavier or darker writing or imprint most frequently appeared to be on the top of the lighter impression.   .   .   .

Grossly improbable, as those accusations of forgery and fraud may have seemed to be, the court was obliged to hear the evidence, starting, as it did, with the confident specific statements of specialists, by the recitation of their experience, qualifying as learned and skilled.— By Hon. George F. Lawton, Surrogate, Cambridge, Mass., in a decision in Matter of Russell, April 13, 1910.

CHAPTER XXI.

WRITING OVER FOLDS IN PAPER

It is sometimes possible to show conclusively that a paper was folded before certain writing was placed upon it, and the proof of this fact may be a matter of vital importance in the investigation of the date of a writing, or in the examination of an alleged fraudulent change in a document. To show that the writing followed the folding sometimes casts grave suspicion upon a document and may even be sufficient to prove that it is fraudulent, or that it contains a fraudulent alteration, addition or interlineation. It has been shown that a fraudulent document was written over a genuine signature by showing that a continuous fold across the sheet *followed* the writing of the signature and *preceded* the writing of the body of the document.

As is well known, a sheet of paper is a compacted mass of short fibers, and when it is folded one side is necessarily compressed and wrinkled and the opposite side pulled apart or actually fractured, and, as paper fibers are only slightly elastic, it is impossible ever to get the parts back into their original condition and relation to each other. The effect of the folding process necessarily depends upon the quality and thickness of the paper, upon the closeness of the fold or amount of pressure put upon the paper when folded, and also upon the number of times that the paper has been folded and unfolded.

[394]

Even one ordinary folding of a sheet of writing paper, pressed down in the ordinary way, inevitably disturbs the fibers on both sides of the sheet, makes the surface uneven and at least to some extent changes the porous character of the folded portion, so that it may distinctly affect the character, direction or width of a line where it crosses the fold. If one or more distinct strokes or parts of letters cross the folded portion of the paper, and particularly if there are other lines for comparison on the same document, which were written before it was folded, it is usually possible to show (see Fig. 28) that part of the writing preceded the folding and part followed it.

It may occur that the writing in question on a document was written so long after the first writing that the folded portion of the paper, which has served as a hinge, is so broken and porous that the pen actually sticks into or through the paper at this point, and a portion of the ink may actually have run through to the opposite side of the sheet. Such a condition would, of course, be unquestionable evidence that the paper was folded before the last writing.

Good paper may be folded many times without being actually fractured, while some papers are broken on one side by one ordinary folding, and therefore the results in writing over the folded portions may vary greatly under varying conditions. Tough, thick papers may not be broken, but it is difficult to make such papers lie flat even after one folding which produces a ridge on the outside of the fold and a hollow on the inside, and this unevenness alone may affect the added writing in such a distinctive way as to show that it was written after the fold was made. Strokes across ridges due to folds are apt to appear widest, because of the obstruction, at the side of the ridge first touched by the moving pen or pencil. It is important that the direction of the stroke should always be considered in such an inquiry.

The concave or inner side of a fold is lower than the other parts of the sheet and with good strong paper a pronounced hollow extends the whole length of the fold on the inner side. If such paper is folded but a few times the paper will not be likely to be broken or made much more porous at the fold, but pen strokes may show gaps or lighter places where the pen jumps over the hollow; or strokes at such a point may show an unusual change of direction just where the fold is situated. The concave or inner side of the fold does not affect a pen stroke in so pronounced a manner as the convex side. In writing over the ridge of a horizontal fold on hard paper the upward strokes in slant writing may be slightly deflected to the right and downward strokes to the left. Upward strokes meet more resistance as the point of the pen as ordinarily held comes more directly against the ridge and is more likely to stick in it and stop.

The surface of hard calendered paper of the ordinary legal and foolscap quality is made smooth by heavy pressure, while the interior of the sheet is more porous. A very few foldings of such paper render it very porous and spongy at the fold, and ordinary fluid ink runs into a fold as it would into a blotter and widens and changes the character of the line at that point in an unmistakable manner. While this effect, as stated above, will show soonest on the convex side of the paper, it will show on either side after a few foldings and unfoldings.

Even a very fine hair line will often show a decided widening just at the fold and the ink from a shaded line will run out both ways at the junction of the shade and the fold. Papers made from wood are easily broken by folding, on account of the shortness of the fibers, and ink lines over folds in such paper are changed in a pronounced manner.

The character of the result of writing over a fold is modified by the character of the ink used. If the ink is very limpid and easily absorbed it will show in a more pronounced manner that, a writing is over a fold than if the ink is thick and heavy. One of the commendable qualities of the commercial writing fluids in common use is that the extreme fluidity of the ink carries it into the fiber of the paper, where it oxidizes and forms a permanent record. This quality makes the ink very sensitive to changes in the porous character of the paper and writing over a fold with this ink is therefore more likely to show a pronounced result. Ink that deposits its color mainly on the surface of the paper, like nigrosine, and all inks of the character that carry coloring matter in suspension instead of in chemical solution, do not show so plainly that a line was written over a fold. These inks in their application to the surface of paper resemble paint, and differ radically from a limpid fluid that is almost instantly absorbed.

When a line is first written and the paper afterwards folded and partly broken, after the ink becomes dry (see Fig. 28) there is a distinct break in the ink film itself, showing a line of unstained paper fiber beneath, the main pen stroke is no wider at the point of fracture on each side, and the broken portion of the paper does not show ink stains excepting on the fractured and frayed ends of the fibers which made up the original line. If the line was made after the fold and the paper is afterwards fractured, the ink stains at the point of fracture will be distinctly wider than the line each side of the broken place. A line which was made before the paper was folded may at first appear slightly wider where it is broken, but careful examination will show that this apparent widening is due entirely to the frayed or loose ends of the stained paper fiber. If a line is completely broken and the ends separated at a fold it may be impossible to determine which was first, the writing or the folding.

The effect of the change in the line over a fold may not be very apparent until the ink has completely oxidized and reached its fullest intensity of blackness. Fresh writing with ordinary fluid ink over a folded sheet will not show distinctly the phenomena described, but the same crossing after the ink turns black may show in a very pronounced manner the characteristics outlined. A pencil stroke over a fold may not be affected to any great extent, but on some kinds of hard paper it may be possible to show clearly that the writing followed the folding. In the investigation of a question of this kind the stereoscopic photo-micrograph is particularly desirable.

Examination of writing over folded paper should be made with a microscope with good light and no opinion should be given until a microscopic examination has been made. Examination with the microscope under a magnification of from thirty to fifty diameters will usually show the conditions with the greatest distinctness.

Illustrations.

The startling clearness with which many of these questions can be illustrated by stereoscopic photomicrographs can only be appreciated by an actual examination of such illustrations. Even those reproduced herewith in half-tone show clearly the fact, but are necessarily much inferior to actual photographs.

Vehement denial is sometimes made of facts that become perfectly evident when thus illustrated and the absence or exclusion of appropriate illustrations may defeat the ends of justice. This unfortunate result is especially liable to be reached in any controversy regarding matters of the character discussed in this and the preceding chapter involving questions of a microscopic character which necessarily are in a measure hidden and indistinct. An investigation of the relation of a writing to a fold in a sheet of paper, or of the sequence of two strokes that cross, are matters to which the average juryman or referee has never given a moment's attention and to ask such men to decide such a question without giving them every possible assistance amounts to a leap in the dark. It will readily be seen by the illustrations shown that many delicate and almost invisible characteristics can be proved so positively that to deny their existence is simply ridiculous.

These stereoscopic photographs should be enlarged from about twenty to sixty diameters, and, with proper care and attention to details, can readily be made by following the directions given in the chapter on photography. In order to view such illustrations the ordinary stereoscope is required, and there are no valid objections to its use if it assists in showing the facts.

There is always violent opposition to any innovation in legal processes, but the science of the law has kept abreast of the progress of the physical sciences only by the recognition and employment of improved methods by means of which the facts may be more clearly shown. If it is made to appear by clear, positive testimony that in certain inquiries a stereoscopic photograph will illustrate, explain and enforce oral testimony and that without this illustration, testimony would in some measure be weakened and made ineffective, the exclusion of such a photograph would undoubtedly in some states afford good ground for reversal on appeal.

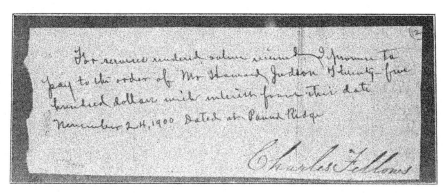

Fɪɢ. 167—An illustration made to show the important bearing that the question may may have as to whether a writing preceded or followed a folding of the paper.

THE STEREOSCOPIC ILLUSTRATIONS.

In Fig. 168 is shown the top of the small "h" in "Charles" where it is broken by the fold, showing clearly that the writing must have preceded the folding.

In Fig. 169 is illustrated the last stroke in the word "from" which shows unmistakably that the writing followed the folding; it therefore necessarily follows that the lines of the body of the note were written after the signature.

In order that the illustrations may be conveniently seen in the ordinary stereoscopic instrument they are printed on a detached folded sheet and enclosed in an envelope inside of the back cover of this book.

Fig. 170 is another illustration of a writing before folding (the upper one) and a writing after a folding of the paper.

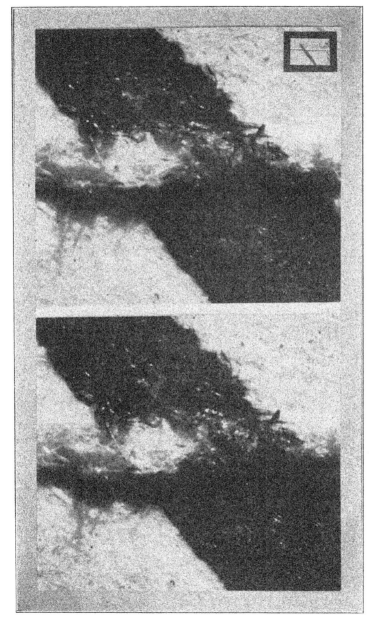

FIG. 168.—Stereoscopic Photo-Micrograph of a written line made before the paper was folded. Fig. 167 shows document complete. Actual size of line shown in small illustration.

Fig. 169.—Stereoscopic Photo-Micrograph of ink line over a fold. Complete form of document shown in Fig. 167.

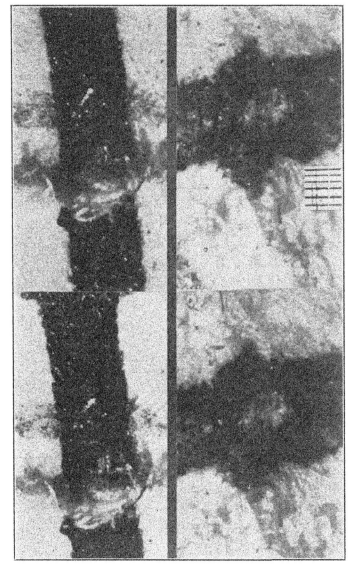

Fig. 170—Stereoscopic Photo Micrograph of ink writing before folding and after folding. Lines in actual size shown in small illustration.

CHAPTER XXII.

ERASURES AND ALTERATIONS IN DOCUMENTS

If for any reason a document is under suspicion it should in all cases be thoroughly examined for the purpose of discovering any suspicious erasures or alterations that it may contain. Fraudulent changes naturally are made in such a way as to avoid detection and may not be discovered if attention is not directed to this particular subject[1].

Many questions of importance arise regarding alterations in documents and the questions are presented in a great variety of forms. It may only be necessary to determine whether a change or erasure has actually been made[2], or it may be a matter of great importance to show

---

[1]ERASURES. . . . the question has also seriously been considered whether an expert may testify as to the existence or time of erasures, alterations, or interpolations. Such testimony is often not to be distinguished practically from testimony deciphering illegible writing, which has uniformly been held proper. There is, at any rate, no scintilla of reason for doubt.—Wigmore on Evidence, Vol. III, Sec. 2027 (1904).

[2]The question, what are really the words in a written instrument, when they are doubtful either on account of the obscure manner in which they are written, or because of an uncertainty on the face of the writing, whether any of them have been stricken out or altered, by the maker, is a question of fact; and if such question arises in a cause being tried by a jury, this question of fact should be submitted to the jury, and the evidence of experts on the question, what are the words in the writing, ought to be received; and if the court refused to permit such evidence to go to the jury, this court ought to reverse such action of the court below.—Beach vs. O'Riley, 14 W. Va., 55 (1878), L. R. A., 65, 155.

The alteration or interlineation should be explained by the party claiming the benefit of the paper, and if it is suspicious in appearance and satisfactory explanation is not made, the proper conclusion is a conviction of fact against the instrument.—Catlin Coal Co. vs. Lloyd, 180 Ill. 406 (1899).

[404]

what was first written. Sometimes the whole inquiry is regarding the change in a word, or even of one figure or part of a figure in a date or an amount, and again it may be possible to prove that a whole document, with the exception of the signature, has been erased and a new and fraudulent document written above the genuine signature. Wills, notes and other important documents have been manufactured in this way[1].

The most common and clumsy form of erasure is by abrasion, by which method the paper fiber itself containing the ink is actually removed taking the ink with it. Such erasures are usually perfectly apparent when carefully examined but may be so skillfully made as to escape detection on first view. If the attempt has been made to write with ink over such an erasure the resulting conditions will usually show very plainly that an erasure was first made, because it is inevitable that the operation of making the erasure has so disturbed the fiber (see Fig. 31) that the paper is more porous and the ink makes a mark distinctly different from that on other portions of the same sheet.

The line is to some extent wider and rougher than it would otherwise be and the ink runs out sidewise forming a series of minute points extending in both directions from the stroke. The ink line is also usually somewhat dulled in color and without lustre, but may be a deeper black than on undisturbed portions of the paper. Writing over an erasure will sometimes show through on the opposite side of the sheet. The attempt may have been

---

[1]These questions had for their object to elicit testimony tending to show that the note was written over the signature of Allen, and after it was written.—Dubois vs. Baker, 30 N. Y. (361) 1864.

made to smooth or rub down the erasure before writing, and if this is skilfully done on good paper the ink line at such point may show but little if any difference from a normal line until it is looked at under proper magnification. A microscopic examination of the paper will always show a distinct difference in the quality of the line due to the disturbance of the fiber and the roughening of the surface of the paper.

Examination should be made with good light falling on the document at various angles and with the microscope tube or magnifier held at various angles to get an exact view of the gloss or lustre of the paper surface, and examination should always be made under various degrees of magnification. Too high magnification may be as undesirable as that which is too low. The slightest disturbance of the surface of smooth paper can readily be detected by holding the sheet so that the angle of reflection from the portion in question is exactly on a line with the eye. The portion disturbed will look darker simply because it will not reflect as much light as the smoother portions of the paper.

Examination should also be made by transmitted light which may show what otherwise is not clearly seen. A transmitted light photograph of a portion of the document (see Fig. 6) including the place in question affords an effective means of comparing the transparency or opacity of various portions of the paper. This test is more fully outlined in the chapter on photography[1].

---

[1]The clumsy attempt is sometimes made to obliterate part of a writing by covering the first word or character written by a blot or by smearing it over with ink, thus covering it up and making it illegible. The changed word or character is then written above or at one side. If the ink in the first word written had become fixed in the paper before the change was made, a view of the part by strong transmitted

One of the most common of forgeries is the "raised" check, draft, or other commercial paper which is made to represent a larger sum than when it was signed. This is a very dangerous kind of forgery as the signature which it carries is genuine and when a paper is presented for payment or credit special attention is naturally directed only to the signature.

Genuine documents are sometimes so carelessly drawn that the amount is increased by simply adding words before or after the smaller amount first written, and then adding ciphers to the amount written in figures or, if necessary, changing the amount in figures. In this way "Twenty-four" is made to read "Twenty-four hundred" or "Twenty-four thousand," or "One hundred" is changed to "Twenty-one hundred." If, however, papers are properly drawn it is impossible to make such changes without first making some kind of an erasure.

There have been numerous cases in which notes, orders, receipts, and other papers were purposely drawn in such a manner that they might easily be changed after being signed or paid. This is accomplished in some cases by writing the amount only in figures when the paper was signed, or by leaving open spaces in amount lines that later could easily be filled in. Adding ciphers of course multiplies by ten and amounts like 100 or 1000, written only in figures, are easily changed to 400 or 4000 by changing the one to a four simply by the

light, by the use of a focusing glass or by looking through a tube to cut off all side light, will often render the first word written perfectly legible. The lines first written, although completely covered, will be more opaque than the other parts and can thus be seen and read. This method of examination with a strong light and focusing glass or a tube is frequently of great assistance in examining various questions in connection with many classes of disputed documents.

addition without erasure of the first part of the four to the figure 1. In the same manner the figure 1 may be changed to 7 or 9, and 3's may be changed to 8's.

If a document has been raised by simply adding to it a word or a figure which has not required any erasure it may be impossible to show that any change has been made. If the change or addition has, however, touched any previous writing it is usually possible to show an unnatural order in the writing. In some cases, for example, it is possible to show (see Fig. 33) that a figure 4 or 9, or 7, was made from a figure 1 by showing that the left side of the figure was made last or added to the figure 1, or the last or added part may have been written with a different kind of ink. A fraudulent addition, if in words, will almost invariably show a different slant or size or a general unnaturalness that indicates a different time of writing, or, as stated, the added part may be written with an ink that shows a lack of uniformity or continuity when compared with the ink first used.

If before a change is made a previous writing must be erased, the operation of producing such a forgery is necessarily made much more difficult, but it is not by any means prevented. Even school children know that there are certain cheap preparations on sale in stationery stores that will successfully remove ordinary ink writing. These chemical preparations are of great assistance to the forger, and make it easily possible in many cases for him to remove previous writing and make a check, note, receipt or contract read as he desires to have it read.

These chemical erasures may affect the document in such a way as to show clearly that it has been tampered with, but when skillfully made they may not be discernible by ordinary observation. All such chemical preparations have a tendency to produce on white paper, after the lapse of some time, a pale yellow stain[1]. On all smooth or calendered papers the application of any liquid is at once apparent, especially the application of a strong chemical solution which at once attacks the sizing, dulls the finish and loosens up the paper fibers which have been compacted by the calendering process. On some papers such chemical solutions remove the sizing so effectually that ink "runs" or spreads out as in blotting paper in a perfectly evident manner. Chemical erasures show least upon heavy, rough linen or bond paper, which, unfortunately, is the paper generally used by banks for checks and drafts and other commercial papers.

In such parts of a writing under examination the exact tint and lustre or gloss of the ink should be compared under various conditions and angles of light, as also the quality and exact width of the various strokes of the writing of the part in question. Tests for evidences of chemical erasures with litmus paper may furnish useful information, and some kinds of erasures, for a long time, can be detected by the distinct odor of chlorinated lime. Tests with iodine vapor, if properly made, will show chemical erasures and other disturbances of paper surfaces, but such tests inevitably deface a docu-

---

[1] Ordinary iron inks are not "eradicated" or removed by the application of the so-called ink eradicators but are simply decolorized and under some conditions the color can be brought back to a sufficient extent to make the writing legible again, as shown in Fig. 4. This result is accomplished by subjecting the writing in an enclosed receptacle to the fumes of strong ammonia sulphide. The erased writing cannot always be brought back but in some cases can be and with startling results.

ment. Delicate stains due to chemical erasures are sometimes effectively proved by photography (see Fig. 4)
which may show slight differences in tint with unmistakable distinctness. The photographic methods to be
employed for this purpose are outlined in the chapters
on photography and ink.

Unfortunately a large proportion of modern blank
forms of checks, drafts and other negotiable papers are
made exactly as the forger desires in order that it may
be easy to make fraudulent changes. In the first place
they are printed on rough surface, high quality, bond
or linen paper on which even erasures by abrasion can
be made quite successfully, and chemical erasures leave
almost no trace and can hardly be detected. In the
second place a large proportion of such forms are lithographed on wet paper which process of wetting makes
it impossible to discover any evidence of a subsequent
wetting when a chemical erasure is made.

In addition to these conditions favorable to the forger
many of the printed devices intended to prevent raising
not only do not serve as a protection but may actually
assist in making such a change appear regular and
genuine. One device often employed consists of some
kind of a design printed on the surface of the paper.
Some of these are simply parallel, straight or curved
lines, while others are elaborate designs, or the words
making up the name of the bank, printed small and close
together so as nearly to cover the whole surface of the
paper and give a tint to it. These designs or lines are
supposed to be printed in an ink that is removed by any
chemical agent that will remove writing ink and with
the thought that such an erasure would thus become

perfectly apparent by also taking away the lines. This would be the result if the ink is removed by clumsily smearing the chemicals over the whole field of the writing, as an office boy might do it, but when only the lines themselves are taken out only a small portion of the design is removed, which is easily restored, and, when overwritten with the new or added words, the change can hardly be discovered and the printed tint actually assists in hiding the changes[1].

Another device which has been widely used is the check punch by the use of which the amount in figures is punched out of the paper either by small perforations arranged in the shape of figures, or the complete figure is cut out. Although this method has been very popular it is not only ineffective but also actually aids a forger through enabling him to give an added air of genuineness to a fraudulent document (see Fig. 8) after filling in the genuine amount punched out which, by using a similar machine, is a very easy and simple operation.

Another almost universal practice in this country that greatly assists the forger is the printing of the word "Dollars" at the extreme right hand side of the blank form, leaving a long space usually covered only by a single ink line. This open space is an invitation to add

---

[1] The older methods of preventing counterfeits by the properties of the paper itself are the use of a special watermark and the Willcox process of applying colored fibres on the surface. Forgeries are guarded against by Ballande's method using a paper containing calomel on which the authentic writing is done with a solution of alum and sodium hyposulphite; Zeiss's method consisting in printing the paper with three colors, one visible and fast, another over this one which is visible and easily removed, and a third invisible but darkened by writing materials, and Haskins and Wells's method using a paper containing 5% phosphate of iron, 2% phosphate of manganese, and 5% potassium ferro-cyanide, which is stained by acids, alkalies or salts.— Berlin Centralblatt, through Paper Making, 26, 541-3, Dec., 1907, and Chemical Abstracts, Vol. 2, No. 4, p. 586, Feb. 20, 1908.

"hundred" or "thousand" to a small amount or to make any change desired after the necessary erasure with chemicals.

Some business forms have a protective stub which is torn off to the proper line, but with these after being "raised" the whole stub is torn off; others have separate printed forms for different amounts and this is no doubt the most effective protection, but the method is not practical. Still other forms are printed on a paper which is supposed to be discolored by chemical applications, others are written with "safety ink," which is usually India ink or ink made of carbon which can not be removed by chemicals but, under some conditions, can be removed by mechanical means as it is not absorbed in the paper. There is also in use a machine that embosses and prints across the face of a check or draft "Not over One Hundred Dollars," or a similar line, which, while the machine is in good order, is an effective protection. Representatives of competing machines are, however, showing how it is possible to make a fraudulent change of amount when a machine has been in use for a long time and the ink has become nearly dried up. These machines should be in good condition in order fully to serve the purpose for which they are designed.

The question of raised checks and drafts is a very practical one to the banker. As a rule he loses what he pays on such documents and must constantly be on guard. The method and procedure that he should employ in order to avoid the paying of raised papers are, as far as the conditions will allow, those that should be employed in an exhaustive examination of such suspected documents.

A few quick tests that can be applied to suspected papers of this kind are: (1) an examination of the whole paper surface by reflected light, (2) comparison of the line quality of the several parts of the amount in words and comparison of the line quality of name of payee and words of amount line, (3) examination of the number on the document in order to discover if it is made with rubber stamp or shows any irregularity, (4) comparison of exact tint and quality of ink in amount line with other parts, (5) comparison of width of pen lines or pen strokes of the various parts and search for any irregularities due to differences in sizing or surface of the paper on different parts of document, (6) search for discolorations due to chemical erasures, (7) examination of back of document in field where suspected writing appears for evidence of embossing or erasures, (8) examination of style, slant, size and speed of writing of amount in words and figures compared with writing on other parts of document, (9) careful examination of amount in figures for evidences of lack of uniformity, (10) examination for odor of ink eradicator, (11) observation of amount line and amount in figures by transmitted light with sun shining directly on the document. The final step to be taken in some cases, and the best of all, is to call by long distance telephone the parties who drew the paper.

The banker labors under several difficulties. He usually is hurried when forged paper is presented and must make a quick decision, knowing that unwarranted suspicion of a document may never be forgotten and may lose a good patron, and also fully realizing all the time that he may pay out good money on a fraudulent paper. If a paper is suspected some excuse for delay must be made until it can be properly examined. Most raised papers are handled or, in the forger's vernacular, "laid down" by a comparatively new depositor who has previously opened an account and made deposits and drawn checks until he has become known, so that when the time arrives for him to present his fraudulent paper he needs no identification. These facts would seem to suggest the importance of investigating all new customers[1].

It is not generally known what an enormous amount is lost every year on forged and "raised" documents. Bankers and business men do not even tell each other and often a clever swindler actually leaves a trail of fraudulent paper from the Atlantic to the Pacific. Not banks alone but hotels and many business houses of all kinds are thus constantly victimized. If there is no clew the victim quietly charges the amount to his loss account as part of the cost of experience and does not advertise the fact that he has been swindled.

A central clearing house for forged paper, properly

---

[1]Certain practices can hardly be too strongly condemned. One of these is paying money to unidentified strangers on "O. K.'d" endorsements. In such a transaction reliance is solely on the handwriting and if a forger is skillful enough to forge the name on the face of the document he can put the same name on the back. Another dangerous practice is the sending out of money on written orders where handwriting alone must again be depended upon. Under the present practice of keeping only one signature, and often a very poor signature, for handwriting comparison it is dangerous to depend exclusively upon such comparison.

On the third of July, 1909, two forged "O. K.'d" checks for $2600 were paid by a Rochester bank on the same day, and on the eighteenth of December of the same year, five forged "O. K.'d" checks, aggregating $7840, were paid by five different banks of the city of New Orleans.

Another objectionable practice that may open the door to fraud is the selling of New York exchange to strangers.

conducted by one skilled in classifying and identifying disputed documents and especially handwriting, would save banks and hotels hundreds of thousands of dollars every year. It is said that every such forger is convicted sooner or later, and this is no doubt true as forgery in so many cases seems to be an unconquerable habit, but in the meantime the losses amount to an enormous sum. It is positively known that clever swindlers of this class have operated for more than ten years before they were finally caught[1].

No devices or methods of procedure would be an unfailing protection against fraud, but open temptation could be partially removed and many losses prevented if all checks, drafts and orders for money, and especially bank drafts, were printed and drawn in such manner as to make changes difficult instead of easy as now is often the case.

---

[1]Forgers who make a practice of defrauding the banks of the smaller cities, first establish confidence with the officials of the institution they intend to plunder. This is done in a very simple manner, but one that generally proves successful. Several weeks before the forgery is attempted the advance agent of the gang hires and opens an insurance or real estate office in the vicinity of the bank. At the latter place he makes a number of bona fide deposits and has some business transactions, which are simply the transfer of money from one city to another. Then when he is beyond suspicion he lays down for collection a draft for a large sum, which bears the forged signature of a genuine depositor at a bank in a distant city. Upon the presentation of the paper the officials telegraph to the bank it is drawn upon, inquiring if the person or firm whose forged signature it bears is a depositor in good standing there. The answer being satisfactory, at least three-fourths of the amount called for by the check is willingly advanced by the bank of deposit, to the forger's trusted agent. In due time the counterfeit is forwarded for collection through the regular business channels, and when it finally reaches its destination its character is discovered. The insurance or real estate office has in the meantime collapsed, and the forger and his tools have vanished. A smart gang, with a dozen or more advance agents, have been known to dupe in a single year over forty banks throughout the country, netting, with a small outlay, about $160,000 by their operations.— Professional Criminals of America, by Thomas Byrnes, late Chief of Police, New York City, second edition, p. 18.

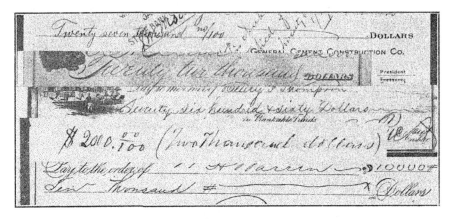

Fig. 171—The Amount Lines of Five "Raised" papers[1].

All such business forms that pass from hand to hand should be printed on dry, very smooth and perfectly white calendered paper, not of the very highest quality, with an ample field of pure white paper surface above and below the amount line. The word Dollars should not be printed in drafts and important papers but should be written immediately after the amount in words, and the amount in figures with the dollar sign should follow close upon the same line. This writing of the line con-

---

[1]The first draft illustrated was drawn on The State Bank of Chicago, Jan. 29, 1909. It was certified, then raised to twenty-seven thousand dollars and deposited in the Illinois Trust and Savings Bank and $17,000 drawn against it.

The second illustration is from a Bank of Woodland, Woodland, Cal., draft drawn for twelve dollars raised to twenty-two thousand and cashed in gold at the Nevada Bank, San Francisco. Charles Becker, the celebrated forger, was finally convicted of forging this paper.

The third raised paper was drawn by The Philadelphia National Bank for seventy-six dollars, raised to seventy-six hundred and paid in New York.

The fourth raised paper is from a note raised from two hundred to two thousand dollars. After being photographed in enlarged form it was not presented for payment.

The fifth specimen is from a draft by the German American Bank, Sidney, Ohio, raised from ten to ten thousand dollars and negotiated in Buffalo, N. Y.

taining the amount in words, the word Dollars, and the amount in figures should be begun at the extreme left of the paper and should be written continuously with the parts close together until all are written. Any protective embossing should follow immediately upon the same line in the writing space if there is room, or across the line of writing if there is not room for it in the blank space. To raise such a paper from a small to a large amount would necessitate the erasure of at least part of the line of writing including the word dollars and the amount in figures, instead of removing a single wavy or straight line between the amount in words and the printed word "Dollars" at the extreme end of the line.

It is not often that a fraudulent paper is first presented to the bank upon which it is drawn and these extra precautions are really for the protection of others. It is objectionable and unpleasant to put into the hands of every innocent customer a paper all plastered over with perfectly evident precautions against forgers and for this reason many effectual methods for the prevention of check raising cannot be employed. Some of the devices in use convey disagreeable suggestions and even if effective would not be universally adopted. Banks and business men, however, are quick to make any change for the common good and a few by careless practices should not continue to subject others to constant danger of serious loss[1].

---

[1]Many valuable suggestions regarding the general subject discussed in this chapter as well as many other questions relating to forgery and questioned documents generally may be found in "Der Nachweis von Schriftfalschungen u. s. w.," by Prof. Dr. M. Dennstedt and Dr. F. Voigtlander, Fredrich Vieweg und Sohn, Braunschweig, Germany, 1906. Dr. Dennstedt is director of the State Chemical Laboratory at Hamburg.

Illustrations.

The facts regarding erasures and alterations in documents can usually be discovered and shown if suitable photographs are promptly made. Mere enlargements on a small scale or on a large scale by the bromide process from a small negative may show nothing if the work is not done with an intelligent understanding of the problem. An examination of some of the accompanying illustrations in half-tone of delicate microscopic facts shows what is possible. The subject must be studied from the standpoint of lighting, color and degree of enlargement and in some cases it is possible, only by actual experiment to determine what is best. Whatever is done should be done promptly.

Fig. 172—Pencil erasure photographed by strong side
light showing by shadow in indentation
the erased figure "3."

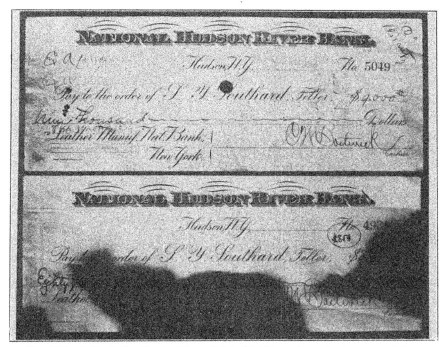

FIG. 173—A Bank Draft raised from $51 to $9,000; and one that a gang of forgers in the same case attempted to raise but did not do a good job the first time and then had the assurance to burn away a portion and "take the paper back where it was bought and have it redeemed." The upper check, raised from $34 to $9,000, was the one on which Alonzo J. Whiteman, the celebrated forger, was convicted. It was deposited and drawn against in Buffalo, N. Y.

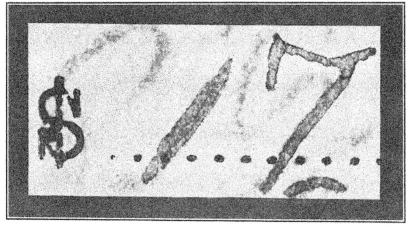

Fig. 174—The amount "11" changed to "17" by addition to top of figure "1" in a series of "raised" notes. This exhibit is from case illustrated in Fig. 29.

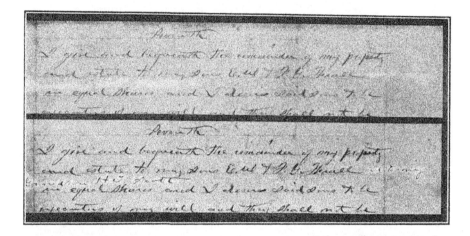

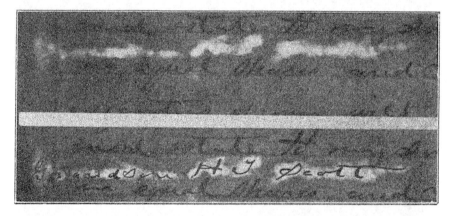

Figs. 175, 176—Abrasion erasure in a will in which the shape of the erasure, as illustrated by a transmitted light photograph, showed that the erasure fitted the words which it was claimed the will contained when it was executed. Fig. 175 shows the full width of the page in reduced size showing the transmitted light photograph and below the same photograph with the words written in that it was alleged the will originally contained. Fig. 176 is an enlarged portion made with more contrast to show more clearly the shape of the erasure which it will be seen exactly matches the name of H. T. Scott. The photographs were made by Mr. J. F. Shearman, handwriting examiner and photographer, Wichita, Kansas.

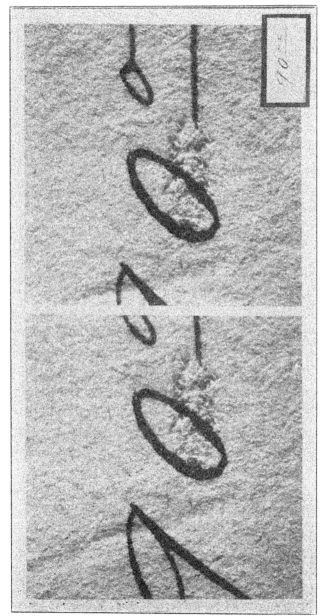

Fig. 177.—Stereoscopic Photo-Micrograph of abrasion erasure same as illustrated in Fig. 31. The startling stereoscopic effect is seen even in the half-tone cut when viewed in the stereoscope. This illustration shows how the slightest disturbance of the paper surface by any means or for any purpose can be effectively shown. This and other stereoscopic illustrations are printed on a detached folded sheet and inserted inside of back cover.

CHAPTER XXIII.

QUESTIONED ADDITIONS AND INTERLINEATIONS

The validity of a document is sometimes questioned because it contains parts in the form of interlineations or additions which may greatly change, extend, or limit its effect and value. In such a case the question to be determined is whether the document was continuously written and completed before execution, or whether the addition or interlineation is a fraudulent writing which the document did not contain when it was signed. Such questions are the basis of much litigation.

Changes or interlineations in a will should be described at the end of the will itself before execution, but this commendable practice is by no means universal and it frequently becomes necessary to determine whether interlined or added parts are genuine or fraudulent. Numerous careless practices in the drawing of wills are an open temptation to fraud. Many important wills not only contain erasures, additions and interlineations but are written on two or more sheets of paper loosely fastened together, and in one important case the attestation clause and the signatures of the witnesses were on a separate sheet from the will itself bearing the signature of the testator. These practices make it easy to make a fraudulent addition or interlineation or even to substitute whole pages.

If it is possible that the interlined or added part may be in a different handwriting then careful study and comparison must be made as with a simulated forgery, but often the part in dispute is concededly written by the writer of the remainder of the document, and the order, date and continuity of the writing are the questions to be investigated.

If an interlined part immediately precedes the signature, as is often the case, careful examination should be made to see if any parts of this writing cross or touch any stroke of the writing of the signature itself. If there are such crossed lines they must be examined with great care and thoroughness as outlined in a preceding chapter. It is not easily understood without actual experiment and examination with what clearness and certainty (see Fig. 29) it can often be shown which was the last stroke made in such a case. Crossed lines may also point to unnatural order of writing of other parts of the document and it should be carefully examined throughout with this point in mind.

The question whether any part of the writing followed the folding of the paper should also be carefully considered if that fact has any bearing on the genuineness of the document or shows anything irregular in its preparation. This question is often of great importance and such points may be entirely overlooked if a document is not systematically examined in every particular.

If it is claimed or must be maintained that the writing in question or any suspected part was written at the same sitting as the remainder of the document and with the same pen and ink, then the class, condition, tint and shade of the ink must be carefully examined throughout the whole document. The portion in dispute and those preceding and following it should be photographed in several ways, as directed in the ink and photography chapters, to discover possible differences in tint. As it is difficult if not impossible to distinguish tints by artificial light, unless the differences are very pronounced, the ink lines should be examined in daylight with the color microscope and magnified to an extent which best shows the exact tint and shade. Somewhat distinct differences in shade or tint are not discernible except under proper magnification, and then the conditions and light must also be favorable.

If a color microscope is not available, then two ink lines of equal strength should if possible be found lying close together, one disputed, one undisputed, which can both be brought for comparison at one time into the field of the ordinary compound microscope. Hand magnifiers are not always corrected for color aberrations and must not be relied upon exclusively in determining tints.

The ink in such a questioned writing should always be chemically tested by the application of suitable reagents to determine whether it shows the same color reactions as the ink in other parts of the document. If inks of different chemical constituents have been used, although their color as shown in the writing be the same, such chemical tests properly and carefully made, as outlined in the chapter treating the question of ink, will show conclusively that they are different.

If it is claimed that the writing was with the same pen then a number of the unshaded and shaded strokes of the questioned writing should be carefully measured and averaged for comparison with similar measurements of other parts of the document. A microscope with filar-

micrometer attachment (see Figs. 35, 49) is necessary
for this work.   Line widths, which in unshaded strokes
range in extremes from about one-thirtieth up to one
two-hundredth of an inch, can easily be measured.   With
this instrument measurements in divisions of twenty
thousandths of an inch can readily be made, and this
high division renders it possible to compare with extreme
accuracy the average widths of the normal, minimum,
and shaded strokes in the regular writing and in the
questioned interlined or added writing.   The upward
normal strokes show approximately the width of the pen
point, and, if measured in both writings and compared
(see Figs. 36, 75, 78), any difference can be conclusively
shown.

The difference in width of lines made with fine pens
actually varying as much as fifty per cent., is not plainly
apparent until the lines are measured.   The microscope
attachment referred to is indispensable for such examinations as it enables even those without experience in
such matters to read and verify these measuremnts.
Differences in line width in such parts may be apparent
to the unaided eye and in this case definite measurements confirm and enforce the conclusion.

The question is sometimes presented as to whether
several book entries, charges, credits or debits, were made
in the regular course of business on the dates they bear
or were fraudulently made at one time at some later
period to show some desired result.   In such a case it
is highly probable that there will be greater uniformity
in the fraudulent additions than in the regular writing.

This unnatural uniformity may show, (1) in the tint
or condition of the ink, (2) in the quality of line, (3) its

width, (4) its smoothness or roughness, (5) in the size of the writing, (6) in its position, especially its vertical alignment, or (7) in the size, position and arrangement of figures, ditto marks or abbreviations. Such continuous writings, whether with pencil or pen, will almost certainly show less variation in numerous ways than if written at different times, with the writing instrument in various conditions and the writer necessarily surrounded by differing circumstances of time, position, light, haste and care, which variable conditions inevitably affect the result. Some of these habits of uniformity differ in different individuals and the basis of comparison in such an inquiry should, if obtainable, be other similar work by the same writer.

If the task of the forger is to add a considerable amount of writing to a document and thus change its significance the task is, as a natural consequence, vastly more difficult than simply to write a signature under such conditions. Even with the same materials and under the same external conditions, it is exceedingly difficult to produce such an addition without making some conspicuous differences, which, when pointed out and properly interpreted, are perfectly apparent. This difference can usually be shown even if it has been possible to match the exact tint of ink, quality of line and width of strokes, which, after the lapse of even a little time, is exceedingly difficult if not actually impossible.

Another interesting kind of forgery by addition of a fraudulent part is that in which a document is written over a genuine signature. Old documents containing genuine signatures in which a blank space was carelessly left above the signature are sometimes used to make fraudulent notes, agreements or contracts, all the document being cut away but the signature and the blank paper above it upon which the subject matter is written. Such fraudulent documents have been written over signatures carelessly written on blank paper, or fraudulently obtained, and, at least in one instance, illustrated herewith, a document was made out of a page of an old

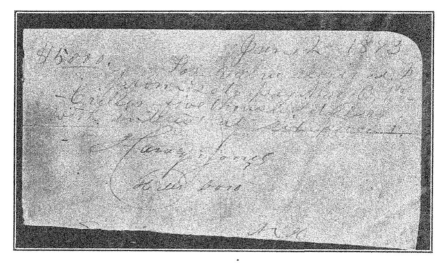

FIG. 178—A disputed note in a New Hampshire case written above a signature in an old style autograph album. The sheet had a "silvered" edge and the one round corner and the mark of the binding at the left and a part of what was the original date line at the bottom can be seen even on the half-tone cut.

style autograph album, a note for a large amount having been written above the genuine signature.

If it is claimed, as is usually the case, that both the signature and the body of a suspected document of this class were written at the same time and place, the ink of the two parts should be carefully tested in every way possible as with a disputed interlineation. If the writing of the body of the document and the signature touch at any point this may show, by examination of the crossed strokes, that the signature was undoubtedly written first.

The writing of both the signature and the subject-matter over any continuous folds in the paper should be examined for the purpose of determining, if possible, the order of the writing and the folding. If the signature extends across a well defined fold over which the writing of the subject-matter also extends and it can be clearly shown that the signature was written before the folding and the writing above the signature after the folding (see Fig. 28) then these facts alone would show that the document is not genuine.

A third indication of a lack of genuineness in such a document is a crowded or unnatural arrangement of the words written in before the genuine signature. This crowding in of writing immediately above the signature may be shown by comparison with the other parts of the document, or the curving of the last line of writing up above the signature may show that the signature must have been there first, or the line would not have been written so as to avoid it.

In some instances the fraudulent writing is begun too high and the last lines are written with the words wide apart and arranged in such a way as to show the attempt to fill up the open space above the signature. The signature may be too far to the left to be in a natural position or, in some instances, it may be too far away from the body of the document to look natural and as if written in the usual manner after the writing it follows. The lower parts of long letters in the writing over the signature may be abbreviated in an unnatural manner to avoid running into or touching the signature, or such letters may be bent to the right or left for the same reason.

The paper on which such a suspected document is written should, if possible, be followed to its source. It may be possible to show that the paper is actually a part of a legal blank or document used for another purpose and its foldings or worn portions or discolorations may point to its former use. The edges of the paper should be carefully examined to see if it was cut by hand and to determine what part of the sheet it came from, and both sides of the paper should be carefully examined for evidences of unequal soiling or discoloration due to

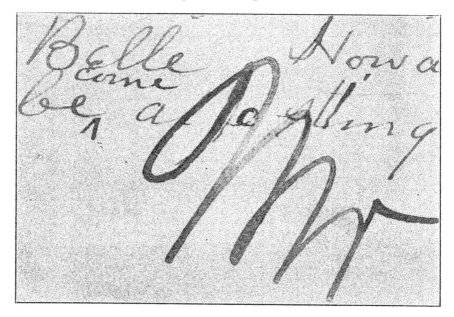

Fig. 181—Exhibit from Matter of Kirkholder estate tried in Buffalo, N. Y., 1908, photographed by Mr. William J. Kinsley, Examiner and Photographer of Questioned Documents, New York. It was proved that the writing of the body of a will was written over what purported to be a will signature. The alleged signature was preceded by the abbreviation "Mr." and the word "attestting" was written over the capital "M."

its position as part of a previous larger sheet used for some other purpose.

It is also possible that a genuine signature over which a fraudulent document is written may be so old that, like the selected model in a traced forgery, it may show a change in handwriting inconsistent with the date of the document. This is especially true if the writing is by one well advanced in years whose condition of health may have greatly changed between the actual date of the writing of the signature and the date of the fraudulent paper.

FIG. 181-a—An illustration made to show change by erasure and addition of stroke. Transmitted light photograph showing erasure of top of "3" and "crossed" line over "4."

CHAPTER XXIV.

The question of age has been discussed incidentally in several preceding chapters but the subject is here somewhat more fully treated and some of the matters previously referred to are briefly reviewed.

No matter how suspicious the circumstances surrounding a fraudulent document, or how incredible the story of how it was found, or how generally improbable the alleged act may be, it usually becomes necessary first or last to prove the fraud, if it is to be proved at all, from the document itself. One of the first of the questions that naturally arise in such an inquiry is whether it is possible to show that a fraudulent document is not as old as it purports to be. This cannot always be done, but the question should always be investigated in a thorough, systematic manner.

Questions of age enter into the study of disputed documents in many ways. The most common inquiry is, as has been said, whether a document is actually as old as its date would indicate, but it is also sometimes very important to show the probable date of an undated document. Another frequent subject of investigation is whether several documents, or several writings bearing different dates, are not actually of the same age, having been fraudulently produced all at one time; and then occasionally the other question may arise as to whether a document is not older than it purports to be.

[431]

In bankruptcy cases and settlements of estates the important question may arise whether certain entries or memoranda in books of account were actually made in due course of business on the dates they bear, or whether they were made at a subsequent period for the fraudulent purpose (see Fig. 77) of showing a certain result at the date of settlement.

Letters are sometimes produced as evidence to support other claims and it becomes necessary to determine whether they were written at the time alleged. The attempt is sometimes made to prove the date of an undated letter by producing the postmarked envelope in which it is said the letter was mailed. As briefly described in a preceding chapter, a postmark often makes an indented imprint on an inclosed letter (see Fig. 24) and in such a case it should be ascertained whether the postmark and the indentation on the letter match each other in position, intensity and size. If the postmarking was so heavily done that it shows through on the back of the envelope then a letter which is said to have been inclosed in it must necessarily show a postmark indentation.

The actual age of a document is ascertained by a study of all the means by which it was produced, and all the external evidence bearing on the question should be carefully investigated. The phraseology throughout and the subject matter of the document should be examined with reference to all the known conditions and facts that may be connected in any way with the case. It frequently happens that names of persons, firms, or corporations, names or numbers of streets, or references to events or transactions in a questioned document, have a conclusive chronological significance and prove that such a document was made before or after a certain definite date. Even a postage stamp may have a most important date significance.

The age of a typewritten document should be carefully tested by a study of that subject as outlined in a subsequent chapter. More and more this subject is coming to be of importance as bearing on the date of documents; the most short-sighted and incriminating blunders have been made in the production of fraudulent typewritten documents under the common delusion that typewriting cannot be identified.

It is also quite possible that a study of the handwriting of a document may throw some light on the question of its date. If the handwriting is unknown or in dispute, then this phase of the subject should, of course, receive the most careful attention. Many writers, particularly those who write well and freely, are from time to time making slight but persistent changes in their handwriting. These changes are usually few in number compared with all the characteristics of the writing and do not change the general style, but are often sufficient, with adequate material for comparison, to show conclusively that a writing was made before or after a certain definite time. An interval of five years or even less, under certain health conditions, may show a number of permanent and significant changes.

Writers differ greatly in the permanency of their writing in this regard, but if the circumstances permit it, the question should always be carefully considered in estimating the age of a document. Fraudulent notes against estates for thousands of dollars have been manufactured, purporting to be many years old, but with forged signatures the design and form of which proved unmistakably that they were simulations of a genuine signature of a period twenty years or more after the alleged date of the notes.

References to alleged promises, contracts or incidents are sometimes made in added postscripts to old letters. The additions may have been made by the writer of the original letter into whose hands it has come. Examination of such a writing should include careful attention to the writing over folded portions of the paper, exact tint of ink, width of pen strokes, style, speed and care of writing, and relevancy of the matter in question.

The approximate age and fraudulent date of a document can often be shown by an examination of the paper on which it is written. Many wills and other important documents have been written on paper which it has been the fraudulent document. In the chapter on paper this the fraudulent document. In the chapter on paper this subject is more fully treated.

In many instances the fluid ink on a document purporting to be several years old has not reached its ultimate intensity of color and changes and actually turns black after the document is brought forward. This is a matter which should, of course, receive the closest scrutiny at the earliest possible moment. A verified and dated color reading of the ink should at once be made with the color microscope in order that it may be compared with a similar reading at a later time.

Hundreds of thousands of dollars have been paid for spurious letters and writings of various kinds purporting to have been written by famous people. The most astonishing credulity is shown by purchasers of documents of this kind. These spurious papers are cherished with the greatest care, apparently with no suspicion that they were manufactured to be sold like certain imitation antique furniture. To be above suspicion, ancient documents should have a connected and authentic history[1]. In many instances the most superficial tests will show that such alleged ancient documents are undoubtedly fraudulent.

The attempt is sometimes made to make fraudulent documents look old by soiling and discoloring them in various ways, and a bleaching agent may be applied to the writing to make it appear to have faded. Such an artificial document will almost certainly show suspicious inconsistencies and should be compared with undoubtedly genuine papers of the date it bears. Artificial aging may be overdone, and a paper purporting to be ten or a dozen years old may in some ways have the appearance of one that has been written fifty or seventy-five years.

Writing that is actually old has certain distinctive characteristics that are not easily imitated. Old ink lines

---

[1] But the collector must be warned to be constantly on his guard against forgeries. There are great quantities of spurious specimens in circulation. The French (though their laws are severe against all frauds) are wonderfully clever in manufacturing autographs. This probably accounts for the number of interesting French documents of the great characters of the last century, from Louis XIV. to Napoleon, always on sale at very moderate prices. There are many forgers, too, in our own country as clever as "Jim the Penman." * * * A very little study of the subject, however, will enable the amateur to distinguish spurious writings from originals. In the first place a careful examination will immediately afford many points of evidence either for or against the genuineness of any autograph. There is something unmistakable to the practiced eye in the real article which rarely deceives it. If the paper were taken out of a book some faint indications of this would probably be apparent—e. g., the impressions of the bindings or the printed letters, etc. And if a genuine letter of the supposed writer of the document in question could be compared with it, all doubt would be removed by attention to the feel of the papers, watermarks, etc.—Autograph Collecting, by Henry T. Scott, London, 1894, pp. 4, 5.

have a peculiar appearance under magnification; they usually have lost all trace of actual pen furrows, and the ink lines are cracked and broken and often stand up from the paper in a peculiar manner, caused no doubt in large measure by changes in humidity and the swelling and shrinking of the paper. In an inquiry of this character it is very important to get actual old papers for purposes of comparison.

As has been said before, much time is lost in all kinds of questioned document inquiries by not at once seeking out proper standards of comparison. This should be done in all such investigations instead of spending the whole time looking only at the questioned paper. A proper standard will often open up an investigation that will lead to evidence of great value. Like the other subjects previously discussed, investigation of this matter of age of a document should be taken up and carried through following a definite routine in order that nothing may be overlooked.

CHAPTER XXV.

QUESTIONED TYPEWRITING[1]

There is an increasing use of the typewriting machine for the production of spurious papers; this is due to the great increase in use of the typewriter generally and to the erroneous idea that fraudulent typewriting cannot be detected. Whatever the cause that may have led to it, the use of the typewriter for the production of fraudulent writings of all classes has certainly created an urgent necessity for means that will lead to the identification of such documents, the determination of their dates, and the discovery of their authors. Many fraudulent typewritten papers have no doubt entirely escaped attack and served their evil purposes because it was assumed that their genuineness could not be impeached.

Confirmatory typewritten documents of various kinds are frequently brought forward to sustain signature forgeries and other fraudulent claims and it is often a matter of great importance to learn where they came from and when they were written. The public generally

---

[1]The principal part of this chapter was first printed in the "Albany Law Journal," Volume 63, Number 11, and was afterwards reprinted in the "Chicago Legal News," May, 1906, and in the "Typewriter and Phonographic World," of November, 1906. That part of the chapter referring particularly to the question of fraudulently dated typewritten documents, was first printed in the "Typewriter and Phonographic World" of April, 1907, and afterwards reprinted in the "American Lawyer," of June, 1907. In Band I, Nr. 3, of "Archiv für Gerichtliche Schriftuntersuchungen," Leipsig, 1909, both articles were printed with illustrations.

and many lawyers who have not investigated the subject
hold the opinion that the typewriter has no individuality.
Fortunately this is not true, and the typewriting machine
does not always afford an effective protection to the
criminal. On the contrary, the typewriting of a fraudulent document may be the direct means by which it is
traced to its source and shown to be what it is. This is
especially true of typewritten anonymous letters and
fraudulent typewritten documents containing considerable matter, the correct identification of which has heretofore depended entirely upon other means.

Without careful investigation it is impossible to say
what can be determined from the examination of any
particular piece of typewriting, but it is important that
those whose interests are attacked by such documents
should know that typewriting can sometimes be positively identified as being the work of a certain particular
typewriting machine, and the date of a typewriting in
many cases can be determined with certainty. A knowledge of these two facts by those who try cases in courts
of law would in many cases lead to the discovery of the
truth and prevent miscarriages of justice.

The importance of this new field of inquiry is becom-
ing recognized by typewriting men, who have shown
much interest in these investigations, the results of which
are here reported, and have rendered valuable assistance;
indeed, without their co-operation, the work could not
have been done[1]. There is naturally no lack of interest

---

[1] The erroneous idea is generally accepted by the public as a fact
that the typewriting machine is of great assistance to those who set
about the manufacture of fraudulent documents.

Those connected with the typewriter industry should endeavor to
correct this mistaken notion. The typewriter is not only not an ally

by lawyers having actual typewriting questions in hand, or by lawyers' clients whose property, whose character or whose liberty has been assailed by fraudulent typewritten documents.

Typewriting questions are presented in a great variety of ways. In the first place, it is often necessary simply to ascertain the date of such a writing. It may also be a matter of great importance to learn whether a document was all written at one time, or written at different times on the same machine or at different times on different machines. The inquiry sometimes arises as to whether fraudulent typewritten pages have been substituted in wills, whether paragraphs or interlineations have been added to old letters or deeds and contracts after execution, or whether modifying conditions have been added to receipts and similar vouchers.

Sometimes the question is simply whether a document was written on a certain kind of machine, and then again whether it was written on a certain particular typewriter which may be one of a number of suspected machines. Different habits of touch, spacing, speed, arrangement and punctuation may also tend to show that a document was not all written by one operator or that a collection of documents was produced by different operators, all

---

of the forger, but may be made the direct means of his downfall in many cases if the subject is properly investigated.

Any one knows that a typewritten document dated early enough would necessarily be fraudulent, and it is equally true that a document dated long after typewriters came into use may show a kind and style of typewriting that could not have been produced on the date the written instrument bears. Typewriter men should counteract this mistaken notion that they are putting into the hands of the evil-minded a dangerous tool. The interests of justice would be promoted if there could be published an authoritative chronologically arranged collection of typewriting specimens.—Typewriter and Phonographic World, Vol. XXIX., No. 4.

of which facts may be of great importance as bearing on the genuineness of a document in question. Even the number of threads to the inch in the ribbon, as shown in the type impression, plainly seen and accurately measured by the microscope or in the enlarged photograph, may show that a typewritten addition or interlineation is fraudulent.

Where the subject-matter of a questioned document is typewritten and bears a date long previous to the time when it was actually produced, the question naturally arises whether an examination of the typewriting may not prove that it could not possibly have been written on the date it bears. Fortunately there are many typewriting characteristics that have a definite date significance, and this question of the age or date of typewriting is here first considered.

A fraudulent document is usually dated back to some selected time when certain circumstances or occurrences tend to confirm the fraud. Such documents may actually bear a date twenty years before the time when they were actually written, and if it can be shown that such a paper could not have been written on the date it bears, the forgery is proved. Those whose interests lead them to investigate the subject should not be discouraged because they at first obtain no assistance from those who naturally would be supposed to have at hand the technical information required. Many who are interested in typewriters in a commercial way have had no occasion to give special attention to this phase of the subject and may inform those who seek information that the attempt to determine the date of a typewriting is an entirely hopeless task. There are necessarily cases where any attempt in this direction is fruitless, but this fact can only be ascertained by a careful investigation.

It is a matter of common knowledge that typewriters of the various kinds were not manufactured before certain dates and that changes and improvements are constantly being made in the various kinds of machines in use that may show conclusively that a document must have been written after a certain definite date. As an illustration, the Smith-Premier narrowed its capital letter designs in 1896. A document in an important Wisconsin case contained hundreds of capital letters; it was dated 1893; it was written on a Smith-Premier typewriter and the capitals were all of the narrow design,—the conclusion that it could not have been written in 1893 was irresistible[1].

These progressive changes, which have been made in

[1]The case of Peshtigo Lumber Co. vs. Robert O. Hunt et al. was tried before Honorable Charles M. Webb, of the Wisconsin Supreme Court, without a jury, at Grand Rapids, Wisconsin, in the summer of 1903. During the progress of the trial the question arose as to the genuineness of a typewritten document introduced in evidence. The document bore the date of August 7, 1893, and the determination of the actual date of the typewriting became the main question at issue in the case.

After a vigorously contested trial it was shown conclusively: first, that the document was written on a Smith-Premier typewriter, second, that it must have been written after 1896, and third, that it was actually written in 1903, a few months before the date of the trial, on a certain sample machine sent out on approval by a Milwaukee typewriting company, which machine was found and brought to court.

Mr. Justice Webb in the course of his able opinion says of this document: "It further appears that defendant Hunt, during the month of April, 1903, by himself or through the agency of some other person, falsely made and prepared what purported to be a typewritten copy of the record in its altered form . . . as of the date of August 7, 1893."

This final decision was reached notwithstanding the fact that at the outset it was considered almost a hopeless task to attack the typewritten document. At the beginning of the inquiry those interested to set aside the fraudulent paper held the common opinion that it is exceedingly difficult if not impossible to identify or show the date of a questioned typewritten paper.

typewriters from the time they were first put on the market, are in the design, size and proportions of the type faces, the length of the line that the machine will write, the vertical spacing between the lines, the number of characters on the machine and in a great number of other particulars, some of which may affect the written result only indirectly. As has been said the mere length of a typewritten line may show that a writing could not have been done at a certain time. Again, it may be proved or admitted that a paper was written on a certain particular machine, and the typewriting may show a combination of individual characteristics, defects and conditions that did not develop in that machine until long after the date of the document in question. It is not often necessary or possible to show by the typewriting itself and that alone exactly when a paper was written, but it may be possible to show conclusively that it could not possibly have been written until after a certain definite date.

Unlike machines of a different character, a typewriter makes a continuous record of its own history and to read this history it is only necessary to have at hand a sufficient amount of the continuous writing of the machine. The active life of a typewriter ranges, perhaps, from five to twenty years and during this period its work gradually deteriorates, from the condition which satisfied the inspectors at the factory down to work so inferior that the machine is discarded. It is easy to understand how a document written on a certain machine and dated back would not match the condition of the machine at the pretended fraudulent date. The faces of many letters inevitably become broken, worn or battered, and, with successive dated specimens of work of the machine at hand for comparison, it can be shown with absolute certainty when defects first appeared. These facts can often be shown so convincingly that they cannot be successfully denied[1].

The first fact to be considered in investigating the date of a typewriting is to find when a certain kind of machine, the work of which is in question, first came into use, and then it is important to learn and to be able to prove when any changes were made that affected the written record. Naturally the most important special points for consideration are the design, size and proportions of the type faces. There have been constant changes in these particulars on all the older machines on the market, and in such an investigation it is simply necessary to have for comparison authentic, dated specimens from the particular kind of machine the work of which is under investigation.

Fortunately, the Remington typewriter, which has been longest on the market, shows continuous changes during its long history that indicate unquestionably many fixed dates in the work of this machine. These changes were made in the natural course of the improvement of the typewriter, but the result is just as useful

---

[1]Now a large amount of typewriter work done in Mr. Rust's office was produced here. It had been produced in court already in agreements written at the same time, almost with the dates of these receipts, and not one of them has any such characteristics.—Levy vs. Rust, New Jersey Chancery, 49 Atlantic, 1025.

He testified, and his evidence is not disputed that the letters and affidavits showed that the type used in printing them was of the same class and size, that certain letters (type) were defective, broken and out of repair, that certain other letters were out of alignment, and the spacing between certain letters was too great; that these peculiarities and defects appeared in the affidavits and typewritten letters and the addresses referred to which were typewritten.—State vs. Freshwater, 30 Utah, 446 (1906).

in determining the date of a typewriting as if made definitely for this explicit purpose.

The interests of justice would be served if all manufacturers would deliberately make such slight changes at intervals of not more than five years, even when improvements and changes in the machine did not actually require it. There would also, no doubt, be some advantage in a business way to the manufacturer in being able to ascertain the age of his machines simply by inspecting their work, and some few changes have been made in type designs for this particular purpose. All changes in type designs and sizes are inconspicuous and entirely unknown to many who are identified with the typewriting industry.

A consecutive arrangement of specimens of dated writings from a certain machine will also show the exact date when each new ribbon was put on the machine or other changes were made, and a fraudulently dated document may not match the condition of the work of the machine in this regard on the date it bears. The machine may also have been repaired between the alleged date and the actual date of the writing, a fact which would change the written result and the fraudulent document would not then correspond to the writing done before the repairs were made.

Perhaps the most important typewriting inquiry to be considered is that of identifying a typewritten document as the work of a particular individual machine. There are often two steps in such an inquiry, the first being the determination of the fact that the document was written on a certain particular kind of machine and the second, that it was written on a certain individual machine.

These two questions are quite closely related and, strange as it may seem, in some instances it is easier to answer the second question than the first, especially if the document is brief and does not show all the characters and is written on an old machine.

Typewriting individuality in many cases is of the most positive and convincing character and reaches a degree of certainty which may almost be described as absolute proof. The identification of a typewritten document in many cases is exactly parallel to the identification of an individual who precisely answers a general description as to features, complexion, size, etc., and in addition matches a long detailed list of scars, birth-marks, deformities and individual peculiarities[1].

In identifying a typewriting, as in determining its

---

[1] In Judge Tarrant's court, yesterday the attorney for the plaintiff asked to have a juror, naming the man, withdrawn from the panel. The request was granted and the juror was excused. Thereupon it became necessary to postpone the case.

This action occurred in the case of James L. Gates against the estate of George Hiles, in which the sum of $20,000 is involved. The action was brought by Mr. Gates against the estate to recover money alleged to be due under a contract. The plaintiff claimed that in 1891, a contract was made between him and Mr. Hiles, whereby, in considcration for certain lands, Mr. Hiles would hold Mr. Gates harmless for a judgment of about $20,000 secured against him in the state of Florida. The judgment was not satisfied by Mr. Hiles and Mr. Gates was obliged to pay it. Thereupon Mr. Gates sued to recover the amount.

In the trial of the case, Mr. Gates introduced what purported to be a letter press copy of the contract dated 1891, as the original had been lost. . . . An expert in typewriting was called as a witness and testified that the alleged contract could not have been made earlier than 1896, a year after Mr. Hiles' death. He gave an extended lecture to show how typewritten letters vary when made on different machines, or on the same machine at different times.

The court granted an adjournment until 2 o'clock Tuesday afternoon and continued it to yesterday morning on a second request. A third continuance was refused and to avoid endeavoring to rebut testimony which was unexpected, the attorneys took advantage of the unusual proceeding of asking the withdrawal of a juror.—Milwaukee "Sentinel," February 21, 1907.

date, the type faces naturally afford the greatest field for study, and, while the various typewriting machines approximate the same style, no two standard machines are alike in this regard (see Figs. 15, 42) except some few recent machines produced under the same management. A large majority of machines of all kinds, probably over ninety-five per cent., use what is called a "pica" style of type. To the printer this indicates a certain definite size of type body, made of exactly the same size by all type makers; but in typewriting it indicates approximately the size of the type face itself and as it is the kind of type most used on all machines it consequently is that most frequently found in a questioned document.

There is a great diversity of taste as to the best designs for letters. No two type-engravers exactly agree as to the proper proportions of the various characters used in printing; and the result is that there are almost innumerable styles of printed letters of all sizes. This is true of typewriting letters as well as of ordinary print. The various typewriter manufacturers, while following a style similar in general features, have aimed at a certain individuality in design of letters and have vied with each other in producing legible, graceful forms.

Another important point not generally understood is that the mechanical requirement in the spacing of typewriting makes it necessary that all letters, capitals and lower case, narrow and wide, shall be given the same lateral space. This in ordinary typewriting is one-tenth of an inch, and thus arose the necessity for new designs of special letters, the effort being directed to gaining the appearance of uniformity in spacing by making the very narrow letters wider and the very wide letters narrower than in ordinary print while still maintaining legibility and a pleasing appearance. To meet this demand an entirely new class of engravers has been developed and modern typewriters show the result of their work.

A comparison of typewriting with ordinary printing, spaced according to the actual width of the letters, will show what a marked change has been wrought in letter designs, and this gradual development in letter designs and proportions makes it possible, in many instances, as has been outlined, to give to a piece of typewriting a very definite date in comparison with the work of other machines of the same kind, in addition to showing that a document was written on a certain kind of machine.

The gradual deterioration of the work of a typewriter gives to it that individuality which distinguishes it from the work of other machines of the same kind and also affords the means, as described above, by which it is possible, knowing that a document was written on a particular machine, to ascertain when it was written. This latter fact is shown by collecting specimens of the work of the machine in question arranged in exact chronological order, which will show the development of certain irregularities or defects that only become permanent after certain definite dates, and a comparison of these specimens with the document in question may show, for instance, that abnormal characteristics due to accidents or use which did not actually develop until after January or February, 1910, all appear in a document on the same machine dated December, 1908.

As a means of identifying the particular machine

upon which a writing was done or determining its date the examination of the type impression should be made in five ways:

First, the design, size and proportions of all the characters. Second, the relation of the character as printed to adjacent characters or the vertical and horizontal alignment. Third, the vertical position of the character in relation to the line of writing—that is, its perpendicularity or slant to the left or right. Fourth, the comparative weight of impression of the upper, lower, right or left sides of each character, or, as the machine adjusters describe it, how the type stands "on its feet." Fifth, the condition of the type faces and the presence of defects, bruises, or "scars" in the letters due to wear or to accidents.

Divergences from perfect conditions in these five directions make it possible to examine and describe the characteristics of the work of a typewriting machine in great detail. If typewriting shows clear impressions and includes numerous characters and there are at hand proper standards of comparison, it becomes possible to show with the highest degree of certainty by the combination of these five classes of characteristics, that a document was or was not written upon a certain machine. Photographic enlargements of from two to four diameters are desirable in all cases, and are necessary if typewriting characteristics are to be effectively shown.

The first particular specified above, the design, size, and proportions of the type faces, identifies a machine as of a certain kind or differentiates it from others of a different kind and also from others of the same kind carrying a different style of type. Differences may be small and not observable under ordinary view, but if they actually exist they differentiate two machines as certainly as if they wrote two different languages having totally different letter designs.

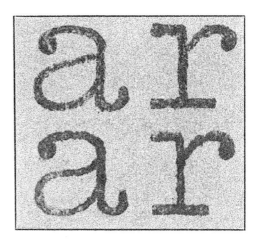

Fig. 179—Enlargement to show slight but distinctive divergence in design of Remington and Monarch letters.

The second point is that of alignment. Typewriter types are either fastened on a type wheel or sleeve or, as is usually the case, are attached to the ends of printing arms or type-bars. It is impracticable to attach and adjust these separate types by any method so that after actual use the printed letters continue to bear an exact relation to each other like printing types, and divergences from exact horizontal and vertical alignment, which in their combinations extend into the thousands, show unmistakable individuality[1]. Entirely new machines usually show slight but persistent differences which are readily seen upon close examination.

In alignment each character may occupy any one of nine positions. In ordinary typewriting each letter occupies an imaginary square, ten to the inch horizontal-

---

[1]The fact that the letters in typewritten matter are in exact lines vertically as well as horizontally is sometimes of importance in determining whether a disputed interlineation was a part of the original writing before the paper was taken out of the machine. It may be easy to show that an interlineation is out of vertical alignment with the writing it precedes and follows.

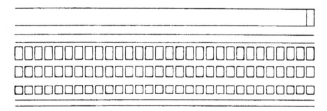

Fig. 180—Alignment Test Plate on Glass, ten to an inch, for illustrating defects in alignment.

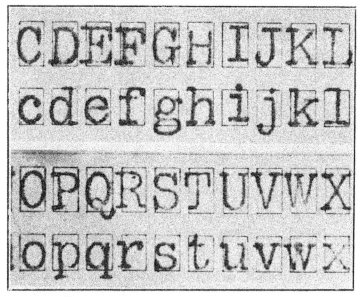

Fig. 181—Alignment Test Plate over typewriting showing letters out of alignment and defective letters.

Fig. 182—Enlargement with Test Plate over Letters.

ly and six to the inch vertically, typewriting letters being in line both ways. When in perfect alignment, the letter occupies the middle of such square, and when out of alignment may be in either of the four corners, or either side of the middle position or either at top or bottom, above or below the middle, making nine positions in all, or eight possible divergences from normal in this particular alone. Divergences in alignment and perpendicularity in a shift key machine affect both capitals and small letters or other companion characters, since the two characters are on one piece of metal, while in a double-case machine the two letters are independent. Careful examination of this point is usually sufficient to distinguish the work of a single case machine from that of a double case machine which has a separate key for each character.

The third possible divergence, the perpendicular position of the letter in relation to the line, is of great value in individualizing a machine, and it is very seldom that machines, even when new, are perfect in this particular. This characteristic may not seem very pronounced until typewriting is enlarged, when it can be seen by any one, and it is a characteristic that is fixed and continuous and is not

Fig. 183—Typewriting Protractor for measuring siant of divergent letters.

materially changed by variations in speed or methods of manipulation.

Examination of the work of any typewriter that has been in actual use will illustrate the fourth variety of

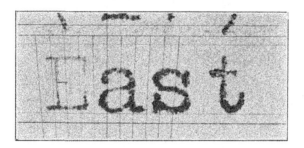

Fig. 184—Typewriting Protractor, Fig. 183, photographed over divergent capital E out
of position four degrees.

divergence specified, the lack of uniformity of the
impression of the different parts of the several characters. Typewriter faces are not flat but are concaved
to conform to the curve of the printing surface of the
platen or roller. When properly adjusted all portions
print uniformly, but
when slightly out of
position in any direc-
tion the two curved
surfaces are not par-
allel and thus do not
come together with
uniform pressure,
the result being a
difference in intens-

Fig. 185—Upper and lower case W's printing
heavily on left.

ity in different parts of the impression, especially in light
impressions[1].

Individuality in a typewriter is shown most conclusively by the fifth point, that is, the combination of diverg-

[1]It is easy to understand that differences in intensity of different
portions of the type face may not be seen in a heavy impression. With
a new and heavily inked ribbon or when struck with much force the
whole type face may print when it is quite uneven. This is one of the
variations in typewriting that should be carefully noted.

ences and defects due to imperfections in the letters as originally made, accidental collisions of the types with each other or with metallic portions of the machine, and to ordinary wear. If two machines of the same kind were perfect to begin with and in perfect condition—which is never found to be the case when they are critically examined—the work from one could not be distinguished from that of the other until actual use had affected them differently. The work of any number of machines inevitably begins to diverge as soon as they are used, and, as there are thousands of possible particulars in which differences may develop, it very soon begins to be possible to identify positively the

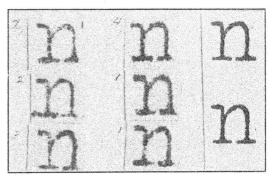

Fig. 186—One of a number of defective letters tending to identify a disputed typewriting. The "x" letters disputed, "a" standard, and two letters on right perfect letters from new machine.

work of a particular typewriter if the writing in question includes clear prints of a sufficient number of the characters and a sufficient amount of genuine writing is furnished for comparison.

The principles underlying the identification of typewriting are the same as those by which the identity of a person is determined or a handwriting is identified. The identification in either case is based upon a definite combination of common or class features in connection with a second group of characteristics made up of divergences from normal features which thus become individual peculiarities.

The mathematical principles outlined in the fourteenth chapter show how remote is the possibility of coincidence of even a few scars or deformities on a person, and coincidence of scars and deformities are as remote with typewriters as with persons[1].

The problem is easily stated and its solution is not difficult. Suppose a typewriter has three broken letters, three letters out of alignment, three letters printing "off their feet," and one out of slant. As was the case in considering this subject in relation to handwriting, the mathematical probability of a combination of just these characteristics is found by first determining how frequently each characteristic will be found and the continued product of the separate probabilities will show how frequently they will all unite in one event.

If it be granted that in every ten machines (five hundred would be nearer the fact) a certain letter face is broken or worn in a definite way this will give, in the

---

[1]Although disputed typewriting is comparatively new in courts of law the question has arisen in numerous important cases in the past few years. Some of these are here briefly mentioned:

Hunt vs. Peshtigo Lumber Co., Marinette, Wisconsin. Tried at Grand Rapids, Wisconsin, 1903. James L. Gates vs. George Hiles Estate, tried at Milwaukee, Wisconsin, February, 1907. The Gamey Investigation, at Toronto, Canada, in 1903, of charges by R. R. Gamey, that he had been offered a bribe of $3000 by Provincial Secretary J. R. Stratton to vote with the Liberal Party. Eleven anonymous typewritten letters were under investigation in this case.

In the "Lilley Investigation," Washington, D. C., conducted by a committee of congress in March, 1908, a question arose regarding two anonymous typewritten letters. In the Schooley-Crawford will case tried at Scranton, Penn., the question regarding the identity of typewriting arose. The identification of typewriting was also an important feature of the case of United States vs. Everding, tried in Washington, D. C., January, 1909. The Groves case at New Brunswick, N. J., in May, 1910, was a typewriting inquiry, and the Glazier Insurance Assignment investigation at Chelsea, Mich., 1910, was based on a number of disputed typewritten assignments.

problem stated above, three fractions of one-tenth. Then if it be assumed that of every ten machines one of the three selected letters will print off its feet or heavy at top, side or bottom in a definite way, and of every ten machines one of the three selected letters will be out of alignment in a certain definite way, and on one of every ten machines a particular letter will be out of slant in a definite way, this will give ten fractions of one-tenth, and the continued product or mathematical probability of these particular divergences all uniting in one machine is represented by a fraction with one for a numerator and ten billions for a denominator.

The question and its solution can be put in another form which will show in another way how positive typewriting identification may be. As a problem let it be assumed that a clear specimen of typewriting shows, for example, twenty distinct characteristics as described above, and that it was written on a Remington machine. Assuming that it would be possible to make a great collection of all the machines ever constructed by this company the task then would be to find from the number the machine on which the specimen was written.

It would be necessary to take the first characteristic and put in one group all the machines writing that particular feature and exclude all the other machines. Then the second characteristic would be considered and from the first group it would be necessary to put together only those machines showing both the first and second features, then with the group remaining the same is done with the third and so on up to the twentieth. Finally every machine must be excluded that has defects or individualities not shown on the specimen, and it is easy to understand how each characteristic would decrease the number of machines in the group until finally the machine would be found upon which the specimen was written.

Illustrations.

Appropriate photographic enlargements and illustrations are essential if the facts are to be shown in a disputed typewriting case; and this is particularly true if such a case is to be tried before a jury. The few halftone illustrations printed herewith will show in a measure what is possible, but, as with other subjects in this book, it should be understood that in the restricted space and the method available only a suggestion can be made as to what is possible with large, clear photographs showing every detail.

It is not possible to print reference material relating to all machines in use, but what is shown will suggest in a general way what can be done and will furnish a basis for some investigations.

The degree of enlargement desirable depends upon conditions, but from two to four diameters is usually sufficient. Much typewriting is with blue and purple ribbons, and appropriate light filters or color screens are absolutely necessary if photographs are to be clear enough to be of any use. It is waste of time and money to attempt to get photographs of such documents from ordinary photographers who do not possess the necessary apparatus.

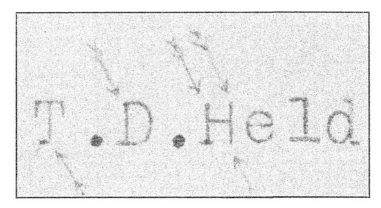

Fig. 187—Typewriting characteristics due to accidents.

Fig. 188—Defective letters on a new machine.

Fig. 189—Disputed and Standard letters "off their feet" printing heavily on right side.

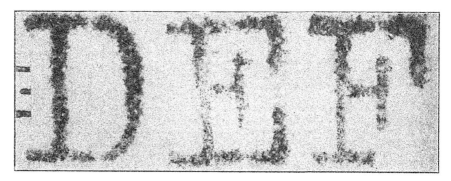

Fig. 190—From exhibit in case of Hunt vs. Peshtigo Lumber Co., Grand Rapids, Wis., showing capital E out of alignment.

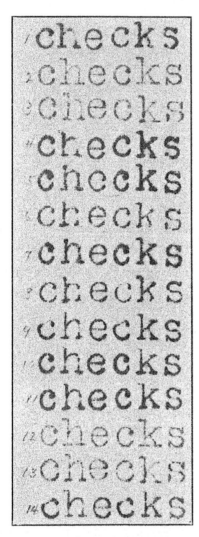

Fig. 191—This illustration represents two specimens from each of seven machines of the same kind and shows how it is possible from a few letters to identify typewriting. The pairs it will readily be seen are 1-4, 2-12, 3-13, 5-7, 6-8, 9-14, 10-11.

Characteristics.

In the first pair, one and four are examples of defective alignment, broken letters and letters printing "off their feet." Numbers two and twelve show the work of a machine nearly in perfect condition and more than these six letters would be required to identify work from it. Three and thirteen show two letters out of alignment. In five and seven the h is defective and the k prints high. Six and eight show a broken h, differing from one and four, and also a broken k that prints too high. Nine and fourteen show an unmistakable broken c and an e printing too low. Ten and eleven show both staffs of the h broken, k light at top and e mashed on right side.

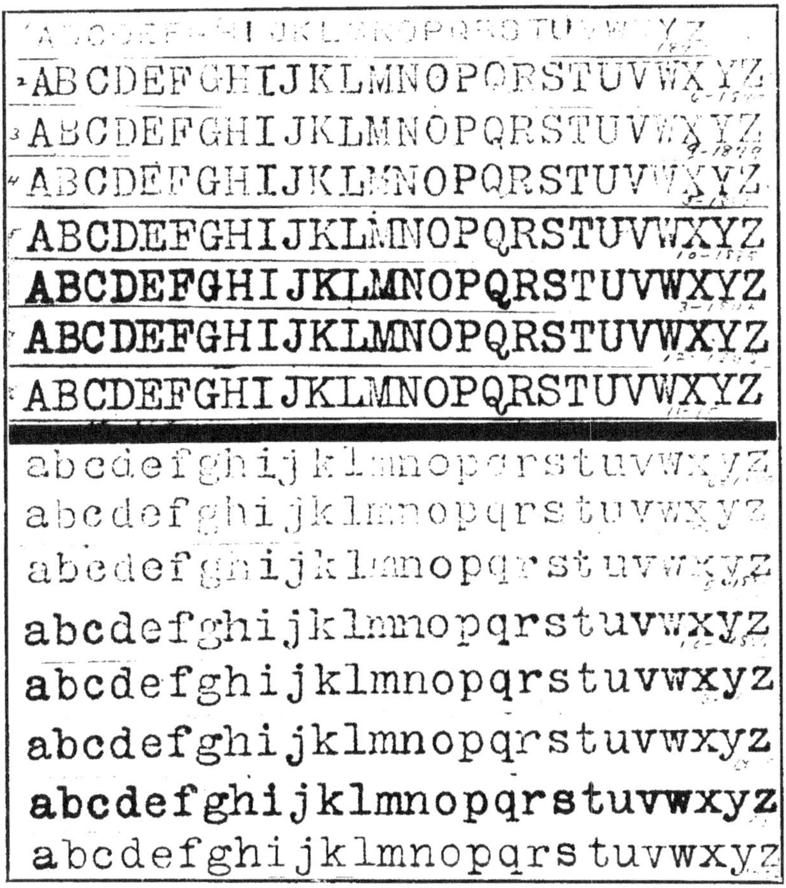

Fig. 192—Specimens of Remington Inspection Slips from 1879 to 1906.

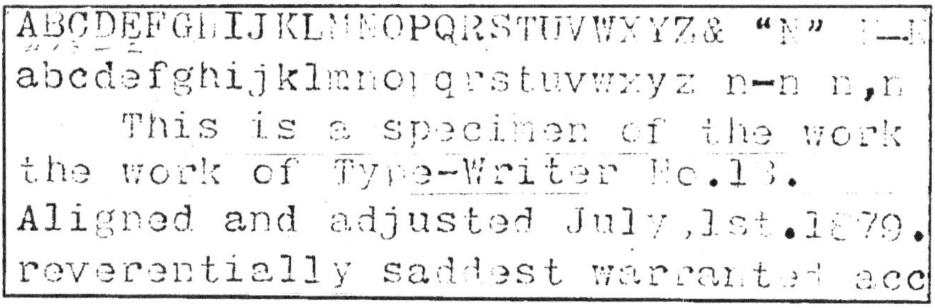

Fig. 193—Remington Inspection Slip from Machine No. 13, July 1st, 1879.

```
qwertyuiopasdfghjklzxcvbnm
QWERTYUIOPASDFGHJKLZXCVBNM
23456789-0;¾.,"#$%_&'(),:.?
Rem #10 #72730 2-9-10
```

```
qwertyuiopasdfghjklzxcvbnm
QWERTYUIOPASDFGHJKLZXCVBNM
23456789&/( )%#$:-?_;
Smi-Pre #10 #38793 2-16-10.
```

```
qwertyuiopasdfghjklzxcvbnm
QWERTYUIOPASDFGHJKLZXCVBNM
23456789-;/,"#$%_&'():.?
Under #4 #284996 2-9-10
```

```
qwertyuiopasdfghjklzxcvbnm
QWERTYUIOPASDFGHJKLZXCVBNM
234567890-¢;,"#$%_&'()*:?
L.C.S.#2 #71921. 2-21-10.
```

```
qwertyuiopasdfghjklzxcvbnm
QWERTYUIOPASDFGHJKLZXCVBNM
234567890-;/.,"#$%_&'():¾?
Mon #3 #49298 2-9-10
```

```
qwertyuiopasdfghjklzxcvbnm
QWERTYUIOPASDFGHJKLZXCVBNM
1234567890@$%*/¢#()?":;
Oliv #5 #295863 2-9-10
```

```
qwertyuiopasdfghjklzxcvbnm
QWERTYUIOPASDFGHJKLZXCVBNM
234567890-;,"#$%_&'()*:?
Roy #1 #36413. 2-9-10.
```

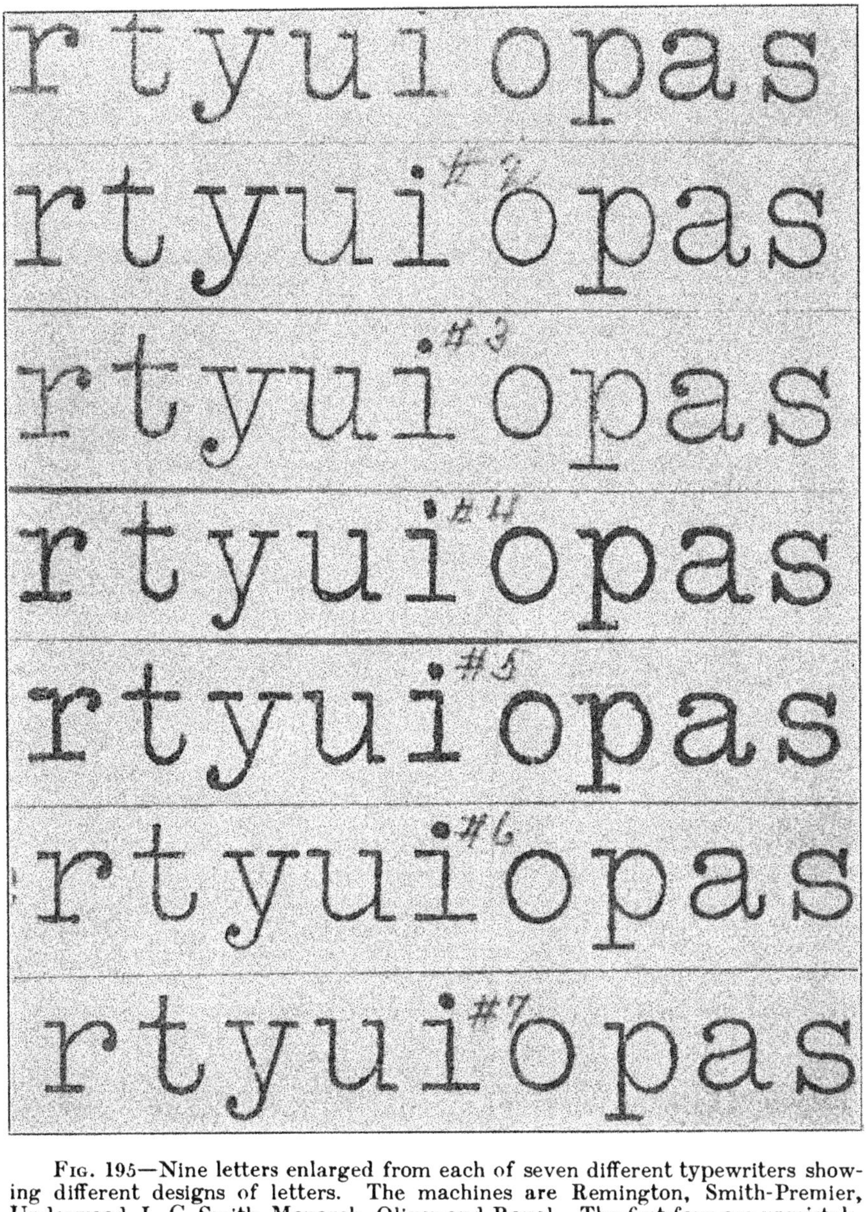

FIG. 195—Nine letters enlarged from each of seven different typewriters showing different designs of letters. The machines are Remington, Smith-Premier, Underwood, L. C. Smith, Monarch, Oliver and Royal. The first four are unmistakably different in many ways; in one and five the "r" and "a" are not the same and in six and seven the small "t," "u" and "a" are not the same. The small letters in No. 2 it will be observed are larger than the specimens from the other machines.

Easter Sunday, 1909.

Dear Mrs. Wilson:
    I am the person who had the unpleasant task of removing your
late husband from this world.
    In this connection my chief regret was in robbing your little
girl of her father, but as things go the innocent must frequently
suffer with the guilty.
    I am not in a position to adequately recompense her, but I have
promised to do what I can for her, and that I have done. You

While this money is only a small amount, it shows how I feel in
this unhappy matter and I much desire that it go to its proper destination
Perhaps someday I shall be able to do something handsome for Vera.
    Many people say "Everything happens for the best". When we think of a
our griefs - you of yours, xxxxxxxxxxxxxxxxxxxxxx I of mine, it is
hard to realize this, yet way down deep I have faith it is so, and that
        "TO KNOW ALL IS TO FORGIVE ALL"

FIG. 196—The beginning and ending of an interesting typewritten letter from the murderer to the wife of the victim in the noted "Wilson murder case," Philadelphia.

POSTAL TELEGRAPH (•) COMMERCIAL CABLES

TELEGRAM

CLARENCE H. MACKAY, PRESIDENT.

Postal Telegraph-Cable Company (Incorporated) transmits and delivers this message subject to the terms and conditions printed on the back of this blan

COUNTER NUMBER.	TIME FILED.	CHECK	

the following message, without repeating, subject to the terms and conditions printed on the back hereof, which are hereby agreed

190

    Loud voted for this $1,476,396.-60 graft, in the Naval Committee.
    There is a story in circulation that the Holland people got a
    prominent attorney to become a candidate against Loud last time
    that Loud finally agreed to vote for the submarines upon deal
    that the attorney withdraw- the attorney withdrew.
        Subscribe for N.Y. HERALD and Washington POST,
        Loud can be defeated on this proposition alone by you,
        Watch Congressional Record.
        Have your local papers play up proposition.
        Have them write Loud for explanation and whether the
    withdrawal story is true.

FIG. 197—One of the anonymous typewritten letters in the "Lilley Submarine Boat Investigation," Washington, D. C , 1908. Before the inquiry was concluded the actual writer confessed, confirming the previous testimony identifying the machine upon which the writing was done. The investigation was conducted by a committee of the House of Representatives of which Hon. H. S. Boutell, of Illinois, was chairman.

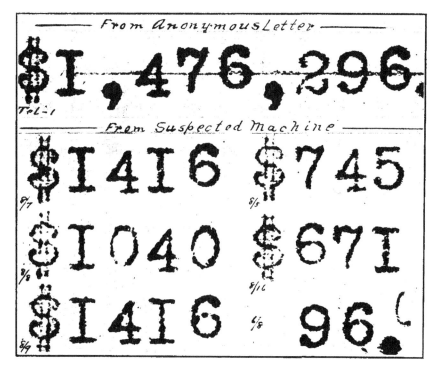

FIG. 198—Anonymous and Standard typewriting from an exhibit in the Lilley Investigation, Washington, D. C., 1908.

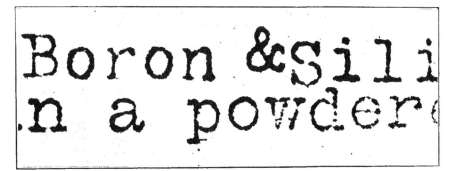

FIG. 199—From exhibit in case of United States vs. Everding, Washington, D. C. Henry E. Everding, of Philadelphia, a patent attorney, and Ned W. Barton, an examiner in the Patent Office, were convicted, Jan. 1909, of "altering certain records in the United States Patent Office." It will be seen from the small "r" that the interlined matter was by a different machine.

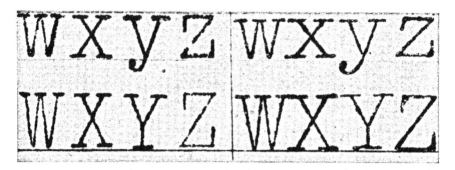

Fig. 200—Exhibit showing difference in size and designs of Smith-Premier (at left) and Remington typewriting. Smith-Premier small letters $78/1000$ high; Remington $68/1000$.

Fig. 201—From exhibits in case tried at Olean, N. Y., July, 1910. Standard typewriting on left, disputed on right.

FIG. 202.—Stereoscopic photo-micrograph of the faces of typewriter type, showing the effect of wear and accidents, by which the work from such a machine can be positively identified. One letter new and unused, one showing one "scar" and one much battered. Some detail is lost in the process of engraving. This illustration and the other stereoscopic views are printed on a detached sheet at the end of the book.

CHAPTER XXVI.

A QUESTIONED DOCUMENT CASE IN COURT

Before an expert or opinion witness is allowed to testify the law requires that he be "qualified" in a legal way to give such testimony. This qualifying process consists in showing that the witness has had such preparation and experience as legally qualifies him to give an opinion in court on the subject in dispute.

Instead of simply asking the witness to state his qualifications, as is sometimes done, it is much better to draw from him the necessary information by a few properly arranged questions. The jurors do not always understand that this qualifying of a witness is a legal requirement, and if a witness is required to say off-hand and at considerable length what his qualifications are and his experience has been, the act sometimes appears to them like an exhibition of self-conceit. This is a particularly unfortunate impression to give as an introduction to testimony.

At the same time it is important that the jury should be informed in considerable detail as to the qualifications and experience of a witness who is to give opinions, which information can be brought before them in an entirely unobjectionable way by a series of questions as suggested. This information as to qualifications should usually be brought out before the jury and entered on the record, even if opposing counsel is willing to admit that the witness is a qualified expert. This is important in case of appeal, when the printed record alone must be depended upon, and also that the jury may know at the time testimony is given what preparation and experience the witness has had that may give weight to his testimony, or, on the contrary, show how meagre his qualifications may be for giving an opinion on the subject in dispute.

After the witness is shown to be qualified he is asked if he has made a comparison of the disputed and standard writings in the case or examined the matter in dispute. Upon saying that he has, he is then asked if he has reached a conclusion as to the matter in dispute and if so what that conclusion is. Following this somewhat formal series of questions which bring out the essential facts, the witness should be requested to give, and should be afforded ample opportunity to explain, the reasons and basis for the opinion given[1].

This latter is the really important function of the

---

[1]It may be stated as a general rule that the value of opinions given by experts depends upon the experience and knowledge which they have and evince concerning the matters about which they testify and the reasons which they assign for it.—Cyclopedia of Law and Procedure, Vol. XVII, p. 268 (17 Cyc.).

Handwriting is an art concerning which correctness of opinion is susceptible of demonstration and I am fully convinced that the value of the opinion of every handwriting expert as evidence must depend upon the clearness with which the expert demonstrates its correctness. . . . The appearance or lack of one characteristic may be accounted to coincidence or accident but, as the number increases, the probability of coincidence or accident will disappear, until conviction will become irresistible.—Gordon's case, 50 N. J. Eq. 397, 26 Atl. 268 (1893).

The evidence of experts is neither intrinsically weak, nor intrinsically strong; its value depends upon the character, capacity, skill, opportunities of observation, the state of mind of the expert himself and on the nature of the case, and of its weight and worth the jury must judge without any influencing instruction, either weakening or strengthening from the court.—Coleman vs. Adair, 75 Miss. 660 (1898).

And in Collier vs. Simpson, Tindal, C. J., ruled that counsel might ask a witness, who was called to testify as an expert, ":bis judgment

expert witness, especially in a questioned document case where a tangible thing is actually before the jury. Just at this point there comes to the competent witness who seeks to show the fact, and to the attorney on the right side of the case who has technically qualified himself, the opportunity to assist the jury in reaching a correct conclusion as to the matter in dispute.

The primary purpose and function of questioned document expert testimony is not to foist a ready-made opinion on court and jury, but to assist the jury in reaching a correct interpretation of the facts before them. The importance of the bare opinion given by the witness should be constantly minimized and the reasons for the opinion should be elaborated and emphasized. Naturally those arrayed against the facts strenuously object to this part of effective testimony even to the extent of arguing that all reasons for opinions must be brought out on cross-examination. It is easy to understand how brief, under such circumstances, a cross-examination of an intelligent and effective witness would be. When such testimony is hampered and

and the grounds of it." The value of an opinion may be much increased or diminished, in the estimate of the jury, by the reasons given for it.—Keith vs. Lothrop, 10 Cush. (Mass.) 457 (1852).

Appellant then proposed, by further questions, to have each of these witnesses state the grounds upon which this opinion was based, and to point out and explain to the jury the differences which they detected and which induced this belief on their part. An objection on the part of counsel for appellee to this line of interrogation was sustained by the court.

The value of an opinion may be much increased or diminished in the estimate of the jury, by the reasons given for it (Keith vs. Lothrop, 10 Cush. (Mass.) 457).

The closing sentence of this quotation from the Massachusetts case seems to us to suggest a most potent reason in favor of the admissibility of such evidence. To withhold it from the jury would be to deprive them, to a large extent, of the very facts best calculated to enable them intelligently to weigh and determine the value of the opinion expressed.—Kendall's Ex. vs. Collier, 79 Ky. 446 (1895).

restricted it is always to the advantage of the party who is seeking to distort or hide the truth. Two mere opinions in conflict may neutralize each other, but this is not usually true of two reasons.

This reason-giving part of expert testimony should not be an unbroken monologue by the witness nor, what is worse, should it be a succession of assents by the witness to testimony which is really given by counsel in the form of a series of long, technical questions. Either of these methods is tiresome and ineffective. Counsel should have a series of questions prepared that will bring out in proper order the main points of the testimony and should also be prepared to ask for explanations or repetitions when they are necessary. Salient points can be greatly enforced by well-timed and correctly phrased inquiries. At this juncture a thorough and ready knowledge of subjects under discussion is of great value to a lawyer. If thus qualified he, as well as the witness, can put just the shade of emphasis on a statement that it requires and with the assistance of an intelligent witness can actually lead the minds of jurymen from ignorance to knowledge, from doubt to belief[1].

In a handwriting case of importance, where the jury must make a careful study and comparison of the writing

[1] It is then a duty resting upon the legal profession to remove the public suspicion directed against this species of evidence by removing its cause, and this can only be done by a higher standard of professional ability and ethics in this field. A knowledge of the detailed rules governing expert testimony, the nature of this species of evidence and its relation to the judicial investigation, the general principles of the sciences most frequently appealed to in judicial proceedings, such as medicine and handwriting, in their legal aspects, should be as requisite to a legal education as a knowledge of contracts or real estate. These subjects should be taught in the law schools and should be requirements for admission to the Bar.—The Law of Expert Testimony and the Proposed Changes Therein, Edward Lindsey, LL. B.; the "Legal Intelligencer," Dec. 5, 1902.

in question, duplicate photographs of the disputed writing and the same number of photographs of at least part of the standards should be provided. If there are many different photographs they may be mounted in photograph books made for such purpose, but it is generally better and more convenient to have them backed and hinged as is suggested in the chapter on photography, and then numbered or lettered in regular order.

In some cases it is desirable to bind all photographs together in detachable covers and have an extra photograph of the disputed writing separate from the others so that it may be more readily compared with any of the other photographs. Under some conditions it is desirable to mark plainly all photographs of standard writings in ink of one color and the photographs of the disputed writings in ink of a different color. All details should be arranged so that there will be no confusion, no opportunity for misunderstanding and no loss of time. Each juryman's set of exhibits, when there are several separate photographs not bound together, should be inclosed in a strong envelope or other suitable receptacle.

In some cases only one set of photographs are necessary but where the question is one mainly of handwriting an ample number should be provided. Sixteen complete sets of photographs allow one set for each juryman, one set for the court, one set for the witness and one set each for the opposing attorneys. In case one set for every two jurymen is provided only ten sets in all are required.

It is not usually necessary to mark all the sets of

photographs in evidence. It is customary to mark one complete set as regular exhibits and the others are proved and used as duplicates. In some instances photographs are simply used as illustrations, exactly as a chart or blackboard would be used, and under such conditions are only marked for identification[1].

Photographs may be admitted without objection but it is usually necessary to prove them. This is done by the one testifying who made them that he made them and that they are "correct." The witness tells what the photograph is made from, whether it is smaller, the same size or larger than the original and how much if at all it differs in size. Three or four questions are usually sufficient to prove ordinary photographs.

If photographs are unusual in any way then the process of making them should be described in detail. A photograph is considered to have been made by one technically qualified to do such work who can testify that it was properly arranged in position before the camera, accurately focused, and then given the proper time of exposure. It is not essential that the plate be developed by the one who proves the photograph or that the prints should be actually printed from the negative by him, if he has inspected the negative to see that it is an accurate reproduction of the original, and inspected the prints to see that they are accurate impressions of the negative. Photographs are sometimes admitted on

---

[1]The next objection was that an expert witness was allowed to explain upon a blackboard his meaning and the reason for his opinion. We think there was no error in this. Of course the whole class of expert evidence is exceptional. And as experts are to give opinions, it is right that they should explain the reasons for them.—McKay vs. Lasher, 19 N. Y. S. Rep. 816 (1888). Followed in Dryer vs. Brown, 52 Hun, 327 (1889).

the evidence of those who did not make them if it is shown that they are accurate reproductions of the original.

When photographic illustrations are provided and are in the hands of the jury it may not be necessary to use a blackboard or chart, although in important and difficult cases it often saves considerable time and strengthens testimony somewhat to make a few general illustrations as testimony is being given that all may see and understand at once.

. It is usually preferable to use paper rather than a blackboard so that the sheets may be numbered and preserved for cross-examination or future reference. Cheap white paper, like that upon which newspapers are printed and about 24 by 36 inches in size, is best for the purpose. A soft marking crayon of large size should be used and illustrations should be made large and distinct. Colored crayons are sometimes useful for special illustrations.

Where numerous exhibits are referred to, constant care should be exercised by counsel and witness that numbers of exhibits always be given or that papers be described so that the record of the case may be intelligible. This is particularly important in the event of an appeal of the case where the record of the testimony must be depended upon entirely. Cases have been lost on appeal because important testimony, as reported, was mere gibberish and absolutely unintelligible. This was not the fault of the reporter but of the witness and of counsel. A statement that "this is identical with that" means nothing whatever on the record, and when counsel says, "Look at the exhibit in your hand and tell me, etc.," a report of such testimony may be entirely meaningless. Exhibit marks should be written plainly and carefully and should always be given either in question or answer or both so that the testimony as reported may be clearly understood by one reading it.

Where lay witnesses are to testify as to handwriting in connection with experts who will go into details, it is best usually that the lay witness should testify first. When writing is carefully analyzed and reasons and explanations are given with considerable minuteness and such testimony is given in advance of the testimony of lay witnesses who cannot make this analysis, the lay witnesses are sometimes embarrassed and their testimony weakened because they are unable to enter into the matter as has already been done. Opinion testimony of lay witnesses is usually most effective and much less vulnerable when of a general character and when based on general resemblances or differences. Such testimony frequently has little technical value but may have much force before a jury especially when the witness is well known[1].

Practical questioned document investigation has two phases, the discovery of the fact and the proving of it. It avails but little to discover that a document is a forgery, or to reach a conclusion that a suspected document is genuine, if finally the fact cannot be presented to those who are legally to decide the matter so that they too will reach a correct conclusion. But little is accom-

---

[1]The impressions of the immediate friends of Morris are strongly against the genuineness of the disputed signatures. Usually such impressions are more reliable than the reasons given for them, and in ordinary cases they are valuable.—Matteson vs. Morris, 40 Mich. 57 (1879).

plished if only the investigator sees and understands what he finds out; a bare opinion is not worth much in any court. Nor is an opinion worth much backed up by fantastic, hazy, expert theories that do not appeal to sensible men. The best reasons for an opinion are good, clear illustrations that appeal to the intelligence through the sense of sight.

Appropriate illustrations enable court and jury to see for themselves and understand that upon which a judgment must be based. Naturally those arrayed against the facts, who object to illustrations as well as to reasons, would, if possible, dull the hearing, dim the vision and muddle the understanding of all those who are finally to pass judgment on the question at issue. This unfortunate result may be brought about in effect by throwing around questioned document testimony such restrictions that those who are to decide cannot distinguish the good from the bad.

Much of the discussion of conflicts of opinion testimony begins with the assumption that those who listen to it are totally unable to distinguish between a reasonable opinion and an unreasonable opinion; it is assumed that one may exactly offset the other. Would it not be better to set out with the assumption that if an opinion cannot be supported by reasons intelligible to the ordinary man then it will be given no weight whatever?

As is well known the theory of expert testimony in general is that in a trial at law questions regarding subjects that the ordinary man knows nothing about must be referred to specialists who come into court and give opinions which it is assumed are based on knowledge unknown to the ordinary man and reached by a process

that he may not be able to follow. It is easy to understand what little force testimony strictly in this class
may have if a contrary opinion is given by another
witness of equal standing. Opinion testimony regarding
disputed documents when given without reasons is exactly of this class and, like similar testimony on other
questions, may be and oftentimes is absolutely worthless.
It is, however, not necessarily worthless for the reason
that it belongs to an exceptional class of testimony
dealing with questions that in many cases permit of a
reasonable and tangible interpretation, not only within
the comprehension of a man of average intelligence, but,
by means of illustrations, actually before him in visible
form.

From these facts it follows, therefore, that in testimony regarding the genuineness or falsity of a document the clear illustration and logical interpretation of
the physical evidence from which the opinion is drawn
is the vital part of the process. This is the view of the
subject now taken by most courts, and this view brushes
aside a great mass of discussion in the decisions and the
text-books that has served only to befog the whole
question.

Reduced to its briefest statement the enlightened view
is, If testimony regarding disputed documents or any
expert testimony is reasonable and convincing then it
will be so considered. The giving of reasons is necessary, as Professor Wigmore succinctly and sanely puts
it, because, "Without such re-enforcement of testimony
the opinion of experts would usually involve little more
than a counting of the numbers on either side."

HANDWRITING is an art concerning which correctness of opinion is susceptible of demonstration and I am fully convinced that the value of the opinion of every handwriting expert as evidence must depend upon the clearness with which the expert demonstrates its correctness. . . Thus comparison is rated after the fashion of circumstantial evidence, depending for strength upon the number and prominence of the links in the chain. Without such demonstration the opinion of an expert in handwriting is of a low order of testimony, for, as the correctness of his opinion is susceptible of ocular demonstration, and it is a matter of common observation that an expert's conclusion is apt to be influenced by his employer's interest, the absence of demonstration must be attributed either to deficiency in the expert or lack of merit in his conclusion. It follows that the expert who can most clearly point out will be most highly regarded and most successful.— *Gordon's Case, 50 N. J. Eq. 397, 26 Atl. 268. 1893.*

APPENDIX

FINGER PRINTS.

There is a constantly increasing use of finger prints as a means of human identification, and space is taken to describe a new photographic method of comparison which removes the objection of the personal equation of the witness, which must be present in the method necessitating the drawing by hand of the outlines of an indistinct print.

As will be seen by the illustrations, in the proposed new method the imprints to be compared are photographed with a superimposed glass plate ruled with uniform squares. By making a suitable enlargement and then numbering and lettering the squares, as is shown in the illustrations, it becomes possible to compare the characteristics as they appear in any similar squares, and it is also possible to describe definitely the square to which reference is made. Thus attention can be directed to square "6-D," or any other square on the photographs of different prints, to discover whether or not the impressions were by the same hand.

One of the illustrations shows black on white, the other white on black. It will be observed that the impressions in general outline are not quite identical in size, but after a little study it cannot be doubted that the two impressions must have been made by the same hand. Not only this, but it is clear that no two human hands in all the world can be just alike in all these complex particulars.

Fig. 203—Two thumb prints from the same thumb photographed under glass carrying uniform squares to facilitate comparison.

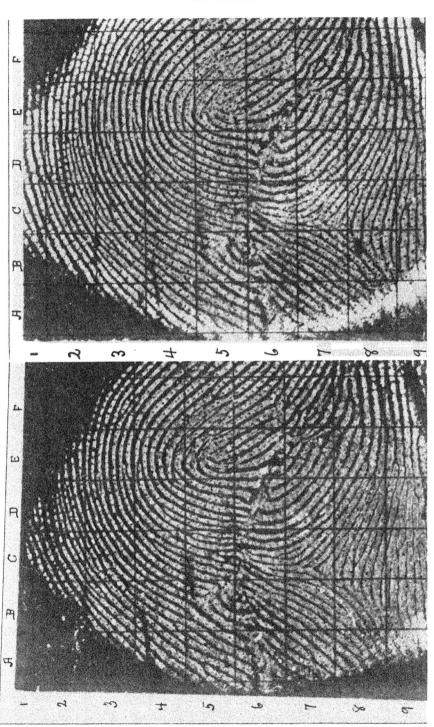

Fig. 204.—Thumb marks photographed under ruled squares.

BIBLIOGRAPHY

ARRANGED ALPHABETICALLY BY AUTHORS

Ames on Forgery. By Daniel T. Ames. Ames-Rollinson Company, New York: 1900.

The Origin and Progress of Writing. By Thomas Astle, Esq., F. R. S., F. S. A., and Keeper of the Records in the Tower of London. London: 1784.

The Autographic Mirror. Vol. I., Vol. II. Autographic Letters and Sketches of Illustrious and Distinguished Men of Past and Present Times. Cassell, Petter & Galpin, London and New York: 1864.

L'Autographe. (December, 1863-October, 1865.) Les editeurs: H. DeVillemessant. G. Bourdin, Paris: 1864, 1865.

Manipulation of the Microscope. By Edward Bausch. Bausch & Lomb Optical Company, Rochester, N. Y.: 1897.

The Universal Penman. Engraved by George Bickham, London: 1743.

Les Révélations de l'Écriture D'Après un contrôle scientifique. Par Alfred Binet. Félix Alcan, Paris: 1906.

The Detection of Forgery. By Douglas Blackburn and Captain Warthman Caddell. Charles and Edwin Layton, London: 1909.

Bibliographie der Graphologie, Von Hans H. Busse, München, 1900.

Butterworth's Universal Penman. By E. Butterworth. London: 1799.

The Microscope and its Revelations. By W. B. Carpenter. Eighth Edition, 1901.

Lectures on the Art of Writing. By Joseph Carstairs. London: 1814.

Forty Centuries of Ink. By David N. Carvalho. The Banks Publishing Co., New York: 1904.

Alphabets of Characters. By Joseph Champion. London: 1735.

The Handwriting of Junius, Professionally Investigated. By Mr. Charles Chabot, Expert. With Preface and Collateral Evidence by the Hon. Edward Twistleton. London: 1871.

A Booke Containing Divers Sortes of Hands, etc. Set forth by Iohn de Beau Chesne and M. Iohn Baildon. Imprinted at London by Thomas Vautrouillier dwelling in the blackefrieres, M. D. LXXXI. (This curious book is in the Library of Congress, Washington.)

The Story of the Alphabet. By Edward Clodd. D. Appleton & Co., New York: 1900.

Fair Writing. By Edward Cocker. London: 1657.

A Text-Book of Paper-Making. By C. F. Cross and E. J. Bevan. Third Edition, E. & F. N. Spon, Ltd., London, Spon & Chamberlain, New York: 1907.

Modern Microscopy. By M. I. Cross. Third Edition, 1903.

The History of Ink. By Thaddeus Davids & Co. New York: 1860.

The Writing Schoolmaster. By John Davies of Hereford. Sold by Michaell Sparke at ye blue Bibell in greene Arbor, London: 1631. (A copy of this book is in the Library of Congress, Washington.)

Dean's Analytical Guide to the Art of Penmanship. By Henry Dean. New York: 1805.

The Instructor, or American Young Man's Best Companion. By George Fisher. Philadelphia: 1737.

American Text-Book for Letters. By Nath'l Dearborn. Boston: 1846.

Der Nachweis von Schriftfälschungen, Blut, Sperma usw. unter besonderer berücksichtigung der photographie, von Prof. Dr. M. Dennstedt und Dr. F. Voigtländer. Friedrich Viewig & Son, Braunschweig: 1906.

Photography for Students of Physics and Chemistry. By Louis Derr, M. A. S. B. The Macmillan Company, New York: 1906.

Practical Penmanship. By B. F. Foster. Published by O. Steele, Albany: 1832.

Foster's System of Penmanship. By B. F. Foster. Published by Perkins, Marvin & Co., Boston; Henry Perkins, Philadelphia: 1835.

"Junius" Revealed. By his surviving grandson, H. R. Francis. Longmans, Green & Co., London: 1894.

Bibliotics or the Study of Documents. By Persifor Frazer. J. P. Lippincott Company, Philadelphia: 1901.

Les Ecrits et les dessins dans les Maladies Nerveuses et Mentales. Dr. J. Rogues de Fursac. Masson et Cie, Editeurs, Paris: 1905.

Finger Prints. By Francis Galton, F. R. S., etc. Macmillan & Co., London and New York: 1892.

Decipherment of Blurred Finger Prints. By Francis Galton, F. R. S., etc. Macmillan & Co., London and New York: 1893.

Finger Print Directories. By Francis Galton. London: 1895.

Calligraphotechnia or The Art of faire writing, etc. By Richard Gethinge. Sold by —— Humble at the white-horse in Popes head alley over against the roiall Exchange in London: Anno Domini 1616.

Registry of Water Marks and Trade Marks. Andrew Geyer, Publisher, New York: 1906.

The Writing Reader. By T. Gilbert & F. Prass. Published for the Authors by D. & J. McLellan, New York: 1858.

Chemistry of Paper-Making. By Griffin & Little. H. Lockwood, New York.

Handbuch für Untersuchungsrichter als System der Kriminalistik von Dr. Hans Gross. 4, Auflage J. Schweitzer Verlag (Arthur Sellier). München: 1904. English translation by J. & C. Adam, Lawyers Co-operative Publishing Co., Rochester and New York.

Disputed Handwriting. By William E. Hagan. Banks & Brothers, New York, Albany, N. Y.: 1894.

Classification and Uses of Finger Prints. Third Edition. By E. R. Henry, C. V. O., C. S. I. Darling & Son, Ltd., London: 1905.

L'Art De Juger Du Caractére Des Hommes Sur Leur Ecriture. Paris: 1816. [Anonymous but written by L. J. F. Hocquart.]

Three-Colour Photography. By Arthur Freiherrn von Hübl. A. W. Penrose & Co., London: 1904.

The Origin and Progress of the Art of Writing. By Henry Noel Humphreys. David Bogue, London: MDCCCLIV.

Miscellaneous Papers and Legal Instruments under the hand and seal of William Shakspeare, including the Tragedy of King Lear and a small fragment of Hamlet, from the Original MSS. in the possession of Samuel Ireland. London: 1796.

The Confessions of William-Henry Ireland. Ellerton & Byworth, London: 1805.

The Theory and Practice of Handwriting. By John Jackson, F. E. I. S. Sampson Low, Marston & Company, Ltd., London: 1893.

The Art of Writing. By John Jenkins. Cambridge, Mass.: 1813.

Die Mikrophotographie, von Dr. Paul Jeserich. Verlag von Julius Springer, Berlin: 1888.

The Mystery of Handwriting. By J. Harington Keene. Lee & Shepard, Publishers, Boston: 1896.

Pens, Ink and Paper. A Discourse upon the Caligraphic Art with Curiosa and an Appendix of Some Famous English Penmen. By Daniel W. Kettle, F. G. R. S., Cosmographer. London: 1885.

Natural-Color Photography. By Dr. E. König. Translated from the German, with additions, etc., by E. J. Wall, F. R. P. S. Dawbarn & Ward, Ltd., London: 1906.

Die Schrift bei Geisteskrankheiten ein atlas mit 81 Handschriftproben, von Dr. Rudolf Köster. Verlag von Johann Ambrosius Barth, Leipzig: 1903.

The Manufacture of Ink. Translated from the German of Sigmund Lehner, with additions by William T. Brannt. Henry Carey Baird & Co., Philadelphia: 1892.

The Flying Pen, or New and Universal Method of Teaching the Art of Writing, etc. By James Henry Lewis. London: 1806.

The Royal Lewisian System of Penmanship, etc. By James Henry Lewis. London: 1816.

Measurement of Light and Colour Sensations. By Joseph W. Lovibond, F. R. M. S. George Gill & Sons, London.

Contributions to Photographic Optics. By Otto Lummer, translated by S. P. Thompson. New York: 1900.

De Re Diplomatica. By Mabillon. Paris: 1681.

The Origin and Progress of Letters and A Compendium Account of the most celebrated English Penmen with the Title and Character of the Books they published. By W. Massey. London: 1763.

An Inquiry into the Authenticity of Certain Miscellaneous Papers and Legal Instruments [Shakespeare Forgeries]. By Edmond Malone. London: 1796.

Archiv für Gerichtliche Schriftuntersuchungen und verwandte Gebiete. Heft 1, 2, 3, 4. Herausgegeben von Dr. Georg Meyer und Dr. Hans Schneickert. Verlag von Johann Ambrosius Barth, Leipzig: 1907, 1908.

Sur la Methode vicieuse des expertises en écriture. By L'abbe Michon. Paris: 1880.

Inks, Their Composition and Manufacture. By C. Ainsworth Mitchell and T. C. Hepworth. Charles Griffin & Company, Ltd., London: 1904.

The Autograph Miscellany. Netherclift & Durlacher. London: 1855.

Lehrbuch der Mikrophotographie, von Dr. Richard Neuhauss. Verlag von S. Hirzel, Leipzig: 1907.

Handbuch der kriminalistischen Photographie, von Friedrich Paul. J. Guttentag, Verlagsbuchhandlung, Berlin: 1900.

Payson & Dunton's Copy-Books. By J. W. Payson and Seldom Dunton. Boston: 1851.

Theory and Art of Penmanship. Payson, Dunton & Scribner's Method of Teaching. Crosby & Ainsworth, Boston: 1862.

Graphics, a Popular System of Drawing and Writing. By Rembrandt Peale. Philadelphia: 1842.

The Juvenile Penman or Practical Writing Book Engraved on Brass. By A. Picket. New York: 1817-18.

Potter's System of Penmanship. By S. A. Potter. 1864.

Rand's System of Writing. By B. H. Rand. Philadelphia: 1834.

La Photographie Judiciaire. R. A. Reiss. Charles Mendel, Editeur, Paris: 1903.

What Handwriting Indicates. By John Rexford. G. P. Putnam's Sons, New York: 1904.

The Philosophy of Handwriting. By Don Felix de Salamanca. London: 1879.

Die Eisengallustinten. Grundlagen zu ihrer Beurtheilung. Osw. Schluttig und Dr. G. S. Neumann. Zahn & Jaensch, Dresden: 1890.

Handwriting and Expression, translated and edited by John Holt Schooling, from the third French edition of l'Écriture et le Caractère par J. Crépieux-Jamin. Kegan Paul, Trench, Trubner & Co., Ltd., London: 1892.

A Guide to the Collector of Historical Documents, Literary Manuscripts and Autograph Letters, etc. By Rev. Dr. Scott and Samuel Davey, F. R. S. L. London, S. J. Davey, The Archivist Office, 47 Great Russell Street, Opposite the British Museum: 1891.

Autograph Collecting. By Henry T. Scott, M. D. L. Upcott Gill, London: 1894.

Universal Palaeography. By J. B. Silvestre. Paris: 1839-41. London: 1850.

Spencerian Copy-Slips. By Platt R. Spencer and Victor M. Rice. Buffalo: 1848.

Spencerian Key to Practical Penmanship. By H. C. Spencer. Ivison, Blakeman, Taylor & Co., New York and Chicago: 1866.

The Manufacture of Paper. By R. W. Sindall, F. C. S. D. Van-Nostrand Co., New York: 1908.

'According to Cocker," The Progress of Penmanship from the Earliest Times. By W. Anderson Smith. Alexander Gardner, London: 1887.

B. F. Stevens' Fac-similes of Manuscripts in European Archives Relating to America, 1773-1783. 25 Vols. London: 1889.

The Alphabet. 2 Vols. By Isaac Taylor. London: 1883.

Manual del Perito Caligrafo. By Enrique Sanchez Terrones. Imprenta De Fortanet, Madrid: 1902.

Handbook of Greek and Latin Palaeography. By Sir Edward Maunde Thompson. 1893.

Kompendium der Gerichtlichen Photographie. By Wilhelm Urban. Leipsig: 1909.

A B C of Photo-Micrography. By W. H. Wamsley. Philadelphia: 1902.

Manuscripts, Inscriptions and Muniments. By Henry Smith Williams. Merrill & Baker, New York: 1907.

Universal Classic Manuscripts. Vols. I, II. Fac-similes from Originals in the Department of Manuscripts; British Museum. With Descriptions, Editorial Notes, References and Translations by George F. Warner, M. A., Ass't Keeper of Manuscripts British Museum. M. Walter Dunne, Publisher, Washington and London.

INDEX

Abrasion erasures, see Erasures.

Additions, fraudulent, 75; and interlineations, 4 2 2; often made to wills, 422; test of ink on, 424; see Erasures.

Admission of Standards, 16; Law in various states, 17; see Standards.

Age, tremor of, 117-119; shown by design of letters, 169.

Age of Documents, 6, 9, 10, 431; study of subject of age, 432; shown by typewriting, 433, 440, 447; by handwriting, 433; by ink, 8, 434; by contents, 432; by paper, 434; simulated age by artificial means, 435.

Age of Writer, may affect standards, 21, 23, 105; shown by system, 185, 216; may show age of document, 433.

Age of Writing, shown by ink, 74; by copying pencil, 167; by figures, 187; by system, 167-195; artificial aging, 435.

Alignment of Writing, in Angular system, 107; irregular in tremor of age, 119; of illiterate writing, 121; definition, 123-125.

Alterations, documents containing, 6, 8, 75; see Erasures.

American Handwriting, many changes in, 168; main divisions of, 170; changes in, 173, 174, 175; lack of knowledge of, 208.

Angular Writing, movement in, 107; may show through disguise, 144, 192; a distinct woman's hand, 173; illustration of, 184; shows sex in anonymous letters, 315, 316.

Angularity, an important characteristic, 173, 188; illustration of different systems, 225.

Anonymous Letters, see Letters.

Anxiety, of forger affects result, 120, 252; in pencil forgery, 165; limits skill, 205, 236, 239, 243, 252; in traced forgery, 269, 279.

Arnold's Ink, 338.

Arrangement of Writing, conditions governing, 141; unconsciousness of, 141; anonymous letters, 312; in forgery over genuine signature, 428.

Astle, Thomas, 193.

Attention to details, evidence of forgery, 251.

Autograph album signature, forged note over, 427.

Autographs of noted persons often forged, 9, 192, 194, 373, 434.

Badlam, C. G., 189.

Bank Clerk, time only for "general appearance," 245.

Banks, only one standard signature kept, 19; depositors' signatures often poor standards, 25; loss on "raised" paper, 412; quick tests the banker may use, 413; should investigate new customers, 414; certain practices condemned, 414; blank forms that make forgery difficult, 416; see Erasures.

Bausch, Edward, 71.

Bausch & Lomb Magnification Table, 85.

Bertillon Measurements, small number of, 233.

Binet, Alfred, 318.

Black-board, use of in court, 472; N. Y. law on, 471.

Black-hand letters, 11, 325.

Bleaching Agent, 435.

Blotter impression and original, 313, 329.

Boyer case, Buffalo, N. Y., 292, 297; illustration of, 103.

Burbank case, illustrated, 114, 115, 265; Mr. Justice Ward's charge in, 258.

Bureau of Standards, certify lenses, 51; certify measures, 95.

Burr, Professor George L., on palaeography, 195.

Burtis case, quotation from opinion, 120; illustrated, 263; opinion in, 275.

Byrnes, Thomas, 415.

Bankers, practice regarding standards, 19, 28; signature cards not good standards, 25; interest in raised papers, 412; quick tests to discover fraud, 413; certain practices condemned, 414.

Caliper, micrometer, 97, 364.

Camera for document photography, 40, 54-64.

Camera Lucida, 83; drawing with, 115.

Capitals, use of in holograph forgery, 254.

Care of Questioned Documents, 1.

Carelessness, shows genuineness, 120; shown by pen pressure, 134; in holograph documents, 251; in ending strokes, 115, 118.

Certainty of proof of forgery differs, 14.

Characteristics, see Writing.

Check Protectors, 46, 411.

Chemical Abstracts, Vol. 2, No. 4, 411.

Chemical applications to produce appearance of age, 435.

Chemical Erasures, in standards, 27; reproduced, 43; in documents, 408.

Chemical Tests, when to be made, 1, 341, 385.

Classes of Questioned Documents, 6-15.

Coincidence, of two writings, 12; accidental, when possible, 211; improbability of two persons, 183, 227; exact, very improbable, 277.

Coleridge, Mr. Justice, 31, 33, 213.

Color Filters, 67, 68, 345.

Color Microscope, use of, 74, 102; description of, 355; illustration of, 357; examination of interlineation, 424.

Color, study of, 356; delicate tints recorded, 358; comparison of, 359; three color illustration, 361; age of ink shown by, 362.

Comparison, careful, to be made, 244; Professor James on, 257.

Comparison, a process of reasoning, 212, 257, 260.

Comparison of Hands, 16; not at first allowed, 30-34; not like other expert testimony, 260.

Composition, in holograph forgery, 254.

Conflicts of Expert Testimony, 474.

Connections between letters, 226.

Continuity, to be investigated, 8; shown by photographs,

43, 65; lack of, shown by pen, 158; lack of, in pencil writing, 163; shown by line or stroke, 242; of holograph document, 251; of questioned addition, 424; tests of continuity, 425.

Copy Book Forms, alone do not identify, 214; not exactly followed, 231.

Crawford-Schooley case, 290.

Crossed Lines, press copy not to be made, 4, 387; to be observed, 9; in altered documents, 9; photographs of, 48; illustration of, 75; sequence of writing shown by, 375; sometimes impossible to answer, 375; order of writing may be vital, 376; crossed line characteristics, 377; a microscopic question, 378; as affected by use of blotter, 380; lapse of time affects question, 378, 382; sequence shown by ink borders, 382; with nigrosine ink, 75, 383; conditions affecting result, 385; possibility of error, 386; made with pencil, 389; pencil strokes over ink, 389; ink lines over rubber stamp, 390; to show comparative age, 391; in Russell case, Boston, 393; in forgery over genuine signature, 423, 428.

Date of Standard writing, 18.

Date of Writing may be important, 216.

Dates of Documents from handwriting, 22.

Day vs. Cole, case of, 297.

Dearborn, Nathl., 189.

Demonstrative Evidence, by photographs, 36; by microscope, 70; by instruments, 89; of documents, 212, 257, 260, 399, 474.

Design of Letters, see Form.

Details, attention to in forgery, 251, 253.

Defacing of Paper to hide forgery, 8, 435.

Dennstedt, Dr. M., 348, 417.

Disguised Writing, definition, 11, 12, 233; proof of, 13, 14; in request writing, 23; usually only superficial, 144; by changing slant, 201; difficulty of, 226, 305; a double process, 233; thought to be easy task, 306; gives thought to conspicuous features, 308.

Disguised Letters, 11; see Letters.

Dividers, to be used with care, 2.

Documents, care of, 1; unnecessary folding of, 1, 2; glass covers for, 2; dangerous tests not to be permitted, 4; to be put in custody of court, 4; classes of questioned, 6; defaced to hide character, 8; alleged ancient, 10.

Document Camera, illustrated, 40, 54, 61; description, 53.

Document Photographs, 55-69.

Drawing movement, in forgery, 73, 118, 238, 253.

Education, degree of, in anonymous letters, 305, 314.

End strokes, importance of, 115, 118.

England, changed handwriting procedure, 16.

English Handwriting, development of, 192, 193.

Enlargements, necessity for, 38, 39, 48, 57, 62, 124, 390, 399.

Entire Document, see Holograph.

Envelopes, to show date, 10, 366, 432.

Erasures, on standards, 27; shown by photography, 44; by abrasion, 44, 88, 405; and changes in documents, 404; methods of examination, 406; "raised" papers, 407; by "ink eradicators," 408; devices to prevent raising, 409; quick tests to discover "raising," 413; to restore writing, 409.

Errors due to insufficient standards, 19, 28; due to haste, 125; due to conditions, 199; mistaking general for individual characteristics, 206; from "general appearance," 212; possible under some conditions, 241; in identifying anonymous letters, 304, 322; see Pretenders.

Essenhower, see Messchert.

Evidence, force of, in forgery cases, 14.

Examinations, should be prompt, 15; at two sittings, 7, 243; purposeless of no value, 15, 125, 213; to be made with care, 243, 246, 253.

Expert Testimony regarding documents, enforced by instruments, 89; of varified quality, IX; regarding document permits of illustration, 89, 190; regarding documents not like other expert testimony, 260.

Eye, limit of vision of, 71.

Eyesight, poor, may cause distortions, 119; too poor to do retouching, 120, 202.

Famous People, writing often forged, 192, 373, 434.

Feigned Writing, 12.

Feminine characteristics, see Sex.

Figures, questioned, 255-257; show age of writer, 187.

Filar Micrometer, 81, 100; measurements with, 82; to measure pen strokes, 159; use in crossed line inquiries, 378; to test questioned additions, 424.

Finger Prints, 479.

Folds in Paper, writing over, 9, 48, 394; relation to writing shown by microscope, 73; illustration of, 74; examination of, 88; ink affects result, 397; pencil line over, 398; stereoscopic illustrations of, 399, 400, 401; in forgery over genuine signature, 423, 428; across questioned postscripts, 434.

Foreign Writing, persistence in later style, 169, 170; traces of easily recognized, 175, 182; errors in identifying, 207; see German.

Forger, task of, 234; gives painful attention to details, 200; not satisfied with careless, distorted writing, 202; conditions surrounding, 236; self-conscious, 239; strain, fear and anxiety of, 243, 252.

Forgery, proof of, 1, 3, 7, 210, 259; definition of, 13, 233; certainty of proof, 14; various degrees of perfection, 14; proved without comparison, 18; proof of usually by comparison, 18; characteristic movements of, 111, 112, 113, 115; mainly of forms, 115, 238; tremor of, 117, 118; anxiety produces poor result, 120; line quality shows, 133; often inclines upward, 140; with pencil uncommon, 164; of unfamiliar system very difficult, 183, 185; may on first view appear genuine, 199, 214; reason for difficulty, 226; conditions surrounding, 236; actual forgery poor work, 237; may be intrinsically bad, 245; more formal than genuine, 279; great sum lost in forgery, 414; "clearing house" for forgeries, 414; business forms to prevent forgery, 416; writing over genuine signature, 426; of writing of celebrated people, 192, 373, 434.

Form, this only thought of in forgery, 106, 115, 137, 252; original background of a handwriting, 168; only one of writing characteristics, 173; copy book does not identify, 214; great variety of, 217, 218; simplest part of forgery, 238; may have great significance, 241; may show nationality, 242; in traced forgery may be closely followed, 267; only considered in traced forgery, 270.

Freedom in Writing, shows genuineness, 106, 120, 133, 140.

General Appearance, 32; defined, 212; may mislead, 213, 244; affected by connections, 226; the first test, 244; bank clerk must depend upon, 245; too much time given to, 253; alone may show traced forgery to be genuine, 267.

Genuineness, how shown, 7; proof of, 19; evidences of, 119, 133, 140, 202, 203; shown by number and character of characteristics, 208, 259; hasty opinion not to be given, 245; shown by freedom, 251, 280, 255.

Genuine Writing, not admitted for comparison, 16.

German, writing characteristics of, 206, 312; accent not easily changed, 196; quotation marks in, 312.

Grammar, in holograph forgery, 254; in anonymous letters, 305.

Graphology, and arrangement, 145; errors of, 208; general appearance of, 212; Keene quoted, 213; and anonymous letters, 318; weakness of, 318, 319.

Gross, Dr. Hans (Berlin), 268.

Grounds of Belief, see Reasons.

Habits, writing, how acquired, 141; unconsciousness of, 143, 190; opposite do not exist, 201; not easily changed, 202; always to be compared, 241; variation in holograph documents, 251.

Handwriting as means of identification, 10; two questions regarding, 11; not disguised, 12; natural and unfeigned, 12; complex character of, 141; proof of may be a farce, 16, 18; of different dates may vary, 20; affected by conditions, 21; individualized from beginning, 21; scientific examination of, 105; movements in, 106; forms of not the only characteristics, 106; nervous organization basis of, 106; speed an important characteristic, 111; original styles, 183; "on the wall," 195; identity, how shown, 210, 259; how varied, 230; a complicated act, 239; a coordinated movement, 240; most difficult to imitate, 240; identity same as personal, 259; change in may show age of document, 433; proof of, 473.

Handwriting Evidence, serious character of, 243.

Handwriting Investigation, method of, 243; how to submit questions, 246; points to consider, 246-249; same to prove genuineness as forgery, 255.

Hasty Judgment, danger of, 7, 243, 304.

Hesitation, may be evidence of forgery, 245, 252, 254.

Hewitt Will case, pens in, 158.

Hidden Characteristics, 190.

Holland J. G. "Sevenoaks" referred to, 57.

Holograph, Documents, class of, 6; vulnerable if not genuine, 9, 240; forgery of very difficult, 251; procedure regarding, 250, 253.

Howland, Sylvia Ann, case, 277 Prof. Pierce's testimony in, 285; illustrations of, 301.

Hübl von, on color photography, 346.

Humidity, affects ink, 354; affects paper, 435.

Humphreys, Henry Noel, 168.

Hyland case, 263.

Identification, from disguised writing, 14; from handwriting may be positive, 14; principles of, 226; from writing, 24, 197.

Identification by handwriting, 6, 10, 212, 227; by disguised signature, 13; by unaccountable variation, 217; slight from traced forgery, 280.

Identity of two signatures, may be suspicious, 18, 254, 279; legal opinions on, 274-276; significance of, in alleged tracing, 281, 282, 283, 284; of position of forgeries, 281; exact identity proof of forgery, 282; in Boyer case, Buffalo, N. Y., 284; shown by photography, 287.

Identity of Writer, shown by combination of features, 210; by comparison with standard, 227; how shown, 230; and difference, study of, 260.

Idioms, in holograph forgery, 254; in anonymous letters, 315; see Subject Matter.

Illiterate, clumsy hesitation of, 105; tremor of, 117, 121; and anonymous letters, 313.

Imitating, affects freedom, 243.

Inconspicuous Characteristics, importance of, 308.

Individuality, of writing, 21, 22, 105, 138, 184, 190, 197; how shown, 212; of a particular letter, 215; positive character of, in writing, 217; of writing same as of person, 259; cause of, 184.

Ink, special care of on document, 4; color of observed on first view, 8; may show age of writing, 8; and alterations, 9; uneven distribution on drawn forgery, 47, 73; and questioned documents, 249, 330; opportunity for charlatans, 330; common classes of ink, 331; sediment in, 76; to ascertain composition, 333; nigrosine ink, 336; German article on, 336; English inks, 338; how same class of inks may differ, 339; changes in bottle, 340; manner of making tests, 341; effect of blotter, 343; photographic tests, 344; age of ink, 74, 102, 348; Dr. Dennstedt on, 348; age of colored inks, 349; lead pencil writing, age of, 350; to find and show if ink has not matured, 350; bearing on alleged old writing, 351; rate of development of final color, 352; use of color microscope, 355; employment of Lovibond glasses, 356; method of measurement of color, 358; age not to be told by one examination, 360; changes unmistakable, 362; proportions of "black" inks in common use, 362; fluidity of, 397; changes over erasure, 405; over chemical erasure, 409; to be tested and examined by daylight, 424; appearance of old ink lines, 435.

Instruments, description of, 89-104.

Interlineations, fraudulent, 9, 75; in wills, 422; see Additions.

Intuition, not to be relied upon, 213, 245.

Ireland, William Henry, the literary forger, 192, 194, 373.

Involuntary Characteristics, 12, 190.

Iodine Test, for erasures, 409.

"Italian Hand," 171, 172, 192.

"J" in old "round hand," 191.

James, Professor William, 143. 201, 234, 258, 323.

Jastrow, Professor Joseph, 205, 239.

Judd, Professor C. H., 106, 143, 240.

Judge, to enlarge powers of, 323.

Junius, handwriting of, 260.

Juxtaposition, for comparison, 41; of typewriting, 57; Wigmore on, 41; to show identity or difference, 323.

Keene, J. Harrington, 213, 319.

Kinsley, William J., 326, 429.

Kynast, Richard, on inks, 336.

"L. R. A.," quoted, 17, 33, 39.

Lay Witnesses on handwriting, 473.

Lenses, perfection of, 51; for document photography, 58.

Letters, anonymous, 6, 10; Black-hand, 11; by those under suspicion, 11; one standard may be enough, 19; like holograph forgery, 252; arrangement of parts, 142; system features important, 185; often work of insane, 302; strange facts about, 303; identification not usually difficult, 305; not well disguised, 306; points to be considered, 307; inconsistent with each other, 307; assumed illiteracy in, 314; how to find standards, 321; method to be followed, 322; and envelopes connected by postmarks, 432.

Letter Designs, not the only characteristics, 106.

Limitations, of expert ability, X, 29, 209, 241, 375.

Line Edges, character of, 131; conditions affecting, 132.

Line Quality, 23; shows speed, force, freedom, 114; how produced, 116, 117; in forgery, 137; affected by pen position, 127; in traced forgery, usually bad, 269, 286; shown in Figs. 53, 54.

Line Widths, measure for, 96; of shades, 136; increased over erasure, 405; in questioned additions, 159, 424.

Literary Ability, in anonymous letters, 305.

Lovibond, J. W., 356.

Mabillon, 195.

Magnification table, 85.

Magnifying Glasses, kinds, 91.

Malone, Edmond, 373.

Marks and Scars, identification by, 211, 227-235, 259.

Masculine Characteristics, 315.

Materials, may show fraud, 6; in holograph forgery, 254.

Mathematical Calculations, and disputed writing, 217; in Howland case, 277.

Measurements, instruments for, 92; certified by bureau of standards, 95; of shaded strokes, 136; to show size of writing, 146; of pen strokes, 159.

Messchert case, 112; illustrations of, 294, 295.

Meyer, Dr. George, 336.

Microscope, and questioned documents, 70; makes evidence visible, 70; and photography mutually helpful, 73; shows pen lifts and erasures, 73, 77; degrees of magnification, 78; special for documents, 4, 80, 81, 102;

special foot for, 41, 82; magnification table, 85; stereoscopic miscroscope, 86; law
of, 87; simple microscopes,
91; for color examination,
74; 102, 355; to prove genuineness, 245; in crossed line
inquiries, 378; in writing
over folds in paper, 398.

Mitchell, C. A., 336.

Model Writing, may be of wrong
date, 22; may not be accurately followed, 266, 278; not
usually found, 267; for traced
forgery, 267; may be put in
case, 267; may be of wrong
date, 273; choice of, may be
wrong, 273; finding of strong
proof of forgery, 278.

Movement, unnatural shown by
photographs, 57; shown by
microscope, 73; like drawing
in forgery, 117, 118; more
defective than form in forgery, 252; defined, 106; defee-
tive in forged, 106, 253; in
best writing, 108; variation
in number of movements,
111; affected by shading, 139;
in different systems, 173, 179,
181; affected by anxiety, 238;
difficult to imitate, 238;
shown by strokes, 242; imitation of in holograph document, 251; in traced forgery,
286.

Münsterberg, Prof. Hugo, 205.

Muscular Habits, 106.

Muscular Skill, in writing, 105;
may be too great in forgery,
116; necessary in forgery,
238.

Nationality, shown by handwriting, 170.

Nigrosine Ink, 333, 335, 336.

Nibs, marks of, 155.

Obscene, anonymous letters, 10.

Occupation, shown by writing,
144, 184.

Offhand Opinions, not to be
given, 28, 125, 209, 243; given
by volunteers, 304.

"O. K.'d" forgeries paid, 414.

Old Writing, shown by photography, 44; shown by ink, 435.

Order of Writing, see Crossed
Lines.

Original Hands, 183.

Palaeography, the study of, 194,
195.

Paper, size, shape and color to
be observed, 8; made after
date of document, 10; shown
by photographs, 46, 48; instruments for measuring, 98;
ink over folds, see Folds; examination of, 249; of holograph forgeries, 254; and
questioned documents, 363-
373; evidence sometimes conclusive, 363; characteristics
that identify, 364; thickness
test with micrometer calipers, 364; history of printed
forms, 365; identification by
matched perforations, 366;
matching of paper and en-
velopes, 10, 366, 432; matching of torn edges, 368; ascertaining date, 369; date by
watermark, 369; process of
manufacture, 370; dated
watermarks, 46, 371; forged
watermarks, 372; used in
Shakespeare forgeries, 373;
books on paper making, 374;
fiber disturbed by erasure,
405; in forgery over genuine
signature, 429.

Parr case, illustration of, 264,
296.

Patched Writing, 18, 136; see
Retouching.

Patrick case, see Rice case.

Payson, Dunton & Scribner, an
American hand, 172, 176, 177.

Pen and Alterations, 9.

Pen Position, in pencil writing, 22; variation in, 126-131; may indicate forgery, 136, 137.

Pen Pressure, in pencil writing, 22; of forgery, 117, 254; definition of, 132-134; variety of, 132; in forged writing, 136.

Pen Strokes, width of, 82, 96, 155.

Pen, points of, 154; width of point, 155; stub, 130, 156, 157; writing identified by pen, 157; in Hewitt will case, 158; stylographic, fountain, gold, quill, 160, 161; change of, affects writing, 200; identity of, in questioned additions, 424.

Pen-Lifts, in forgery, 73, 115, 116, 137, 245, 252; in genuine writing, 121, 122, 123, 173; in traced forgeries, 269, 272.

Pencil Marks, on questioned document, 77, 273.

Pencil Writing, forms and pen pressure in, 22; erasures shown by photographs, 45; outline for forgery, 77; often questioned, 162, 164; how produced, 162; direction of stroke, 163; continuity of, 163; photographs of pencil forgery, 64, 166; with copying pencils may show age, 167; easily forged, 270; suspiciously retouched, 270; copy for traced forgery, 273; over fold in paper, 398.

Personal Characteristics, significance of, 230.

Personality, Human, cause of variety, 217; like handwriting, 218; identity of, 227, 230.

Personal writing characteristics, 11, 197, 210, 211; individual forms, 215.

Photographs, necessity for, 36-43, 245; objections to, 37, 51;

law of, 38, 39; stereoscopic, 47-49, 399; by side light, 50, 65, 66; transmitted light, 45-47, 67; photo-micrographs, 47, 60; directions for making, 53-59; juxtaposed, 41, 56, 57, 323; enlargements, 38, 47, 48, 56, 58, 59; reversed, 67; color filters, 67, 68, 345; show pen-lifts of forgery, 116; of pencil forgeries, 166; opinions not to be based on exclusively, 166; of holograph forgery very important, 254; of traced forgeries, 286; size of photographs desirable, 286; of traced forgery under ruled squares, 289; duplicate, for jury, 470; proof of in court, 471; Exclusion of, 324

Physical Condition of Writer, if unusual, should be known, 216.

Pictorial Effect, elements of, 212; see "general appearance."

Pierce, Prof. Benjamin, 277, 285, 293.

Pin Holes to be observed, 8.

Postmarks, see Envelopes.

Postscripts may be fraudulent, 434.

Preliminary Examination, 7, 15, 16, 243, 268, 304, 341.

Probability, calculus of, 227-235; Professor Newcomb's law, 228; of handwriting identity, 230, 231, 235; in Sylvia Ann Howland case, 277.

Projection Lantern, 57.

Proof of Handwriting, how made, 7; often a farce, 16; how positive, 211.

Proportion of Writing, may be important characteristic, 147; in different systems, 148, 173, 177; may show identity, 215; one cause of variation, 218.

Protractor, use of, 101; illustration of, 150.

Psychology of Writing, 106, 143, 201, 205, 234, 239, 240, 258, 323.

Punctuation, in holograph forgery, 254.

Pye, Frank, case, 297.

Questioned Writing, may be recognized at once as fraudulent, 18; in pencil, 22; date may show it is fraudulent, 24; see Writing; case in court, 466.

Quill Pen Writing, characteristics of, 161.

"Raised" Checks, etc., 9, 46, 407; see Erasures, Alterations.

Reasons, the essential part of expert testimony, 30, 36, 70, 89, 209; Twistleton on, 211; for identity, 215, 227; always important, 242; Mr. Justice Ward on giving, 258; Professor Wigmore on, 259; legal opinions on, 467; illustrations, the best, 474.

Request Writings, 24; suggestions regarding, 25.

Retouched Writing, how to show, 47, 57; how to examine, 273; evidence of fraud, 120, 136, 245, 254; in pencil written document, 165; in traced forgery, 270; discussion of, 270-272.

Reversed Photographs, 67.

Rice-Patrick case, 111; opinion in, 274; illustrations, 30, 298, 299.

Rood, on color, 360.

Round Hand, spacing of, 150; slant of, 151; the early American hand, 171; examples of, 185, 186.

Russell case, Boston, 393.

Scars, see Marks.

Scientific Comparison, 260.

Schneickert, Dr. Hans, 336.

Scientific Method, excludes intuition, 213; in examining writing, 241; starts with no presumption, 255.

Schooley-Crawford case, 290.

Scott, Henry T., 435.

Scott & Davey, 194.

Seal, how to photograph, 48, 65; illustration, 50, 66.

Self-consciousness, in forgery, 118, 120, 140, 202, 237; lack of shows genuineness, 119; shown by pen pressure, 133; in pencil forgery, 165; attention to details, 202; affects genuine writing, 204; affects all effort, 205; limits skill, 237, 239; see Anxiety.

Sequence of Writing, see Crossed Lines.

Sex, shown by "angular system," 185; in anonymous letters, 306, 315, 316.

Shading, not same in pencil writing, 22; location of shows pen position, 128, 242; distinguished from pen pressure, 134; variations of, 134-140; attempts to explain lack of, 136; may point to forgery, 136; lateral shading on forgery, 137; requires much skill, 139; in different systems, 173, 177; one variation, 218.

Shakespeare Forgery, 192, 194, 373; the Shakespeare system, 193.

Shattuck, George H., 191.

Shearman, J. Frank, 292, 420.

Signatures, disputed, 5, 7; one may not be adequate standard, 19; formal and informal, 20; to documents of varying importance, 20; and other writing, 20; bearing on proof of other writing, 20; forged documents over genuine, 405, 426; movements in should be counted, 116; showing tremor of age, 119; may be unusual and genuine, 213.

Simulated Writing, definition, 7, 12, 136, 236; movement of, 115; illustration of, 260.

Simulated Forgery, of signature, 7.

Size of Writing, a characteristic, 145, 146, 147, in old style hand, 177; one variation, 218.

Skill in Writing, great variety in, 105, 109; an important characteristic, 110, 111, 133; too much may show forgery, 116; one cause of variation, 218; in anonymous letters, 305.

Slant, . cause of, 108; a fixed habit, 151; peculiarities of, 152, 153, 173; changes appearance, 201.

Slant, significance of, 214; change of, a favorite disguise, 311.

Smith, W. Anderson, 192.

Spacing, of writing, 149; in different systems, 150, 173.

Speech, and writing compared, 197.

Speed, in writing, 110; shown by strokes, 113, 242; changes in, in forgery, 117; in genuine signatures, 119; slow in "vertical," 181.

Spelling, in holograph forgery, 254; in anonymous letters, 307.

"Spencerian," proportions of, 148; spacing of, 150; an American hand, 172-177; some features of, 185.

Standards of Comparison, 16-35; seeking out, one of first steps, 16; in some states not admitted, 16; best, 18, 20; date of may be important, 18, 20, 23; number necessary, 19; of different classes, 21; for pencil

writing, 22, 23; instructions regarding "request" writing, 25; bank standards frequently inadequate, 19, 26, 28; forged or changed standards, 26, 27; necessity for, 435.

Standard Dictionary, 345, 359.

Standard Writing, only that to be used that can be proved, 7; often inadequate, 304; in anonymous letter cases, 321; adequate amount to be supplied, 19, 208; how much necessary, 19; always to be sought, 436.

Stealth, a condition of forgery, 236.

Stenographer, not to deface disputed paper, 5.

Stenographic Record, suggestions regarding, 472.

Stephen's ink, 338.

Stereoscopic Illustrations, 47, 48, 50; how made, 49; law reference, 49; in writing over folds in paper questions, 399; duplicates in envelope at end of book.

Stereoscopic Microscope, illustrated, 86; use in pencil forgery, 166; in crossed strokes inquiries, 389.

Stub, of check book, matched perforations of check and stub, 366.

Stub Pen, writing of, 130, 156, 200.

Subject Matter, in holograph forgery, 254; to show age, 432; see Idioms, Spelling, Use of Capitals.

Suicide letters, 326.

Superimposing, in traced forgery inquiries, 288.

Systematic Procedure, always desirable, 15, 125, 213, 243, 246, 253; in examining alleged old writing, 435.

Systems of Writing, and holograph documents, 9, 168; alone do not identify, 214.

System of Writing, should be known, 168, 214; do not produce identity, 230; traces remain, 208; divergences from, 210; effect of foreign, 196; puts impress on writer, 231; shown by forms, 242.

Telegraphers' Writing, 144, 184.

Terminals, show speed, 115; importance of, 118.

Tests of Handwriting testimony, 27; unfair tests, 29, 237.

Torn Paper, matching of, 368.

Traced Forgery, of signature, 7; shown by identity, 18; illustrations of, 102; definition of, 136, 266; varying pressure on, 134; too much alike, 198, 245, 274; mathematical calculations regarding, 235; not usually well done, 266; movement chief defect of, 267, 268; main defects in, 268; legal opinions on, 274-276; not identical with model, 278; how to illustrate, 279, 285; position on document suspicious, 281.

Tracing Process, evidence of, 273; in "Day vs. Cole," 274; inherent evidence of fraud, 278.

Transmitted Light, photographs by, 45, 46, 61, 67; examination by, 406.

Tremor, natural, 113, 120; of fraud, 111, 114, 115, 116, 117; of age, 118, 119, 120; shown by pen pressure, 133.

Twistleton, Hon. Edward, 35, 211, 260.

Type Printing to show date, 10.

Typewriting, disputed documents in, 6; shown by photographs, 48, 57; illustration, 58; examined by microscope, 77; instruments for examination of, 101; may show age of document, 433; questioned, 437; the various questions about, 439; changes in type of, 441; shows its own history, 442; identifying work of particular machine, 444; Wisconsin cases, 441, 445; letter designs, 466; deterioration produces individuality and has date value, 447; the five "individualities" of type impression, 448; alignment illustrations, 450; slant, 451; uniformity of impression, 452; defects, 453; principles of identification, 453; typewriting cases, 454; illustrations, 456-465.

Unconsciousness of Writing habits, 141, 144, 196, 201, 207; of angularity or roundness, 226; in general, 239.

Undisguised Writing, identified by "general appearance," 212.

United States dated watermarks, 371.

Uniformity of Writing, varies with different writers, 281.

Uttering, proof of, 14.

Van Deventer case, 262.

Variation in Genuine Writing, 20, 196; through age and conditions, 21; causes of, 199, 200, 204; lack of in complete forged documents, 203; in holograph documents, 9, 253; begins from beginning, 231; due to age, 22; slight, inevitable, 275; may show age of document, 433.

Variety of Forms, vast number, 217; how produced, 218; with different writers, 214; of certain letters, 215; illustrations of, 221-225.

Vertical Writing, movement in, 106; proportions of, 148; spacing of, 150; beginning of, 173; characteristics, 180, 181,

182; questions regarding, 192; failure, of, 182.

Vernier, illustration and description, 99.

"W" date value of form of, 190.

Watermark, to be looked for, 8; shown by photographs, 45; imperfect specimen, 369; how produced, 370; dated, 46, 370, 371; earliest English, 372.

Weight of Evidence, difference in, 7, 14; depends on number and character of parts, 227; sometimes weak, 241; increased by reasons, 260; always to be considered, 322.

Whitman, Alonzo J., case, 324, 325, 419.

Whitney, W. R., 374.

Wigmore, Professor John H., 17, 33, 41, 259, 404.

Wills, often forged, 7; careless practices regarding, 422.

Women, writing of, see Sex.

Woodman, A. G., 374.

Writing, characteristics of, 7, 12; persistence of, 21; classified, 28, 196; defined, 105, 209; vary in significance, 105, 322; pen pressure an important, 132; shading, 134-140; how produced, 141; in various systems, 173; significance of, 190, 197, 217, 322; variation of, 196; individual and general, 206, 304; significance of, vital problem, 209, 210; inevitable and not sought for, 218.

Printed in Great Britain
by Amazon

45478548R00294